DATE DUE

DEC - 5 1995	
OCT 2 9 1998	
NOV 1 6 1998	

BRODART   Cat. No. 23-221

The Arctic

A HISTORY

The Arctic
A HISTORY

RICHARD VAUGHAN

ALAN SUTTON

First published in the United Kingdom in 1994
Alan Sutton Publishing Limited
Phoenix Mill · Far Thrupp · Stroud · Gloucestershire

First published in the United States of America in 1994
Alan Sutton Publishing Inc · 83 Washington Street · Dover · NH 03820

British Library Cataloguing-in-Publication Data
A catalogue record for this book is available from the British Library

ISBN 0 7509 0177 2

Library of Congress Cataloging-in-Publication Data applied for

Typeset in 11/12 Ehrhardt.
Typesetting and origination by
Alan Sutton Publishing Limited.
Printed in Great Britain by
The Bath Press, Avon.

Contents

Illustrations

Plates

Maps

Tables

Acknowledgements

First and foremost, I thank my daughter Nancy for enhancing the book with her hand-drawn and labelled maps. My wife Margaret has also contributed much to this book by putting in many hours of work on the word processor, and by her forbearance, advice, and help of various kinds. My son David read and criticised Chapter 8 and sent me newspaper cuttings. Terence Armstrong, of the Scott Polar Research Institute, Cambridge, patiently read through the entire manuscript and made many helpful suggestions. Eugene Potapov, of St Petersburg, has read through several chapters and also lent me books and periodical material not otherwise available in England. Peter Speak and Piers Vitebsky of the Scott Polar Research Institute have most helpfully answered my queries. Two reference works proved of exceptional value in the writing of this book: H.G.R. King's bibliography of the Arctic (1989) and A.M. Prokhorov's encyclopedia (1988).

The following institutions have made their facilities available to me and I wish to thank their staff for much friendly help: The Arctic Centre, the Department of History and the University Library of the University of Groningen, Holland; the library of the University of York; the Department of History and the University Library of Central Michigan University at Mount Pleasant, Michigan; the Scott Polar Research Institute, Cambridge; and the Kirkbymoorside Branch of the North Yorkshire Library, which has also obtained much inter-library loan material for me.

Finally, I thank the staff of Alan Sutton Publishing for their very substantial contribution to the creation of this book.

ONE

Inhabitants of the Tundra

Adventurous white men and women may trek across the floating pack ice of the Arctic Ocean to the North Pole, voyage through America's ice-choked Northwest Passage or along the Northern Sea Route from Arkhangel'sk to Vladivostok, or mine coal in Spitsbergen. They may ski across the Inland Ice of Greenland or set up scientific stations on drifting ice islands north of Alaska or Siberia. But only in the far north of Norway and of Russia have Europeans permanently settled in the Arctic. Otherwise white people are mere visitors there. Nowadays, they have built military bases and even great cities like Noril'sk in the Arctic, but the individuals in them do not usually remain for more than a few months or years at a time. Moreover, these modern settlements draw their life blood from outside the Arctic, for they are entirely dependent on the outside world for food, fuel and other necessities. The only people who really do live in the Arctic, the only true and genuine human inhabitants of the Arctic, are its native peoples, the Eskimos or Inuit, the Sami or Lapps, the Nentsy or Samoyeds, the Chukchi, and others who live in the tundra north of the forest zone or taiga. With some exaggeration, they could be termed the real owners of the Arctic. These peoples, who inhabited the Arctic long before the first white people arrived there, form the subject of the first and last chapters of this book because they stand at the beginning and present-day end of the history of the Arctic (on Arctic peoples as a whole see Brody 1973, Graburn and Strong 1973, Marucci 1980; for Asia see Levin and Potapov 1964; for America and Greenland, Damas (ed.) 1984).

THE BERELEKH MAMMOTH TUSK AND OTHER SIBERIAN FINDS

The earliest human penetration of the Asiatic Arctic of which we have convincing evidence occurred around twelve thousand years ago in the north of what later became Yakutia. In 1947 Russian permafrost expert N.F. Grigor'yev inspected and photographed a mammoth 'graveyard' on the upper reaches of the Berelekh River, a left-hand tributary of the Indigirka, at 71° north latitude. This river-bank site is about 250 km (150 miles) south of the shore of the Arctic Ocean, lying opposite that most famous mammoth graveyard of all, the New Siberian Islands (Novosibirskiye ostrova) (Map 2). It was subsequently excavated by a team of biologists and palaeontologists from the Yakutsk section of the Soviet Academy of Sciences. They found thousands of bone fragments, most of which belonged to some 120 different individual mammoths, and unearthed numerous worked flints left by the animals' human predators. Early man, then, had pursued his prey well north of the Arctic Circle. In 1965 Russian ornithologist Vladimir E. Flint met with graphic confirmation of this Stone Age man-mammoth connection when, in the settlement of Berelekh, he was given by a local inhabitant a fragment of a mammoth tusk which had come from the river bank about 50 km (30 miles) above the village. It was 56.5 cm (22.25 in) long and on it was engraved the unmistakable outline of a mammoth. Its radiocarbon date was given as 12,240 ±160 years ago (Vereshchagin and Mochanov 1972, Mochanov 1977: 76–87; and see Kozlowski and Bandi 1984: 367–8; Sutcliffe 1985: 89).

After the Second World War, or Great Patriotic War as it is called in Russia, senior archaeologists seem to have partitioned the then Soviet Union between them. The Berelekh mammoth site and much else besides fell to Yuri Alekseyevich Mochanov, who presided over the archaeology of Yakutia. Beyond his territory to the east lay Chukotka, the domain of his colleague Nikolai Nikolayevich Dikov, whose *Ancient Cultures of North-Eastern Asia* was published in Russian in 1979. He could not, like Mochanov, describe Asia's most northerly Palaeolithic site so far discovered, but his share of the Siberian Arctic proved equally exciting. He was able to report the 1975 discovery on Wrangel Island (ostrov Vrangelya), 130 km (80 miles) north of the north coast of Siberia and, like Berelekh, at 71° north latitude, of an assemblage of stone tools, found at a site called the Devil's Ravine (*Chertova ovraga*). These he described as 'Palaeoeskimo' because they closely resembled artefacts from sites in Alaska and Greenland dating from about the same time. They were called Palaeoeskimo because their makers were thought to have been the ancestors of the Eskimos of today. But now the scene has changed from 12,000 to a mere 3,500 years ago. The mammoth is extinct and the Wrangel Island Palaeoeskimos are sea mammal hunters. Dikov (1971) was also able to report on the life of the prehistoric hunters of the Arctic coast of mainland Chukotka, nearly opposite Wrangel Island and only some 250 km (150 miles) from it, at about the same time. Their activities are vividly portrayed by a group of drawings on rock faces in the valley of the Pegtymel' River in northern Chukotka (Map 2). These show indisputably that wild reindeer were being hunted with dogs and the aid of something very like skis in spring, and from boats – some of which look uncommonly like kayaks propelled by double-bladed paddles – in the autumn, with spears and harpoons. Whales were hunted too, from boats that resembled umiaks. No artefacts were found to establish the ethnic characteristics of these people, nor suitable objects to date them accurately. They were probably ancestors of the north coastal Chukchi of more recent times.

A most exciting discovery was made between 1987 and 1990 by Russian workers from the Arctic and Antarctic Scientific Research Institute and the Institute of Archaeology in St Petersburg (Makeyev, Pitul'ko and Kasparov 1992). Far out in the Arctic Ocean in 76° north latitude, on ostrov Zhokhova, an outlier of the New Siberian Islands (Map 15), they unearthed tools and animal bones left by Mesolithic people who lived there, or camped there from time to time, about 8,000 years ago, when the sea level was lower than now and Zhokhov Island was on the edge of a low-lying continent supporting a richer flora and fauna than it

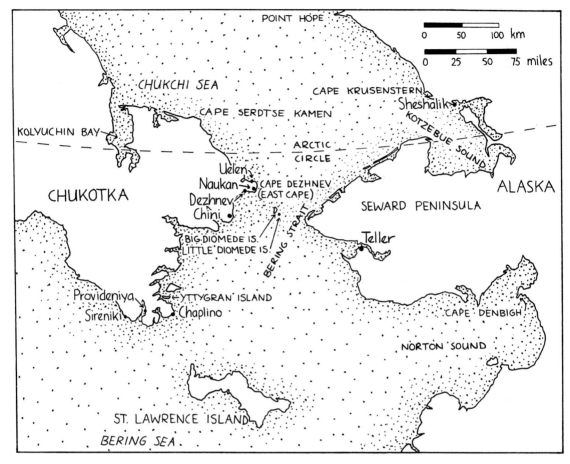

Map 1. Bering Strait.

now does. Of 906 bone fragments identified only one was of a walrus. The most numerous were those of the reindeer (450 fragments) and Polar bear (397), placing these people among the champion Polar bear hunters of all time.

OLD BERING SEA PEOPLE

The appearance of specialized sea mammal hunting communities about 3,500 years ago in northern Chukotka, as evidenced by the Wrangel Island finds and the Pegtymel' petroglyphs, was a big event in the history of mankind. Earlier in his archaeological career, Dikov had excavated an ancient cemetery belonging to a much later culture, the so-called Old Bering Sea Culture, at Chini on the Asiatic shore of Bering Strait about 50 km (30 miles) south-west of the extreme tip of continental north-east Asia, namely Cape Dezhnev (mys Dezhneva), formerly called East Cape. Here, in the summer of 1965, Dikov and colleagues, with assistance from local people, excavated 102 shallow graves in four adjacent cemeteries (Dikov 1974a). The graves were rectangular pits: the bodies had been placed on wood, peat or skin, with their heads to the south. Some graves, strengthened with flagstones, were thought to have been dug in summer. The burials dated from the first to the fifth century AD, that is, from about 1,500 to 2,000 years ago. Dikov deduced from the many artefacts found in the graves at Chini that land and sea hunting were of about equal importance in these people's subsistence. They must have hunted whales, walrus and other sea mammals offshore using a large open walrus-skin-covered boat or umiak and a harpoon with detachable point. Land hunting of wild reindeer with bows and arrows was likewise important. The Old Bering Sea people's quest for food was evidently successful enough to enable them to do other things too. In particular they developed remarkable artistic skills. They carved human figurines from walrus tusks and even took the trouble to decorate everyday objects like ivory harpoon heads with incised lines, curves, circles and dots. The hundreds of such objects now in museums in Russia and America bear witness to a complex spiritual life which lies quite outside our comprehension. No one has any idea of the purpose of many of these artefacts; they can only be described as 'winged objects', or 'ornaments' or whatever.

WHALE ALLEY

Just as enigmatic as the decorative art of the Old Bering Sea people, and even more convincing of surpluses in energy, in time and in manpower derived from sea mammal hunting, and in this case especially whale hunting, is the remarkable cult centre or sanctuary on Yttygran Island (ostrov Yttygran or Sikluk (Siqlluq) in Eskimo) not far north of Provideniya in Chukotka. This site, on a remote and now uninhabited offshore island, cannot be paralleled elsewhere on either shore of Bering Strait. It reminded Jean Malaurie of the megalithic stone alignments at Carnac in Brittany: it is an Arctic Stonehenge. A 300 m long (328 yd) row of about sixty skulls of bowhead whales extends along a grassy strip above the pebble beach. They were arranged in fifteen groups, mostly of two or four skulls each. The skulls, weighing about two tons each, were fixed nose down into the ground. Between the skulls, thirty-four single whale jawbones, fourteen of which are still standing, were planted upright in the ground. In the centre of this monumental alley or row is an amphitheatre surrounded by massive stone blocks in a semicircle 4–5 metres in diameter. In a hearth in this amphitheatre Russian archaeologists found ashes from walrus and seal bones. Near it were found 120 pits, each about one metre deep, partly filled with the mummified meat of whales and walruses. Near them a paved path led up the slope to a stone structure resembling a shrine. On a neighbouring, larger island, opposite this cult centre, thirteen bowhead jaw bones had been set up on headlands, from 3 to 5 km (2–3 miles) apart, in such a way that from any one of these columns its neighbours on either side were visible. Curiously, virtually no whale bones other than skull and jaw bones were found on the site, showing that this was not a butchering place but a ceremonial site to which the skulls and jaws had been brought from elsewhere. Questioned about the origin and purpose of this remarkable monument, the local

Eskimos had little to say, which is surprising because the experts dated it to as recently as the thirteenth or fourteenth century AD. It seems that the ancestors of present-day Asiatic Eskimos built it as a whale cult centre. Possibly an all-male secret society of whale-hunting boat (umiak) teams, drawn from several widely spread settlements, was involved. Perhaps the fifteen groups of skulls represented in some way fifteen umiak crews. Speculation is hampered by the absence of any known parallel to Whale Alley anywhere else in the Arctic (Arutyunov *et al.* 1982, Vasil'evskiy 1987: 83–5, Malaurie 1990: 10).

ACROSS BERING STRAIT: IPIUTAK

It is not to be imagined that the Eurasian Arctic was peopled by a single large-scale migration from that power-house of nomads, central Asia. Rather one has to think in terms of an endless trickle of tiny groups. A trickle whose move northwards was prompted by the pursuit of game as much as by pressure from other peoples. It was facilitated by the great rivers, frozen in winter into ice roads, though patches of thin ice or even open water could make these very dangerous. By four thousand years ago people had appeared on the lower reaches of the Pechora and the Ob', and followed the Yenisey and the Lena to reach the shores of Taymyr (Belov 1956: 21–4). Before about ten thousand years ago the Siberian coastal tundras continued eastwards from Chukotka across what is now the Chukchi Sea. Dry land, now known as the Bering Land Bridge or Platform, or Beringia, then linked the Asian and American continents. Beringia was indubitably traversed and occupied by ancient peoples, who may have penetrated into the American Arctic as early as some twenty-five thousand years ago, if the modified animal bones found at Old Crow Flats on the Canadian side of the Alaskan border really are human artefacts. After about ten thousand years ago, when it was first formed, Bering Strait's 35–86 km (22–53 miles) of open water with its stepping-stone islands, Great and Little Diomede (ostrova Diomida), formed no serious obstacle to humans. When Russians first arrived on the scene in the seventeenth century they found peaceful barter in progress across the strait: the settled, coastal Chuckchi, needing pelts for fur clothing and wood for sledges and boats, obtained these materials partly from the nomadic inland Chukchi and partly from the natives of Alaska on the opposite shore of Bering Strait, who took their seal skins and blubber in exchange. After the Russians had brought iron articles into the area to exchange for furs, groups regularly crossed Bering Strait in either direction for more warlike purposes. In particular, in the eighteenth century, the coastal Chukchi would attack an Alaskan settlement, kill the men, and kidnap the women and children whom they would then barter for reindeer with the inland reindeer-herding Chukchi (Gurvich 1981: 119–21). Against this background it is easy to imagine the passage over the preceding millennia of numerous groups of migrants from Asia to America, from the predecessors of Aztecs and other Indians to those of Eskimos.

Anthropologist Aleš Hrdlička went to look at Bering Strait for himself on 26 July 1926 and wrote in his Alaska diary (1944: 103):

The afternoon brings an exceedingly precious treat, worth all the tribulations. The captain takes me around the Big Diomede. It is cool, but calm and sunny. Sit on boxes at the very fore end of the old *Bear*. See Asia, the two Diomedes, the Seward Peninsula – all in easy reach, like so many features in a big lake. There is no problem here as to human comings from Asia. Such comings when weather was favourable were natural, easy, inevitable. But also, there could never have been any mass migration – the inhospitable ends of the two continents could never have accommodated any large numbers of people.

In 1958, when Dikov and his Soviet colleagues were excavating the prehistoric cemetery at Uelen on the extreme north-eastern point of Asia, American archaeologist J. Louis Giddings, then professor of anthropology at Brown University, Providence, Rhode Island, was collecting prehistoric skulls and artefacts on the raised beaches at Cape Krusenstern, on the opposite shore of the Chukchi Sea. Although Giddings, like Dikov, has added immeasurably to knowledge of the ancient peoples of Bering Strait, they and the other archaeologists of their day destroyed a great deal of what they found. Nowadays they might be condemned as vandals. Giddings (1968: 349) himself explains his recognized procedure:

> Ideally, an archaeologist with the necessary time and funds would plan to dig the whole area of a site like this, level by level, scanning each layer across its entire breadth and removing from it the artefacts left by the people of its time before digging lower to the next, clearly separate level containing artefacts of an older generation of culture. . . .

Giddings had been introduced to Arctic archaeology in 1939 at Point Hope on the north-west Alaskan coast by Froelich Rainey, professor of anthropology at the University of Alaska at Fairbanks, and Helge Larsen, curator at Denmark's National Museum in Copenhagen (Giddings 1968: 114–25). He took part then in their discovery and excavation of an outsize prehistoric Arctic village consisting of over six hundred rectangular houses, each dug 2 or 3 ft into the ground, on ancient beach ridges. They called the previously un-named site Ipiutak, from a neighbouring sand bar of that name, and so the people and culture they had discovered became known as Ipiutak. By the time the archaeologists had finished their work at Point Hope in 1941, 138 graves had been excavated as well as numerous dwellings. The dead were either buried in driftwood coffins in graves up to one metre deep, or simply laid out on the surface, the heads mostly towards the west. In three coffin burials, carved ivory eyeballs with jade pupils had been inserted in the eye sockets, perhaps pointing to the closing of the body openings to prevent the ingress or egress of evil spirits. Interestingly, a local Point Hope Eskimo knew of a legend about a man with ivory eyes. In many important respects the Ipiutak People resembled those of Chini on the other side of Bering Strait, subsequently investigated by Dikov. The Ipiutakers also hunted both on land and sea, apparently living at Ipiutak while hunting seals and walruses in the summer, and pursuing caribou inland in winter. They too were intensely artistic, placing small, beautifully engraved ivory carvings of human heads and animals in their burials and also engraving ivory objects in everyday use like snow goggles. The Ipiutakers lived at the same time as the Chini People, from 1,500 to 2,000 years ago. They did not hunt whales and they did not use blubber lamps, but cooked on an open driftwood fire on a hearth in the centre of a square wood-framed dwelling, and they probably had no dogs or sledges (Giddings 1968: 102–27, Bandi 1969: 99–117, Anderson 1984: 88–9).

A SUCCESSION OF CULTURES

The chronological position of the Ipiutakers in the succession of early Bering Sea Arctic cultures was established by Giddings at Cape Krusenstern, 200 km (125 miles) south-east of Ipiutak. Here, from 1958 onwards, in what is now the Cape Krusenstern National Monument, he conducted numerous excavations on a unique series of 114 coastal ridges which run parallel to each other in a wide sweep round the cape. Each ridge is the remains of an earlier beach. As new beaches were formed one after another they were occupied by the sea mammal hunters of the day. The Ipiutakers occupied the beaches numbered 29–35 some two thousand years ago. Giddings identified still earlier cultures on the more landward ridges until on beaches 83–104, over one mile inland, he unearthed the small, delicately chipped stone implements of the earliest occupants of the cape who lived there nearly five thousand years ago. Giddings had found such implements before, south of the Arctic Circle and south of the Seward Peninsula, at Cape Denbigh, and had referred to them as the 'Denbigh Flint complex'. This assemblage of stone tools, or culture, was subsequently found to be an early representative of a wider tradition now called the Arctic Small Tool tradition or, in archaeologists' jargon, ASTt. Considered by many to be Palaeoeskimo or a precursor of Palaeoeskimo cultures, this culture has been identified in sites occupied between five thousand and two thousand years ago right across the Arctic from Wrangel Island to Greenland. Many archaeologists have regarded it as playing 'an ancestral role in the formation of Eskimo culture' (Henry B. Collins in Giddings 1968: xxv); others have argued for a separate origin for Palaeoeskimo cultures. In coastal Arctic Alaska the Arctic Small Tool culture was followed from about three thousand years ago by another that was probably in part derived from it, the Norton culture named from Norton Sound. One of the stages of this culture is represented by the already-mentioned Ipiutakers (besides Giddings 1968, see Bandi 1969, Faynberg 1971, Dumond 1977, McGhee 1978, Damas (ed.) 1984 and Stewart 1989 for this and what follows).

Just as prehistoric Arctic coastal dwellers crossed Bering Strait, they also crossed the straits between the ice-bound islands of the Canadian Arctic Archipelago. Only a quite small number of people were involved at any one time and they may have occupied a given site for only a few weeks, then abandoned it for a thousand years (Schledermann 1990, Helmer 1991). After the disappearance of the Arctic Small Tool cultures in Canada, which archaeologists have speculatively explained as the result of a miniature ice age occurring between 3,500 and 3,200 years ago, a new culture emerged to occupy much of the same huge area, namely the Canadian Arctic and Greenland. This was called the Dorset culture by Canadian ethnologist Diamond Jenness when, in 1925, he was examining artefacts dug up by Eskimos at Cape Dorset in southern Baffin Island. The time span of the Dorset culture has been set at from about three thousand to seven hundred years ago. Its geographical spread included Victoria Island, the eastern Canadian Arctic south to insular Newfoundland, and west Greenland. The Dorset People made snow houses and some more or less permanent winter houses, hunted seals and walrus, and used kayaks. They are included by archaeologists among the Palaeoeskimos.

CIRCUITS OF GREENLAND

Naturally, the hunters who crossed Bering Strait and the many straits between Canada's Arctic islands also crossed the often frozen Nares Strait separating America from Greenland, probably on numerous occasions, beginning about 4,500 years ago and ending in AD 1862. On this last occasion a fifteen-strong band of Baffin Island Eskimos migrated to Avanersuaq in north-west Greenland (Vaughan 1991: 26–8). Some of these prehistoric immigrants from America settled in Avanersuaq (Map 2) but many worked their way north-east along the narrow strip of ice-free tundra round the edge of Greenland's gigantic ice cap or Inland Ice, in all probability following the route taken by the musk ox. This large wooly-haired grazing animal was the principal prey of the earliest people whose remains have been found in Peary Land, northern Greenland, called the Independence People by their Danish discoverer, Eigil Knuth (1967; see too Gessain 1981: 142–205). They and their successors in the same area were named from Independence Fjord, near which the remains of their camps were first found. The Independence People arrived in two waves between 4,000 and 2,500 years ago, and have been linked to the (Palaeoeskimo) Arctic Small Tool tradition. Their numbers may not have exceeded 150 people at any one time. They lived in skin shelters within which were placed their box-shaped hearths made of up-ended flagstones. Without the dogs and sledges and blubber lamps of Eskimos, their survival depended solely on driftwood, which provided them with fuel and tent poles. They camped on beaches at the heads of fjords where timber, torn out of the Siberian taiga by the great rivers and drifted by ocean currents, had accumulated. This cannot happen now, for the fjords are choked with ice, but a few thousand years ago the land here was lower and the climate milder. Knuth found that the first wave of Independence People lived on beaches which are now about 10 m (33 ft) above sea level, and the second wave on beaches around 4 m (13 ft) above sea level.

At about the time when these Independence People, evidently moving round Greenland from Avanersuaq in a clockwise direction, began to colonize Peary Land, other people, likewise assigned to the Arctic Small Tool tradition, may have migrated southwards from Avanersuaq to Disko Bay (Disko Bugt), half-way down Greenland's west coast, and spread thence down the west coast and part-way northwards up the east coast (Fitzhugh 1984, Gulløv 1986, Grønnow 1991). Because many of their stone tools were found near a settlement of that name, their culture was called Sarqaq, which Danish spelling enthusiasts have now altered to Saqqaq. Excavations at two other places on the shore of Disko Bay, Sermermiut and Qeqertasussuk (Grønnow and Meldgaard 1991), have shown that the Saqqaq culture flourished for at least a millennium, starting about 4,500 years ago. Its bearers cooked with heated stones on an open hearth, had dogs but no sledges, and used kayaks. Seal was their most important prey species.

No house ruins at all have been found in west Greenland that date from the five hundred years after the disappearance of the Saqqaq People about three thousand years ago. Traces of two separate and much later occupations by Dorset People in west Greenland have been found, the later one dating from about AD 700–900. These people, too, had penetrated west Greenland from Canada. All these early Greenlandic colonists – Independence People, Saqqaq People and Dorset People – have been included among the Palaeoeskimos. But the next penetration into Greenland was by a new people who have been termed Neoeskimos because many experts consider them to be the direct forebears of virtually all the present-day Eskimos of Alaska, Canada and Greenland. Neoeskimo cultures originated in the Bering Strait area, and whale hunting is their hallmark.

The Old Bering Sea People, who were buried at Chini, and the Birnirk People (Ford 1959) (the whale-bone frames of whose houses can be seen projecting from the ground at Birnirk, now spelled Pigniq, 8 km (5 miles) north-east of Barrow in Alaska), are numbered among the earliest Neoeskimos. From the Birnirk culture, at least in part, evolved a later Neoeskimo, or perhaps more accurately, a truly Eskimo culture, named Thule after a former place name in Avanersuaq, north-west Greenland (Vaughan 1991: 1, 14). The Thule People, originating in Alaska, soon spread eastwards across Canada to Greenland, where they repeated the peregrinations of their predecessors (McGhee 1984, Jordan 1984). A possible explanation for this rapid expansion of Thule People around AD 1000 is that they were pursuing bowhead whales, which a warming climate had allowed to penetrate through the formerly ice-clogged waterways of the Canadian Arctic Archipelago. In any event, they entirely replaced their immediate predecessors, the very different Dorset People, whom the Thule People called Tornit, Tunit or Tunnit and did not recognize as fellow Eskimos. The immediate descendants of the Thule People, now called Inuit in Canada and Greenlanders in Greenland, use to this day many of the sites their ancestors occupied in Canada and Greenland.

In Greenland the Thule People settled in the area of their first arrival, namely Avanersuaq, formerly called the Thule District (Holtved 1944), but also moved round the north and down the east coast, as well as probably penetrating southwards down the west coast, to found other settlements in west and east Greenland. In the west their settlement on the islet of Inussuk (formerly Inugsuk) near Upernavik was excavated in 1929 by veteran Danish archaeologist Therkel Mathiassen. It gave its name to a modified Thule culture called Inussuk which flourished in about AD 1300–1400. On that occasion Mathiassen's field assistant was a young American graduate student of anthropology called Frederica de Laguna. Years later she published a most appealing account of her experiences (de

Laguna 1977). Not far south of Inussuk is Qilakitsoq, meaning the place where the sky is low, a remote and now deserted inlet where in 1978 Danish archaeologists uncovered the remains of a small group of Thule People – six women and two children. Preserved complete in every detail, from the exquisitely sewn fur clothes and boots to the elegant tattooed lines on the women's faces, in the dry Arctic frost, these 'mummies', one of the most notable archaeological finds of all time, now form part of the collections of the National Museum of Greenland in Nuuk (formerly Godthåb). Radiocarbon dates show that it was around 1475 that tragedy overtook a travelling party of women and children on the bleak coast opposite the town of Uummannaq. Death by drowning seems most likely; perhaps their umiak was overwhelmed by a tidal wave caused by a huge block of ice splitting off from an iceberg. Their menfolk, accompanying or following them in their kayaks, must have escaped. They buried them carefully under an overhanging cliff at the top of the tiny beach, heaping boulders over their corpses (Hansen *et al.* 1985, Hansen and Gulløv 1989).

ABORIGINAL PEOPLES OF THE ARCTIC

Thus far the archaeological record, put together mostly from excavations of ancient middens or rubbish tips, of abandoned camp sites and of the remains of dwellings, has made it possible to sketch out tentatively the course of Arctic prehistory. Hereafter, history comes to the rescue, for European and American explorers and travellers to the Arctic have left descriptions of Arctic peoples as they were when first confronted with people of European origin. Although these white people viewed the Arctic peoples through the distorting spectacles of the European mentality, the detailed information which they often give, for instance about their languages, greatly enhances that found by archaeologists. What exactly is an Arctic people? Some North American Indians could well be termed Arctic, but they will not be considered here. Nor will the Aleuts, those sub-Arctic islanders who colonized the Aleutian chain of 104 islands starting apparently from their eastern end, between five thousand and three thousand years ago. The Eskimos might seem to be a quintessentially Arctic people, but some are not Arctic at all: for instance the Pacific Eskimo of the Alaska Peninsula, Kodiak Island, and the shores of Prince William Sound, not to mention the Labrador Coast Eskimo. Kodiak Island is in the same latitude as Scotland.

The aboriginal Arctic peoples have never formed a homogeneous whole. Inevitably they were divided geographically, scattered as they have been all round the shores of the Arctic Ocean. Some wide expanses within the broad area colonized by Eskimos have been entirely unoccupied in historic times, for example most of Ellesmere Island and Peary Land. The so-called North Atlantic Gap which occurs in the distribution of some Arctic animals was also true of people, for no trace of prehistoric occupation has been found in Iceland or the Spitsbergen Archipelago. The aboriginal Arctic peoples were also ethnologically divided into distinct groups like Eskimos, Sami, Chukchi and the rest. Nor by any means did they speak the same language, even though the Eskimos, occupying about half the Arctic, spoke what is virtually the same language throughout most of that enormous area. Actually they spoke two related languages: Yupik in Chukotka and western Alaska; and Inuit-Inupiaq from western Alaska to eastern Greenland. Each contained several more or less mutually intelligible dialects. While only a single language family, Eskimo-Aleut, was represented throughout the New World Arctic, in the Old World the linguistic map was more divided and complex. Chukchi has been placed in the Palaeo-Asiatic language family, the Sami and Nentsy have been classified as speaking Finno-Ugric, and the Yakuts, Turko-Tartar; these two being subsections of the Ural-Altaic language family (Graburn and Strong 1973: 7–8). Finally, the aboriginal Arctic peoples are historically divided in the European record, the Sami having been first encountered by Europeans at various dates between about AD 500 and 1000 and some Inuit groups in Greenland and Canada only after 1800.

In spite of these divisions, the Arctic peoples had much in common, partly because the Arctic environment is similar all round the globe (Graburn and Strong 1973: 6–7). It compelled all Arctic peoples to wear tailored fur or skin clothing and footwear, caused most of them to construct their permanent dwellings partly underground, and forced them to be at least partly nomadic. The distribution of the main species of game, be it animal or bird, is circumpolar, like the Arctic peoples themselves, who have tended to hunt the same animals, especially seals, walrus and reindeer (called caribou in North America), and fish. Most groups specialized in either coastal sea-mammal hunting or inland reindeer hunting or breeding. The dog sledge and the skin-covered boat were almost universal. Social organization was everywhere based on families and kinship groups and, necessarily, on food sharing and economic cooperation. Authority was not institutionalized but successful hunters won respect and influence by sharing their harvest. The permafrost ensured that burials were above ground nearly throughout the Arctic; either stones were heaped over the corpse or it was laid out on a sledge or wooden platform. The deceased was fully clothed and accompanied by his or her belongings, sledge, harpoon and bow and arrow, or sewing kit and woman's knife, though these were put out of commission by being purposely broken or blunted (Gurvich 1981: 124).

Contacts between peoples may be as important as environment in explaining the affinities between them. Striking similarities in material culture between the Nganasans of Taymyr and some Canadian Eskimos have been pointed out: they hunted caribou or reindeer in the same way by driving them into an enclosure, they made bows of deer antlers, their meat-drying racks were of similar construction, and they both used a conical skin-covered tent, the *chum* or *tipi*. Russian anthropologist L.A. Faynberg (1981) was inclined to attribute some of this to possible earlier contacts between the Nganasans and Eskimos, for Eskimos may formerly have occupied the coasts of Taymyr.

These affinities in material culture between Arctic peoples are matched by numerous customs and beliefs shared in common, which they must have inherited from their Asiatic ancestors. Animism, the belief that animals and things are inhabited by spirits, is universal; so is the shaman (Halifax 1980, Vasylov 1984, Hoppál and Sadovszky 1989). He can communicate with the spirits and obtain their help, often by going into a trance and undertaking a soul-flight, perhaps to the moon, and his performances are everywhere associated with his drum. The shaman, common to all Arctic peoples, was already ubiquitous throughout Eurasia in Palaeolithic times. Elaborate songs and legends are shared by all Arctic peoples. It has been shown (Meletinskiy 1981) that similar myths about the raven as demiurge or creator and also as knave or deceiver were recounted among the Chukchi in Chukotka and by both Eskimos and Indians in Alaska. Evidently 'Palaeo-Asiatic' peoples had shared these beliefs in the raven as a first forbear and first shaman. Arctic peoples also share a belief in some form of life after death. The human soul is conceived of as a plurality; one element of it is the name, which was thought to pass from the deceased to an infant child.

The peoples of the Arctic share the remarkable achievement of colonizing thousands of kilometres of Arctic coast and tundra. They have been able to do this by developing food-sharing egalitarian social systems and complex technologies of hunting and transport equipment. Most of them were compelled by scarcity of game to live in small isolated groups, and they soon fell behind other peoples in terms of political, intellectual and material progress. This was

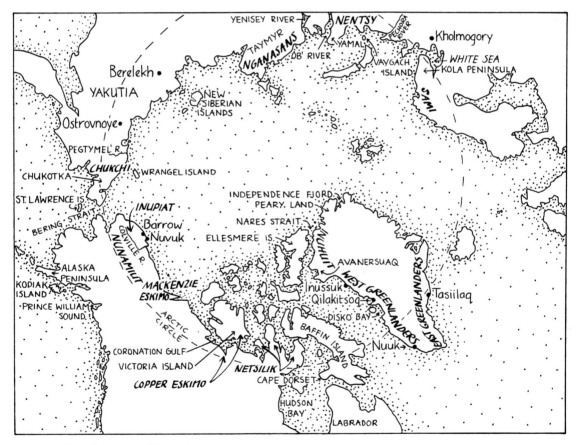

Map 2. Peoples of the tundra.

the price they paid for their success in learning to live in the Arctic. They were still subsistence hunter–gatherers when first confronted by Europeans. Table 1 sets out some data on those discussed below.

Name of people	Date of first contact with Europeans	Person making the first contact	Approximate size of population	Source of population estimate
Sami	before 890	?	32,600 in 1940	Manker 1954:60
Nentsy	Eleventh century	Expedition from Novgorod	9,427 in 1897	Levin and Potapov 1965:105
Nganasans	?	?	876 in 1897	Armstrong 1965: 105
Chukchi	1642	Ivan Verastov	5,000 in 1878–9 12,000 in 1990	Nordenskiöld 1881b: 81–2 Bogoras 1904: 32
Inupiat Eskimos	1826	Thomas Elson	2,000–2,500 in 1853	John Simpson in Bockstoce 1988b: 506
Copper Eskimos	1771	Samuel Hearne	793 in 1941 1,115 in 1963	Damas 1984: 410
Netsilik Eskimos	1829	John Ross	579 in 1923	Balikci 1984: 429
West Greenlanders	1585	John Davis	5,122 in 1789 10,254 in 1890	Kleivan 1984: 597
East Greenlanders	1752	Peder Walløe	413 in 1884 at Ammassalik (Tasiilaq)	Petersen 1984: 638

Table 1.   Tundra peoples mentioned in Chapter 1 with dates of first contact with Europeans and population estimates.

It would be unfortunate if the attempt to describe Arctic societies as they were when first contact with Europeans was made, gave the impression that these societies were static. They were not. Constantly adapting to the demands of their harsh environment, to changes in climate, to fluctuations in numbers of their prey, they were ceaselessly evolving new social and demographic patterns, new weapons and material equipment, and new ideas. Far from being stable, the varying groups into which the Arctic peoples were divided formed intensely dynamic societies, which also repeatedly suffered sudden breaks or discontinuities of one kind or another (Krupnik 1989).

THE SAMI, SOMETIME LAPPS

The Sami may be unique among present-day Arctic peoples in the length of time they have been in the Arctic. They may even have remained in the same place within the Arctic. For they and their immediate ancestors are thought by some to have inhabited the far north of Norway, Sweden and Finland, as well as Russia's Kola Peninsula, at least for the last eight thousand years, that is nearly since the end of the ice age, though formerly their settlement area probably extended further east and south. Although they call themselves Samek or Sameh, in the remote past they were known as Finns, Fenni or Scrithifinni. Later, the name Lapps was used for them. Modern practice varies, but the form Sami (or Saami) seems to be gaining in popularity over Samek, and the word 'Lapp' is now obsolete. The Sami were the only Arctic people of whom the Greeks and Romans had any knowledge, and this was summed up in about AD 550 by the Byzantine historian Procopius. He called them *Skrithiphinoi* and noted that they lived like wild beasts, having neither clothing nor shoes, apart from what they could make from animal skins, and drinking no wine. They obtained no nourishment from the earth and hunting was their only occupation. Later sources and archaeological finds confirm that Procopius's curious word *Skrithiphinoi* for the Sami implies that they had greatly increased their mobility as hunters by learning to run swiftly over the snow on wooden planks or skis, which they probably did not themselves invent (Manker 1954, Whitaker 1955, Manker 1963, Graburn and Strong 1973: 11–33, Spencer 1978, Meriot 1984, Zorgdrager 1984).

Sami subsistence activities were never confined to a single specialization. The nomadic reindeer herding they are popularly linked with was limited to the mountainous border region of northern Norway and Sweden, was undertaken by a minority of Sami only, and apparently became the chief means of livelihood of these Sami only from about the sixteenth century AD. Before then the communal hunt for wild reindeer was a much more important activity. Wooden fences were constructed along the animals' migration routes so that they could be driven into corrals and despatched with spears. Or a fence would be constructed across their route and pitfalls made or snares set in gaps in it. In winter the deer could be rounded up, using men on skis and dogs, and then killed. Domesticated reindeer were used to catch wild reindeer, especially during the autumn rutting season. Snares were attached to the antlers of a tame male deer so that the wild bucks were entrapped when they attempted to fight with it. Or else a man would hide among a group of tame does and spear or shoot the stags that were attracted to them. Although they also hunted wild reindeer, coastal Sami in north Norway and the Kola Peninsula probably depended more on fishing. This was carried out with the aid of small wooden boats made of planks lashed together. In winter, on frozen lakes, nets were set under the ice and hooks and lines used in holes kept open with an ice chisel. In principle, the Sami dwelling consisted of poles arranged round a frame made of curved branches. In summer the poles were fewer and lighter and the covering was of reindeer skins sewn together. In winter the more substantial poles were covered with birch bark and overlaid with turf. At least since the fifteenth century a favourite means of transport was a boat-like wooden sledge pulled by reindeer.

Although the essential unit of Sami society was the nuclear family, which normally shared a single dwelling or tent, these families were linked in wider cooperatives or groups known as the *siida* in the west and *sit* in the east. A *siida* might contain up to twenty related families, and it occupied a defined hunting and fishing territory. It was controlled by a council comprised of the heads of families in it, and this council was responsible for organizing communal hunts, maintaining trapping systems, allocating fishing grounds between families and adjudicating disputes. It also annually elected a head man or chief of the *siida*.

The religion of the Sami, based on animism and shamanism, was broadly speaking common to all the northern peoples of Eurasia. Many natural features and all living beings were believed to have spirits or souls. At particular places in the countryside thought to be frequented by spirits, pieces of stone or wood, sometimes with effigies carved on them, were set up, and sacrifices of reindeer meat and various animals were offered. A miniature forest of reindeer antlers from sacrificed animals often formed a semi-circle round the effigy. To facilitate his entry into a trance and his soul-flight to the world of spirits, the shaman used a 'magic' reindeer-skin drum, which was often covered with tiny figures painted with reddish pigment made from alder bark (Ahlbäck and Bergman 1991). In the ritual bear hunt Sami hunters accompanied by the shaman aroused a hibernating bear and killed it. Then they dragged its carcase ceremonially back to camp for a ritual bear feast, to the accompaniment of special songs inviting the bear's soul not to take revenge and asking its forgiveness. Butchered without damaging a single bone, and then cooked, the bear was served and eaten, to the accompaniment of more songs, by the hunters seated in a circle in a particular order. For three days these hunters remained under taboo and could only return to their own households after a special purification ceremony. The bear's bones were buried. The skin was stretched out and used as an archery target for the women, who were blindfolded for this contest. The husband of the first woman to hit the target was granted the honour of killing the next bear. A bear cult of some kind existed among many aboriginal peoples, especially among those of the lower Amur.

SIXTEENTH-CENTURY SAMOYEDS

The tundra dwellers of northern Russia and Siberia, living north of the Arctic Circle between the White Sea and the Yenisey, have long been called Samoyeds in both Russian and Western European accounts of the region (see Schrenk 1848, Jackson 1895, Hajdu 1963, Prokof'yeva 1964, Vasil'yev and Geydenreykh 1977). Philologists at first treated the word *Samoyed* as Russian in origin and suggested 'self-eaters' or 'people who go together' as possible meanings. The first of these two etymologies was the more favoured, and the Samoyeds were consequently long thought to have been cannibals: a Russian report of about 1560 translated for Richard Johnson claimed that they would feast a visiting merchant on one of their own children and, should he die among them, they would eat his body (Hakluyt 1907a: 467). The word Samoyed has more plausibly been linked with the word Sami and has been variously construed as meaning 'the land of the Sami' (*saam-yedno* in Sami) or 'marsh-dwellers'. The first of these makes sense because the Samoyeds were relatively recent intruders from central Asia into the Russian coastal tundras, where they may have replaced the Sami, causing them to withdraw westwards. At any rate numerous Samoyed legends concern their predecessors in the tundra, who lived in semi-underground houses. The eighteenth-century Russian explorer and academician, Ivan Lepekhin, claimed that the remains of such dwellings, with human artefacts and bones in them, had been found. In any event, modern Russian experts have very prudently abandoned the dubious word, and the Samoyeds are now known as *Nenets* (rendered in English 'Nyanitz' by Trevor-Battye 1895: 131 n.1) in the singular or *Nentsy* in the plural, which are Russianized forms of the name they use to describe themselves, meaning 'people'. The word *Samoyed* is still used as a generic term for the group of related peoples which include the Nentsy, the Nganasans and others.

The earliest accounts of the Nentsy, or Samoyeds as they were then called, made by English and Dutch seafarers in search of the North-East Passage to Cathay, in the sixteenth century, describe a people still virtually in their aboriginal state. Although expeditions from Novgorod had already, before the close of the twelfth century, levied tribute on the Samoyeds as far as their winter quarters on the Pechora River (Platonov and Andreyev 1922: 31), in 1556 they still would not allow Russians to land on the 'Islands of Vaigats', their summer quarters (Hakluyt 1907a: 354). Stephen Burrough, who sailed the pinnace *Serchthrift* as far as Vaygach Island (ostrov Vaygach) in 1556, was told that the Samoyeds had no houses, only tents made of reindeer skins sewn together and stretched over a framework of poles. They used reindeer as draught animals and carried their skin boats on their backs when they went ashore. The captain of a Russian ship, named Loshak, took Burrough ashore to show him a group of about three hundred crudely carved Samoyed idols (Hakluyt 1907a: 347).

> The eyes and mouthes of sundrie of them were bloodie, they had the shape of men, women and children, very grosly wrought, & that which they had made for other parts, was also sprinckled with blood. Some of their idols were an olde sticke with two or three notches, made with a knife in it. . . . Before certaine of their idols blocks were made as high as their mouthes, being all bloody. I thought that to be the table wheron they offered their sacrifice: I saw also the instruments, whereupon they had roasted flesh, and as farre as I could perceive, they make their fire directly under the spit.

Unable to penetrate through the ice at the entrance to the Kara Sea (Map 7), on 23 August Burrough set course for home. The *Serchthrift* reached Kholmogory near Arkangel'sk on 10 September and there the winter was passed. On 5 January 1557, possibly somewhere near Kholmogory, a member of the party, Richard Johnson, attended the seance of a Samoyed priest or shaman and wrote a detailed description of what he saw, apparently some time after the event. The shaman wore a sort of white garland over his head. His face was covered with a piece of 'a shirt of maile' from the links of which dangled numerous small bones and teeth of animals. Using a stick about a span long with a round head covered with deerskin at one end, he beat on a sieve-like deerskin drum, at the same time singing 'as we use heere in England to hallow, whope, or shout at houndes'. The assembled company responded with many times repeated cries of 'Owtis, Igha, Igha Igha' to which the shaman replied 'with his voyces'. This went on and on until the shaman collapsed and lay on the floor on his back as if dead. Johnson's Russian was good enough to communicate with the Samoyeds and for him to be taken by them for a Russian. Asked why the shaman was lying on the ground, an onlooker told him that 'our God' would advise the shaman what they should do and where they should go. After a while the shaman rose to his feet and told them to kill five reindeer, then both he and the rest continued singing as before. Then the shaman pushed a sword into his belly, but no wound was to be seen, nor did

*Plate 1. The ancient Samoyed place of worship (*kapishche*) on Cape Greben, the most southerly point of Vaygach Island, as sketched above by Lieutenant Andreas Hovgaard of the Royal Swedish Navy, during the* Vega's *circumnavigation of Europe and Asia in 1878–9 (Nordenskiöld 1881a: 91) and below by Frederick George Jackson in 1893 (Jackson 1895: 34). Earlier descriptions of this place mention a massive* bolvan *or wooden effigy with seven faces carved on it one below another, 420 smaller wooden idols arranged in rows in a semicircle south of it, a heap of reindeer antlers stacked to a height of over 2 m (6 ft), thirty Polar bear skulls and, a short distance away, twenty smaller idols of stone. The idols were burnt by the missionary Archimandrite Veniamin in the 1820s (Vasil'yev and Geydenreykh 1977: 73–4; see Chapter 12 below).*

he suffer any harm when, after warming the sword in the fire, he inserted it through 'the slitte of his shirt and thrust it through his bodie, as I thought, in at his navill and out at his fundament'. After this, the singing still continuing, the shaman sat on a special seat set against the inside wall of the tent 'called Chome in their language' and took off his head coverings and shirt but still wore his deerskin trousers with the hair on. He continued singing while assistants on either side stretched a deerskin rope across him, which he tied round his neck and under his left arm. Then, after a cauldron of hot water was placed in front of him and a cloth draped over him, the assistants pulled on the rope until Johnson heard something heavy splash into the water. This, he was told, was the shaman's head, shoulder and left arm which the cord had cut off. The curious Johnson was not allowed to look to see if this was true, and the performance came to an end when the shaman emerged in one piece (Hakluyt 1907a: 354–6).

Almost forty years after Stephen Burrough's visit, a Dutch fleet arrived at Vaygach Island. In July 1594 Jan Huygen van Linschoten described the same sacred spot, with its three or four hundred wooden idols, all facing south, surrounded with reindeer antlers. Both in 1594 and again in September 1595 the Dutch made contact near Vaygach Island with the still-heathen Samoyeds, some of whom could speak broken Russian and be understood by the interpreters the Dutch had brought with them. One of these was a Russian, married and living in Holland; another was a Dutchman who had lived a long time in Russia. The Samoyeds had bows and arrows and wooden sledges drawn by two to four reindeer and wore fur clothes with the skin on the outside. Their gloves and hoods were sewn onto their coats. Their swarthy faces bore no sign of beard because, as they explained, they pulled the hairs out to look better. They had pitch-black smooth and straight hair which fell down over their ears. They were alert and quick-moving and leaped about like young stallions. One of them seemed to be a chief: he wore silver ear-rings and different clothes, and the others seemed to obey him. His bow was decorated with gold leaf. They had nothing for sale except walrus teeth, for which they asked almost their weight in gold (Beke 1876: 60, Naber 1914: 75–87, 160–73; Van der Moer 1979: 205–9, 237–43). Such, in the sixteenth century, were the nomadic Nentsy, who summered on the Russian Arctic coast and islands and moved south to winter in the valley of the River Pechora and elsewhere inland. This annual migration, as well as a similar one between Yamal and the valley of the Ob' (Nansen 1914: 26–39), was still taking place three hundred years later.

NGANASAN REINDEER HUNTERS

The Russian anthropologist A.A. Popov made a detailed study of the Nganasans or Nganasany in the 1930s, when they were still almost isolated from European civilization (Chard 1963: 105–21, Popov 1965). They are the most northerly of all Siberian peoples. Numbering around 850 to 900 persons, these nomadic reindeer hunters of Taymyr moved north and south annually following their prey over distances of up to seven hundred miles between the low-lying forest or scrub tundra in the south and the Taymyr highlands or Byrranga Mountains (gory

Byrranga; Map 14). They kept domesticated reindeer for transport rather than for meat – they were hunters rather than herders. Although the Nganasans now share a single culture and language, they are heterogenous and relatively recent in origin. Of three tribes or clans into which they were divided, one originated from a certain Oko, who went to live among the Nganasans in the early nineteenth century. He belonged to a neighbouring people called Dolgans. Another originated from a forest people called Tungus until infiltrated and absorbed by Nentsy in the eighteenth century, and the third probably originated in the seventeenth century from Tungus and from earlier pre-Nentsy tundra dwellers.

Although the Nganasans hunted reindeer individually by means of stalking, their cooperative hunts, which were similar to those of the Sami, were their main source of meat, which was divided equally among the participants in the hunt. In one of these, long poles, each with a white ptarmigan's wing attached to the top, called *makhavki*, and not used anywhere else in Siberia, were employed. When a herd of deer was located, these poles, or similar ones with lumps of turf or reindeer skulls fixed on top of them, were set up in two converging rows leading into a suitable lake. While some hunters in dugout canoes concealed themselves on the opposite shore of the lake, others, with the aid of dogs and reindeer sledges, drove the deer into the funnel-shaped enclosure formed by the poles. Once in the water the deer were killed with spears by the men in the canoes. In winter a similar technique was employed on the open snow-covered tundra using a net about 50 m (150 ft) long held by three or four posts and fixed across the narrow end of two converging rows of *makhavki*. The Nganasans used similar techniques to catch flocks of moulting geese in the autumn (Vaughan 1992: 37–8). They also trapped foxes, and some of them spent the summer fishing in Lake Taymyr (ozero Taymyr) and the rivers flowing into it. They had no fish spear, using instead a gorge, that is a splinter of reindeer leg bone 10–15 cm (4–6 in) long. The bait was fixed to one end, the line firmly attached to the middle, and the gorge then suspended in the water. When the fish swallowed the bait, the gorge stuck in its gullet.

Nganasan society was made up of a network of patriarchal clans which owned or controlled the fishing sites and reindeer-killing places, but their nomadic settlements were often made up of families from different clans. A member of a clan had to select a spouse from another clan. The Nganasans were unusual among Eurasian Arctic peoples in lacking any kind of ski or snow shoe for winter hunting. Their main hunting weapon in the nineteenth century was a bow intricately constructed of pieces of larch wood lashed tightly together, which shot arrows of several types, including one with a two-pronged or forked head for birds. This bow replaced an earlier one made of reindeer antler. The aboriginal dwelling of the Nganasans was excavated into the ground, and built of stones and driftwood covered with turves.

THE CHUKCHI IN THE NINETEENTH CENTURY

The ethnic history of the numerous Siberian peoples who at least partly inhabit the Arctic – the Komi, the Khanty and Mansi, the Yakuts, Dolgans, Yukagirs and the rest (Map 38) – is too complex for a separate enumeration here. But one distinctive and relatively well-documented people cannot be omitted, namely the Chukchi of Chukotka or the Chukchi Peninsula, that is, of the far north-east of Siberia. The English Arctic geographer Clements R. Markham (1921: 16) considered the Chukchi race 'to be the finest on the Siberian coast'. Russian anthropologist Vladimir Bogoraz (Bogoras 1904, Bogoraz 1934; see too Antropova and Kuznetsova 1965), exiled to Siberia for ten years in 1889 after serving a three-year prison sentence in the fortress at Petropavlovsk in Kamchatka for his revolutionary activities, studied the Chukchi in unusual detail. Before him the Swedish explorer Adolf Erik Nordenskiöld had seized the opportunity to investigate them when, between 28 September 1878 and 18 July 1879, his ship the *Vega* was beset in the ice off the north Chukotka coast between Kolyuchin Bay (Kolyuchinskaya guba) and Cape Serdtse-Kamen'. The result was a lengthy chapter in his classic *The Voyage of the* Vega *Round Asia and Europe* (1881b: 70–147) on the 'history, physique, disposition and manners' of the Chukchi. Inevitably the aristocratic Swede's anthropological fieldwork was unsystematic, though his expedition took home a fine collection of artefacts of all kinds including stone hammers with bone handles, bows and arrows, carved ivory figurines and drawings done by Chukchi on paper (Plate 27). He was unable to study Chukchi social organization and intellectual culture, but believed that they had no chiefs or social organization and no crime, and that they were monogamous. He never came across a shaman.

Exactly thirty years before Nordenskiöld's enforced wintering in Chukotka, a similar contingency had overtaken Her Majesty's Ship *Plover*, which was beset in southern Chukotka 300 km (180 miles) due south of the *Vega*'s winter quarters, in a bay which her commander, T.E.L. Moore, named Providence Bay (bukhta Provideniya). On this occasion Lieutenant William Hulme Hooper RN participated in numerous shore parties, travelling as far north as Cape Dezhnev, and compiled a dossier on the Chukchi, or Tuski as he called them, published in book form in 1853 under the title *Ten Months Among the Tents of the Tuski* (Hooper 1853, and see Bockstoce 1988a: 14–25). Hooper and his British shipmates got on famously with the Tuski. When their friend the supposed local chief (*toyon*) Akool became grandfather to a little girl, the *Plover*'s crew fired a 21-gun salute to mark the event. Hooper (1853: 34–6) mistakenly thought the name *Tuski* meant 'brotherhood' or 'confederation', and that the Reindeer *Tuski* or Tuski Proper, nomadic reindeer herders of the interior, were 'evidently the original proprietors or occupants of the soil' (p. 35). Actually the word *Chukchi* means 'rich in reindeer' and Hooper noted that the Reindeer Tuski slaughtered deer for food and clothed themselves in well-cured skins. The Alien or Fishing Tuski spoke a 'dialect evidently first corrupted from the Esquimaux' but with many words adopted from 'the Reindeer tribe', and were 'infinitely inferior both in moral and physical condition to their neighbours' (p. 35). The two groups were on friendly terms and traded with one another, the coastal Tuski bartering seal skins and walrus ivory in return for deer skins and meat from the reindeer Tuski. They were evidently not entirely distinct and Hooper concluded that the Alien Tuski were the result of immigration from America while the Tuski Proper were indigenous. He describes vividly the Tuski's broad, rotund, flat Mongolian faces, those of the women tattooed on the chin with diverging lines, and their ornate knee-length reindeer skin coats, fawnskin shirts, well-made belts and mittens, and handsome boots. He thought them reliable, hospitable and sociable, and believed their society was organized in small egalitarian brotherhoods. However, there were inescapable traces of a social hierarchy among them – a few were much better dressed and 'of a higher condition' than most of their fellows (pp. 59–60). Hooper thus confirmed what the Russian explorer Lieutenant (later Admiral) Ferdinand Petr Vrangel, of the Imperial Navy, had noted on his expedition to Chukotka in 1823, namely that 'a kind of bondage exists both among the settled and the nomade Tchuktches'. He surmised, no doubt correctly, that these apparent household slaves of the wealthier Chukchis were descendants of former captives (Wrangell 1844: 361), for, as noted earlier in this chapter, the Chukchi were obtaining slaves from Alaska in this way in the eighteenth century.

The coastal Tuski dwelling was called a *yaranga*. On a circular or oval frame of whale ribs was stretched a cover of beautifully cleaned and prepared walrus skins. They were translucent and some were very large, up to 70 or 80 ft (23 or 26 m) square, thought Hooper. Ample light came through this roof. Snow was heaped round the outside of the *yaranga* and ropes of hide passed over the roof secured the whole thing to the ground. There was an entrance hall or antechamber, and cubicles for sleeping in were arranged round the inside. The blubber lamp was a large shallow dish with a moss wick which, if properly trimmed, gave out a great deal of heat but no smoke or smell. Outside the *yarangas* in one coastal settlement eighteen or twenty whale skulls were arranged in pairs to rest walrus-skin boats on. Hooper was sure that the Tuski practised polygamy. One wife was head of the *yaranga* and the owner might have two or three others who showed no jealousy. But often a man had a single wife. On average, Hooper reckoned ten persons to a *yaranga* though one, which was extremely neat and clean, housed twenty-six people. On one occasion he describes a six-course Tuski feast to which he was treated (pp. 170–4):

1. A small raw frozen fish on a wooden tray: inedible [*stroganina*: still in use now].
2. A 'mess of green stuff' from a reindeer's stomach, with blubber. 'We didn't like it.' [*mariyalo*: a main source of vitamins in winter.]
3. Boiled seal and walrus meat: tough and tasteless.
4. Cubes of chopped-up black whaleskin: eaten with relish.Cocoa-nut flavour.
5. Boiled reindeer meat. 'We did ample justice' to this.
6. 'Portions of the gum of the whale, in which the ends of the bone lay still embedded': 'perfectly delicious'.

Although some of his Tuski friends had been baptized by Russian priests on trading visits to the fair at Ostrovnoye on the Malyy Anyuy river, a right bank tributary of the Kolyma (Map 38), Hooper believed they were still heathen. He witnessed a religious ceremony performed after his friend Ahmoleen had killed a small whale (pp. 179–81):

Upon the bank above the sea was lit a fire, into which were thrown the entrails of a puppy, just strangled; its carcase was then cast into the wave. Fish, venison, blubber, and some other sorts of food were boiled over this fire, and minced very fine; the head, fins and tail of the whale, were disposed near, and upon them were laid small portions of the cooked food, a few beads, some tobacco, and mites of several other of their most valuable articles. The food, when cooked, was handed round in separate platters to the assembled crowd, each of whom was also presented with a small strip of tobacco; nor was I omitted in this attention, although the latter article had been obtained from me for the purpose. After all had been served, and some time allowed to elapse, the offerings upon the fish, together with pieces cut from its head, tail and fins were consumed in the fire. All was conducted in almost unbroken silence; even the queries, which with ill judgement I presumed upon my friendship to put to Ahmoleen, who was the person principally officiating, were responded to in an under tone; and the company, comprising the greater part of the villagers, seemed impressed with a sense of the sacred nature of the ceremonies. Inside his yarang, Mooldooyah, Ahmoleen's father, whom I have before said I believed to be a shaman, or priest, beat incessantly upon the largest drum I ever saw among the people, chanting monotonously in a succession of quivering notes, and drawling out the words to a great length. The burden of his ditty, which might easily have been taken for a dirge rather than a song of rejoicing, ran very much in this way:– 'Ah.....h mo.....o le.....en, K...à . poo.....ok ah.....h, Wahl.....dah; Mà.....à zi.....n.....kah, Mà.....zi.....n . Kah, Kà.....à poo.....k.....ah, Ka.....poo.....kah.' [Ahmoleen a whale has killed good, good, the whale the whale, &c.] and so on *ad libitum*, with an occasional change into 'Ah.....h.....h.....ah.....ah,' as his breath denied utterance to the words. There was much to strike one as extraordinary in the appearance of this minister of a rude religion. Seated crosslegged in his tent, nude from the waist upwards, his body swaying to and fro with the intonations of his chant, perspiration streaming from every pore of his vast bulk, the huge tambourine filling the entire space with its reverberations, and, above all, the expression of conviction impressed upon his lineaments of the sacred importance of his duty, Mooldooyah acquired a new and imposing character, far different to his ordinary nature.

INUPIAT WHALE HUNTERS OF NORTHERN ALASKA

The Eskimos or Inuit are the most widespread, the most numerous, and the most studied, of all truly Arctic peoples (Rasmussen 1933, Birket-Smith 1936, Oswalt 1979, Damas (ed.) 1984, Kleivan and Sonne 1985, Burch 1988). At the start of historic times their habitual hunting territories stretched from north-east Asia and St Lawrence Island (Sivokak), where they called themselves Yuit, through Alaska, occupied by Yupik in the south-west and Inupiaq or Inupiat in the north, and Canada, where the term Inuit is widely used, to Greenland where the word Kalaallit is coming into use to refer to all Greenlanders. Throughout their extensive territories the Eskimos were divided into small, discrete tribal groups.

Each had a distinct territory and a name composed of the name of their principle settlement or a river or other geographical feature with the suffix –*miut* 'inhabitants of' added (Map 3 below). Thus the Eskimos living at or near Point Barrow, on Alaska's north coast, were the Nuvugmiut after their settlement of Nuvuk. Here, it will only be possible to mention a few of these groups.

HMS *Plover*'s contribution to anthropology in the middle years of the nineteenth century was by no means limited to Lieutenant Hooper's account of the aboriginal Chukchi, for the ship's surgeon, John Simpson, compiled the first systematic report on the north Alaskan Inupiat (Bockstoce 1988b: 501–50 and 1988a: 14–49) while the ship was wintering at Point Barrow in 1852–4 in the vain hope that the lost John Franklin and his men might find their way there. Like the Chukchi, the Inupiat were not quite in their primordial state, for, as Simpson noticed, they already possessed articles of trade of European manufacture and suffered from diseases of European origin. Nonetheless, his balanced, well-informed and dispassionate account was essentially that of an aboriginal society. It set the tone for subsequent European and American perceptions of early Eskimo societies, though many of these were less enlightened than his.

The entire population of north-west Alaskan Eskimos in the mid-nineteenth century was thought by Simpson not to exceed 2,500 persons. At Nuvuk in the winter of 1852/3 there were 54 inhabited dwellings, and at the end of 1853, 309 people were living there, 166 males and 143 females. In seasons when game was scarce, famine occurred, accounting for most of the 27 people who died at Nuvuk in 1853–4 (as against four births) as well as for 40 dead in the neighbouring settlement of Cape Smyth (now Ukpeagvik or Barrow). The dome-shaped wooden winter houses, partly excavated into the ground, were covered with a thick layer of earth, and were entered through a round hole in the floor via a 25 ft (7.6 m) long passageway. The house was warmed to a temperature of 70° F (21° C) by a large shallow stone blubber lamp obtained from 'the eastern Esquimaux, who procure it from a more distant people' (the Copper Eskimos) (Bockstoce 1988b: 528). There was a hole in the centre of the roof of the house, in which a funnel of stiff hide was inserted to serve as a chimney, and a square window 'covered with a transparent membrane stretched into a dome-shape by two pieces of whalebone arched from corner to corner . . .' (p. 528). Behind the house, which was nearly invisible when snow-covered in winter, the framework of tall driftwood posts with cross-bars to keep kayaks, skins, meat and the like out of reach of dogs, showed up conspicuously against the horizon. There were a few larger wooden houses, not covered with earth. This type of building was 'called a Ka-ri-gi' and was 'used by the men to assemble in for the purpose of dancing, in which the women join, for working, conversing and idling, while the boys are unconsciously learning the customs and imbibing the sentiments of their elders' (pp. 531–2). The summer tent or *tupak* was a cone-shaped structure based on four or five 12 or 13 ft (4 m) long poles covered with seal skins, or reindeer skins inland.

A striking feature of the physical apearance of the Nuvuk people was their sooty black hair, 'without gloss and coarse', cut in a fringe across the forehead but allowed to grow long at the sides and back of the head. Their faces were rather broad and plump and they had short, flat noses. Their eyes were of varying shades of brown, which 'generally have a soft expression; some have a peculiar glitter, which we called gipsy-like' (p. 508). The good-natured smiling faces of the men were disfigured, as Simpson thought, by the stone labrets they wore protruding from their face on either side, just below the lower lip opposite the eye-tooth. The most expensive and coveted of these were 'each made of a flat circular piece of white stone, an inch and a half in diameter, the front surface of which is flat and has cemented to it half a large blue bead' (p. 509). Simpson thought it fortunate that the appearance of the women's faces was not deformed by labrets, but instead 'marked with three tattoed lines from the margin of the lower lip to the under surface of the chin', the middle one rather over half an inch broad (p. 511).

Both men and women wore elaborate fur clothing. The man's caribou-skin-hooded parka with hair outside had a fawnskin lining with the fur inwards. The hood and the lower hem of the parka were fringed with wolf or wolverine fur. The trousers were also of caribou skin and the boots were usually made from the dark-coloured skin of the caribou's legs, or else vertical strips of this alternated with white strips from the animal's belly. The soles were of white dressed sealskin and the boots cushioned inside with whalebone scrapings or dry grass. At the 'grand summer dance', the whaling festival or *nalukataq*, which is still held at Barrow to this day, every variety of dress was displayed. The dancers wore headbands supporting eagle's feathers and their faces were marked 'with a streak of black lead, either in a diagonal line across or down one side of the face . . .'(p. 513). Many of the headbands were made of the skin and neck of an animal or bird, with the nose or beak retained so as to project from the centre of the forehead. The long bill of the white-billed diver was conspicuous among them.

Cheerfulness and intense curiosity were the two most evident features of the Nuvuk Eskimos' mentality. Their treatment of their children and womenfolk was favourably commented on. One group travelling in summer with fourteen tents and as many umiaks, or women's boats, were taking with them and caring for a crippled old man, a blind and helpless old woman, another old invalid, two women with sprained ankles, and children of various ages. Their hospitality, both to other Eskimos and to whites, was exemplary. Although there was 'nothing among them resembling acknowledged authority or chieftainship' the 'chief men are called Omeliks (wealthy), and have acquired their position by being more thrifty and intelligent, better traders, and usually better hunters'. Curiously, Simpson did not mention that the Omelik, or better Umialik, was the owner of an umiak or boat used for whaling. He interrogated the Eskimos about their classification and naming of the constellations and learned that the three stars of Orion's belt were three men 'who were carried away on the ice to the southward in the dark winter. They were for a long time covered with snow, but at length, perceiving an opening above them, they ascended farther and farther until they became fixed among the stars' (p. 546).

The Nuvuk people undertook prolonged journeys in the spring after closing their winter houses. They loaded tent, umiak, kayaks and blubber or train oil in sealskin containers on sledges, and travelled eastwards along the coast. Arriving at an unfrozen inlet of the sea, they reversed the mode of transport, packing the sledges and everything else into the umiak and continuing the journey by water. After a ten or eleven day journey they arrived at a bartering place near the mouth of the Colville River. Six or ten hectic days followed, of bartering, revelry and dancing with their trading partners from inland, the Nunamiut or 'inland people' (Gubser 1965). These brought to the mouth of the Colville not only their own produce of caribou skins and coats, otter skins, feathers for arrows and headdresses and the like, but also manufactured goods of Russian origin: iron and copper kettles, knives and tobacco. These last the Nunamiut obtained in the summer on the west coast of Alaska, at Sheshalik in Kotzebue Sound, from the Chukchi, who crossed Bering Strait every summer in several boats with goods to trade. The Nunamiut carried their share of these into the interior and then descended the River Colville with them the following summer.

After bartering some of their trade articles with the Nunamiut, the Nuvuk people carried on further eastwards along the coast to a rendezvous with the Mackenzie Eskimos, who lived in that river's delta. From them they obtained narwhal skins, wolverine and wolf pelts, the soapstone lamps originating with the Copper Eskimos of the central Canadian Arctic, as well as knives, beads, guns and ammunition ultimately deriving from the Hudson's Bay Company. In return for these, the Nuvuk people supplied the Mackenzie Eskimos with the balance of their whale oil, whalebone, walrus tusks and sealskins and some of the goods acquired from the Nunamiut. Tracing the fortunes of a single trade article in this complex bartering network, Simpson described how a knife of Russian manufacture obtained at the Ostrovnoye fair by the reindeer or inland Chukchi would spend a winter with them, a second with the Nunamiut in inland Alaska, a third winter with the Mackenzie Eskimos, and only some time after that would it reach the Copper Eskimos of Victoria Island. The lamps made by the Copper Eskimos, which Simpson had often seen in Chukchi dwellings when the *Plover* was wintering in Providence Bay in 1848/9, would travel by the same roundabout route but in the opposite direction. Though manufactured goods of European origin were being injected into it from either end by the Russians and British this trading system, described so interestingly by John Simpson, was certainly in part aboriginal. A similar one has been described from west Greenland, where it was the Dutch who injected manufactured articles into an Eskimo exchange economy (Gulløv 1987, Kramer 1992). Though between north-east Asia and north-west America articles of trade made lengthy journeys of several years' duration a quarter of the way round the Arctic Circle, each of their carriers had only to travel for a month or two in the summer. As Simpson discovered, this trade circuit had only been recently extended to include the Mackenzie Eskimos. It soon collapsed when, in the second half of the nineteenth century, the Hudson's Bay Company and American whalers and traders cut into it in the east and west respectively (Morrison 1991).

A remarkable feature of the Inupiat life-style was, and still is, the whale hunt, which was not described by Simpson (Spencer 1959: 332–52, Spencer 1984). It could perhaps more accurately be called the cult of the whale. The entire culture and social organization of each whaling community revolved round the communal whale hunt of migrating bowheads, which was carried out in spring and autumn from the ice edge up to ten miles offshore. These people believe that 'these great whales give themselves to their hunters, if they have been hunted by Inupiat rules that govern the relationship between the people and the whales' (Berger 1985: 48). A successful catch provided food and fuel for the entire settlement throughout the winter. The hunt was organized and led by whaling captains called *umialiks*, each of whom owned an umiak and recruited and led its crew. The umiaks, though universally known as women's boats and normally rowed by women, were paddled by a crew of six to ten men. As soon as a passing whale was sighted, the umiaks were launched from the ice edge and the whale was harpooned, then killed with a stone-pointed lance. Dragged onto the ice by the entire community, the 30 ton carcase was butchered there after every person in the entire community had helped themselves to as much of the black skin, or *muktuk*, as they could carry in one container. Afterwards, the meat was stored in ice cellars in the permafrost. Magic and ritual accompanied the whale hunt from start to finish, the umialik acting as a sort of high priest as well as commander. New clothing was sewn for his crew and a new cover for the umiak. After they had eaten a specially prepared meal, the crew went to live in a separate house or *karigi*, and abstained from sexual relations. Songs, charms such as a beetle, a stuffed raven, or the hair of a deceased whaler, amulets and taboos played a crucial role. The umialik's wife took a leading part, and had special ceremonial mittens, which came half-way up her forearm and were trimmed with wolf fur, sewn for her. She sang her own special whaling songs while pouring fresh water on the umiak. When the whale was dragged onto the ice, she greeted it formally, wearing special clothes and with her face made up with soot and grease. She poured fresh water on the whale's snout and blowhole and invited the whale to drink and return next spring. Then the wives of the crew thanked the whale for allowing itself to be captured. The whale hunt continues to this day.

COPPER ESKIMOS

The Inuit of Arctic Canada have been divided into eight or so main groups, each of which was itself composed of up to twenty smaller groups. The Copper Eskimo (Jenness 1922, Damas 1984), whose territory in about 1900 covered the southern half of Victoria Island and a large mainland area to the south of it around Coppermine and Bathurst Inlet, were so named because of their use of copper to make implements. That sharp-eyed traveller Samuel Hearne, who encountered some of them near the mouth of the Coppermine River in 1771, described them briefly, fifty years before they as much as saw another white man (Glover 1958: 108–10). Although their physique, clothes and hunting implements closely resembled those of the Eskimos of Hudson Bay, they did have some distinctive features. The men had 'all the hair of their heads pulled out by the roots' (p. 110), while the women 'wore their hair at full length' exactly as all the other Eskimo women he had seen. The use of copper by these Eskimos also struck Hearne as unusual. The men's 'bayonets' had copper blades 'in shape like the ace of spades' (p. 109) mounted on foot-long handles made of caribou antler, and their hatchets were also of copper, the head lashed to a wooden handle. Among kitchen utensils

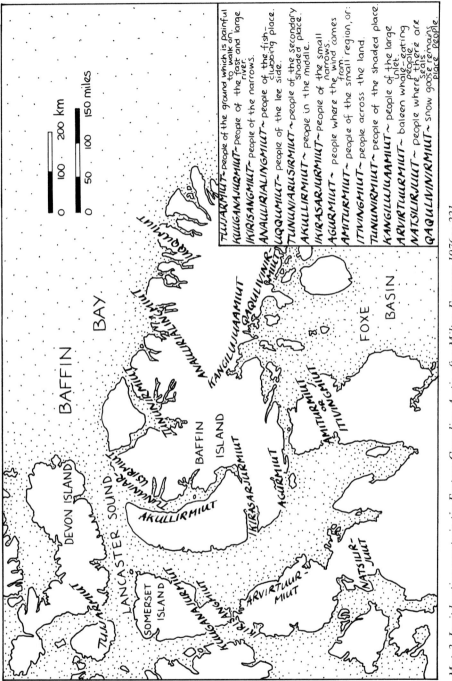

Map 3. Inuit hunting groups in the Eastern Canadian Arctic after Milton Freeman 1976a: 221.

they possessed wooden troughs and dishes, scoops and spoons made of buffalo or musk-ox horn, and large stone bowls 'formed of a pepper and salt coloured stone'. Some of them he thought large enough to hold five or six gallons; all were 'ornamented with neat mouldings round the rim'. Hearne calls these 'stone kettles', but some of them were probably the stone lamps made and exported by the Copper Eskimo. There was an outcrop of the soft stone with a soapy feel called soapstone, necessary for making these lamps and bowls, within the territory of the Copper Eskimos, near the Tree River, which flows into Coronation Gulf from the south.

It was July when Hearne inspected the dwellings of the Copper Eskimos, and he was only able to describe their conical summer tents of caribou skin stretched over wooden poles, and some abandoned semi-underground winter houses, apparently of stone with a conical roof of poles. He saw nothing of the remarkable snow houses built by the Copper Eskimos in winter, well described years later by the Canadian anthropologist Diamond Jenness, who lived with the Copper Eskimos between 1913 and 1918. He describes how rectangular blocks of snow were cut out of a snow drift with a special snow knife. These snow blocks were set together on their sides in a circle and built upwards to form an inward-curving wall. In the best constructed snow houses the blocks formed a spiral pattern and no joint between two blocks came directly above or below another. The centre of the domed roof was formed by a single circular block carefully placed in position from inside the house. Gaps and chinks were filled from outside, a snow sleeping bench was formed inside and a window, consisting of a single sheet of freshwater ice cut out the previous autumn, was set into the wall. When the family moved on, a new house could be made in an hour or so, the ice window being packed on the sledge with the bedding and taken along. Jenness illustrates no fewer than thirteen different types of Copper Eskimo snow dwelling, all of which had more or less lengthy entrance passages built of rectangular snow blocks, with a flat roof. One house, owned by a famous shaman with two wives, was arranged inside so that he slept with a wife, each with her own lamp, on either side of him. Joined on to this house was a larger dome-shaped dance house, and the entrance passage led out from that. Other types of dwelling consisted of two or three separate houses with a single entrance passage dividing into two or three; of a single house with two rooms on either side; or of a large dance-house with up to four individual houses arranged round it, with entrances leading into it (Jenness 1922: 59–76; see also Damas 1984).

THE NETSILIK OR NETSILINGMIUT

The next-door neighbours to the east of the Copper Eskimos were the Netsilik, also called Netchillik or Netjilik (Balikci 1970 and 1984, Remie 1984). When Danish explorer-anthropologist Knud Rasmussen (1933: 218–36) visited them in 1923–4 these isolated people, comprising 150 males and 109 females, were divided into five nomadic bands or hunting groups. The excess of males over females was due to female infanticide, which was so prevalent that Rasmussen thought it might even bring them to extinction. It certainly must have contributed to the forceful abduction of other men's wives, which he found to be quite common among them. The very limited food resources available caused the Netsilik hunter to regard girl children as impossible to provide for except through a prior promise in marriage. If this was not possible, then the child was either smothered or exposed outside the igloo until she died. Rasmussen knew of a Netsilik Eskimo aged about sixty who had had twenty children, ten of whom were girls killed in infancy. In one settlement on King William Island he questioned the women individually and found that, out of a total of ninety-six children from eighteen marriages, thirty-eight were girls killed immediately after birth (p. 226). Infanticide was practised by many other Eskimo groups besides the Netsilik, some kind of population control perhaps being regarded as essential to minimise deaths by starvation (see Schrire and Steiger 1981 and references given there).

The name Netsilingmiut means 'the people of the seal' and they had indeed developed a complex technology for harpooning seals in winter through the breathing holes the seals make and keep open in the sea ice, which may be up to 2 m (6 ft) thick. This winter seal hunt required a large number of hunters operating together so that as many seal holes as possible could be manned simultaneously. So, between December and April, winter camps of snow houses were established out on the sea ice, each comprising several extended families. The hunter, after his dog had sniffed out an active seal hole, would carefully cut away the snow that had accumulated round it and chip away part of the dome of ice that had formed over it. Then he pushed a long curved piece of horn down into the hole to ascertain the exact position the seal would be in when it came up to breathe. After this the snow was packed down again over the ice and a hole made to ensure that the harpoon was thrust in precisely the right direction. The head of the harpoon was removable and attached to a line so that, once the seal was struck, it could be hauled back to the hole to be killed and then dragged up onto the ice to be butchered. The Netsilik hunter did not sit by his seal hole, but stood on a sealskin bag used to carry his equipment, motionless, for hours on end in temperatures down to -50° C (-58° F). At the start of the vigil, a special indicator was carefully placed in the hole. This was made from the stiff leg sinew of a caribou, with a swan's feather fixed to one end. The other end was forked in such a way that the forks caught on either side of the opening and the indicator was held in position thereby, the feather being just visible in the top of the hole. When he saw the feather quiver the hunter would know the seal was there, and would plunge his harpoon down into the hole (Rasmussen 1933: 227–9).

WEST GREENLANDERS

The Eskimos living on the west coast of Greenland (Kleivan 1984, Nuttall 1992) referred to themselves, in the eighteenth century, as *Inuit* (Crantz 1767a: 132). Two missionaries who lived among them at that time, the Norwegian Hans Egede (1745: 100–220) and the German David Cranz (Crantz 1767a: 132–240), both gave detailed descriptions of these almost aboriginal West Greenlanders. Cranz in particular was careful to 'describe only such original savages, as have little or no intercourse with Europeans, and have not yet adopted any of their manners' (p. 157).

At the time Egede wrote, two formerly important subsistence hunts were all but things of the past among the West Greenlanders: whale hunting and the caribou hunt. Instead of being hunted from the ice edge, the bowhead whale was taken at sea by expeditions of up to fifty men and women, the men in kayaks, the women in an umiak. According to Egede (1745: 102), 'When they go a Whale catching, they put on their best Gear or Apparel, as if going to a Wedding-Feast, fancying that if they did not come cleanly and neatly dressed, the Whale, who can't bear sloven and dirty Habits, would shun them and fly from them'. First the men in kayaks would throw their harpoons at the animal. In a successful strike, the harpoon head would bury itself firmly in the whale while the shaft was released and could be recovered. To the harpoon head was tied a long line, at the other end of which was an air-filled buoy made of a whole seal skin. As the whale tired from dragging several such floats, it moved more slowly and could dive less often, if at all. Sooner or later the kayakers would close in and despatch it with lances. Then they donned waterproof suits 'made of dressed seal skin, all of one Piece, with Boots, Gloves, and Caps, sewed and laced so tight together that no Water can penetrate them' (Egede 1745: 103). In these suits, which trapped air round the wearer's body to make him buoyant, they jumped into the sea to flense the whale, dexterously removing the blubber and cutting out the whalebone from the mouth (Egede 1745: 102–3, Crantz 1767a: 121). The caribou hunt was likewise a cooperative affair, men, women and children all taking part and travelling inland from the heads of the fjords for the purpose. The women and children helped surround the caribou and drove them into a defile, where the men lay in wait to kill them. As well as people, white poles, each with a piece of turf stuck on top, were used to help deflect the deer (Egede 1745: 61–2). Danish archaeologists have recently investigated a great summer caribou hunting camp inland from Sisimiut (formerly Holsteinsborg; Map 18) which was used intensively until shortly after 1700. They found rows of man-like cairns (*inussuit*) to deflect the driven deer, shooting blinds, and meat caches (Grønnow 1986).

By far and away the most important animal quarry of the eighteenth-century West Greenlander was the seal. It was absolutely essential for food, clothing, summer tents, fuel for giving light and warmth in winter with the blubber lamp, and, above all, for covering umiaks and kayaks. 'The sea is their corn-field' wrote Cranz (1767a: 130) 'and the seal-fishery their most copious harvest'. Catching seals was 'their staff of life' in which they displayed 'inimitable skill' (p. 135). He waxed enthusiastic over the kayak and its equipment, and over the courage and expertise of the solitary seal hunter who paddled out into the open sea and secured his prey with harpoon and line, using the sealskin float to tire out his prey, which then had to be towed ashore. Cranz enumerated ten different practice exercises for the kayaker, most of which involved not only capsizing and then righting oneself, but disentangling oneself from the line. Other methods of seal hunting included hunting in winter from or through the ice which forms in bays and fjords.

The fur clothing, the boats, the weapons used for hunting, the houses and tents and the diet and feeding habits of the West Greenlander are all described in detail by Egede and Cranz. Seven or eight families would live perfectly amicably together without quarrelling or stealing in one rectangular winter house. The walls were built of stones and turves, the roof of wooden rafters covered with

Plate 2. The West Greenlandic collective caribou hunt as illustrated in Hans Egede's A
Description of Greenland *(1745: 61). The text claims that 'they chase them by Clap-hunting,
setting upon them on all Sides, and surrounding them with all their Women and Children, to force
them into Defiles and narrow Passages, where the Men armed lay in wait for them and kill them'.*

'bill-berry bushes, then with turf' and lastly earth (Crantz 1767a: 139). Cranz admired the neat and orderly manner in which each family kept its furniture and belongings and the way each member of the group assisted the others. He found that these so-called savages were actually 'gentle, quiet, civil and good-natured'. The family groups were 'not knit together by any publick laws and institutions, much less by compulsion, or penalties, but by voluntary agreement and order' so that 'the fictitious suppositions about the state of mankind before the civil police commenced, are not at all confirmed by their state' (pp. 183–4). On the other hand, Cranz attributed the amity, compassion and cooperation on which Eskimo society apparently depended to a mixture of self-interest and fear, lamenting that these qualities were not the product of moral principles (pp. 187–8).

The missionaries deplored what they regarded as the Greenlanders' filthy habits and superstitions. Egede (1745: 139–40) goes out of his way to mention 'a certain illegal Game', fortunately, he thought, played by married men and women only, who during an evening of feasting and revelry would 'fall a Singing and Dancing . . . and in the mean while one after another take a trip with each others Wife, behind a Curtain or Hangings made of Skins at one end of the House, where their Beds are placed and there divert themselves'. But they both commended and described the song contests, when two men settle a quarrel with a 'singing-combat', each in turn composing a satyrical song about the other to the beat of a drum, while the assembled company joined in with a chorus and acted as a jury.

EAST GREENLANDERS

Throughout historic times the pack ice, which drifts southwards perennially down Greenland's east coast, has made it all but inaccessible to conventional European shipping. Hence the Danish attempts to explore the area were necessarily conducted from a base in south-west Greenland using West Greenlandic guides and boats. The first of these explorations was made in 1752 by a Dane in the service of the Royal Greenland Trading Company, at the request of the directors. But Peder Olsen Walløe obtained little information about the inhabitants, beyond firmly establishing their existence (Ostermann 1935, Stefansson 1943: 173–4). The anthropological results of the next expedition, sent in 1829 by the Danish government under Lieutenant Wilhelm August Graah of the Royal Danish Navy were limited because he did not reach the main centre of population at Ammassalik (now Tasiilaq) (Graah 1932). It was left to Danish naval officers Gustav Holm and T. Vilhelm Garde in 1883–5 to give the first detailed account by Europeans of the East Greenlanders as a whole and of their aboriginal way of life (Holm and Garde 1887, Mikkelsen 1934, Gessain 1969, Petersen 1984).

The most thickly populated part of the east coast of Greenland, then as now, was the Ammassalik area, which is roughly on the Arctic Circle. In 1884, 413 East Greenlanders lived here on the shores of three fjords, those of Ammassalik, Sermilik and Sermiligaaq. These people were divided between twelve inhabited places, each having just one winter house. In the summer the five or more families in each winter house would move out into tents and disperse. Most of the East Greenlanders had never set eyes on a white man or woman, and some were astounded to discover that there was another language in the world besides their own. But they had heard a good deal about white people, for they had for years been obtaining European-made goods, such as metal articles and rolled Dutch tobacco, in return for sinews, bear skins and the like. Since about 1800 parties of them had been travelling in their umiaks and kayaks to Nanortalik at the southern end of the west coast of Greenland for this bartering, those from the north taking three or four years over the round trip. Some had even been baptized (Kolsrud 1935). The East Greenlanders were naturally great travellers: after all, they or their ancestors must have circumnavigated much of Greenland to reach Ammassalik from their probable starting point in Avanersuaq. Not surprisingly, they firmly believed Greenland was an island; one of their legends told of a certain Uijartek who had indeed circumnavigated Greenland in an umiak with his wife and child, taking at least two years to do it, in a clockwise direction – south down the east coast, and then northwards up the west coast.

As Graah (1932: 120, 126–7) had already discovered fifty years before Holm, the nineteenth-century East Greenlanders were literally dying of starvation. In 1884 the coast north of Ammassalik was no longer inhabited for this reason: the winter pack ice had blocked the fjords so that the seals disappeared and seal hunting became impossible. But Ammassalik was affected too. In a single house, in the Ammassalik region, in which nineteen people divided between five families lived, supplies of food and fuel for the blubber lamps ran out one winter and could not be replenished by hunting. The first to die of hunger and cold were an elderly couple. Following east Greenland custom their bodies were thrown into the sea. But survivors were soon too weak to dispose of the dead bodies of the deceased and eventually, in April, they were compelled to eat their flesh. Of the two women who survived this horror, one, Keligasak, had participated in the eating of her husband, eight of her children, and four grandchildren.

The habitual division of labour among all Eskimos was that the men alone hunted and the women alone were responsible for turning the results of the hunt into fuel, food and clothing, and for the management of the household. But in east Greenland, where Holm found that there were 114 women to every 100 men in the population, it was not unusual for women to take over the economic and social role of men in settlements where women outnumbered men. In one place in 1884 only five of the twenty-one inhabitants were male. As a result, two young women who had no brothers had been taught by their father to go out seal hunting in kayaks. They could paddle these, and throw harpoons or bird darts, as well as the men. As far as the Danes could tell they dressed like men, behaved like men, and were treated as such by the other inhabitants.

The typical East Greenlandic half-underground winter house of stones, timber and turves contained a single room, 7.5–12.5 m (25–41 ft) long and 4–5 m (13–16 ft) broad, with windows of translucent intestinal seal membranes sewn together, and was inhabited by up to ten families or thirty to fifty people in all. The narrow entrance passage was 6–9 m (20–30 ft) long. Inside, the floor was of flagstones and the walls were hung with seal skins. Along the rear part of this roughly rectangular structure ran a wooden sleeping platform 46 cm (18 in) above the floor divided by sealskin partitions into sections or cubicles, each 1.2 m (4 ft) wide. Each cubicle was occupied by the married members of a single family together with their daughters and small children, that is a man, his wife or wives (bigamy was not particularly rare) and up to six children. The married people slept with their feet towards the rear wall of the house, the unmarried daughters slept at the foot end, and the unmarried men, teenage boys and any guests there might be, slept on a narrow sleeping bench along the front of the house below the windows. Each married woman tended her blubber lamp on a stone support in front of her cubicle and the heat of the several lamps permitted the normal indoor clothing to consist of very scanty sealskin underpants for the adults and birthday suits for the children. In these houses the long dark winter was enlivened by all sorts of entertainments, prominent among them being shamanistic seances, drum song contests, and the telling of lengthy stories with much gesticulation which, if not obscene, were often descriptive of hunting adventures and successes. The game of turning out the lights, otherwise known as wife exchange, was also played by adults, especially when there were guests in the house.

Because of the existence of a recognized probationary or trial period of marriage or cohabitation among young couples, the East Greenlanders' sexual relationships were somewhat kaleidoscopic. It was not altogether unusual for a young man or woman to change partners six or eight times in rapid succession. Ipatikajik cohabited with Igsiavik's third 'wife' while her 'husband' was away fishing, though she had been living with him for six months. Igsiavik sought solace by teaming up with Misuarnianga's second 'wife', who was fed up with her 'husband'. Misuarnianga then challenged Igsiavik to a drum-song contest because he had taken his wife from him. In his turn, Igsiavik wanted to challenge Ipatikajik for taking his third wife from him, but he could not sing. So he persuaded Misuarnianga, with whose mother he had previously been living, to stand in for him. All these three men were between twenty and twenty-five years old. Besides this, some of the best hunters, especially if they were shamans, were notable womanisers. Sanimuinak, aged about thirty, had two wives, Puitsek and Amakotak. He had been married to Puitsek for several years and had two fine sons by her. One day Sanimuinak persuaded Ingmalukutuk to marry Uitinak's wife, who was Puitsek's sister, since on his own admission Uitinak had not caught anything during five days of hunting. In retaliation, Amakotak's mother induced Uitinak to take her daughter over from Sanimuinak, who, she claimed, could not maintain two wives. When he returned from his next trip away, Sanimuinak brought with him a young woman called Utsukuluk, who had been 'married' six times already though she was only twenty years old. Not surprisingly, violent quarrels ensued between Sanimuinak and his first wife Puitsek, and between Puitsek and Utsukuluk. Utsukuluk stayed only a short time before leaving Sanimuinak and taking up with a young man. But this, her eighth attempt at marriage, lasted only three weeks. For her ninth attempt she 're-married' her 'husband' number six, whom she regarded as the best of all her men, even though he had assaulted and beaten her a few times, and had already married again, so that she now became his second wife only. Too much attention must not be given to carryings-on like these, for there were certainly many long-term stable relationships among the East Greenlanders. Marriage as such did not exist. The only thing which might be taken to denote it was the birth of a child: the nuclear family was the ultimate social reality.

TWO

Early Explorers and Colonists

THE UNKNOWN ARCTIC

Naturally the early eastern civilizations of India and Persia, the essentially Mediterranean-based empires of Greece and Rome, and the desert kingdoms of the Arabs, knew little of the Arctic. The ceremonies to welcome the dawn after a long night of darkness, described in ancient Hindi verses, suggest the end of the long Polar night in the far north of Asia. The Persian sacred texts or *Avesta* describe a country where the angry gods sent frost and snow so that winter lasted ten months of the year and sun, moon and stars rose only once a year (Laktionov 1955: 30–6). Among the Greeks, Aristotle and others believed that the inhabited part of the world was surrounded by ocean and that Polar climatic zones were too cold to be habitable. Roman geographers, tending toward popularization, peopled the Arctic with 'the Hyperboreans who inhabit the lands of the north "where the axis of the world is ever turning"' (Kimble 1938: 10–11). Early references to the North, though originally reflecting distant glimmerings of truth, were self-contradictory and fantastic: it was the kingdom of the dead, a bottomless pit or precipice, a frozen sea in perpetual dark night, a land of eternal sun. The most famous geographer of the ancient world, Claudius Ptolemaios or Ptolemy, did not mark the Arctic on his world map, which extended only to 65° north latitude. The crude world maps which were produced in Europe during the thousand years between the collapse of the Roman Empire and the Renaissance either ignored the Arctic altogether or, at best, marked a zone at either Pole as *frigore inhabitabilis* 'uninhabitable because of cold' (Pognon 1984). None of the medieval world maps showed Iceland in the right place or gave it the right shape; and Greenland, if it was marked, was sometimes made into a promontory of the European mainland. The Polar inset to the renowned atlas of the world produced by the Flemish geographer Gerhard Kremer or Mercator in 1569 has an entirely fanciful representation of the area round the North Pole. In part this indirectly derived from a lost work called *Inventio Fortunata*, attributed to Nicholas of Lynn, which was as fanciful as its title implies. The Pole was described as a tall

Plate 3. The north Polar regions as shown on Martin Behaim's globe made in Nürnberg in 1492. This map, as well as Mercator's later one, owed its purely fanciful representation of a circular North Pole surrounded by water, outside which are large land masses intersected by channels, to the lost Inventio Fortunata. *Greenland is shown as a peninsula north of Norway. Inscriptions on the mythical lands round the Pole state that 'the land is inhabited in summer', 'Here white falcons are caught' and 'The longest day is a month long'. (Nansen 1911b: 228.)*

magnetic rock 10 miles across, rising out of the ocean. This ocean was surrounded by a roughly circular ring of land divided into four by wide inflowing channels. In the atlas which appeared in 1595 soon after Mercator's death, this nonsense was repeated, but in 1598 the Dutch cartographer Cornelius Claeszoon had the good sense to leave unexplored areas white on his Polar map (Steinnes 1958, Zögner 1978, Schilder 1984. For this chapter as a whole see Beazley 1897–1906, Nansen 1911, Wright 1925, Newton 1926, Hennig 1936–9, Vaughan 1982).

Cartographic ignorance of the Arctic in early historic times was matched by the ignorance of encyclopedists, geographers, historians and travellers. The few sparse facts these writers record usually contradict one another and are mixed with fancies and part-truths. The sixth-century Byzantine historian Procopius locates the inhabitants of the northern forests who hunt animals and wear fur clothing in a place called Thule, where the sun does not set for forty days in summer nor rise for forty days in winter. But the Irish monk Dicuil, whose information about Thule came from Irish clerics who had been there towards the end of the eighth century AD, firmly identifies Thule with Iceland. He says that the sea is frozen one day's sailing north of there, and describes how there was enough light during a midsummer night to pick the lice off one's shirt. A handful of later medieval writers provide scraps of information about Iceland, a couple mention Greenland, and there are occasional references to Polar bears and whales, travel by dog sleds, and frostbite. At the end of the middle ages the Swedish ecclesiastic Olaus Magnus, who spent the later part of his life in exile from protestant Sweden in Italy, published his *History of the Northern Peoples* in Rome in 1555. This northern geography, written in Latin, repeats many fanciful tales of sea monsters swallowing ships, of pygmies and giants, but adds new material about Arctic regions, some of it acquired by Olaus himself on a journey through Norway and Sweden that took him at least as far north as Tornio, just south of the Arctic Circle (Magnus 1555, Savel'yeva 1983). He tells us correctly that the stars are not visible in Finnmark in northern Norway between May and early August, describes frozen rivers, the trade in furs in the Far North, and the domesticated reindeer of the Sami. He has information about Iceland, which he too identifies with Thule, and even provides an illustration of Mount Hekla.

ARCTIC PRODUCTS IN EUROPE

Although information about the Arctic was scanty, Arctic products were far from unknown in the European middle ages. In the market at Cologne, according to the German theologian Albertus Magnus, walrus hide for making ships' cables was regularly for sale in the middle years of the thirteenth century. Another article of trade was ivory in the form of both walrus and narwhal tusks, much of which, as well as seal and reindeer skin, originated in Greenland (Larson 1917: 142–3, Marcus 1980: 91–2). One of the uses of walrus tusks is shown by the walrus ivory chessmen, probably dating from the twelfth century, which were found in the nineteenth century on a beach on Lewis in the Outer Hebrides. Arctic products also circulated in medieval Europe in the form of gifts and souvenirs and were displayed in public places. A sharp-eyed Venetian traveller noticed a white bearskin rug at the foot of the archbishop's throne in Trondheim cathedral in 1432, and in 1515 Olaus Magnus (1555: 68) saw two Greenland kayaks inside the cathedral of Oslo attached to the wall above the west door. They were said to have been taken by King Hakon IV of Norway (1217–63) when cruising off the Greenland coast with a war fleet. Proof of Greenlandic provenance is afforded by some crude runic letters carved on one of three narwhal tusks given to St Mary's church in Utrecht, Holland, probably by the German ruler Henry IV, who founded the church in about 1080. Two of these tusks are in the Museum of Christian History in the Catharijne Convent in Utrecht. Arctic products also found their way to western Europe as diplomatic gifts. In the eleventh and twelfth centuries Polar bears taken alive in Greenland were presented to Scandinavian monarchs. In the thirteenth century King Hakon IV gave Polar bears to two rulers well known for their menageries. Henry III of England kept his in the Tower of London, along with an elephant given to him by the king of France. A collar and chain, and a long rope so that it could be allowed to swim and perhaps catch fish in the Thames, were provided for the Polar bear. Frederick II, ruler of Germany and Italy, passed his Polar bear on to El Kamil, the sultan of Damascus.

Gyrfalcons (*Falco rusticolus*), especially white ones, were highly prized for falconry by European rulers, but many of them came from Iceland or Norway rather than the Arctic. Either they were Greenlandic breeding birds caught while on migration or wintering in Iceland, or they were caught in sub-Arctic Norway or further south (Vaughan 1992: 80–97). Gyrfalcons were also obtained in Arctic Russia, especially, in the sixteenth and seventeenth centuries, in the Kola Peninsula (Kol'skiy poluostrov) and Pomor'ye (Map 6 below). They were used by the tsar to oil the wheels of diplomacy as well as for falconry. Ivan IV the Terrible, the first Russian tsar, sent a fine white gyrfalcon to Philip and Mary, king and queen of England, in 1556, but the ship carrying it was wrecked on the Scottish coast and 'the whole mass and bodie of the goods laden in her, was by the rude and ravenous people of the Countrey thereunto adjoyning, rifled, spoyled and caried away . . .' (Hakluyt 1907a: 358). Good relations with powerful neighbours like the shah of Persia and the khan of the Crimea were ensured by presents of gyrfalcons: on six occasions between 1616 and 1652 a gift of twenty-eight gyrfalcons was sent from Moscow to the shah of Persia. The tsar's seventeenth-century instructions for obtaining falcons show that special expeditions were sent to their breeding places in the far north, led by the tsar's falconers. An official called the Superintendant of the Falcon Route (*Uryadnik sokolnichyego puti*) had to ensure that the falcons were brought to Kholmogory (Map 7 below), fed on reindeer meat, and sent to Moscow in special enclosed sledges lined with felt, by the first sledge train of the autumn. The birds' attendants were not allowed to smoke or drink while the falcons were in transit. Throughout the seventeenth century between fifty and a hundred gyrfalcons were sent annually by this route to Moscow; later, Siberian birds were obtained as well (Dement'yev 1951: 152–63).

While falcons were a luxury article, furs were widely used for winter clothing in the middle ages. Until the fifteenth century, Novgorod was the great export centre for furs, which were collected by way of trade and tribute from lands far to the north-east of that city, extending across the valleys of the rivers Dvina (Severnaya Dvina), Mezen, and Pechora. German merchants were said to have been able to buy over a hundred thousand pelts at a time in Novgorod at the beginning of the fifteenth century. The furs passed to Western Europe via Lübeck and the towns of the Hanseatic League, but they were not products of the true Arctic. They came from the typical animals of the forest or taiga, notably the sable, squirrel, lynx, marten and beaver, and not from tundra animals like the Arctic fox. At the close of the fifteenth century, Novgorod was conquered by the princes of Moscow and her fur empire came under their control (Khoroshkevich 1963).

MYTHICAL VOYAGES

Most of the early recorded exploring expeditions to the Arctic must be dismissed, either because they did not take place at all, or because they did not reach the Arctic. The earliest of these, the famous voyage of Pytheas, who set out from the Greek colony of *Massilia* or Marseille in the south of France in about 325 BC, is shrouded in mystery because his book *On the Ocean*, which included an account of his northern voyage, has been lost. All we have are the garbled quotations and disbelieving comments of some later Greek and Roman geographers. Nonetheless he has an assured place at the beginning of every history of European Polar exploration (see for example Kirwan 1962, Victor 1964, Mirsky 1970, Mountfield 1974). Pytheas was a noted astronomer who had precisely determined the latitude of his native Marseille, and on his northern voyage he measured the degrees of latitude in four different places. He reached a country six days' sail north of Britain which he called Thule, but the sources only permit a guess as to whether this was Iceland (as Dicuil assumed) or somewhere on the Norwegian coast, as Procopius apparently thought. In any case Pytheas probably never reached the Arctic, but perhaps just touched on the Arctic Circle. Some of the already-mentioned scraps of information about the Arctic known to writers like Procopius, Bede and Dicuil certainly derived indirectly from Pytheas. Of special interest is the observation that one day's sailing north of Iceland brought one to a congealed sea. Does this, as some later writers thought, mean a frozen sea and, if so, did Pytheas see it himself or was he told about it? These questions are unanswerable. No Norwegian would have been able to tell Pytheas about the pack ice, which is, and probably was in 325 BC, 160 km (100 miles) off the north Norwegian coast even in midwinter. On the other hand, an Icelander could have been familiar with the pack ice, but it is almost certain that no one was living in Iceland in 325 BC to tell Pytheas about it. The possibility cannot be entirely ruled out that Pytheas reached the pack ice off the east coast of Greenland: this must be his chief claim to be included in a history of the Arctic (Stefansson 1944: 1–107, Whitaker 1982).

The Irish monks who rowed and sailed out into the stormy waters of the north Atlantic in their cowhide-covered boats or *curachs* certainly reached the Faeroes, the Vestmannaeyjar or Westman Islands, and Iceland itself during the course of the eighth century AD. In these remote islands they set up their monasteries or hermitages, living a life of peace, solitude and meditation. One of them, Cormac, is supposed to have sailed due north for fourteen summer days and as many nights, until he was forced to turn back by swarms of small creatures covering the surface of the sea, which he feared might puncture the skin covering of his boat. Neither pieces of ice nor jellyfish seem a convincing explanation. Another

Irish monk, Abbot Brendan the Navigator of Clonfert, met with a crystal column floating in the sea, which could have been an iceberg, and a tall smoking mountain that could have been Beerenberg on Jan Mayen. He and other early Irish seafarers sprinkle the ocean with fabulous islands: their paradise was an island; they found an island on a pillar, an isle of laughter, and islands of canticles and singing birds (for a recent discussion with references see Le Goff 1990). The nearest they got to the Arctic was probably the south coast of Iceland. As fanciful as these old Irish tales, but more sophisticated, are the voyages attributed by Niccolò Zeno of Venice in his 1558 book to two of his ancestors, the brothers Niccolò and Antonio. In around 1380 one brother is supposed to have sailed to a large island north of Iceland called Frisland. Later joined by Antonio, he sailed to Engroneland, where they found a monastery centrally heated from a hot spring, then voyaged on to Estotiland, one thousand miles west of Frisland. Formerly accepted as genuine, and published as such by the Hakluyt Society in 1873, this narrative has been rejected as spurious by virtually all modern authorities. Likewise spurious is the alleged North Pole expedition of 1360 undertaken by a friar from Oxford. On the other hand it seems that King Christian I of Denmark, acting in concert with the king of Portugal, Alfonso V, did send two German skippers, or 'jolly pirates' as American historian Samuel Morison (1971: 82) calls them, named Didrik Pining and Hans Pothorst, on a voyage 'to seek out new islands and countries in the north' (Vaughan 1982: 323n.). They probably did not reach the Arctic. According to Olaus Magnus they carved a navigation beacon in the form of a compass on a rock called Hvidsærk on the east coast of Greenland; their voyage may have taken place in 1472–3. It seems unlikely that the Portuguese participant in this expedition, Joao Vaz Corte-Real, reached Labrador (besides the references in Vaughan 1982 see Morison 1971: 81–111, Henriksen 1988: 151–6, Monberg 1990).

VIKINGS IN THE ARCTIC

The Viking colonization of sub-Arctic Iceland and southern Greenland did not involve any penetration of the Arctic. These lands lay west and south-west, not north, of the Viking homesteads in south-west Norway. Nonetheless, Vikings did indubitably voyage north of the Arctic Circle. They sailed north or north-east up the Norwegian coast, rounded North Cape (Nordkapp), Norway's most northerly point just north of 71° north latitude, and then sailed south-east to the lands around the White Sea (Beloye more) which they called Bjarmaland. Much of the return trip may have necessitated rowing against the prevailing winds. The voyage to Bjarmaland was described in some detail to King Alfred of England in about AD 890 by the north Norwegian chieftain Ottar, from Halogaland, who was probably not the first Viking to attempt it. His motive in going to Bjarmaland was partly 'to find out how far the land extended due north' and partly to hunt walruses, which had tusks of fine ivory and hides good for ships' cables. Some of these tusks he gave to the king. Other northern products, including furs obtained in tribute from the Sami and the proceeds of whaling, he sold in south Norway, Denmark or England (Jones 1984: 158–62). It seems unlikely that the Bjarmaland

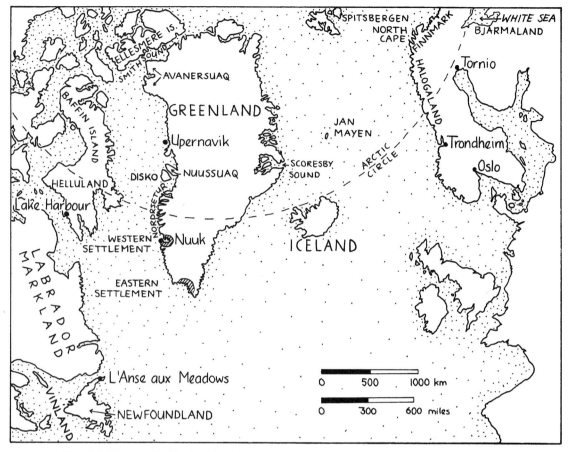

Map 4. Vikings in the North Atlantic.

voyage became a regular trade route, nor did Norwegian settlers arrive in Finnmark until the thirteenth century. But at least three Norwegian kings voyaged to Bjarmaland in the eleventh century, and the motives for going there now came to include revenge for the killing of Norwegians overwintering there (*c.* AD 1220) and plunder, especially the robbing of grave mounds of their treasures. (Tiander 1906 remains the standard work on the Bjarmaland voyages. Besides the works referred to in Vaughan 1982, see now Blom 1984.) According to Adam of Bremen, who knew more about the north than most other medieval chroniclers, King Harald Hardrada of Norway, that last great Viking warrior, who met his death at Stamford Bridge in 1066 at the hands of Harold of England, had led a voyage of exploration northwards into the unknown ocean but withdrew just in time to escape 'the vast pit of the abyss' (Jones 1984: 388).

The Viking settlers in Iceland are also said to have undertaken voyages northward into the Arctic. It may be true that the cryptic entry under the year 1194 in the Icelandic annals 'Svalbard was found' (Svalbard meaning the cold edge or coast), as well as a later mention of it in another Icelandic source, refers to Spitsbergen, but there is no way of proving this. The unanimity of the Norwegian historians of Spitsbergen in their support of the hypothesis that these references are to Spitsbergen is clearly to be explained by the national wish for sovereignty over that archipelago which was realized in 1920 by international treaty. It was only after the 1920 treaty conferred sovereignty 'over the Archipelago of Spitsbergen' to Norway that the Norwegians publicly adopted their own name for it – Svalbard (Østreng 1977: 101; Arlov 1986: 173–5). The British historian of the Vikings, Gwyn Jones (1984: 494), suggests 'eastern Greenland in the neighbourhood of Scoresby Sound' as a more probable location for the Svalbard of the medieval Icelanders. The Viking colonists of Greenland indisputably travelled northwards up the west Greenland coast beyond the Arctic Circle. Indeed it is almost certain that their hunting parties travelled north at least as far as Disko every year to obtain walrus ivory and walrus and seal blubber, as well as probably driftwood. These northern hunting grounds or Nordrsetur extended north from the most northerly Viking farmsteads inland from present-day Nuuk as far as Disko Bay and the peninsula of Nuussuaq, where the ruins of a well-built stone shelter or storehouse, or possibly chapel, are now known as the Bear Trap. Further north than this, 1,000 km (600 miles) north of the Viking settlements, three Norsemen must have overwintered probably in the fourteenth century. They erected three cairns on the island of Kingigtorssuaq just north of Upernavik and just short of 73° north latitude. In one of them a small blackish-green stone only 10 cm (4 in) long, inscribed in runes, had been placed. It was found lying nearby in 1824. It recorded that Erling Sigvatsson, Bjarnè Thordarsson and Eindridi Oddsson built the cairn(s) 'on the Saturday before Rogation Day' (Gad 1970: 137; Stoklund 1982: 199–200). Still further north, archaeologists excavating ruined Eskimo houses have found Viking artefacts which may point to Viking voyages, and perhaps a shipwreck, in the Smith Sound area both in Avanersuaq and in eastern Ellesmere Island. Among these objects are fragments of chain mail, a small wooden box, part of a wooden barrel, a bone comb and two turned ivory chessmen from north-west Greenland (Vaughan 1991: 15); and pieces of woven wool cloth, a lump of chain mail, clinch nails probably from a Viking ship, part of an oak box, a plane, and fragments of a barrel bottom from Ellesmere Island. Several of these finds have been dated to the thirteenth century AD (Schledermann 1982). All of them could be accounted for by a single Viking shipwreck in Smith Sound, but they could also be due to trade, either among Eskimos, or between Eskimos and Vikings. A hint at such trade is given by the find of a hinged bronze bar in an Eskimo house site in north-west Ellesmere Island: it is of the type used by Viking traders. A hint at the presence of Vikings among Eskimo settlements in southern Baffin Island is given by a wooden figurine recovered in 1977 by two archaeology students from Michigan State University who were excavating the floor of an ancient Inuit house near Lake Harbour. This carved figure, only 5.5 cm (2 in) high, is thought to be an Eskimo depiction of a Viking. In style and technique it is a typical Thule culture Inuit doll, but the clothing appears similar to that worn in the thirteenth century in the Viking colonies in Greenland (Anon 1979, McGhee 1987).

VINLAND VOYAGES

While the northern voyages of the Norse settlers in Greenland, which penetrated a long way into the Arctic, were undertaken too late, or too far away from Iceland, to be described in saga, the western or south-western voyages of the Vikings, which took them away from the Arctic, formed the main subject matter of two important sagas, *Eirik the Red's Saga* and the *Greenlanders' Saga*. Written down in Iceland two hundred years or more after the events they describe, which took place in the first twenty years of the eleventh century (AD 1000–20), these saga accounts are muddled, inconsistent and partly fanciful or implausible. It seems likely that the story of the Vinland voyages was originally told in the *Greenlanders' Saga*, where Bjarni Herjolfsson, driven off course in 985 or 986 *en route* to Greenland from Iceland, first sights land in the west, coasts along it, and returns successfully to Greenland without setting foot in America. Fifteen years later, perhaps in 1001, Leif, son of Eirik the Red, resolves to explore this new land and does so after buying Bjarni's boat and obtaining his advice. On this voyage he first sights the mountainous ice-bound land Bjarni had sighted last, lands there, and calls it Helluland or Flagstone Land. It is usually identified with southern Baffin Island. Continuing southwards along the coast, Leif Eiriksson lands again on what was probably the southern part of the Labrador coast. This rather flat, well-forested land, with white sandy beaches, he names Markland or Forest Land. Finally he reaches a pleasant grassy land where a small river flows out of a lake and he and his men resolve to build some large houses and winter there. One evening one of the party, a 'southerner', perhaps from Germany, returns to base reporting that he has found vines and grapes, so this country was called Vinland. *Eirik the Red's Saga* may have been a revised version of the *Greenlanders' Saga* in which it is Leif Eiriksson who accidentally discovers Vinland, while Bjarni Herjolfsson has been entirely left out of the story. Both sagas describe a later – perhaps *c.* 1010 – exploration of Vinland by Thorfinn Karlsefni, who remained through three winters, but then sailed home, apparently because of the hostility of natives whom the Vikings called *skraelings*. These natives, identified by archaeologists as Indians, had been provoked in the first place by the Vikings. In all there were from three to six Vinland voyages in the first twenty years of the eleventh century, and one or two later ones. The main or possibly only overwintering place mentioned in the sagas is Leifsbudir or Leif's Bothy, that is the houses built by Leif. After a long search, in the summer of 1960 Norwegian archaeologist Helge Ingstad found what clearly is the site of Leifsbudir. It is in Épaves Bay at the northern tip of the island of Newfoundland, near the present-day fishing village of L'Anse aux Meadows, 'the Bay of Meadows', and is the only indisputable Viking site so far discovered in North America. It was excavated under the direction of Ingstad's wife Anne Stine from 1961 to 1968, and further excavations were carried out by Parks Canada between 1973 and 1976. The archaeologists have unearthed eight Norse buildings, one a furnace for smelting the local bog iron, and a charcoal pit kiln to make charcoal for smelting. The houses had wooden frames and were walled and roofed with sods – the usual Icelandic and Greenlandic form of construction. Artefacts found include small personal ornaments, iron slag, and leftovers and detritus from ship repairs. One artefact was quite certainly Norse: a soapstone spindle whorl used in the process of twisting raw wool into yarn, identical to one found in a

Norse ruin in Greenland and to others from Viking Age sites in Iceland and Norway. Radiocarbon dates are consistent with occupation in AD 1000–1020, and the small kitchen middens indicate occupation for a short period only. No cowsheds and no burials have been found. The fact that wild vines do not grow in Newfoundland but *are* found a few hundred miles further south may imply that Leifsbudir was only a kind of base camp where the Vikings overwintered *en route* to Vinland itself, or from which they made expeditions to the south. Alternatively, the grapes may have been berries (Morison 1971: 32–80, Ingstad 1969, Jones 1984, 1986. Magnusson and Pálsson 1965 is a handy translation of the sagas, with a commentary. Of earlier studies, Hovgaard 1915 is outstanding. On the Vinland Map, now discredited as a forgery, see Wallis *et al.* 1974.)

Norse Settlements in Greenland

Apart from the wish not to omit a good story, there is no excuse for including Vinland in a history of the Arctic. Iceland, too, is not really Arctic at all and its long history, starting in the ninth century when it was first colonized by Vikings – mainly west Norwegian farmers – will not be considered in this book. That part of west Greenland settled from Iceland in and after 986, though in the same latitude as, or south of, Iceland, and probably enjoying a climate at least as warm as it does now, has a better claim to be considered Arctic. The presence of Inland Ice on the one side and drifting pack ice offshore on the other, helps to keep the mean annual temperature even at the southern tip of Greenland below zero °C by at least a degree or two (28° F), while the mean annual temperature at Akureyri on the cool north coast of Iceland in 1931–60 was a bearable 3.9° C (39° F) (Nordal and Kristinsson 1975: 11). The Vikings who sailed to Greenland with Eirik the Red in 986 to settle down and become Norse colonists and farmers there left Iceland in a fleet of twenty-five ships only fourteen of which reached Greenland. Eirik had spent three years, while exiled from Iceland for manslaughter, exploring the country. The name 'Greenland', which he coined for it, may have been a promotional stunt, but by this time the limited amount of cultivable land in Iceland was already occupied, and the large-scale emigration of several hundred Icelanders with Eirik was due mainly to land hunger. Thanks to the astonishing wealth of detail in the Icelandic sagas we know the names of the main colonists and precisely what land they took (Jones 1986: 187):

> These men who went out with Eirik at this time took land in [the Eastern] settlement in Greenland:
> Herjolf took Herjolfsfjord (he lived at Herjolfsnes)
> Ketil, Ketilsfjord
> Hrafn, Hrafnsfjord
> Solve, Solvadal
> Helgi Thorbrandsson, Alptafjord
> Thorbjorn Glora, Siglufjord
> Einar, Einarsfjord
> Hafgrim, Hafgrimsfjord and
> Arnlaug, Arnlaugsfjord;
> while some went on to the Western Settlement.

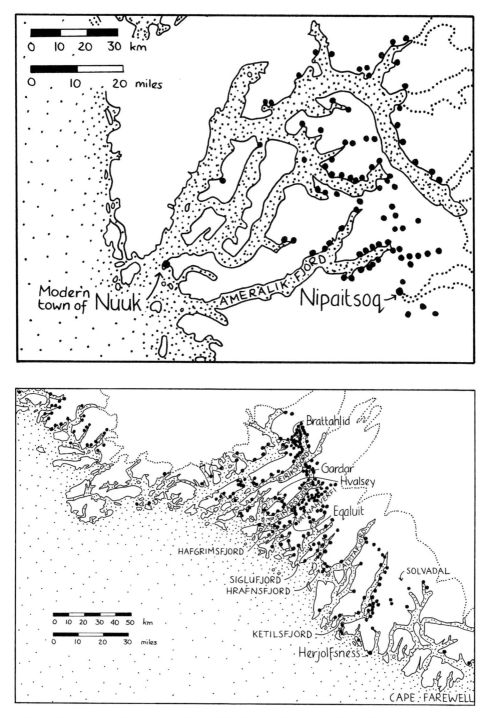

Map 5. Norse sites in Greenland. Above: The Western Settlement; below The Eastern Settlement.

The list docs not mention Eirik the Red, who built himself a fine homestead in the Eastern Settlement at Brattahlid 'steep hillside' far up in Eiriksfjord at least 50 km (30 miles) inland from the line of the coast. Both settlements consisted of scattered isolated farmsteads often miles apart, far up the fjords. The ninety or so farms of the Western (and more northerly) Settlement or Vestribyggd were dispersed between 75 and 100 km (about 50–60 miles) inland around the shores of two or more fjord systems which had their outlets to the sea near the present day capital of Greenland, Nuuk. Between the Western and the Eastern Settlement (Eystribyggd), was a good 400 km (250 miles) of uninhabited coast – uninhabitable for the Norsemen because it lacked suitable fjords leading inland to lowland pastures. At the peak of its economic and demographic development in about AD 1300, there were perhaps 150 occupied farms in the Eastern Settlement, twelve parish churches, a cathedral at Gardar and a convent and a nunnery. The total population of both settlements may at that time have reached about three or even four thousand.

These flourishing Norse colonies in Greenland ceased to exist altogether some time before about 1500. Though Thule or Inussuk culture Eskimos moved south along the coast, past both Western and Eastern settlements, while the Norse were still there and afterwards, their dwellings were on the outer shore, where they could hunt sea mammals, or else further inland than the Norse farms, where they established summer camps to hunt caribou. Only in the 1920s, when the Danish authorities reintroduced sheep farming into the area to shore up the failing Greenlandic economy, were Greenlanders settled on some of the Norse farms, and the impressive ruins of the cathedral and bishop's residence at Gardar were also settled by Greenlanders. They called the place Igaliko 'the deserted cooking place' because they imagined such imposing buildings could only have been where the cooking was done. Thus the ruins of the Norse settlements had mostly been left untouched ever since the farms were abandoned. This created a veritable paradise for archaeologists, or, rather, for Danish archaeologists, for the Danes have monopolized archaeological studies in Greenland just as effectively and jealously as they have trade. They have, however, done the job of excavating the Norse ruins extremely well. Renowned archaeologists like Poul Nørlund described his 1921–32 excavations of Brattahlid, Herjolfsnes and Gardar in the classic *Viking Settlers in Greenland* (1936). Now, the wind of change has blown through the corridors of the Danish National Museum in Copenhagen. A handful of Americans, and even Norwegians, have been participating in continuing research on the Norse settlements, and research, management and even artefacts are now being transferred from Copenhagen to Nuuk, seat of the government of Greenland, still officially called 'the Home Rule Authorities', and of the new National Museum of Greenland (Arneborg 1989). At the same time, new problems for archaeology – and archaeological conservation – have arisen because of the very rapid expansion of Greenlandic sheep farming in the areas of both Norse settlements since 1970.

The Norse farms in Greenland were based on the typical Long House of west Norway and Iceland, consisting of a single long room which could be divided by wooden partitions. The entrance was on the long side of the house, which had rounded corners at either end, giving an oval ground plan. Building materials

*Plate 4. Artefacts from the Norse graveyard at Herjolfsnes in the Eastern Settlement.
Above: Carved wooden crosses. About sixty of these crosses were recovered during the 1921
excavations or before then, mostly laid on the chest of the corpse. A few were inscribed with runes
giving the dead person's name or offering a prayer. Vahl et al. 1928b: 409. Below: Hood with
tippet or liripipe. This type of hood was popular in Europe in the second half of the fourteenth
century. (Vahl et al. 1928b: 411.)*

were turf, stone and timber. Farm buildings, which included cowsheds and barns, were placed near the farmhouse and many farms had drains and water reservoirs. The Passage House was a variant of the Long House in which the rooms were linked by a corridor running the length of the house. It may have been colder winters in the thirteenth century that caused a quite new type of farm to be developed in Greenland, known as the centralized farm: all the rooms were in a single block round the all-important cowshed, which had as few outer walls as possible. Even more so than in Iceland, each Norse farm in Greenland was virtually self-sufficient, and each of the Greenland settlements had a subsistence economy which did not depend on imports and exports. The great bulk of artefacts recovered from the settlements are of local manufacture and origin, both domestic and farm implements being manufactured from driftwood and from locally smelted iron-ore (Jansen 1972). It seems that towards the end the settlers became very short of wood and iron.

Even though the settlers unquestionably used skin clothing, too, woven woollen cloth, made in every farm, was the habitual dress. In 1921 Poul Nørlund excavated what remained of the graveyard at Herjolfsnes after erosion by the sea; the church had been built on a low promontory, stretching seaward at the settlement's most southerly point, as a welcoming beacon for ships approaching from Iceland or Norway. He recovered from the permafrost the everyday clothes in which the dead had been wrapped in lieu of coffins, some probably in the second half of the fifteenth century, near the close of the settlement's five-hundred-year history. When the mangled remains had been unpacked, sorted and treated at the National Museum in Copenhagen there were about thirty well-preserved coats and dresses, seventeen hoods and caps, five hats and six stockings. The material is a four-thread twill which has lost its colour (Nørlund 1936, Krogh 1967: 71–2).

Pollen analysis of peat cores has shown that, in the early stages of Norse settlement, extensive areas of birch and willow scrub, many of them forming regular forests, were cleared to make way for grassland (Fredskild 1981). The homesteaders brought with them cows, sheep, goats, pigs, horses and dogs, but so far no evidence of cats or poultry has been found. Sheep were the most numerous farm animals and were probably capable of remaining outside all winter in mild years. Cows were even more important than sheep, for their dairy products formed an essential part of the settlers' diet. Stalls for ten or a dozen animals have been excavated at many farms. At Gardar, the bishop's farm could house as many as a hundred cows (Hatting 1982). Some of the Norse farmers probably grew corn. The food provided by farm animals was supplemented by products of hunting, and the two most important game animals were the seal and the reindeer. Recent analysis of bone fragments at three Norse farm rubbish tips or middens in the Western Settlement has shown that over half the bones in two of them came from seals, 10–30 per cent in all three were caribou bones, and 10–30 per cent were bones of domestic animals. At neighbouring Eskimo middens seal formed almost 100 per cent of the bone deposits, but the Eskimos only lived there in spring and autumn (Møhl 1982: 286–95). Evidently, whenever a dietary resource in sea mammals was available, the Norse were able to exploit it. They must have eaten whale blubber with just as much relish as the present-day Faeroese.

From the very start, the Norse farming economy in Greenland was probably marginal. The farmer's biggest headache was to grow enough hay on his infield, and collect sufficient from the outfield, to keep his cows alive for the two hundred or so days they had to be kept indoors in the winter. The infields were carefully irrigated in the summer and heavily manured in the winter, but recent research has suggested that the resultant hay was often insufficient (Albrethsen and Keller 1986). Thus the area of infield of two neighbouring farms in the northen part of the Eastern Settlement that could be irrigated – a mere 7 hectares (17 acres) – has been calculated as able to produce 10–15 tons of hay, sufficient for only a moderate daily ration for five or seven cows on the two farms. For this reason it is likely that the majority of Norse farms had recourse to saeters, some of which have recently been discovered and excavated. The saeter is a mountain pasture, in Greenland at 200–400 m (700–1300 ft) above sea level, where a barn and rudimentary living quarters would enable farm staff to take the animals for a brief period in summer to graze the pastures, while winter food supplies for man and beast could be laid in the form of milk products and hay. So far only a few saeter buildings have been unearthed by archaeologists, but the authors of this study predict that the saeter system will be found to have been an essential part of Norse farming in Greenland throughout both settlements.

THE DISAPPEARANCE OF THE GREENLAND COLONISTS

In Vilhjalmur Stefansson's *Unsolved Mysteries of the Arctic*, published in 1939, the disappearance of the Greenland colony took pride of place: it still is an unsolved mystery. Dozens of hypothetical causes for the failure of the Norse farmers to survive in Greenland after about 1500 have been concocted by historians. The simple fact is that one cannot identify the causes of a historical phenomenon until one has discovered exactly what happened; and the chronological course of events in Greenland can never be ascertained because of the inadequacy of the historical sources. The only piece of documention we have from fifteenth-century Greenland is a wedding certificate, issued by the bishop's official at Gardar on 16 April 1409, in which it is stated that the banns for the wedding of Thorsteinn Olafsson and Sigrid Björnsdotter had been called on three successive Sundays, and the wedding celebrated in Hvalsey 'Whale Island' church on 16 September 1408 (Gad 1970: 148–9). There was apparently nothing very wrong with the Eastern Settlement then, and recent excavations seem to show farms in the Western Settlement still flourishing up to about that time. The cryptic assertions of Ivar Bardarson, extant only in a late, garbled copy, that in about 1345 'the skraelings [Eskimos] have the entire Western Settlement; but there are horses, goats, cows and sheep, all wild, and no people, neither Christians nor heathens' (Bardarson 1930: 29), which common sense never found acceptable, have now been invalidated by archaeologists.

Assuming that the settlements survived well into the fifteenth century, one can speculate that they must have been squeezed out of existence thereafter by the inexorable laws of economics and climatic change; certainly not by the Eskimos, with whom the Norse had both friendly and hostile encounters, but no more than that.

Nor, as archaeologists have demonstrated, did English or Dutch pirates or anybody else burn down most of their farms. Rather, the Norse farmers, probably suffering from chronic malnutrition (Lynnerup *et al.* 1991), seem to have dwindled in number and eventually died out, as farm after farm was abandoned, perhaps in the same way as the farm at Nipaitsoq in the Western Settlement, where all the cattle and other livestock seem to have been butchered and consumed during or toward the close of an exceptionally hard winter (Jones 1986: 268–76). All authorities agree that a temperature decline began in west Greenland in the mid-thirteenth century and persisted, perhaps with a pause, until after the end of the fifteenth century. This climatic deterioration may have had a disastrous effect on the farming economy, always somewhat marginal. Probably from about 1300, the economy was contracting, outlying or less fertile farms, some suffering from overgrazing, were being abandoned, and a steady trickle of people may have migrated from the Western Settlement to the Eastern, and even perhaps from the Eastern Settlement to Iceland, if and when shipping was available. Others may have intermarried with Greenlanders. In the same period, the once centralized and powerful Norwegian state, which had taken over Iceland and Greenland in the 1260s, was crumbling. Shipping and trading connections between Bergen and Greenland, guaranteed under treaty with the king, had probably ceased altogether by the fifteenth century.

Shortly before the start of the steady erosion of the farming base of their economy by climatic deterioration, the Norse in Greenland had fallen into the ravenous clutches of the élitist ecclesiastical and royal bureaucracies of Norway. These combined together to suck the economic life blood of the colony. On top of a subsistence economy, it now had the equivalent of a market economy, but one in which surpluses, instead of being sold, were given away to the church and king, bringing nothing of economic value in return. It was these outrageous demands on an ailing economy, made by the priests and royal officials who had taken over the colonies from the farmers themselves, which finally caused the extinction of the Norse settlers. Those twelve fine parish churches and the cathedral at Gardar, built in the twelfth and thirteenth centuries, swallowed up a huge proportion of the colonists' slender agricultural production. By the close of the church-building period about one-third of the best land in the Eastern Settlement had been donated by the farmers to these parish churches; donated by farmers whose fields were barely sufficient for their subsistence, but who were prepared to sacrifice the future well-being of their families and descendants in order to have their souls prayed for in the churches and thus improve their chances of eternal salvation (Gad 1970: 130). While the local churches thus overburdened the Norse farming economy, the proceeds of the sea mammal hunt, which might have been traded against useful products, disappeared into the treasuries of pope and king. In 1327, six years' worth of tithes, paid by the see of Gardar to be shared between the Norwegian king and the pope, amounted to about 373 walrus tusks. The 186 animals must have been caught by the Nordrsetur hunting expeditions over a six-year period (Gad 1970: 136–7). Thus the Norse settlers in Greenland disappeared from history, victims of climatic change and human avarice and élitism (besides references already given, see too McGovern 1981, Jones 1986: 101–14, Berglund 1986, Fyllingsnes 1990, McGovern 1991 with references).

RUSSIAN COLONIZATION

Although Russian northward expansion consisted mainly in the imposition of tribute in furs and the development of trade, these activities were accompanied by settlement. The basis for the Russian colonization of the European Arctic was created in the twelfth to fifteenth centuries by the city republic of Novgorod, founded in the tenth century by Swedish Vikings or warrior-merchants and named by them Holmgard 'Island Garth'. This expanding mercantile republic set out to conquer the territories surrounding it, and soon developed into a flourishing commercial centre. But her outward thrusts were blocked in the west by the powerful kingdoms of Sweden and Norway, while Novgorod was squeezed from the south, especially in the thirteenth century, by the Tatars, organized into fighting groups or hordes by leaders like Jenghiz Khan. Thus the economic empire of Novgorod developed northward and eastward from the great city. The first area to be settled by her noblemen and peasants was the southern shore of the White Sea. A document of 1137 shows that Novgoroders were already active along the rivers flowing into the White Sea, namely the Onega, Dvina (Severnaya Dvina) and Pinega, where many peasants settled, and had reached the Dvina mouth. In the fifteenth century they founded the famous Solovetskiy monastery on the Solovetskiye Islands (ostrova Solovetskiye) in the White Sea (Beloye more). A document of 1264 shows that part of the south coast of the Kola Peninsula was already then numbered among Novgorod's territories; and a series of campaigns in 1271–1323 probably consolidated her control of the eastern end of the peninsula. In the second half of the fifteenth century the Solovetskiy monks had extended their domain along the south coast of the peninsula. But the colonization of the Kola Peninsula, which lies almost entirely north of the Arctic Circle, did not really get underway until the sixteenth century, when the area was penetrated by Russians from outside the Novgorod area, whose homesteads are said to have increased in number from three in about 1565 to ninety-four in 1607. In 1582 the tsar's government in Moscow appointed a *voyevoda* or military governor at Kola (Platonov and Andreyev 1922: 37–46). Monks followed: the monastery at Pechenga in the far north of the peninsula on the Norwegian frontier was founded in 1532–3. In 1562–4 Father Triphon and his monks turned up at the fortress of Vardø in Norway in their boats with a cargo of fish, and probably walrus tusks and hides, for sale (Platonov and Andreyev 1922: 7–17).

Just as after the fifteenth century Russians from Moscow and elsewhere replaced Novgoroders in the Kola Peninsula, so in the other great field of Novgorod's northern expansion, namely Pomor'ye, her conquests were taken over by the tsars of Moscow. Pomor'ye was the rather ill-defined region of coastal tundra that extended from the White Sea toward the Urals. Beyond it lay the region around the Pechora river, and an equally ill-defined region called Yugra or Yugria, which straddled the northern tip of the Urals. As early as about 1096 a certain Guryat or Yurat Rogovich from Novgorod was familiar with Yugra and the Pechora region, and mentions the Nentsy tribes inhabiting the area and the wealth of furs obtainable from it. Evidence is scanty, but Novgorod seems to have penetrated Pechora and Yugra and to have levied tribute in furs, not without opposition, in the course of reconnaissance raids in 1187 and 1193. In a 1264

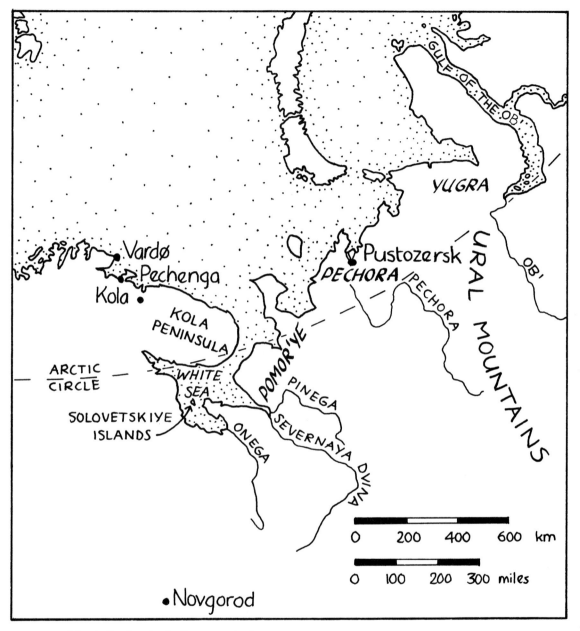

Map 6. Russians in the European Arctic.

treaty both Pechora and Yugra are named among Novgorod's territories. In 1363–4 the chronicles mention an armed expedition from Novgorod to the River Ob' led by Aleksandr Abakumovich. On reaching the Ob', one detachment turned upstream while the other continued downriver to the Gulf of the Ob'. The proceeds of this expedition enabled the leaders in the following year to build a stone church dedicated to the Holy Trinity in Redyatina Street, Novgorod. Novgorod's last expedition to Yugra was in 1445. Twenty years later the voyevoda or military governor, Vasiliy Skyaba, was in Yugra at the head of his troops collecting tribute for the prince of Moscow, and Novgorod was in fast decline. In 1478 she surrendered her independence to the Prince of Moscow, Ivan III, who, in 1498, despatched a small army four hundred strong to Yugra. After building the fort of Pustozersk on the Pechora, this expedition crossed the Urals in winter to assert Russian power more effectively in the lower Ob' valley. The combined effect of these occasional raids or expeditions and the steady movement northwards of colonists, many of them peasants, was to bring the whole of the Russian European Arctic from the Kola Peninsula to the Gulf of the Ob' under the control of the tsar of Russia in Moscow. Though colonization continued long afterwards, this control was already achieved by about 1600 (Platonov and Andreyev 1922, Belov 1956: 28–37, Vernadskiy 1961, Armstrong 1965, Lantzeff and Pierce 1973: 22–50, Skrynnikov 1982: 98–104).

THREE

Trade Routes Through the Ice

By the Treaty of Tordesillas in 1494 the pope divided the world into a Spanish and a Portuguese half, the Spanish having the western and the Portuguese the eastern hemisphere. This arrangement was made at a time when the Portuguese and the Spaniards, aided and inspired by Genoese navigational skills, were inaugurating Europe's conquest of the rest of the world; the Spanish in America from 1496 on, the Portuguese in Africa and the East. The aspiring and vigorous would-be maritime nations to the north of the Iberian Peninsula, the French, English, Dutch, and Danes, excluded in this way from exploring and trading expeditions to the south, directed their attempts to win a share of this new-found wealth in overseas empires towards the east, west and north. The initial aim was to obtain access to the fabled wealth of the Far East, of Cathay or China and Cipango or Japan, by finding a route there outside the control of the Spanish or Portuguese. Such a route, it was hoped, might be found to the north of Asia or, after its existence became clear, to the north of the American continent. Either way, explorers were confronted with the Arctic, forming an icy barrier across their routes, which they penetrated at their peril and lingered in only to search for valuable minerals, for their expeditions were financed by merchants or rulers intent on profits. For a hundred years or more, from around 1500, repeated attempts were made in vain to penetrate through the ice along the North-East or North-West Passage, or even directly northwards over the Pole. Then, toward 1600, the Dutch and the English challenged and defeated the Spanish and Portuguese on the high seas and fought their way through the southern oceans to the East and West Indies, to India and into the Pacific. After about 1620 interest in a passage through the Arctic subsided – except for sporadic English expeditions to Hudson Bay – until it was revived in the nineteenth century (Scoresby 1820a: 1–91, Hakluyt 1907a, 1907b and 1907e, Taylor 1930, Kirwan 1962: 26–51, Morison 1971, Rasky 1976, Day 1986).

JOHN AND SEBASTIAN CABOT

John Cabot's real name was Giovanni Caboto. Born and bred in Genoa at the same time as Christopher Columbus, he moved to Venice and, failing to arouse Spanish or Portuguese enthusiasm for his projected voyage westwards to Cathay, he settled with his Venetian wife and three sons in Bristol, hoping that the English, being at the end of the spice line and therefore having to pay high prices, would jump at the chance of a short cut to Cathay. On 5 March 1496 King Henry VII issued letters patent empowering John Cabot and his sons 'to saile to all parts, countreys, and seas of the East, of the West and of the North, under our banners and ensignes . . . upon their owne proper costs and charges', and giving them 'licence to set up our banners and ensignes in every village, town, castle, isle, or maine land of them newly found'. They were to pay one-fifth of all their profits to the crown, and the king strictly forbade any other of his subjects to visit lands discovered by John Cabot or his sons without their express permission (Hakluyt 1907e: 83–4, Williamson 1962: 204–5). After an abortive first attempt in 1496, Cabot sailed due west from Dursey Head, Ireland, in the *Mathew*, keeping the North Star on his starboard beam until he made landfall, perhaps somewhere on the northern peninsula of the island of Newfoundland and possibly within a few miles of L'Anse aux Meadows, on 24 June 1497. After a brief excursion ashore to erect a crucifix and the banners of St George and St Mark for England and Venice, Cabot explored the coast northwards before returning to Bristol. A third voyage in 1498 with five ships ended in disaster. Only one ship returned and Cabot himself may have perished. His son Sebastian was actively involved in further expeditions to Newfoundland between 1500 and 1510. In 1502 the king rewarded 'the merchants of Bristol that have been in the newfounde lande' with £20, and at about this time the first English company for overseas trade was set up. Based at Bristol and apparently organized by Sebastian Cabot, this syndicate of 'Company Adventurers to the New Found Land' included some Portuguese settlers in the Azores. It is not clear how far the discovery of a route to Cathay was an aim of these voyages, because by 1504 Bristolians were already bringing back cargoes of fish and fish liver from Newfoundland (Williamson 1962, Quinn 1974: 94–103, 131–59, Marcus 1980: 168–70).

THE MUSCOVY COMPANY

The Cabots had failed to find a route to Cathay by sailing westwards from Bristol, but Sebastian Cabot, after a spell in Spanish service, returned to England in 1548 to be appointed 'grand Pilot of England' with a salary from the crown of 'one hundreth, threescore & six pounds, thirteen shillings and foure pence' (Hakluyt 1907e: 91–2). He now persuaded London merchants to finance a voyage eastwards to Cathay, through what came to be called the North-East Passage, and set up for the purpose another trading company, with himself as governor, called 'the companie of the Marchants adventurers for the discoverie of Regions, Dominions, Islands and places unknowen' (Haklulyt 1907a: 232). The hypothesis of a passage to Cathay along the north coast of Russia was not new, for it had been under discussion since the mid-fifteenth century (Savel'yeva 1983: 44) and was supported by the Russian savant Dmitriy Gerasimov in 1525 (Belov 1956: 40–5). The first part of the passage, the voyage round the northern tip of Norway, namely North Cape (Nordkapp), to the White Sea (Beloye more) was very well known, having been accomplished by Norwegian (including Ottar in the ninth century), Danish, Dutch and Russian seafarers (Belov 1956: 75). The intended voyage to Cathay, which Sebastian Cabot and the London merchants launched in May 1553, was thus not altogether a leap in the dark, but it was the first English voyage of Arctic exploration. It was to be undertaken by a fleet of three ships under the command of 'Sir Hugh Willoughby, Knight, Captaine generall' and Richard Chancellor, pilot general of the fleet. These two, the masters and master's mates of the three ships, and four others, formed a council of twelve persons to be in overall control of the expedition. The fleet, which was provisioned for eighteen months to allow for a possible overwintering, was made up as follows:

The *Bona Esperanza*, Admiral of the fleet, 120 tons, with a pinnace and a boat. The 38 persons on board were Hugh Willougby himself, the master and his mate, six merchants and thirty 'Mariners and officers' including two surgeons, a master gunner, boatswain and mate, four quartermasters and mates, two carpenters, a purser, a cook and his mate and others.

The *Edward Bonaventure*, 160 tons, with a pinnace and a boat. Among the fifty persons on board were Richard Chancellor and the ship's master Stephen Burrough.

The *Bona Confidentia*, 90 tons, with a pinnace and boat. The ship's company of twenty-eight persons included three merchants.

A few days before it sailed Sebastian Cabot issued instructions for the expedition in great detail (Hakluyt 1907a: 232–41). The fleet was to keep together so that the councillors could assemble aboard the Admiral of the Fleet whenever the captain general so wished. Morning and evening prayers were to be held on every ship and no 'blaspheming of God, or detestable swearing [was to] be used in any ship, nor communication of ribaldrie, filthy tales, or ungodly talk to be suffred in the company of any ship, neither dicing, carding, tabling, nor other divelish games. . . .' The sky-blue uniforms or 'liveries in apparel' issued to the mariners were to be kept by the merchants and only issued and worn on the captains's orders. Good behaviour toward local people was enjoined, though there would be no harm in taking or alluring a man or woman on board and even making them drunk with beer or wine, to obtain useful information and perhaps tempt people to inspect their wares. The local people were on no account to be trusted and were not to be given the impression that their commodities were actually wanted. Detailed reports were to be made about islands and their inhabitants, what their products were and what commodities they lacked and 'what mettals they have in hils, mountaines, streames, or rivers, in, or under the earth'. Moreover, Cabot warned the expedition that:

. . . there are people that can swimme in the sea, havens, & rivers, naked, having bows and shafts, coveting to draw nigh your ships, which if they shal finde not wel watched, or warded, they wil assault, desirous of the bodies of men, which they covet for meate: if you resist them, they dive, and so will flee, and therefore diligent watch is to be kept both day & night, in some Islands.

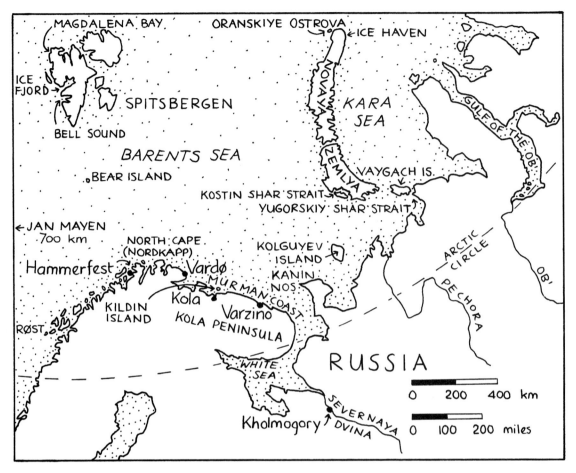

Map 7. The North-East Passage.

The fleet sailed from London in 1553 and was given a stately farewell by the court as it passed by Greenwich on 11 May, the mariners resplendent in their blue uniforms. Courtiers looked on from windows and towers and the common people crowded the shore. The ships fired their guns in salute. Progress was slow up the east coast of England. On 19 July off the Norwegian coast a pinnace was sent ashore to the island of Røst, where the people interrupted their haymaking to welcome the Englishmen. During the night of 2–3 August the fleet was dispersed by a storm, just after a consultation at which it was resolved that, if this happened, every ship would make for the Danish royal fortress of Wardhouse or Vardø in Finnmark. Richard Chancellor in the *Edward Bonaventure* waited at Vardø a week before continuing on his own to the White Sea, where he found his way to the mouth of the Dvina (Severnaya Dvina). There his crew wintered while he sledged to Moscow and opened up a profitable trade between England and Russia and, indirectly, Persia, which largely compensated Cabot's company for the failure to find a route to Cathay. In 1555 the company was reconstituted by royal charter, empowered to trade anywhere in the world not frequented by Englishmen before 1553, and granted a monopoly of trade with Russia and all areas 'lying Northwards, North-westwards, or North-eastwards' (Hakluyt 1907a: 318–29). It became known as the Muscovy or Russia Company. Sir Hugh Willoughby and his companions in the *Bona Esperanza*, with the *Bona Confidentia* in company, had become hopelessly lost in 1553. Overshooting the rendezvous at Vardø, the ships sailed out eastwards into the Barents Sea. Eventually on 14 August they reached a low-lying coast where the water was too shallow to get ashore. This was perhaps Kolguyev Island (ostrov Kolguyev), though Novaya Zemlya has been suggested. On 18 September the two ships anchored in a good harbour at Varzino on the Murman Coast (Murmanskiy bereg) of the Kola Peninsula (Kol'skiy poluostrov) where 'very evill wether, as frost, snow and haile, as though it had beene the deepe of winter' (Hakluyt 1907a: 253) persuaded them to winter. Parties were sent out south-south-west, west and south-east to search for people, but found none. There, apparently in the early months of 1554, all sixty-six persons on the two ships perished, almost certainly of scurvy, though legend had Sir Hugh 'congealed and frozen to death' (Hakluyt 1907e: 121) as he sat at his cabin table writing his journal, and the crewmen likewise frozen in lifelike attitudes, plate in hand or spoon in mouth (Rasky 1976: 88), 'others opening a locker, and others in various postures, like statues' as the Venetian ambassador, making the most of a good story, put it (Powys 1928: 15). Sir Hugh's journal contains no worthwhile information about the tragedy (Hakluyt 1907a: 244–54); his record-keeping seems to have been as incompetent as his navigation. Russian fishermen came across the corpses in 1554. The two ships were recovered, but lost in a storm while being brought home (Hakluyt 1907b: 265–7; Hakluyt 1907a: 232–329, Willan 1956: 1–9). This was the first attempted overwintering in the Arctic by the burgeoning seafaring nations of Western Europe, and the first of many Arctic disasters to come.

The setback of 1553 did not deter the Muscovy Company from organizing further attemps to find a north-east passage to Cathay. In 1556 Stephen Burrough took the pinnace *Serchthrift* east as far as Novaya Zemlya and Vaygach Island (Hakluyt 1907a: 333–52). He was helped and guided by the Russian seafarers who had probably been making regular annual voyages to the Rivers Pechora and Ob' from ports on the Murman Coast and White Sea since at least 1517 (Belov *et al.* 1980: 109). After escaping from a 'monstrous heape of ice' which threatened to overwhelm them, Burrough and his crew had a terrifyingly close encounter with a whale, which came so near that they could 'have thrust a sworde or any other weapon in him, which we durst not doe for feare hee should have overthrown our shippe; and then I called my company together, and all of us shouted, & with the crie that we made he departed from us . . .' (Hakluyt 1907a: 345). On 22 August the lengthening nights of approaching winter, the 'great and terrible abundance of ice', and the continual strong easterly and northerly winds, persuaded Burrough to turn back (Hakluyt 1907a: 350–1). He set course for the mouth of the River Dvina, and sailed into it to winter at Kholmogory.

A further expedition 'for discovery of Cathay' was launched by the 'company of English Merchants for discovery of new trades', that is the Muscovy Company, in 1580 (Hakluyt 1907b: 203–44). The fleet consisted of two barks; the *George* of London, Captain Arthur Pet, with a crew of nine men and a boy, and a burden of 40 tons; and the *William* of London, Captain Charles Jackman, crewed by five men and a boy, carrying 20 tons. Arthur Pet in the *George* was appointed 'Admiral, to weave the flagge in the maine top' and Jackman, Vice Admiral (p. 205). They were to proceed beyond Vaygach and the River Ob' directly to Cathay. Even if they found trading opportunities, or were forced to winter *en route*, they were to continue to Cathay, having been 'victualed for two yeres and upwards, which you may very wel make to serve you for two yeres and a halfe' (pp. 207–8). Pet and Jackman were furnished with a profusion of optimistic instructions drawn up by John Dee, Richard Hakluyt and other armchair geographers of the day. In Cathay they were to collect 'the seeds of all strange herbs & flowers', obtain a map of the country, and take notes on the defences of towns, naval forces, and weapons. The lengthy inventory of things they were instructed to take to Cathay included clothing and cloth of every kind: 'Frizadoes, Motlies, Bristow friezes, Spanish blankets', felts, hats, quilted caps, knitted socks, silk garters, perfumed gloves, 'velvet shoes and pantophles', purses and nightcaps. Hardware included pewter bottles, flagons and spoons, Venetian glass, English glass, 'Looking glasses for women, great and faire', 'spectacles of the common sort'. Others of Christall trimmed with silver', knives and gold and silver coins of every kind, locks, keys, hinges, bolts and hasps. The list is endless. They were even advised to take marmalade, barrelled figs, raisins, prunes, olives and other delicacies with which to entertain important persons coming aboard, as well as a map of England and 'the large Mappe of London to make shew of your Citie'. All the meticulous forethought was in vain. The expedition got no further than its predecessor, turning back at Vaygach Island after failing to penetrate the pack ice of the Kara Sea. These elaborate English expeditions to find a north-east passage to Cathay achieved nothing new. All they did was follow Russian seafarers part of the way along the route regularly used by them from the White Sea to the Gulf of the Ob' (Obskaya guba).

THE DUTCH TRY FOR CATHAY

The rise of Holland as a sea power accompanied her hard-fought independence from Spanish rule proclaimed in 1581, and followed closely on Elizabethan England's maritime expansion. Though the Dutch search for a north-east passage began later than the English one, and was equally unsuccessful in reaching Cathay, Dutch Arctic exploration was more far-reaching – thanks mainly to Willem Barentsz and Jacob van Heemskerck. Barentsz, who came from the Frisian Island of Terschelling, was probably the greatest sixteenth-century Arctic explorer. He combined outstanding navigational skills with excellent leadership, and had the courage and resolution necessary for the navigation of unknown ice-choked seas. Van Heemskerck, according to American historian John Lothrop Motley (1904: 354–5), was 'incapable of fatigue, of perplexity or of fear'. No wonder the monument to him in the Oude Kerk in Amsterdam commemorated his life, after he was killed destroying the Spanish fleet at Gibraltar in 1607, with the words 'The man who ever steered his way through ice or iron' (Powys 1928: 72). The three successive annual voyages of 1594–7 to the far north-east in search of a passage to Cathay led by Barentsz, Heemskerck and other seamen from the northern Low Countries, resulted from the initiatives of merchants and seafarers in the southern Low Countries. Most influential of these were the Brussels-born Olivier Brunel and the Antwerp merchant Balthasar de Moucheron. Their initiatives were perhaps prompted by their exclusion in 1580 from the Lisbon market as a result of the union of Spain and Portugal, which made some other access to Far Eastern markets essential to them. Olivier Brunel had already lived for some years in Russia, and had participated in Dutch trade with Russia via the Kola Peninsula and the White Sea in the 1570s. He had also journeyed overland and by sea to the River Ob' while in the service of the Russian family firm of Stroganov. De Moucheron financed his expedition of 1584, which was apparently aimed at the North-East Passage and Cathay. But this time Brunel did not even reach the Ob'. Setting out from Kola, he called at Kostin Shar Strait (proliv Kostin Shar) in the southern island of Novaya Zemlya, perhaps in the hope of obtaining a Russian escort for the further voyage to the Ob'. Finding no one there, he sailed south to the mouth of the Pechora. There, some of the crew were accidentally drowned and, in all probability, he was drowned with them (Muller 1874: 21–34, Naber 1914: xxvii–lxiv, Horensma 1985, Niedekker 1989). Soon after this, the fall of Antwerp to Spain in 1585 caused de Moucheron and other merchants to flee to Middelburg and Amsterdam in the Dutch Republic. He now became the main promotor of Dutch attempts to find the North-East Passage.

De Moucheron's intention in 1594 was to mount an expedition jointly with the States, or parliament, of Zeeland, but the States of Holland and the municipality of Amsterdam insisted on joining the venture too, and de Moucheron was relegated to the position of adviser. The instructions approved by the States General of the United Netherlands on 16 May 1594 show that there were in fact two separate expeditions. One, commanded by Willem Barentsz in the *Mercurius* of Amsterdam accompanied by *De Swane*, a Terschelling fishing-boat; the other consisting of *De Swane* of Veere in Zeeland and the *Mercurius* of Enkhuizen commanded by Cornelius Cornelisz Nay. The three ships and the fishing-boat were to sail in company until past the North Cape, when Barentsz was to lay course to Novaya Zemlya and attempt to find a route to Cathay round its northern tip, as proposed by the influential Amsterdam geographer Petrus Plancius. Nay was to make for Vaygach, following the route used by the Russians and English, and try to find a passage eastwards to Cathay through one or other of the straits at either end of that island. With help from the Russians, Cornelius Nay passed successfully through the strait at the southern end of Vaygach, called Yugorskiy Shar, and worked his way through the Kara Sea ice pack until his two ships broke out on 9 August into open water 20–30 miles offshore. 'We met with no more ice, or any sign of it, only a spacious open sea with a swell such as oceans have everywhere, and a great depth, for we could not touch ground with the lead', wrote Jan Huyghen van Linschoten on board the *Mercury* of Enkhuizen. 'So now there is absolutely no further doubt', he added optimistically, 'that the passage to China is free and open' (Naber 1914: 100, Van der Moer 1979: 215). Instead of following their instructions to proceed on eastwards, Nay and his shipmates, convinced they had found the long-hoped–for passage, turned joyfully home. In actual fact they had gone no further in 1594 than had Pet and Jackman in 1580. Meanwhile, Barentsz in the *Mercury* of Amsterdam traced the hitherto unknown west coast of northern Novaya Zemlya northwards to its most northerly point, where on 31 July he named some islands after his prince, William of Orange (Oranskiye ostrova). Prevented from penetrating eastwards or south-eastwards through the pack ice of the Kara Sea by his crew, who refused to go further, he returned south along Novaya Zemlya's west coast and the fleet, reunited west of Vaygach, sailed for home convinced of success. But the seven-ship expedition optimistically despatched by the States General in 1595 belied this. Reaching Vaygach only on 24 August, far too late in the season, they found their way barred by ice, and returned home disappointed of their hoped-for trade with China (Beke 1876, Naber 1914, Naber 1917, Van der Moer 1979).

After this fiasco, both the States General and the States of Holland discussed the possibility of a further expedition in 1596, but neither was prepared to put up the funds. Instead, the States General offered a reward of 25,000 guilders to the discoverer of the North-East Passage. Even before this, Amsterdam had resolved to go it alone, and made up to 12,000 guilders available for a two-ship expedition in 1596, one to be commanded by Jacob van Heemskerck with Willem Barentsz as navigating officer, and the other by Jan Cornelisz Rijp. The search was to be pursued via the northern tip of Novaya Zemlya, the events of 1595 having confirmed Petrus Plancius in his conviction that this more northerly route was the correct one. The explorers left Vlieland on 18 May 1596 and followed a more northerly course than any expedition so far. After seeing ice floes floating like swans on the dark green sea, they discovered Bear Island on 9 June, and chased and slaughtered a Polar bear, which was swimming in the sea, with muskets, halberds and hatchets. Continuing northwards, or even north-north-westwards, after sailing for some days in fog and drizzle they sighted on 17 June a high snow-covered land to the south-south-west, which they called Spitsbergen ('sharp' or 'pointed mountains'). They thought it was part of Greenland; it was in fact the extreme north-west tip of Spitsbergen, and the Dutch, after exploring some capes and islands on the north coast and erecting a board displaying the arms of Holland, turned south and returned to Bear Island, sailing southwards along Spitsbergen's west coast and noting its main geographical features, including Magdalena Bay (Teeth Bay), where they took possession for Holland, Ice Fjord or Isfjorden (*de Grooten Inwyck*), and Bell Sound or Bellsund (Brown 1920: 23). At Bear Island on 1 July the two ships parted, Rijp returning north towards Spitsbergen and Barentsz bearing east for Novaya Zemlya. Repeating his 1594 voyage to the northern tip of Novaya Zemlya, Barentsz rounded it, but his ship, surrounded and pounded by masses of ice, became beset on 26 August 1596 in a bay called Ice Haven (bukhta Ledyanaya Gavan') some 100 km (60 miles) down the east coast of Novaya Zemlya from its northern tip. In spite of the early death of the carpenter, which reduced their number to sixteen persons, the crew succeeded in building themselves a substantial wooden house ashore from logs and other driftwood found on the beach and planks from the ship. On 24 October all the personnel took up residence in the house, some having up till then slept in the ship. There they lived, warmed by a fire fuelled with driftwood, whose smoke ascended a chimney in the centre of the structure, and lit by lamps fuelled with bear fat, until 14 June 1597. On that day, abandoning their ship, which was still stuck fast in the ice, they set out in two open boats and voyaged 'in the ice, over the ice and through the sea' for some 2,400 km (1,500 miles) round the northern tip of Novaya Zemlya, down the west coast, past Cape Kanin Nos. They were welcomed at Kola on 30 August by their colleague of the previous year, Jan Cornelisz Rijp, who was there on a trading voyage. On this boat journey, during which they received help on several occasions from Russian seafarers, three of their number perished, one of them Barentsz, who was buried on the west coast of Novaya Zemlya, leaving twelve survivors to return to Amsterdam on 1 November wearing their Novaya Zemlya attire and white fur hats. A journal describing their experiences in vivid detail was kept at the time by one of their number, Gerrit de Veer, who had also taken part in, and kept a journal of, the 1595 expedition. His account of all three voyages, the first described from Barentsz's journal, was published in Dutch in 1598 and became the Arctic best-seller *par excellence*. It was translated into French, German, Italian and Latin before 1600, into English in 1609, into Russian in 1936 (Vize 1936), and reprinted many times. To this day it remains one of the most readable, lively and perceptive eye-witness accounts of Arctic exploration ever written (Beke 1853, 1876 and Naber 1917). The deep impression it made on the Dutch national consciousness was reinforced in 1819, when the most popular Dutch poet of the time, Hendrik Tollens, celebrated the overwintering in verse in his *Tafereel van de overwintering der Hollanders op Nova Zembla in 1596 en 1597*. Dutch interest in a northerly route to Cathay continued long after the 1596–7 expedition. Voyages along the north coast of Russia were made in 1611 and 1625 and to the Davis Strait area in 1614–16 (Muller 1874: 162–88, Hacquebord 1986), and several attempts at sailing due north to find the so-called Trans-Polar Passage were made in the early seventeenth century.

RELICS OF BARENTSZ

No other Arctic explorer that we know of rounded the northern tip of Novaya Zemlya for two-and-three-quarter centuries after Barentsz and Heemskerck. Then, on 7 September 1871, a Norwegian captain, Elling Carlsen, sailing out of Hammerfest in the sloop the *Solid*, reached Ice Haven, and on 9 September discovered a wooden house at the head of the bay that could be none other than Barentsz's winter quarters of 1596–7 (Beke 1876: xliv–xlix). The roof had fallen in and the structure was partly filled with gravel and ice but the clock, pots and pans, books, implements, tools and weapons were just as the Dutch had left them. Captain Carlsen drew up a list of the articles he and his crew removed from the site during three successive visits (Anon. 1876: 270; see too de Jonge 1873):

> Iron frame over the fireplace, with shifting bar; two ship cooking-pans of copper, found standing on the iron frame, with the remains of a copper scoop; copper bands, probably at one time fastened round pails; bar of iron; iron

crowbar; one long and two small gun-barrels; two bores or augers, each three feet in length; chisel, padlock, caulking-iron, three gouges, and six files; plate of zinc; earthenware jar; tankard, with zinc lid; lower half of another tankard; six fragments of pepper-pots; tin meat-strainer; pair of boots; sword; fragments of old engravings, with Latin couplets underneath them; three Dutch books; a small piece of metal; nineteen cartridge cases, some still full of powder; iron chest, with lid, and intricate lock-work; fragments of metal handle of same; grindstone; an eight-pound iron weight; small cannon-ball; gun-lock, with hammer and flint; clock, bell of clock, and striker; rasp; small auger; small narrow strips of copper band; two salt and pepper pots, about eight inches high; two pairs of compasses; fragment of iron-handled knife; three spoons; borer; hone; one wooden, and one bronze tap; two wooden stoppers for gun muzzles; two spear or ice-pole heads; four navigation instruments; a flute; lock and key; another lock; sledge-hammer head; clock weight; twenty-six pewter candlesticks and fragments, six in a complete state of preservation; pitcher of Etruscan shape, beautifully engraved; upper half of another pitcher; wooden trencher, coloured red; clock alarum; three scales; four medallions, circular, about eight inches in diameter, three of them mounted in oak frames; a string of buttons; hilt of sword, and a foot of its blade; halberd head; and two carved pieces of wood, one with the haft of a knife in it.

An Englishman who was at Hammerfest when Carlsen returned there in November 1871 bought these relics from him for 10,800 Norwegian crowns and passed them on to the Dutch government for the same price. Since then many have been exhibited in the Rijksmuseum in Amsterdam and in the Naval Museum at The Hague. But the plundering of the remains of Barentsz's winter house continued. Another Norwegian walrus hunter, M. Gundersen, searched the site in 1875 and recovered a broken chest containing two maps and a Dutch translation of the log of Pet and Jackman's voyage, which Barentsz had obtained from Richard Hakluyt. These, and Gundersen's other finds, are in the museum at Hammerfest. In 1876, the Englishman Charles L.W. Gardiner, as a result of more systematic excavations, found still more artefacts, including 120 wax candles, a lead inkstand, two goose feather pens, and a powder horn containing a piece of paper on which Barentsz and Heemskerck had written a brief signed statement explaining the circumstances in which they had built the house and subsequently left it in two small boats, leaving their ship still stuck in the ice. Gardiner presented his finds to the Dutch government, receiving a gold medal in return (Beke 1876: Postscript, Nordenskiöld 1881a: 300–1, de Jonge 1877).

In his cargo Barentsz was carrying trade goods destined for China, some of which, notably cloth and clothing, were unpacked and divided among the overwinterers, who used them for bedding and extra clothing. There were also bundles of engraved prints, which were brought ashore from the ship and then left behind in the wooden house in June 1597. These had amalgamated into solid papier-mâché blocks during nearly three centuries of alternate freezing and thawing in the Arctic. It took the Rijksmuseum authorities in Amsterdam another century to get round to separating and restoring these prints, a delicate task which was begun in 1977. It involved, in the case of a typical block of fragments of prints, separating a total of 114 fragments comprising nine lower halves of the *Standardbearer* by Hendrik Goltzius of Haarlem, nine lower halves of his *Captain*, six lower halves of his *Maria Magdalena*, and so on. In the end, about four hundred copies of 150 different prints were recovered. Best represented were costumes and landscapes, but the heroes of ancient Rome did well too, and there were thirty copies of Jacques de Gheyn's *The Great Lion*. In this gold mine for art historians, twenty-four copies were identified of a hitherto unknown *Judgement of Paris* (Braat *et al.* 1980).

The final episodes in the plundering of the remains of Barentsz's wintering hut began in 1933, when a geological expedition from Leningrad's Arctic Institute led by B.V. Miloradovich visited it and was able to unearth a few more artefacts – wooden clogs, a last, a copper jug, an axe, a key and a spear point (Belov 1977: 66–7). Their photograph shows that not a log or a plank was then still standing (Braat *et al.* 1980: 44). Their finds are preserved in the Museum of the Arctic and Antarctic in St Petersburg. Whatever they missed will surely have been found by the three Russian expeditions led by amateur archaeologist Dmitriy Fedorovich Kravchenko to Ice Haven in 1977, 1979 and 1980. They systematically excavated an area of 50 sq m (538 sq ft), once occupied by the wooden hut, down to a depth of 20 cm (8 in). With the help of a metal detector, they found still more artefacts, including parts of a compass, the butt of a musket, scissors and other instruments, boat hooks, fragments of glass dishes, and tin plates, all of which are now in the Historical Museum at Arkhangel'sk. Members of these expeditions searched for Barentsz's grave and, in 1989, some who were also members of Moscow's 'Dolphin' aqualung diving club found the remains of Barentsz's ship at the bottom of Ice Haven. The expeditions produced a couple of riddles among the finds at the site of the hut: a human lower jaw bone which Moscow's Institute of Forensic Medicine thought was that of a young woman, though no women accompanied Barentsz and Heemskerck; and a Dutch copper coin which numismatists at the State Historical Museum in Moscow and the Hermitage in St Petersburg dated to the first quarter of the seventeenth century – after Barentsz's time! (Kryuchkin 1981, 1982.)

NORTH-WEST TO CATHAY

In the sixteenth century, undismayed by John Cabot's failure to discover a westerly passage to Cathay, the merchants and rulers of Western Europe mounted repeated attempts to find it. In the 1520s King Francis I of France encouraged the Italian Giovanni da Verrazano, who was funded by a group of Italian bankers in Lyons, to search the coast between Florida and Newfoundland for a strait leading to Cathay. His rival, Emperor Charles V, ruler of Spain, encouraged the Portuguese pilot Estevan Gomez and the Spaniard Luis Vacquez de Ayllon to do the same. In the 1530s Jacques Cartier explored the Gulf of St Lawrence on behalf of his king Francis I, in the vain hope that it might lead to Cathay (Morison 1971: 277–429, Thomson 1975: 7–14). By the time the English became interested, in the 1560s and 1570s, it was clear that, if a North-West Passage existed, it must be north of Labrador, through the Arctic.

English interest in the North-West Passage was aroused in Queen Elizabeth I's reign by Humphrey Gilbert, who not only wrote a 'discourse . . . to prove a passage by the North-West to Cathaia, and the East Indies' (Hakluyt 1907e: 92–120), but in 1565 petitioned the queen for an expedition to discover 'a passage by the Northe to go to Cataia'. He offered to lead it in person in return for a monopoly of all trade through the passage for his lifetime and one quarter of all English customs duties on imports through it (Morison 1971: 497). His discourse was published in 1576, at which time, partly under its influence, the first sixteenth-century English voyage in search of the North-West Passage was being launched. Between 1576 and 1616 a series of voyages in search of the North-West Passage were made: those of Martin Frobisher in 1576, 1577 and 1578, John Davis in 1585, 1586 and 1587, Henry Hudson in 1610, and William Baffin and Robert Bylot or Billet in 1615 and 1616. These repeated efforts, none of them successful, were financed by a group of businessmen based in London, known as merchant adventurers. Prominent among them were William Sanderson, Thomas Smith, Dudley Digges, John Wolstenholme and Francis Jones (Markham 1921: 104–11).

Although no passage was found, the names of both seamen and merchants, spread over the map, bear witness to their contribution to European geographical knowledge of the Arctic: Frobisher Bay and Baffin Bay, Hudson Bay and Hudson Strait, Smith Sound and Jones Sound, and Baffin Island (now Qikirtaluk), to name but a few. These men were optimists and opportunists, for whom the discovery of a route to Cathay was more an attractive and exciting prospect with which to enlist the support of court and country, than an end in itself. The essential requirement was, of course, profit, to be made either by finding new outlets for English woollens, through the opening up of new, populated lands, Cathay included, or through founding settlements, or by the discovery and exploitation of natural resources, whether in the form of valuable ores or animals and fishes. Frobisher's thrust toward Cathay was blunted, then forgotten, in the excitement of discovering gold; Davis's third expedition was partly financed by having two of the three ships break off to fish for cod, while Davis alone did the exploring. Davis, after somewhat perfunctorily exploring both sides of the strait named after him, wrote optimistically to secretary of state Francis Walsingham on his return from his first voyage that 'the north-west passage is a matter nothing doubtfull, but at any time almost to be passed, the sea navigable, voyd of yse, the ayre tollerable, and the waters very depe' (Markham 1880: xix). Though on his third voyage in 1587 he sailed north up the west Greenland coast nearly as far as Upernavik, and later passed across the entrance of Hudson Strait, Davis made no further progress toward finding a passage to Cathay (see Markham 1880, Markham, C.R. 1889, Morison 1971: 583–616). Nevertheless, his optimism encouraged the London merchants, after organizing themselves into a Company for the Discovery of the North-West Passage, to send out Henry Hudson in 1610 and Thomas Button in 1612 to search for it. In 1614 they despatched a certain Captain Gibbons or Gibbins, but he 'only reached the coast of Labrador, where he took shelter in a bay, and remained there so long that his crew named it 'Gibbons his hole'' (Markham 1881: xxx). Undismayed, the North-West Passage

Map 8. The North-West Passage.

Company hired William Baffin (pilot) and Robert Bylot (master) to continue the search in the *Discovery*, which had been on this quest since 1610. In 1615 these two contented themselves with minor explorations in Hudson Strait, through which Hudson had sailed in 1610, but in 1616 they sailed north through Davis Strait, up the west Greenland coast to the head of Baffin Bay, and then south along the eastern shore of Baffin Island. Baffin discovered three openings or sounds in the bay named after him, which he named after his patrons Smith, Jones and Lancaster. Though he did not enter any one of them, he reported so bluntly and firmly in the negative to John Wolstenholme on his return that no further attempts to find the North-West Passage north of Davis Strait were made for two centuries. 'I entend to shew the whole proceeding of the voyage in a word: as namely, there is no passage nor hope of passage in the north of Davis Straights', he wrote (Markham 1881: 150. For this paragraph see Markham 1880, Markham 1881 and Christy 1894). For the next two centuries all attempts to find the North-West Passage were made through Hudson Bay, yet the passage, when it was eventually found in the nineteenth century, led off from Lancaster Sound.

FROBISHER'S FOLLY

As ex-pirate Martin Frobisher sailed down the Thames from Deptford on 8 June 1576 with his fleet of three small ships bound for the North-West Passage, Elizabeth I waved farewell to them from her palace window at Greenwich. The voyage was financed by Michael Lok and other London merchants who set up a joint-stock Cathay Company for the purpose. Only Frobisher himself in the bark *Gabriel* reached the inlet or fjord in south-east Baffin Island, now Frobisher Bay, which he hopefully believed to be the passage to Cathay. One ship was lost in a storm *en route* and the other, discouraged by the ice off south-east Greenland, turned back for home. Frobisher's 1576 voyage was notable for the first recorded encounters of Europeans and Eskimos, but these were by no means entirely friendly. Though the Eskimos allowed themselves to be entertained on board ship and friendly bartering took place, 'five of our men going ashore were by them intercepted with their boat, and were never since heard of to this day againe' (Hakluyt 1907e: 196). Frobisher tried hard to recover the missing men, for the *Gabriel*'s crew of eighteen was now reduced to thirteen, but to no avail. A hostage he had seized with his kayak was taken back to England, where this 'strange infidel' (p. 197) caused a sensation. A greater stir arose from a piece of black rock brought back by the expedition which, after several rejections, was eventually pronounced by an alchemist of the day to contain gold. A second voyage 'pretended for the discovery of a new passage to Cataya' (p. 199), but actually instructed to bring home a cargo of the ore, was mounted by an enlarged 'Company of Cathay' and was led by Frobisher to the same place in 1577. This time, besides the two barks *Gabriel* and *Michael*, he was 'furnished with one tall ship of her Majesties, named The Ayde, of two hundred tunne' (p. 199), and took with him some 120 men in all. A list of victuals taken for 115 men mentions 5 tons of beef for three months, 16 tons of biscuit for 140 days, 80½ tons of beer for six months, at one gallon per man per day, and 2 tons of butter, at ½ lb per man per day (Stefansson 1938b: 97–9). The events of the second voyage showed that North-West Ore, as it came to be called, had been given precedence over the North-West Passage. In other words, the quest for Cathay had degenerated into a gold rush. In spite of his best efforts, Frobisher failed to discover anything about the fate of the five missing men, except to find some of their belongings in abandoned Eskimo tents, namely a canvas doublet 'made after the English fashion, a shirt, a girdle, three shoes for contrary feete, and of unequal bignesse' (p. 215). Although fights with the Eskimos occurred, ethnographic information about them was recorded by a certain Dionise Settle, who accompanied the expedition. Both he and Martin Frobisher thought that the Eskimos were cannibals, and that the five men who had disappeared in the previous year had been eaten. Dionise Settle has left a colourful account of the 1577 voyage. He describes his first encounter with the Arctic on 4 July in the pack ice off southern Greenland as follows: 'Here, in place of odoriferous and fragrant smels of seweete gums, & pleasant notes of musicall birdes, which other Countreys in more temperate zones do yeeld, wee tasted the most boisterous Boreal blasts mixt with snow and hail, in the moneths of June and July, nothing inferior to our untemperate winter . . . '(Hakluyt 1907e: 139). The voyage was successful, and while the Cathay Company conducted further assays of the ore, which showed a high content of both gold and silver, it set about organizing, for 1578, one of the largest Arctic expeditions ever mounted. This comprised fifteen ships and some four hundred men and received its instructions and half its funds from the queen. It was to open up mines wherever the ore could be found, but especially on Kodlunarn Island, on the northern coast of the mouth of Frobisher Bay, where the 200 tons of ore brought back in 1577 had been mined, and plant a settlement of a hundred men. Only after the mining was in full swing was the further exploration of Frobisher Bay, still thought to lead to Cathay, and still unexplored, permitted. In the event, no overwintering party or colony was established but a house was built on the highest point of a small island 'to the ende we might prove against the next yeere, whither the snow could overwhelm it, the frost break it up, or the people dismember the same'. They left in it bells, knives, 'pictures of men and women in lead, men on horsebacke, looking glasses, whistles and pipes. Also in the house was made an Oven, and bread left baked therein for them to see and taste' (Hakluyt 1907e: 265).

But there was no fourth Frobisher expedition in the following year, to investigate how the house had weathered the Arctic winter and how the local Inuit had treated its contents. The 1,350 tons of worthless rock shipped home that autumn of 1578 was enough to ruin any hope of further financial support. The first serious attempt to find the North-West Passage, which began with the discovery of a wide opening on the American coast, namely Frobisher Bay, ended without any exploration of the 200 km (150 miles) between it and the head of the bay (Hakluyt 1907e: 131–281, Stefansson 1938, Morison 1971: 500–51, Kenyon 1975, Fitzhugh and Olin 1993).

The Frobisher expeditions had a curious sequel. In the spring of 1861, when American Arctic explorer Charles Francis Hall (see Chapter 8 below) was travelling with Eskimos in Frobisher Bay, he was told that white men had entered the bay with their ships a very long time ago. An aged Eskimo woman was able to provide additional details which caused Hall to marvel at the accuracy of Inuit oral tradition, for he very soon realized that the white man's ships referred to were those of Martin Frobisher, 285 years before! The old lady, whom Hall judged to be one hundred years old, correctly stated that ships had arrived in three successive years and that several Inuit had been killed. She revealed to Hall what he assumed to be the truth about the five sailors lost on the first expedition (Hall 1865: 279).

> *Oral* history told me that five white men were captured by Innuit people at the time of the appearance of the ships a great many years ago; that these men wintered on shore (whether one, two, three, or more winters, could not say); that they lived among the Innuits; that they afterward built an oomien (large boat), and put a mast into her, and had sails; that early in the season, before much water appeared, they endeavored to depart; that, in the effort, some froze their hands; but that finally they succeeded in getting into open water, and away they went, which was the last seen or heard of them. This boat, as near as I could make out at the time, was built on the island that Frobisher and his company landed upon, viz., Niountelik

On 11 August 1861 Hall landed on Niountelik Island and was thrilled to find a heap of weathered, lichen-covered coal which must have been left there by Frobisher. Soon afterwards, he landed on neighbouring Kodlunarn Island 'White Man's Island', and there found a mine evidently dug by Frobisher's men, the ruins of the house built in 1578, and a curious trench dug on the shore of the island in which, according to Hall's interpretation of his Eskimo informants, the five English sailors left behind by the first expedition had built themselves a ship in which to sail home (Hall 1865: 257, 267–8, 278–80, 363–6, 426–8, 436–8, 550–3). Hall carefully labelled the precious Frobisher relics he had been able to collect on Kodlunarn Island, which included fragments of pottery, glass, and tile, a piece of cord and pieces of wood and coal, and sent some to the Royal Geographical Society in London and others to the Smithsonian Institution in Washington. At the time Vilhjalmur Stefansson published his *The Three Voyages of Martin Frobisher* in 1938, neither of these revered institutions could trace the whereabouts of their Frobisher relics. As if to make amends for this apparent negligence, between 1981 and 1991 the Smithsonian Institution conducted detailed archaeological work on Kodlunarn Island and published the results in a splendid volume in 1993 (Fitzhugh and Olin 1993). The authors raise the interesting possibility that the five men mentioned in Inuit oral tradition may have been inadvertently left behind by Frobisher's third and last, rather than his first, expedition.

HENRY HUDSON

Henry Hudson was a daring explorer and a brilliant navigator. His exceptionally wide experience was gained from four voyages to four different regions, three of them in the Arctic, and was backed by the erudition of his Dutch friends, the cartographer Jodocus Hondius and the already-mentioned Petrus Plancius. But he suffered from a serious defect which eventually led to his death as a result of a mutiny: he was no leader of men. Already on his second voyage in 1608 trouble occurred between him and his crew. Why else should he, on his own admission, have given the ship's company a certificate of his 'free and willing return' to

England? During his last, fatal voyage in 1610–11, on which he discovered Hudson Bay, the crew, dispirited by the ice and fog of Hudson Strait, refused to go further, but changed their minds after Hudson explained his plans with the help of a chart. Then, in September, when he was working his way to and fro in James Bay, no doubt to establish whether or not it was a cul-de-sac, Hudson found himself faced with another mutiny during which the mate, Robert Juet, was revealed as the ringleader. But Hudson, instead of clapping him in irons or even executing him, merely deposed him from his position of mate, appointing Robert Bylot in his place. Finally, one day in June 1611, when the *Discovery*, after leaving her winter quarters, was moored to an ice floe somewhere in James Bay, mutiny again reared its ugly head, this time to more effect. Hudson was seized, bound and bundled into the ship's boat or shallop, along with his son John and six crew members, two of whom were sick. Before the mutineers cut the shallop free and sailed away, the ship's carpenter, Philip Staffe, loyal to Hudson, insisted on joining him there and sharing his fate. No convincing evidence of the exact nature of that fate has ever been found. The *Discovery* was piloted home successfully by Robert Bylot. Four of the mutineers were killed in a clash with Eskimos on Digges Islands, Juet and another died a natural death on the way home, and eight survivors reached Ireland half starved. Neither the boy, Nicholas Syms, nor Robert Bylot, seem to have been under suspicion of mutiny. When the other six survivors were examined under oath by the authorities of Trinity House, Hull, on 24 October 1611, they did their best to exculpate themselves by blaming the mutiny on their dead shipmates, Henry Greene and William Wilson, who had been among those killed by the Eskimos. According to one of the six, Abacuk Pricket, whose journal with its famous account of the mutiny has survived, Robert Bylot had nothing to do with it: the mutineers had relied on Robert Juet's 'judgement and skill'. Another of the six claimed that Robert Bylot was privy to the plot. With a considerable show of solidarity, five of the six admitted that Hudson and the others were ejected from the ship by common consent, but insisted they had acted, as it were, in self defence. They claimed that Hudson was issuing more than a fair share of provisions to himself and his favourites and that in any case these were insufficient to feed them all. Thus, they had acted as they did 'to saue some from Starving' (Christy 1894b: 629–34). When eventually brought to trial in the Court of Admiralty at Southwark on 24 July 1618, at least three of the alleged mutineers, Abacuk Pricket, Edward Wilson and Francis Clemens, were found not guilty of 'feloniously pinioning and putting Henry Hudson master of the *Discovery* out of the same ship with eight more of his company into a shallop . . . without meat, drink, clothes or other provision, whereby they died' (Powys 1928: 197).

What contributed most to the mutineers' escape from justice was that Bylot and Pricket were able to convince the merchants, with the help of Hudson's charts, that the North-West Passage was all but found. Both were in the crew of the *Discovery* in 1612, when it was sent back to Hudson Bay under command of Thomas Button, not, be it noted, to search for Henry Hudson and his colleagues, who are not mentioned in the expedition's official instructions (Christy 1894b: 636–8), but to sail westwards across the bay and, hopefully, continue on through the passage. The instructions did, however, advise Button to 'be careful to prevent all Mutynie amongst your people . . .' (p. 638). He was the first to reach and explore the western shore of the bay, where he wintered in the mouth of the Nelson River (Christy 1894a: 162–200).

Besides the North-East and North-West Passages, a third possible short-cut to Cathay had been suggested in 1527 by a Bristol merchant then living in Seville called Robert Thorne, who became famous for the bold but dubious statement that 'there is no land uninhabitable, nor Sea innavigable' (Hakluyt 1907a: 228). He urged that the attempt should be made to discover 'if our Seas Northward be navigable to the Pole, or no' (p. 229). Petrus Plancius and others thought they were, arguing that any ice would melt during the long Polar summer. Henry Hudson had first emerged from obscurity in 1607 when the Muscovy Company sent him north as captain of the *Hopewell*, with a crew of ten men and a boy, the boy being his son John, to find this northern or Trans-Polar Passage. He failed, his way blocked by ice at or beyond the northern tip of Spitsbergen, 'the land called Newland by the Hollanders'. Hudson added nothing to the explorations of van Heemskerck and Barentsz of 1596, apart from the discovery, on his voyage home, of Jan Mayen, which he named Hudson's Touches. Still on the track of Barentsz, in 1608 Hudson took the *Hopewell* to Novaya Zemlya, again on behalf of the Muscovy Company, to search for the North-East Passage. Then on 8 January 1609 he contracted with the Amsterdam branch or chamber of the Dutch East India Company to 'search for a passage by the north, round the north of Novaya Zemlya' (Naber 1921: 88–9) in the company's ship *De Halve Maan* (*The Half Moon*). In spite of the fact that Hudson's instructions explicitly forbade him to 'think of any other route or passage except the abovementioned one north and north-east of Nova Zemlya' (p. xxii), he turned back in the first half of May somewhere beyond the North Cape of Norway (Nordkapp), probably well short of Novaya Zemlya, possibly under pressure from a mutinous crew, and sailed off south-westward across the Atlantic to discover and name the Hudson River, which he at first hoped might be the North-West Passage. One can well understand why Hudson's feats of navigation persuaded the English merchants to sign him on for a further search for the North-West Passage in 1610, this time to discover if any of the inlets seen by John Davis might lead to it. That was his fatal voyage to Hudson Bay (on Hudson's voyages see Asher 1860, Powys 1928, and, for his voyage for the Dutch, Naber 1921).

JENS MUNK

Combined into a single kingdom with Norway since 1397, Denmark had more important Arctic interests than either England or Holland. Possession of the port of Vardø in Finnmark, one of the kingdom's key fortresses and itself in the Arctic, enabled the Danish king to levy tolls on and participate in the growing trade with Russia via the North Cape, and involved the Danes closely in attempts to find the North-East Passage. Moreover, the Danish king naturally assumed responsibility for the 'lost' Viking colony in Greenland which 'has ever belonged to and been the rightful property of the Norwegian crown' (Gad 1970: 190). In the sixteenth century King Frederick II of Denmark (1559–88), who called himself 'lord of the sea' (Hansen 1965a: 50), tried, on three separate occasions, to send an expedition to Greenland to this end. In 1582 he attempted to hire Martin Frobisher, and in 1583, Olivier Brunel, to lead an expedition there (Gad 1970: 190–8). In the seventeenth century King Christian IV (1588–1648) of Denmark, intent on creating a Danish maritime empire, gave 'our dominion' of Greenland high priority, organizing expeditions there in 1605, 1606 and 1607. The first two were led by a Scotsman, John Cunningham, who was a captain in the Royal Danish Navy. An Englishman from Hull, James Hall, who served in the Danish navy as mate or *styrmand*, acted as pilot of all three. The declared object of the third, which however never reached west Greenland, was to find Eiriksfjord, where the Viking settlement was thought to have been. Having established his sovereignty over Greenland, of which the 1605 expedition had taken possession on his behalf, Christian IV turned his attention to the north-east. Already in 1599 he had personally sailed with his fleet round the North Cape as far as Kildin Island (ostrov Kil'din) off the Murman Coast. Now, in 1610, he sent a two-ship expedition to Novaya Zemlya to search for the North-East Passage. The captain was an experienced seaman called Jens Munk or Munck, who had gone to sea as a ship's boy aged twelve in 1591, sailed with the Portuguese to Brazil, with the Dutch to England, to Iceland on his own account, and to Spain with a Danish firm. In 1609 he had extricated himself and his crew but not his ship from the ice encircling Kolguyev Island. Ice barred Jens Munk's way to the North-East Passage in 1610, but Christian IV, who promoted him to be captain in the Royal Danish Navy in 1611, accepted his plan for a Danish attempt at the North-West Passage in 1619.

Munk, who had been in London and Amsterdam in 1616–17, and was certainly familiar with contemporary geographical ideas, realized that the English had still not thoroughly explored the west coast of Hudson Bay. His expedition was seen off by Christian IV himself from the royal naval shipyard in Copenhagen. It sailed in two Danish naval ships, the frigate *Enhiorningen* (*Unicorn*) and the sloop *Lamprenen* (*Lamprey*). Munk took two books with him: the Bible and a fifty-page notebook, not yet written in except for the heading in Munk's hand 'Description of Jens Munk's voyage to the North-West Passage which he began on 9 May 1619 to search for China' (Lauridsen 1883: LV). In that book, which still survives in the Royal Library at Copenhagen, Munk kept the journal of his momentous and tragic voyage to Hudson Bay, which he published in 1624 with the title *Navigatio Septentrionalis* (*Voyage to the North*). It is one of the most vivid and poignant works in the literature of the Arctic (Lauridsen 1883; English translations, Gosch 1897b, Kenyon 1980). The outward voyage was uneventful enough in spite of the fog, ice and currents in Hudson Strait, and some serious navigational errors made by Munk's English (or Scottish?) first mate William Gordon. Sailing south-westwards across Hudson Bay, Munk took his ships into an excellent winter harbour inside the mouth of the Churchill River, which he called Munkehavn. It was on the left bank of the river, one-and-a-half miles upstream from the modern town of Churchill.

In spite of a three-mile trek ashore in November to search for natives, which was made extremely difficult by their lack of skis or snow shoes, the Danish

Plate 5. Jens Munk's winter harbour in the mouth of the Churchill River, Hudson Bay, where he and sixty-four companions were struck down disastrously by scurvy in the early months of 1620. His two ships are here shown anchored on the left bank of the Churchill River while crewmen fell timber (non-existent now at Churchill), bury a dead comrade, bring home game and, beyond the ships, hunt a Polar bear in a boat. Details like the trees, which should be coniferous, and houses, which should be the merest huts and further inland, are fanciful. Contemporary illustration from Munk's own narrative published in 1624. (From Birket-Smith 1929: 152.)

explorers made no contact with the local inhabitants. During the autumn some hares and willow grouse were shot and foxes caught. At the year's end only two men had died, but by the middle of February 1620 scurvy was affecting all but seven of the sixty-five overwinterers, and twenty were already dead. In spite of some mild weather, liberal rations of beer and wine, and Munk's personal care of the sick, which included collecting berries ashore in March when the snow had melted, fatalities continued. The expedition's well-stocked medicine chest was of little use. The bottles were labelled in Latin and the surgeon, who was neither a trained physician nor even an educated man, had to get the priest to translate the labels for him. By mid-April both surgeon and priest, as well as William Gordon, were dead, and deaths continued until early June, when only Munk and three others remained alive. In spite of what he thought was the final entry in his journal on 4 June ending with the words 'Herewith, goodnight to all the world;

and my soul into the hand of God' (Gosch 1897b: 48), Munk lived to bring the
Lamprey safely back to Norway with a crew of two (one of the three survivors of
early June having meanwhile died). He was ordered by King Christian IV to lead
another expedition in 1621 both to finish the exploration of the western coast of
Hudson Bay which he had scarcely begun, and to recover the *Unicorn*. This
second expedition never took place, apparently because of a predictable difficulty
in recruiting crews, but Jens Munk did draw up a list of essential requirements for
it which reflects his ideas about the cause of the disaster in 1619–20. It included
'good medical men, especially for scurvy', 'smoked meat in place of salted',
sheepskin clothing, stockings, socks, shoes and boots, blankets and overcoats, and
'skis or snow-shoes for travelling on snow' (Gosch 1897b: xxxviii–ix; Lauridsen
1883: XLVII–VIII; for Munk, besides works already cited, see Birket-Smith
1929, Hansen 1965, 1970).

THE HUDSON BAY CUL-DE-SAC

Once Baffin had declared in 1616 that there was no passage in Baffin Bay, and
Hudson, Button and Munk had between them explored most of Hudson Bay
without any sign of a passage in 1610 and 1620, London merchant adventurers
seem to have lost interest in the North-West Passage. But hopes of finding it were
still entertained by private individuals and provincial towns, and in 1630 a
seafaring burgess of Kingston-upon-Hull, named Luke Foxe or Fox, persuaded
his own city fathers, in the shape of the Master and Wardens of Trinity House,
Hull, one or two influential London merchants, and eventually King Charles I
himself, who lent Foxe the good ship *Charles*, to support a further exploration of
Hudson Bay in search of the North-West Passage. No sooner did the Company of
Merchant Adventurers of Bristol hear of this than they persuaded a certain
Thomas James to undertake a search for the North-West Passage on their behalf,
and lent him their ship, the *Henrietta Maria*. Thus in 1631 two separate, single-
ship expeditions sailed round Hudson Bay in an anti-clockwise direction, one
ship named for the king of the day, the other for the queen. Neither Foxe nor
James distinguished themselves by important new discoveries: their explorations
merely confirmed that there was no easy way out of Hudson Bay. The king sent
both captains off with a map of the discoveries of their predecessors, the royal
instructions, and a letter to the emperor of Japan. They met on 30 August 1631
somewhere off the south-west shore of the bay, when Captain Foxe was
entertained on board the *Henrietta Maria* by Captain James. Although Foxe says
that he 'was well entertained and feasted by Captain James' he complains that,
while they dined between decks, the *Henrietta Maria* took in 'so much water as
wee could not haue wanted sause if wee had had roast Mutton' and that she took
'her liquor as kindly as our selues, for her nose was no sooner out of the pitcher,
but her nebe, like the Ducks, was in't againe' (Christy 1894b: 358). Foxe thought
James was 'no Seaman' (p. 359) and that the time he spent with James 'was the
worst spent of any time of my discouery' (p. 360). Foxe's exploration of Hudson
Bay was more thorough and extensive than James's, though it was completed in
the one summer season. He even poked into two outlets north of the bay, Roe's

Welcome Sound and Foxe Channel. James overwintered at Charlton Island in the bay that now bears his name, adopting the original but risky expedient of sinking his ship to protect her from winter ice. Fortunately he was able to raise her the following spring. Buildings were put up in the forest and James caused the surgeon to 'cut the haire of my head short, and to shaue away all the hair of my face, for that it was become intolerable, and that it would be frozen so great with Icesickles'. Foxe's vivid narrative of his voyage makes light of difficulties and contains many charming passages describing his surroundings and the weather. 'This morning the Sunne lickt up the Fogge's dew as soon as hee began to rise and made a shining day of it' (p. 296). James's narrative is such a catalogue of incessant dangers, miseries, accidents, difficulties and hair's-breadth escapes from the ice that one can only, with Foxe, question his seamanship. He even entitled his book *The Dangerous Voyage of Capt. James*. This contrast between the two narratives is, of course, due to differences of personality rather than sailing conditions, which were the same for both (Foxe 1635, James 1633; Christy 1894 prints both narratives). Foxe's discourteous remarks about James coupled with his evident skill as a seaman prompted Canadian journalist Frank Rasky (1976: 233) to quote Macaulay's dictum at the head of a chapter light-heartedly entitled 'The Foxe-James Yacht race to Cathay': 'There were gentlemen and there were seamen in the navy of King Charles. But the seamen were not gentlemen, and the gentlemen were not seamen.' James has one claim to fame not shared by Foxe. It has been argued that the description of the ice in Coleridge's *Rime of the Ancient Mariner*, especially the following verses, was in part inspired by his narrative.

> And now there came both mist and snow,
> And it grew wondrous cold:
> And ice, mast-high, came floating by,
> As green as emerald.
>
> And through the drifts the snowy clifts
> Did send a dismal sheen:
> Nor shapes of men nor beasts we ken –
> The ice was all between.
>
> The ice was here, the ice was there,
> The ice was all around:
> It cracked and growled, and roared and howled,
> Like noises in a swound!

After a pause in the seventeenth century, the search for a North-West Passage leading out of Hudson Bay was resumed intermittently in the eighteenth century. At times it was fostered by the Hudson's Bay Company, though no mention of the passage was made in the company's charter of 1670. In 1719, a leading company official, James Knight, led a two-ship expedition into the bay with the aim of expanding trade, searching for valuable minerals, and finding the North-West Passage. No more was heard of it until its remains were found on Marble Island off the bay's north-west coast in 1767. Long before then, in the 1730s, Arthur Dobbs had revived the idea of a North-West Passage, and persuaded both the Hudson's Bay Company and the British government to send expeditions to Hudson Bay to find it. In 1745 an Act of Parliament offered a reward of £20,000 for the discovery of a North-West Passage via Hudson Strait, but it continued as elusive as ever (Williams 1962, Rich 1958, 1959, Newman 1985). As for the North-East Passage, after the Russians had conquered Siberia that became a domestic Russian affair, and their search for what they later called the Northern Sea Route was pursued in the eighteenth century more vigorously than ever. Meanwhile, though neither passage had been discovered, the search for them had prompted the exploration of large parts of the Arctic and directly brought about the discovery by Europeans of Baffin Bay and Hudson Bay, as well as of Spitsbergen.

FOUR

The Massacre of the Bowhead in the Atlantic Arctic

The only large species of whale endemic to the Arctic, the bowhead or Greenland whale, *Balaena mysticetus*, once teemed along the edge of the pack ice in many parts of the Arctic. It could have constituted a huge renewable natural resource. Its protective layer of blubber or fat, between 25–50 cm (10–20 in) thick, yielded high quality oil when melted down or tried out; a medium-sized bowhead of 15–18 m (50–60 ft) in length producing 20–30 tons of oil. The three hundred or so plates of baleen or whalebone in its mouth, used to strain out the plankton on which it feeds, had considerable commercial value. Some of the native peoples of the Arctic subsisted for generations on the bowhead, using every part of the animal to supply almost all their needs. The European commercial whale hunters flensed or stripped off the blubber to make oil, cut out the whalebone, and abandoned the rest. While native peoples, here and there in the Arctic, killed tens of whales in a year, the whalers of Western Europe were taking hundreds every year. Between 1600 and 1900 the bowhead was all but exterminated throughout Arctic seas, save for a remnant population around the north coast of Alaska (see Chapter 8 below), and a few scattered individuals elsewhere. In this chapter the history of three centuries of whale killing in the Atlantic Arctic by people of European origin will be considered (Zorgdrager 1720, Scoresby 1820, Conway 1906, Brinner 1913, Jenkins 1921, Lubbock 1937, de Jong 1972, 1978, 1979, Jackson 1978, Watson 1981 and Vaughan 1983).

THE SPITSBERGEN OIL RUSH

Long before the Muscovy Company obtained a royal charter from Queen Elizabeth I on 12 February 1577 granting it a twenty-year monopoly for 'the killing of whales within any seas whatsoever' and for the making of train oil from the whales (Willan 1956: 133), the Basques (Vascos) from French and Spanish

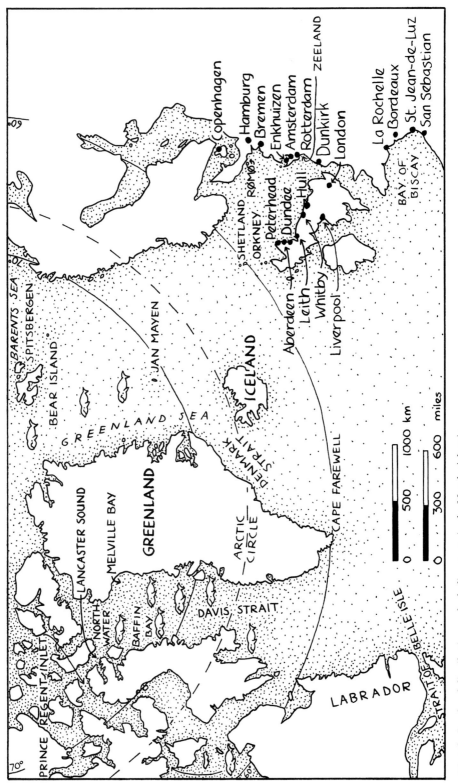

Map 9. Bowhead distribution and whaling ports in the North Atlantic.

Biscay ports, especially St Jean-de-Luz and San Sebastian, had pursued the great right whale or nordkaper *Balaena glacialis* in the Bay of Biscay, and in the Atlantic as far as the north or Labrador shore of the Strait of Belle Isle. Here, from about 1530 onwards, they established whaling stations at Red Bay and elsewhere and successfully hunted bowheads as well as nordkapers, sometimes trying out the oil ashore (Tuck 1981; see too Ciriquiain-Gaiztarro 1961). At this time both whalebone and whale oil, probably from nordkapers rather than bowheads, were being imported into Hull from the far north of Norway, but these products were perhaps being traded for English cloth at Vardø (Map 6), rather than obtained from whales caught by men from Hull. Still, the Muscovy Company was concerned enough about possible infringements of its monopoly to prosecute some of these 'interlopers' in the High Court of Admiralty (Willan 1956: 135–40, Gillett and MacMahon 1980: 143–5). It was also making detailed plans in 1575 for a whaling voyage to Russia via Vardø to which its agent in Russia, William Burrough, contributed a brief memorandum. The voyage would require a two-hundred-ton ship manned by a crew of fifty-five, including 'men skilful in the catching of the Whale', 'out of Biskaie' (Hakluyt 1907b: 161–3, 169), that is, Basque harpooners and other experts. But the company still had not started to hunt whales in 1594, when the Dutch killed the first known whale to fall victim to Europeans other than Basques, on the Arctic coast of Russia (Naber 1914: 56). Francis Cherry (or Cherie) imported 1,311 lb (595 kg) of walrus ivory ('morsse teeth') from Arctic Russia in that same year (Willan 1956: 263). Still, the company caught no whales, not even when, in 1607, Henry Hudson reported that King's Bay (Kongsfjorden) in Spitsbergen was alive with them: one even bumped gently against his ship, the *Hopewell*, and made it list (Asher 1860: 14, Powys 1928: 33). Instead, it was the unfortunate walrus, then present in a huge herd on the north-east coast of Bear Island, that claimed the company's attention. As Jonas Poole put it, 'It seemed very strange to us to see such a multitude of Monsters of the Sea, lye like Hogges upon heapes' (Purchas 1906a: 267). In 1603 a single piece of tusk was picked up there; in 1604 the heads of fifteen walruses were hacked off and taken back to England; in 1605 more were killed, to yield 11 tons of oil from their blubber 'and three hogs heads of their Teeth'; and in 1606 seven or eight hundred walrus yielded 22 tons of oil (Purchas 1906a: 293, 265–74). Interlopers from Hull were on the scene almost as early as the Muscovy Company: Thomas Marmaduke sailed the *Heartsease* to Bear Island and then north to Spitsbergen in 1609, a year before the company's ship *Amitie*, master Jonas Poole, mate Nicholas Woodcock, with a crew of thirteen men and a boy, also sailed north from Bear Island to Spitsbergen, where they killed over a hundred walrus and collected quantities of whalebone on the shore. It was only in 1611 that the Muscovy Company finally implemented its 1575 plan by sending two ships to Spitsbergen to kill whales, on board one of which were six Basque harpooners from St Jean-de-Luz. One whale and five hundred walrus were killed, and some oil tried out ashore, but both ships were lost. It was fortunate, but humiliating, for the company, that Captain Thomas Marmaduke, with Nicholas Woodcock as pilot, was in the offing. After a lively altercation in which Poole sustained injuries to his head, ear, collar bone, ribs and back, Marmaduke agreed to rescue the Muscovy

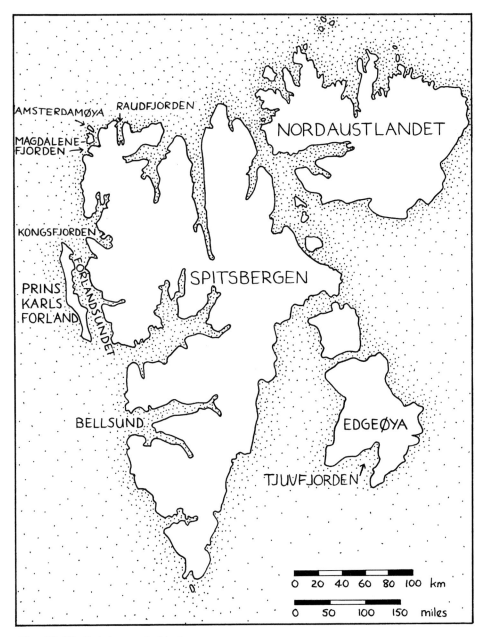

Map 10. The Spitsbergen Archipelago.

Company's ninety-nine men and its cargo of train oil, and took them safely back to Hull in his ship the *Hopewell*. The cargo was charged for at £5 per ton (Purchas 1906b: 34–41; for this paragraph see Conway 1906: 38–50).

While on one occasion in about 1600 the town council of Motrico in northern Spain was unable to meet because the mayor and other town worthies were all away whaling in Terranova (Labrador), by 1612 the whales had all but disappeared from Labrador, and in that year the first Basque whaler from San Sebastian arrived off Spitsbergen (Ciriquiain-Gaiztarro 1961: 254, 275–80), piloted there by Nicholas Woodcock. It was very successful, and, spurred by an oil-hungry market, a veritable fleet of whaleships converged on Spitsbergen in 1613. San Sebastian sent ten, which reported whales so crowded together 80 leagues off the coast that one could scarcely see the sea for them. St Jean-de-Luz, Bordeaux and La Rochelle each sent one or more, the Bordeaux ship piloted by Englishman Alan Sallowes; Amsterdam sent two ships with twelve Basques on board; and twenty English seamen helped to man the Enkhuizen ship captained by Englishman Thomas Bonner. Other Englishmen were among the crews of two Dutch ships chartered by Dunkirk shipowners. Though there are six contemporary accounts of the events at Spitsbergen in 1613, no one has yet puzzled out exactly what happened, nor how many ships were there, though a minimum of twenty-six seems certainly established. The Muscovy Company, warned of the probable presence of 'foreign' ships that year, armed itself with a new royal charter granting its members the exclusive right to hunt whales in Spitsbergen waters. It sent a fleet of seven ships from London in May 1613 with 'prouision necessary for the killing of the whale' and twenty-four Basques 'experienced in that facultie' (Markham 1881: 54). The Admiral or flagship of the fleet was the *Tiger*, of 260 tons burden and twenty-one guns, with chief pilot William Baffin on board. The interloper of previous years, Thomas Marmaduke, now in the employ of the Muscovy Company, was captain of the Vice-admiral, the *Mathew*, of 250 tons. While the *Mathew* remained anchored throughout June in Sir Thomas Smith's Bay, which now forms the northern part of Forlandsundet, her Basque harpooners hunted whales off the northern tip of Prince Charles Foreland with the shallops, and other crewmen had set up a try-works ashore where they were kept busy at the 'furnaces and coppers' nonstop in the continuous daylight from 5 p.m. on Sunday to midnight the following Saturday (Markham 1881: 59). By 6 July the *Mathew* was fully laden with 184 tons of oil and five thousand pieces of whalebone in bundles of fifty. Meanwhile the *Tiger* had warned off seventeen foreign whaleships up and down the west coast of Spitsbergen. Either their cargoes were confiscated and they were forced to leave forthwith, or in some cases they were allowed to stay, provided they surrendered a portion of their catch to the Muscovy Company. For example, the captain of 'the great ship' from St Jean-de-Luz, of 800 tons burden, Miguel de Aristega, was allowed to continue whaling in Bell Sound on condition he gave the English half the oil he obtained. The two Dutch ships in Bell Sound were among those forced to leave after surrendering oil and whalebone already taken aboard, as well as the dead whales floating at their ships' sides ready to flense. Miguel de Aristega must have been pleased to see them go. He claimed that the Hollanders had insulted him and would only allow him to remain and continue whaling on condition they worked together, the Hollanders contributing their three shallops and the Basques seven. Their joint catch would be shared equally, and the Hollanders would have the first whale killed entirely to themselves (Markham 1881: 38–79, Conway 1904: 28–38, Conway 1906: 51–64, Purchas 1906b: 47–60, Naber 1924: 96–100, Barthelmess 1987).

Instead of profits, the Muscovy Company made a loss of £3,000–£4,000 on the 1613 Spitsbergen whaling season. Perhaps it spent too much time driving off its rivals? In 1614 the size of the company's fleet was doubled and it was authorized to annexe Spitsbergen in the name of King James I. The Dutch responded to the English threat by forming themselves into the Noordsche Compagnie or Northern Company (Muller 1874, de Jong 1972) under a charter from the States General of January 1614, giving its members the sole right to trade and hunt whales on all coasts between Novaya Zemlya and Davis Strait, including those of Bear Island, Spitsbergen, Greenland, and others to be discovered. Organized into a group of more or less independent chambers or branches, one for each town or group of towns, with Amsterdam dominant, the Northern Company was a cartel which aimed to control production and prices by allocating catch quotas, and tried to obtain a monopoly of train oil imports into Holland. It armed the fleet of eleven ships it sent to Spitsbergen in 1614 and persuaded the States General to send three warships to convoy them. They were too strong for the English, who allowed them to hunt whales unmolested that year in the northern bays round Amsterdam Island.

The events of 1613 had marked the start of the century-long struggle between England and Holland for mastery of the world's seas. Another maritime power, Denmark-Norway, appeared on the scene soon afterwards. King Christian IV, preoccupied in 1611–13 by his war with Sweden, sent a naval squadron to Spitsbergen in 1615 to assert his ancient rights to what was generally regarded at that time as part of Greenland. He circulated the governments of Europe early in 1616 prohibiting all 'foreign' whaling there, renamed Spitsbergen Christiansbergen, hired some Basque whalemen, and persuaded a German merchant settled in Copenhagen called Johann Braem to help him take up whaling on his own account. By 1622 Johann Braem had taken over the king's whaling enterprise and formed a Danish-Basque whaling company under royal charter with exclusive whaling rights in Spitsbergen (Dalgård 1962). Other countries were interested in whaling, too. In 1629, in the king of France's name, Cardinal Richelieu chartered a French northern whaling company headed by the Basque Jean Vrolicq. As it happened, none of the European powers was able or willing to take effective possession of Spitsbergen: neither the Dutch, who discovered it in 1596; nor the Danes, too weak to maintain an effective presence there; nor the English, whose claim was based on the bizarre notion that the low-lying coast sighted but not landed on by Hugh Willoughby in 1553, probably Kolguyev Island, was actually Spitsbergen (Naber 1924: 100–3 and Conway 1904: 35–8).

JAN MAYEN

The rivalry in the Arctic between different whaling concerns was not only between one ruler or country and another, but also between different groups of merchants from the same country. Occasionally it broke out into deeds of violence. For example, in 1625 the Muscovy Company commander, Captain William Goodlad, returned to Bell Sound, Spitsbergen, to find that whalemen from Hull and York, arriving there first, had taken away eight shallops, burned the casks, smashed much of the equipment of the try-works, and demolished the buildings which had been left behind there by the company in the previous year (Conway 1904: 174–5). But usually there was room for all, each group of merchants keeping to its own bay year after year. Moreover, the whaling grounds, at first limited to the bays and fjords of the west Spitsbergen coast, were soon expanded. As the years went by, whales became scarcer inshore and more and more were hunted and killed in the open sea or along and in the pack ice between Spitsbergen and north-east Greenland: bay whaling was supplemented and eventually replaced by sea whaling and ice whaling and the blubber was no longer tried out in Spitsbergen, but taken back to the whaler's home port to be rendered down. Moreover, right at the start of the hunt for the bowhead, the pressure was taken off Spitsbergen by the 'discovery' in 1614 of the rich whaling waters around Jan Mayen by Jan Jacobsz May on his return voyage from an attempt on behalf of the Noordsche Compagnie to find a northern or Trans-Polar Passage. Actually the thirty-mile-long island, dominated by the spectacular volcanic cone of Beerenberg, seems already to have been discovered and named on at least three occasions: by Henry Hudson in 1607, who named it Hudson's Touches; by Thomas Marmaduke of Hull in 1611 or 1612, who named it Trinity Island after the church of the Holy Trinity in Hull; and by Jean Vrolicq in 1612, who named it Pico and later the Isle of Richelieu. Jan Mayen was also called Sir Thomas Smith's Island by the English and Mauritius Island or Mr Joris Island by the Dutch. The sole right to its whale fishery was granted by King James I to the corporation of Hull in 1617 or 1618. No wonder it is referred to in Dutch sources as the *Eylant in questie* – the disputed island (Scoresby 1820b: 154, Muller 1874: 188–95, Brander 1955: 34–8, de Jong 1972: 194–200). In 1616 the abundance of whales allowed thirteen Dutch ships, four ships from Dunkirk, and single ships from London and Hull, to hunt whales there successfully: there were enough for everyone (Brander 1955: 49–79).

THE HUNT AND THE TRY-WORKS

The shore-based bay fishery of the early days of Spitsbergen whaling was described in detail by Robert Fotherby, an employee of the Muscovy Company (Markham 1881: 72–9). The whale's characteristic v-shaped spout or blow made it visible from several miles away. As soon as a whale entered the bay, several shallops would row out rapidly towards it. Usually it submerged again before the rowers could get near. They would proceed circumspectly, trying to follow its wake to be as near as possible when it surfaced again. When this happened, they would row resolutely towards it and the harpooner, standing ready in the bow of the shallop, would throw the harpoon at it. The whale would submerge, taking the harpoon and the rope attached to it with it, and the men in the shallop would have to pay out the rope, neatly coiled in the stern, as quickly as necessary – up to 100 fathoms (56 m) of it or more, depending on how deep the animal dived. In any case the whale would drag the shallop along with it, perhaps for a mile, before it would surface again to breathe, and the shallop could then close with it and the crew would stab it with their long lances. The wounded whale would writhe and thrash its tail, sometimes smashing the shallop or maiming or drowning some of the men, and its blow would become reddened with blood. It would sometimes drag the shallop three or four miles (4–6 km) in all from the spot where it was harpooned. Once dead, the whale was secured with a rope round the hinder part of its body and towed tail-first, by several shallops made fast to each other, to the stern of the whaleship.

The dead whale now had to be stripped of its blubber, or flensed. While one man in a shallop kept it close to the carcase with a boat hook, another would stand in the shallop or on the whale. This man 'cutts and scores the fatt, which we call blubber, in square-like pieces, 3 or 4 feet (1–1.5 m) long, with a great cutting knife' (p. 75). An iron hook was then lowered at the end of a rope, made fast to one of the rectangular pieces of blubber, and raised slowly while the cutter separated it from the flesh. Once separated, the piece of blubber was lowered into the water and fastened by a rope passed through a hole made in one corner of it. The pieces of blubber were attached one to another and towed ashore with a shallop, ten or twelve at a time. Next they had to be chopped into smaller pieces, each about 1½ in (4 cm) square, the whale's tail or fin being used as a chopping-block, while the two furnaces, each with its copper try pot or kettle, were got ready. Because oil dripped continually out of the blubber while it was being chopped up, the pieces were thrown into a shallop, raised from the ground to the same height as the copper, to collect the oil, and from there the blubber and oil were ladled into a tub suspended by a derrick or small crane. When filled, this tub was swung over one of the coppers and emptied into it. Once sufficiently boiled, the hot oil was ladled into another shallop half filled with water, to cool it. The remains of the blubber pieces, called fritters, which were brown and looked as if they had been fried, were also taken out of the copper with a copper ladle and the oil was strained through wicker baskets standing over the same shallop. 'And out of this shallop the oile runneth into a long trough, or gutter of wood, and therby is conveyed into butts and hogsheads, which, being filled, are bung'd up, marked, and rowl'd by, and others set in their place' (p. 77).

Finally the baleen or whalebone in the whale's mouth had to be cut out. While the dead whale was still secured to the ship's stern, the enormous head was cut off the carcase and towed ashore with a scallop until it ran aground. Then at high water it was dragged further ashore with a capstan so that, at low tide, men with hatchets could cut out the baleen plates, five or six at a time. These had to be scraped clean, rubbed in sand to remove the grease that settled on them from the sea while they were being brought ashore, and tied up in bundles of fifty, each numbered and marked with the Muscovy Company's trademark.

After the middle of the seventeenth century, when the shore-based Spitsbergen whale fishery came to an end and most whales were killed away from the shore, the dead whale was secured and flensed alongside the ship and the blubber was hauled onto the deck of the whaler, to be chopped into small pieces and stowed away in casks in the ship's hold.

MARKETS FOR WHALING PRODUCTS

Whaling in the early seventeenth century was no gilt-edged investment. A good catch brought substantial profits, but losses were frequent. Train oil, derived from the whale, had three main uses, in all of which it had to compete with vegetable oil, especially rapeseed. It was used as a raw material in the soap industry, as an additive in the leather and textile industries, and as a means of lighting oil lamps. Both in Holland and England the soap industry was by far the most important market for train oil, but the notion that the best quality soap could only be made from vegetable oil was stoutly upheld by the soapmakers of Westminster and Amsterdam. The former planned in the 1630s to phase out train oil altogether in favour of home-crushed rape oil; the latter persuaded their town council in 1621 to prohibit the use of train oil for soapmaking. They firmly insisted that the best soap was made from vegetable oil and that the best soap was made in Amsterdam. Fortunately for the whalers, the soapmakers in Rotterdam and elsewhere in Holland were happy to use train oil (Jackson 1978: 19–21; de Jong 1972: 263–6).

The other whaling product was baleen or whalebone. In the middle ages this is said to have been used to make plumes for the helmets of knights, for it proved a good deal more durable in combat than real feathers. In 1624, in an effort to enlarge the market for whalebone, the Noordsche Compagnie asked an English craftsman called John Osborn, a worker in horn and ivory then living in Amsterdam, to see if it could be used as a substitute for those materials, or in any other way. He found that it could be scraped, polished and pressed, and readily made into frames for mirrors and portraits, knife handles, measuring rods and walking sticks, and used for decorating mantelpieces. Separate pieces could be pressed together to form a solid block, and medallions with designs of women, lions and satyrs and so on in high relief could be made after the whalebone had been softened in hot water and then stamped or pressed into a copper mould. The prices paid for whalebone soon rose, and Osborn was suitably remunerated by the company (de Jong 1972: 178–9). By the second half of the seventeenth century whalebone could represent a fifth of the profits from a whaling voyage (Bruijn 1981), and it had begun its long career in women's clothing, being used for hooped petticoats and skirts, heavily boned bodices and corsets, and the rest. Considerable ingenuity continued to be devoted to finding new outlets for it. The nineteenth-century English whaling captain and historian William Scoresby jun. gives details of the following patents taken out in his time (Scoresby 1820b: 436–7):

1. Mr Bowman, of Leith, obtained a patent, bearing date 30th of October 1807, for the adaptation of whalebone to the manufacture of 'hats, caps, and bonnets for men and women; harps for harping or cleansing corn or grain; and also the bottoms of sieves and riddles; and girths for horses; and also cloth for webbing, fit for making into hats, caps, &c.; and for the backs and seats of chairs; sofas, gigs, and other similar carriages and things; and for the bottom of beds; and also whalebone reeds for weavers.'

2. A patent was granted to Mr Samuel Crackles, of Hull, brush-manufacturer, 'for a method of making and manufactuing brushes from whalebone;' dated November 3. 1808.

3. Mr H.W. Vander Kleft, of London, procured a patent, bearing date August 17. 1813, for the invention of a 'walking staff, calculated to contain a pistol, powder, ball, and screw telescope, pen, ink, paper, pencil, knife, and drawing utensils;' the exterior of which may be covered or veneered with prepared whalebone.

4. A patent has also been granted to Mr R. Dixon, 49, High Holborn, London, for an improvement in the mode of manufacturing portmanteaus and travelling trunks, by the use of whalebone.

SMEERENBURG

At the start of the shore-based Spitsbergen whale fishery the Dutch selected a low-lying gravelly tongue of land extending from the south-east corner of Amsterdam Island, in the extreme north-west of Spitsbergen, for their main whaling station, and used it from 1619 until the 1660s. In *The Arctic Whalers*, published in 1937, Basil Lubbock calls this whaling station 'The extraordinary blubber town of Smeerenburg' and claims that, at the height of seventeenth-century whaling, 'as many as 300 whalers were anchored opposite their own capstans, coppers and blubber houses' and 'from 15,000 or 18,000 men' were 'busy at the oil cookeries, besides shopkeepers, vintners, tobacconists, bakers and all kinds of artisans' (Lubbock 1937: 76). Between 1979 and 1981 Groningen University's Arctic Centre sent three expeditions to Smeerenburg, led by geographer-historian Louwrens Hacquebord, to excavate what was left of this supposed Arctic metropolis (Hacquebord 1980, 1981, 1984; Hacquebord and de Bok 1981; Hacquebord and Vroom 1988). Using archive sources as well as archaeology, Hacquebord cut Smeerenburg down to size. Far from being a town, it was more like a typical Dutch single-street village, and it was a seasonal settlement only. Ranged along a low ridge behind the shore were the eight try-works belonging to the different chambers of the Noordsche Compagnie, two of which have long ago been washed away by the sea. Each try-works comprised a large double boiler, formerly holding two coppers or try-pots with a furnace underneath, and behind it one or two substantial wooden sheds, called tents because they replaced what were originally tents, in which the shore workers or landsmen lived while the oil was being tried out. Excavation showed that each chamber had sleeping-places for twenty-four to thirty try-works hands, and eight to ten places for craftsmen: fewer than two hundred men were sleeping ashore at Smeerenburg at any one time. The buildings were strictly for accommodation and industrial use. There was a fort for two guns, but no shops, and not even a church. Archives showed that not more than fifteen whaleships would have anchored in Smeerenburg Fjord in any one summer in the 1620s and 1630s, when activity there was probably at its peak. In the environs of the whaling station, the Dutch researchers discovered and excavated 101 graves (Maat 1981). The archaeological finds from these and the other excavations included fragments of tiles, bricks and glass; 446 fragments of clay pipes dating from 1610 to 1670, many having the maker's monogram stamped on the base of the bowl; numerous objects of wood and metal; as well as shoes, a felt hat, knitted woollen caps, socks and other clothing, and a besom made of willow branches, brought from Holland to sweep the place clean.

WINTER IN THE ARCTIC

Both the English and Dutch whaling companies seriously considered the possibility of leaving overwintering parties behind at their Spitsbergen whaling stations when their fleets left for home in the autumn. In 1623 an offer to overwinter by Dutch volunteers was turned down by the Noordsche Compagnie's directors. In 1626 a plan was considered by the company for twenty-five men to overwinter: they could find out whether Spitsbergen was habitable in the winter, hunt bears and foxes perhaps for the financial benefit of the company, and increase train oil production by beginning to hunt whales before the company's fleet arrived in the spring. But this plan, as well as a proposal for overwintering in 1628 because of conflicts with Basque whalers, was rejected (Hacquebord *et al.* 1989: 24–5). Meanwhile, in England, the Muscovy Company was said to have made repeated attempts to organize an overwintering party at one of their Spitsbergen establishments, probably in Bell Sound. The offer of substantial rewards to any volunteers who might come forward fell on deaf ears. The company then persuaded some convicted criminals under sentence of death to act as wintering caretakers for it, in exchange for rewards and a reprieve. But even these men, on arrival at Spitsbergen and seeing 'the desolateness of the place' (White 1855: 264), changed their minds and insisted on being taken home, where, however, the company secured their pardon. Apparently in the mid-1620s an inadvertent overwintering by 'nine good and able men' left behind by the master of one of the company's whaling ships ended in disaster – they 'all dyed miserably upon the place'.

Unbelievably, the same thing happened again in 1630, the same master being responsible! Gunner's mate Edward Pellham and seven shipmates, 'being employed in the service of the Right Worshipfull Company of Muscowie merchants, in the good ship called the *Salutation*, of London' were sent ashore by the master 'for the hunting and killing of some Venison for the ship's provision' (White 1855: 259) and then negligently left behind when the *Salutation* sailed for home toward the end of August. Against all expectations, having no provisions and having made no preparations for overwintering, they all survived, to be rescued by the first returning whalers from Hull on 25 May 1631. These men were well led by Edward Pellham and they were determined and resourceful. Their morale was excellent. It was bolstered by a religious conviction reflected in the title of Pellham's book: *God's Power and Providence; Shewed, in the miraculous preservation and deliverance of eight Englishmen, left by mischance in Green-land, Anno 1630*. They prayed regularly, but they also took active measures to ensure their survival. They built a cosy, well-insulated living-room inside one corner of the large 'tent' or shed at the company's Bell Sound whaling station. Bricks were used to line the wooden outside wall of the shed to make two of the walls of this room. The other two walls were double ones made of deal boards, the space between them filled with sand. Four wooden two-man cabins were made for sleeping in, the bedding of reindeer skins proving very warm. The men had two mastiffs with them, trained to bring down deer, and this ensured them an initial supply of venison which was supplemented by walrus meat. In the new year these supplies were running low, but on 3 February 1631 two Polar bears were seen approaching the tent and ''twas a measuring cast which should be eaten first, Wee or the Beares, when we first saw one another; and we perceived by them, that they had as good hopes to devour us as we to kill them' (pp. 254–5). One of these bears, a female, they killed with their lances; the other, a cub, fled. 'And upon this Beare we fed some twenty days, for she was very good flesh and better than our Venison' (p. 279). Having exhausted this bear meat, the castaways feared that they would have to consume a reserve supply of roast venison they had stored away in a cache the previous autumn.

> Amidst these our feares, it pleased God to send divers Beares unto our Tent, some fortie at least as we accounted. Of which number we kill'd seven: That is to say, the second of March one; the fourth, another; and the tenth a wonderfull great Beare, six foote high at least. All which we flayed and roasted upon woodden spits (having no better kitchen-furniture than that, and a frying pan we found in the Tent). They were as good savory meat as any beefe could be. Having thus gotten good store of such foode, wee kepte not our selves now to such straight allowance as before; but eate frequently two or three meales a-day, which began to increase strength and abilitie of body in us.

After the bears, Arctic foxes were seen near the tent, and some fifty of these, which made excellent eating when roast, were trapped. While Pellham attributed the survival of himself and his companions to God, one has to point out the vital role played in this by his own undoubted courage and powers of leadership, as well as by the presence of the Muscovy Company's whaling station. It provided them with excellent accommodation in the shape of the tent, and materials to construct an inner living space. It also gave them all the firewood they needed. For this they broke up seven of the company's shallops, which they considered too damaged to be serviceable in the coming season, as well as a good many casks and planks, stowing the timber away above the roof beams of the tent 'so to make the outer Tent the warmer, and to keep withall the snow from dryving through the tiles into the Tent' (p. 272). Finally, Pellham reported that 'our greatest and chiefest feeding was the Whale Frittars, and those mouldy too, the loathesomest meate in the world' (p. 254). These leavings from the trying-out process had been flung on the ground in heaps and constituted their only food on their self-appointed fast days, Wednesdays and Fridays, for some three months or so before the appearance of that providential bear on 3 February.

It was probably the survival of these eight Englishmen in 1630–1 which persuaded the directors of the Noordsche Compagnie to change their minds about overwintering, especially when, in August 1632, Basque whalers ransacked their installations on Jan Mayen after the Dutch had returned home. At the end of the 1633 whaling season specially prepared and provisioned seven-man wintering parties were left at Smeerenburg and at Jan Mayen. At Smeerenburg the overwinterers were supplied with quantities of hard bread, biscuits, butter, cheese, oatmeal, peas, dried fish, bacon, beer, brandy, French wine, salt, olive oil, sugar, lemon-juice, twenty pounds of tobacco and six dozen pipes, prunes, raisins, ginger, pepper, nutmeg, cinnamon, cloves, mace and mustard seed, as well as coal, peat, firewood and all kinds of utensils. Ably commanded by Jacob Segersz van der Brugge, who wrote an almost daily journal (Naber 1930: 77–159 and Conway 1904: 67–168), the six Dutch and one Norwegian (Atlov 1987:10) Smeerenburg overwinterers survived there until 27 May 1634, when the first of their returning compatriots found them in good health. Scurvy had affected them, the cook especially, but had been successfully warded off by the eating of what fresh food they could find, namely scurvy-grass or *Cochlearia*, and the meat of the many Arctic foxes they trapped. Bears they killed in plenty, but did not eat. The contemporaneous Dutch overwintering on Jan Mayen was a disaster (Naber 1930: 21–76). When the returning whalers arrived there on 4 June 1634 all seven men were found dead; one, who had died first on 16 April, was in a coffin, while the others were lying in their bunks. 'One still had bread and cheese by him, another a tankard, a third had a jar of ointment by him some of which he had been using to smear his gums . . . and a fourth had been reading a book' (Naber 1930: 69). Scurvy certainly affected the Jan Mayen winterers, but they may have died from trichinosis as a result of eating insufficiently cooked bear meat. Before news of this catastrophe was brought back to Holland by the returning whaling fleet in autumn 1634 a second overwintering party was left at Smeerenburg, but this, too, ended disastrously. In 1980 the grave of this second group of seven overwinterers was found, and the bones of five of them showed signs of severe scurvy. Nothing was left of the bones of the other two (Hacquebord 1989, 1991). These were the last whalers to attempt to pass the winter on Spitsbergen.

In the nineteenth century the enforced overwinterings of whaleships caught in the Baffin Bay ice at the end of the whaling season were usually accompanied by outbreaks of scurvy among the crews, and many lives were lost. The *Dee* of Aberdeen (Troup 1987) left her home port on 2 April 1836, made her way up the west Greenland coast, and crossed to the Canadian side of Baffin Bay. There she caught four whales and picked up three dead ones, but ice blocked her homeward voyage and she was soon beset. During the winter she drifted slowly southwards with the ice, eventually escaping into open water on 16 March 1837 in 62° north latitude. By the time she reached Aberdeen on 5 May 1837, thirty-seven of her forty-nine crewmen had died of scurvy. In spite of public outcry, shipowners continued to send whaleships to Baffin Bay with far less than twelve months' supply of provisions, and with inadequate supplies of antiscorbutics, and similar tragedies continued to occur. In 1866–7 the Hull whaler *Diana*, in spite of her auxiliary steam engine, was caught in the same way, losing her captain and a quarter of her crew to scurvy (Smith 1923, Credland 1979). Meanwhile, in the 1850s, overwintering by English and American whalers in Cumberland Sound

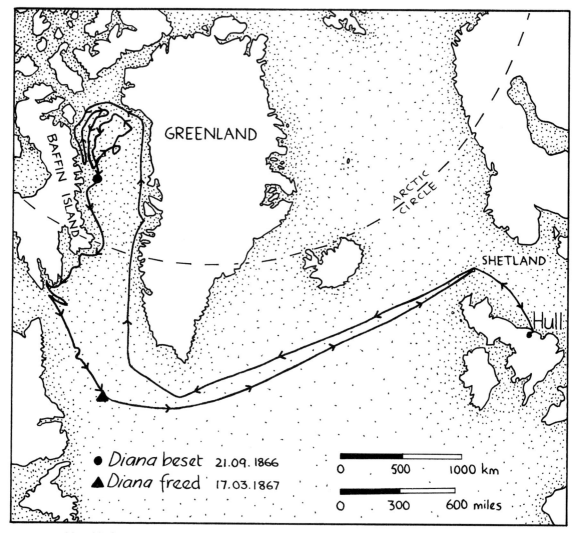

Map 11. Course of the Diana, *1866–7.*

had become almost routine: stores for at least twelve months were taken and Eskimos hired to obtain fresh meat (Ross (ed.) 1985: 155–73). In Hudson Bay, where whaling began in 1860, there were more overwinterings than single-season voyages (Ross 1975).

LAWS OF THE WHALE FISHERY

The law-abiding, regulation-minded Dutch and Germans drew up and agreed on suitable rules for whaling before the close of the seventeenth century. This 'Greenland Law' originated with the Dutch in the middle years of the century, when they first began to hunt whales along and in the ice pack. Inevitably, ships became stuck or beset in the ice and were crushed from time to time. Often the crews managed to save themselves and their stores by moving everything onto the ice before the ship went down. According to the Greenland Law, a whaling captain who came across sailors who had lost their ship was bound to take them aboard his ship; but when he met with another ship, that ship was bound to take half the men who had been saved, unless it already had shipwrecked seamen on board, in which case the two ships would divide all the castaways equally between them. When either of these two ships met another ship, the castaways were again to be equally divided between the two ships, and so on. If the castaways had saved any of their stores, these provisions were to be taken with them and used exclusively by them. But if they had been unable to save any provisions from their wrecked ship, they were to be fed by their rescuers, who would then expect them to work like other seamen. Provided a captain or his representative stayed by his wrecked ship, he could decide when and by whom his stores would be saved. But a captain who came across a wrecked ship deserted by its crew had the right to save whatever he could by way of stores, spars, rigging, sails or cargo, provided, on returning home, that he surrendered half of it to the owners of the wrecked ship. Once killed, a whale was the property of the persons who killed it, so long as any of them remained by it. If deserted, even though made fast to a piece of ice, it became the property of the first person to take possession of it. But if it was made fast to the shore with a grapnel or anchor, and properly marked with a buoy or flag, it remained the property of the person who made it fast. Perhaps typically, the English and Scottish never found it necessary to lay down any whaling laws, except that all were agreed that 'a fish in any way in possession, whether alive or dead, is the sole and unquestionable property of the persons maintaining the connection or possession', and 'a loose fish, alive or dead, is fair game' (Scoresby 1820b: 319. On the Greenland Law see Scoresby 1820b: 312–33, Lindeman 1869: 11–13, de Jong 1978: 124–43). There is evidence that, in spite of the absence of a written law, the crews of shipwrecked British whalers were, as a rule, equally distributed among as many ships as possible in the British whaling fleet (Ross (ed.) 1985: 14, 75, 96).

SHIPWRECKS IN THE ICE

Losing a ship in the ice was almost a routine happening for a whaleship owner. Between 1661 and 1718 an average of 149 Dutch whalers sailed each year for the Greenland Sea, except in 1665–7 and in 1672–4, when Dutch whaling was interrupted by wars with England. Of these ships, approximately one in twenty-five did not return, and losses averaged six ships per year (de Jong 1979: 145–6). In 1678 the Dutch lost eighteen ships out of 110; in 1685, twenty-three of 212 (de Jong 1978: 420). Since the whales were often in company, the whalers tended to be in groups and the crew of a ship that went down could usually escape over the ice to another ship. But substantial loss of life occurred in 1777 in the Greenland Sea, when some fifty whalers were beset on 24 June in about 75° north latitude on the Greenland side of the sea. As they drifted south and west with the ice in which they were trapped, some ships managed to escape, but twenty-seven remained beset: seven Hollanders, eight British ships, two Swedish, one from

Bremen and nine from Hamburg. These continued to be driven south, down the east Greenland coast and through Denmark Strait towards Cape Farewell. One of the more informative descriptions of the disaster was that edited in German from the journal of the commander of the Dutch ship *Wilhelmina*, Jakob Henrick Broertje, which was supplemented by the detailed verbal report of three German sailors in the crew. The *Wilhelmina* had Iceland in sight on 24 August. Other ships were sighted, then lost to view. On 30 September the *Wilhelmina* was suddenly crushed by the ice, the crew barely escaping onto the ice with their lives, and having no time to save provisions. They made their way to another ship, which was also beset. Soon fifty men from yet another wrecked ship came walking over the ice, and 286 hungry men were crowded onto a ship normally crewed by around forty. They were only five or six miles (8 or 10 km) from the east Greenland shore, in 63° north and within sight of open water, when this ship went down too, and the survivors had to make their way over ice and through water with the aid of shallops. They eventualy landed somewhere near Cape Farewell, where they were surprised to receive a friendly welcome from the Greenlanders. In all, seven Dutch and seven Hamburg ships were lost. The crews of two of these made their way over the ice to two ships which found a way out of it. Of the 450 or so men from the other twelve wrecked ships, fewer than 150 reached safety in Greenland. This loss of three hundred men represents one of the worst tragedies, in terms of human lives, in the entire history of whaling (Lindeman 1869: 37–46, Oesau 1937: 236–44, Falk 1983: 83–138, de Jong 1979: 115).

On average, one out of every seventeen whaling voyages west of Greenland ended in the loss of the ship (Ross (ed.)1985: 3). The worst whaling season of all was probably that of 1830, when nineteen out of ninety-one British whalers which sailed to Baffin Bay were lost altogether. Many others were badly damaged, and twenty-one ships returned home 'clean', that is without having killed a single whale. At this time the whalers usually made their way up the west coast of Greenland between the shore-fast ice and the pack ice on the sea, past ever-dangerous Melville Bay, and then sailed across what they called the North Water to whale-rich waters around Lancaster Sound and south of there. On 23/4 June 1830 a long line of whalers, making their way slowly along the Melville Bay coast in this way, was overtaken by a storm from the south-west, which began to drive the pack ice into the bay. At the head of the fleet five Scottish ships and one French, the *Ville de Dieppe*, were moored one behind the other along the ice edge when an enormous floe smashed into them, one after another. In fifteen minutes one ship had many of her timbers broken, another was saved by being lifted right up onto the ice, and the other four were smashed to pieces. Masts were snapped off, decks broken, and sailors leaped out onto the ice. The *Rattler* of Leith became what was said to have been the most complete wreck ever known: she was turned inside out, and her stern was sheared off and carried a gunshot distance away by the ice. The *Achilles* of Dundee had her sides almost pressed together. Not far off, on 2 July, the *Progress* of Hull 'was crushed to atoms'. Another ship was literally buried under masses of ice, and only the tops of its masts were visible afterwards. In the first week of July upwards of a thousand men were camping out on the ice, which they jocularly called Baffin Fair. Provisions and casks of rum were taken from the wrecks, many of which were set on fire. There was singing and dancing, and games, and other frolics on the ice, but only a handful of deaths: almost all the castaways were taken home on the ships that escaped the ice (Leslie *et al.* 1835: 448–58, Lubbock 1937: 278–84). By contrast, in 1835–6 at least 135 men died on board whalers wrecked or forced to winter in Davis Strait and Baffin Bay (Tillotson 1870: 117–18).

HISTORY OF THE WHALE HUNT

During the seventeenth century the Dutch continued to hunt whales successfully in Spitsbergen waters, and increasingly hunted them in and along the edge of the Greenland Sea ice pack. Especially after the collapse of the Noordsche Compagnie in 1642, the annual number of whaleships sent out steadily increased. In 1684 a total of 246 Dutch whalers were hunting bowheads between Greenland and Spitsbergen and between 70° and 80° north latitude. Officers and crews, including many commanders, were soon being recruited for the Dutch fleet from offshore islands all along the North Sea coast from Walcheren in Zeeland to Rømø (now in Denmark), while from the 1640s the German port of Hamburg, followed later by Bremen, also began to send whalers to Spitsbergen, or the Greenland fishery as they called it. The highest number of Hamburg whalers at sea in any one year was eighty-three in 1685 (Oesau 1955: 71). Meanwhile, after the 1630s, the English dropped out of the race for about a hundred years, their efforts apparently hampered by the Muscovy Company's desperate attempts to maintain a monopoly, by the preference of the home market for seed oil, by the continued importing of train oil from Holland and by their conservatism in clinging to the Spitsbergen bay fishery once most of the whales were to be found in the open sea or pack ice (Jackson 1981). From the 1690s, the Dutch, again followed by ships from German ports, began to sail along the west Greenland coast and developed trading contacts with the Greenlanders as a side-line to whaling. By 1720 the Dutch had opened a new whale fishery west of Greenland in Davis Strait and Baffin Bay (Reeves *et al.* 1983, Ross (ed.)1985, Vaughan 1986), as opposed to the existing one east of Greenland. In 1721, 151 of their ships sailed west of Greenland, and only 107 east of Greenland. Nevertheless, in the half century thereafter, most of the 150–200 ships the Dutch ports sent out each year until the 1770s sailed east of Greenland (de Jong 1979: 150–1, Table 2; also Dekker 1971).

European whaling from the continental ports of Amsterdam, Hamburg and others was interrupted by the French Revolutionary Wars and then given the *coup de grâce* by the continental Blockade organized by Britain and her allies against France. Neither the Dutch nor the German whaling industry enjoyed more than a temporary revival after Napoleon's fall in 1815. The last Dutch whaler sailed to the Arctic in 1862, but only to hunt seals (de Jong 1978: 459); the last Hamburg whaler in 1861 (Oesau 1955: 86). It was now the turn of the English and the Scots. In the 1730s and 1740s up to six whalers sailed from London to the Arctic annually, but the number rose rapidly after 1749, when the government subsidy or bounty on tonnage was raised to 40 shillings a ton on whale ships of over 200 tons burden. This coincided with a rapid expansion of the market for whale oil as industrialization and urbanization increased the demand for street lighting and oil lamps. London's whaling fleet increased to over fifty ships a year in 1785; other ports had joined her in the 1750s – Liverpool, Whitby and Hull in England, and Dundee and Peterhead in Scotland. Between 1815 and 1820 these and other English and Scottish ports sent around a hundred ships annually to the Greenland Sea, and fifty or more to the offshore waters of west Greenland. After 1818–20, this whale fishery was extended to offshore waters on the western side of Baffin Bay. In the nineteenth century both English and Scottish whalers sailed from their home ports with a skeleton crew and stopped at Orkney or Shetland to make up the full complement of forty to fifty men. Hull soon became the premier whaling port in the British Isles: in the years 1810 to 1818 inclusive her whalers made 481 whaling voyages to the Arctic. Her nearest rivals were London with 161 voyages, Aberdeen with 98, and Whitby with 80 (Rowley 1982: 50). By 1826 this whaling boom had thronged the town of Hull with traders using whaling

Plate 6. The Dundee steam whaler Arctic *with boats fast to a 'fish', as the bowhead was called by the whalers. The whale in the right foreground has been harpooned by two of the boats, which have accordingly hoisted their fishing flags or jacks. The harpooner or harpooneer in the bow of a third boat is shown firing his harpoon gun. To show that its boats are fast, or attached by line and harpoon to the whale, the* Arctic *flies her jack from the mizzen mast. Each whaler had a distinctive fishing flag; the* Arctic's *was a five-pointed blue star on a white background. As usual in nineteenth-century illustrations of Arctic whaling, the ice is fancifully given high sharp points and looks quite unlike the pack ice formed by loose floes in which whales were often found. The* Arctic, *of 439 tons burden, was owned by Alexander Stephen and Son. She was built in 1867 and crushed by the ice and lost in Prince Regent Inlet in 1874. (From Markham 1875: facing p. 50.)*

products: ten brush-makers, three comb-makers, six soap manufacturers, eight stay-makers, two whalebone-cutters, six umbrella-makers, fourteen oil merchants and so on (Rowley 1982: 33). But British Arctic whaling was soon thereafter in steady decline. Whitby and London ceased in the 1830s, and Hull dropped out in 1869, leaving Peterhead to persevere into the 1890s and Dundee until 1913 (Clark 1986). These Scottish ports survived commercially only by hunting seals as well as whales. In 1874 the Dundee fleet of eleven steam whalers killed 46,252 seals which yielded 577 tons of oil, as against 174 whales yielding 1,290 tons of oil. The seal catch was valued at around £30,600 and the whale catch (oil and whalebone together) at about £87,500 (Henderson 1972: 24). By the beginning of the First World War in 1914, Arctic whaling in the North Atlantic had come to an end. The last bowhead whale fishery to be exploited in this area was that of Hudson Bay, into which between 1860 and 1915 American, English and Scottish whalers made 146 voyages (Ross 1975).

THE DESTRUCTION OF THE BOWHEAD

The size of the original bowhead population in the North Atlantic is unknown, but some idea can be given of the size of the whalers' catch. Between 1661 and 1800 the Dutch whaling fleet killed at least 65,234 whales between Spitsbergen and Greenland, almost all of them bowheads (de Jong 1979: 157–60, 162–4), and the total kill of whales by all whalers in Davis Strait and Baffin Bay, including Hudson Bay, between 1719 and 1915 has been put provisionally by Canadian whaling historian W. Gillies Ross (1979) at 29,966. These numbers do not include whales that were struck, got away, but then died. Moreover, whales killed east of Greenland by English, Scottish, German, Danish and other whalers, and those killed by the Dutch before 1661, are not included. Whatever the exact kill, the stock of bowheads was much diminished by this slaughter (Bree and Hacquebord 1988). The size of the whales killed declined dramatically: in the ten years 1675–84, each whale killed by Dutch whalers produced an average of 40.76 barrels of chopped-up blubber, while a century later, in the ten years 1770–9, the average was a mere 30.05 barrels (de Jong 1979: 177–8). By the time whaling ceased, Atlantic bowhead populations had been reduced almost to the point of extinction. In the eighty or so years since then, they have shown little sign of recovery: the seemingly renewable resource may prove after all to have been non-renewable. Canadian researchers reckoned in 1983 that there were only a few hundred bowheads at most in the Baffin Bay area and stated that 'there is no reliable and consistent evidence of appreciable recovery in absolute abundance of any Eastern Arctic stock' (Reeves *et al.* 1983: 5). The bowhead population east of Greenland seems to have fared even worse. A Soviet report claimed in 1986 that bowheads had been sighted in the Spitsbergen area on only nine occasions in the previous four decades, but a school of seven had recently been seen and photographed west of Severnaya Zemlya (Map 12) (*Soviet Weekly*, 1 February 1986). Perhaps there is a slim chance that the 'few tiny remnant groups in what used to be the main breeding grounds in the Greenland and Barents seas' (Watson 1981: 73) will survive, prosper and multiply.

FIVE

Russians in the Arctic

THE CONQUEST OF SIBERIA

Just when most of the European Russian Arctic had been taken over and in part colonized by Russians from Novgorod in quest of valuable furs, the aggressive, expanding Russian principality based on Moscow moved into the area, and by force of arms annexed both Novgorod and her fur trade. The city fell in 1478, and the new ruler of the area, Grand Prince Ivan III Vasyl'yevich of Moscow, who called himself 'Lord of Yugra' (Map 6), following Novgorod's precedent, despatched an expedition in 1499 across the northern Urals into the lower Ob' area; that is, into Asia and Siberia. But Moscow was far too distant and far too involved in fighting for her life against Tatar neighbours to contemplate further Siberian expeditions at that time. Nor was the tide of emigrant peasants and cossacks, already moving east to escape oppressive social systems, as yet flowing powerfully enough to reach out into Siberia: first the Urals had to be colonized and the frontier march with Siberia settled. While this steady colonization continued, Ivan IV the Terrible, the first Russian tsar, conquered and subdued the Tatars of the Volga, based on Kazan, in 1552. During the next thirty years he encouraged Russian expansion eastwards by authorizing the Stroganovs, a powerful family of merchant-miners whose interests stretched from Kola and the lower Ob' in the Arctic to the Kama river valley in the western Urals, to send troops and build strong points east of the Urals. These tentative moves into Siberia culminated in 1581–4 with the brief but famous campaign across the Urals of the Cossack leader Yermak Timofeyevich. He conquered the Tatar khanate of Sibir' (Siberia) in the Irtysh Valley after defeating the khan's forces at the fortress of Sibir' near modern Tobol'sk, but died defending his conquests. Yermak had inaugurated one of the most remarkable expansions of a single people in all history: the Russian annexation of Siberia. This enormous tract of mountain, steppe, taiga or coniferous forest, marsh and tundra stretched for 5,000 km (3,000 miles) from the Urals to the Sea of Okhotsk. It was occupied here and there by native peoples scattered in tiny groups. These had no political, economic or effective military means of opposing the Russian advance. They were powerless when an armed Cossack band arrived and began taking hostages as a means of compelling them to pay the *yasak*, or tribute in furs, which the Russians themselves had been forced, long before, to pay to the Mongols. In the early days

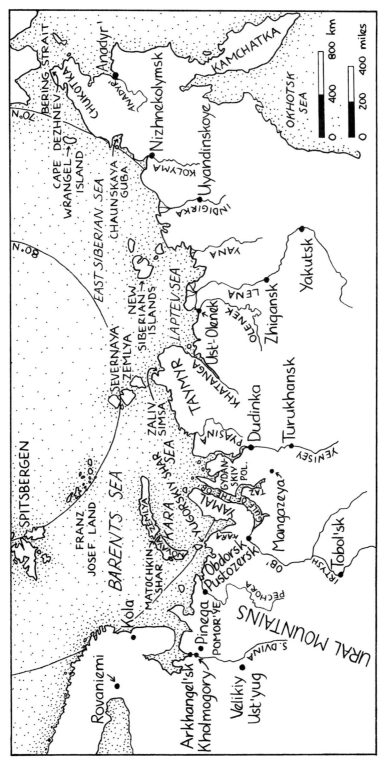

Map 12. The Russian Arctic.

of the conquest at least, the Russians used alcohol as an ally. Apart from the outlying regions of Taymyr and Chukotka, the conquest of Siberia was completed by the time the Russians had moved south from the Anadyr' Valley and reached Kamchatka in 1697. It had taken barely a hundred years.

Siberia was annexed by small bands of well-armed servicemen, either irregular troops called Cossacks, or regular troops called *strel'tsy*, accompanied by *promyshlenniks* or trappers, by traders or merchants' agents, and by government officials. The far-flung, foot-slogging rovings of these detachments were directed from Moscow, for the machinery of conquest was driven by the furs they collected for the government from the native peoples as tribute, and those the government collected from the Cossacks and promyshlenniks in the shape of a tax of one in every ten furs they obtained on their own account. The system was based on a grid of tax- and tribute-collecting stations set up along the river valleys. Often beginning as *zimov'yes* or wintering cabins built of logs, these were usually strengthened into *ostrogs* or forts, and some became regular towns (Fisher 1943, Armstrong 1965, Lantzeff and Pierce 1973, Forsyth 1992).

Moscow's Siberian fur empire, which flourished throughout the seventeenth century, was at first chiefly based on one animal, the sable (*Martes zibellina*). This is a member of the weasel family with highly prized, reddish-brown and black fur, endemic to the Eurasian taiga and a sub-Arctic, rather than Arctic, animal. In the mid-seventeenth century up to 145,000 sable pelts were sent annually from Siberia to Moscow, but only a handful of other pelts (Nikitin 1987: 71). In 1641, for example, animals other than sable were represented by 27 red foxes, 1 Arctic fox, 3 beavers, 7 wolverines, 20 ermines and 180 squirrels (Safronov 1980:26). The only one of these animals that inhabits the tundra north of the tree line is the Arctic fox. It later became an important fur animal, but the initial attraction of the Siberian Arctic was the availability there of ivory in the shape of walrus tusks and, later, mammoth tusks. The Arctic is represented in Siberia by a narrow strip of marsh and tundra along its northern coast from Yamal to Chukotka, comprising the southern shores of the Kara Sea, the Laptev Sea and the East Siberian Sea, all of them southern outliers of the Arctic Ocean, as well as the offshore islands and archipelagos (see Armstrong 1975, Nikitin 1987, Safronov 1980, Skrynnikov 1982, and especially Belov 1956).

MANGAZEYA

The building of fortified towns at strategic points quickly enabled the Russians to consolidate their hold on Siberia. In the Arctic, or at least close to the Arctic Circle, Obdorsk (now Salekhard) was built in 1595 at the mouth of the Ob' and an *ostrog*, or fortified settlement, was built at Mangazeya in 1601 by a force sent from Tobol'sk by the government in Moscow, which also appointed *voyevodas* or military governors to supervise the collection of tax and tribute. Mangazeya perhaps took its name from the name of the tribal group of Nentsy living in the area.

A settlement of some kind already existed on the site of Mangazeya, at the confluence of the River Taz (which flows into a gulf forming a branch of the Gulf of the Ob') and the River Mangazeya, in the 1570s, even before Yermak's irruption into Siberia. The Soviet archaeologists (Belov *et al.* 1980, 1981) who excavated the site of Mangazeya during four summer field-work seasons between 1968 and 1973 found the remains of at least four buildings pre-dating the construction of the ostrog in 1601. Doubtless the site had been used by seaborne traders and promyshlenniks from Pomor'ye and especially from Kholmogory, who, in the sixteenth century, regularly sailed thence to the Pechora, through Yugorskiy Shar Strait and across the Yamal Peninsula via rivers, lakes and portages to reach the Gulf of the Ob', bringing back cargoes of furs. Already in 1588 Giles Fletcher, an English envoy sent by Queen Elizabeth I to the Russian Tsar Theodore (Fedor) Ivanovich, reported in his description of the country that 'the best Sable furre groweth in the countrey of Pechora, Momgosorskoy [Mangazeya] and Obdorskoy' (Hakluyt 1907b: 293). From Mangazeya travel to the Yenisey at Turukhansk with the aid of portages was relatively simple. The rapid development of Mangazeya into the first real town in the Arctic in the years after 1600 was due as much to its position on one of the main routes into Siberia as to the extraordinary wealth in furs of its hinterland.

Like other Siberian towns, Mangazeya was built of wood: wooden fort, wooden churches, wooden houses, and streets paved with logs. The site extended for 270 m (295 yd) along the high right bank of the River Taz. It was on the border between tundra and taiga. By taking cores out of the oldest living trees in the area and comparing their growth-ring patterns with those of logs from Mangazeya, archaeologists established the exact age of the trees felled to construct the town. Most of them were between one hundred and three hundred years old. The oldest was a larch tree which started to grow in 1225 or thereabouts and was felled in or soon after 1628 (Belov *et al.* 1980: 103). Typically of old Russian towns, Mangazeya was built in two sections, with an open space between. The *kremlin* or citadel, on the highest part of the site, based on the original ostrog, contained the principal church, gaol, and voyevoda's house, all within square wooden walls with towers at each corner. The other section was the *posad* or town proper, unfortified, carefully planned, with paved streets, and divided into industrial, commercial and administrative and residential quarters. Mangazeya was a medium-sized Siberian town, garrisoned by fifty to sixty-five soldiers or *strel'tsy* and containing in its prime in the 1630s, according to the archaeologists, between 715 and 748 permanent residents and hosting up to 1,500 visitors annually (Belov *et al.* 1981: 11). The finds show that in winter the inhabitants moved about with skis and reindeer sledges and whiled away the time playing chess with finely carved wooden or bone chessmen.

Mangazeya's history was brief but colourful. Soon after its construction was completed in about 1630, a private quarrel between its two voyevodas, accompanied by artillery duels, reduced the market hall and much of the town centre to a heap of rubble. Then, in 1642, a disastrous fire destroyed the citadel. Rebuilding soon made good this destruction and Mangazeya remained active and populous throughout the 1650s. But then decline set in, and the end came quickly. In 1672 all 446 remaining inhabitants were evacuated to Turukhansk (Belov *et al.* 1981: 5). The 'boom town of seventeenth-century Siberia' (Fisher 1944) was no more. What is the explanation of this sudden collapse? It was certainly not due to the tsar's decree of 1619, closing the sea route to Mangazeya to keep out English and Dutch fur traders. The difficulty in getting food supplies there, and the threatening hostility of the local Nentsy, may have played a part. More important was the over-exploitation and consequent exhaustion of the sable resources of the area, combined with the restructuring of Siberian communications after the opening up of the Lena Valley. It was not Mangazeya, but Yakutsk on the Lena, founded in 1632, that became the great Siberian transport centre in the eighteenth century.

RELIGIOUS DISSENTERS

From the time of Ivan the Terrible (1533–84) onwards a trickle of religious dissenters made their way into Arctic Siberia and formed small isolated settlements there, where they were free to maintain their own way of life and beliefs. Many of them, known as Old Believers, split off from the orthodox church in the schism of 1658, and one of their leaders, the Archpriest Avvakum, was exiled to Pustozersk on the lower Pechora and burnt at the stake there in 1681 (Armstrong 1965: 91). Best known of the remote Arctic settlements founded by these people was Russkoye Ust'ye at the mouth of the Indigirka, where as late as 1912 the political exile Vladimir Zenzinov found the ancient Russian language and customs still in use among colonists who had apparently arrived there, possibly by sea, in the seventeenth century. They constituted for a long time what was said to be the most northerly white man's settlement in the world (Zenzinov and Levine 1932, Armstrong 1965: 63–4, Levin and Potapov 1964: 106–7).

FORGOTTEN EXPLORATIONS

The wandering Cossacks and promyshlenniks who penetrated headlong through the Siberian wilderness did so in the main along rivers. These afforded them easy access to the Arctic Ocean, through the ice-filled waters of which they had no hesitation in sailing from one river mouth to the next. Their mastery of waterways resulted from their seafaring skills and traditions, for most of them came from Pomor'ye in the Russian European Arctic, and depended on a wooden sailing ship, the koch. With its shallow draught and rounded sides, which enabled it to make its way through shoals and between ice floes, and its single mast carrying a square-rigged sail, the koch required a six- to twelve-man crew and could carry around thirty passengers and up to 30 tons of cargo. Cossack detachments travelling overland often included a shipwright and carried the necessary tools so that, when a river was reached, trees could be felled and a koch built. This was put together with wooden dowels instead of iron nails, and reindeer skin could take the place of canvas for the sail if necessary. With this simple but effective ship, and probably with the aid of a primitive compass, the Russians set out to conquer the Arctic Ocean, not so much as explorers, charting new discoveries, but rather as travellers and traders, hurrying from one place to another in quest of furs and ivory. Often no record was made of their voyages. In 1940 and 1941 a Soviet survey party found the remains of a campsite on the most northerly of a group of islands off the north-east coast of the Taymyr Peninsula, the ostrova Faddeya, and the remains of a wooden hut were discovered on the mainland coast of zaliv Simsa, not far off. Subsequent investigation produced numerous artefacts: copper pots, crosses, chessmen, an axe, human bones and 3,482 Russian coins dating from the reigns of seven tsars ending with Mikhail Fedorovich Romanov (1613–45). Expert opinion at first pointed to an unrecorded, forgotten, eastward-bound circumnavigation of the Taymyr Peninsula by an exploring party in about 1617–19. Later, doubts about this were raised and a counter-suggestion made: the expedition had been westward bound and may have dated from about 1640. In any event, though no written record of any such voyage can be found, here was irrefutable evidence that Russian seafarers had sailed along the shores of the Taymyr Peninsula in the first half of the seventeenth century at least as far as its north-easterly extremity (Armstrong 1958: 133–44, Barr 1991c: 12–13).

One of the earliest voyages along the Siberian shores of the Arctic Ocean on record was undertaken by a trader from the Dvina area called Kondratiy Kurochkin, who in 1610 sailed northward out of the mouth of the Yenisey as far as the mouth of the Pyasina River in the Taymyr Peninsula. In 1632 a winter house or zimov'ye was built on the Lena, just north of the Arctic Circle at Zhigansk, and in 1633 the Cossack Ivan Rebrov descended the river to its delta and sailed eastward thence to the Yana River, where he built an ostrog. On subsequent travels, Rebrov voyaged further east along the Arctic Ocean as far as the Indigirka, where he founded the settlement of Uyandinskoye, well within the Arctic Circle, in 1638. Another Cossack, Yelisey Buza, with six servicemen and forty promyshlenniks, sailed through the Lena Delta, reached the mouth of the Olenek, wintered there, and then returned to Zhigansk. When in 1642 the Cossack Mikhail Stadukhin sailed along the coast from the Indigirka Delta to the mouth of the Kolyma River, Cossacks and promyshlenniks had traversed over 1,600 km (1,000 miles) of the Siberian Arctic coast, all of it north of 70° north, within a single decade. These Cossacks were in the service of the government in Moscow and we are reasonably well informed about their exploits because their petitions for arrears of pay were filed in government archives.

The culmination of seventeenth-century Arctic exploration in Siberia came in 1648 with the famous expedition, often misleadingly referred to as that of Semen Dezhnev, which sailed out of the Kolyma River, eastwards along the north coast of Chukotka, round the extreme north-eastern point of Siberia (now Cape Dezhnev (mys Dezhneva), formerly East Cape), and sailed south through Bering Strait to the mouth of the Anadyr' River. Russian historians have considered this 'absolutely one of the greatest geographical discoveries of the seventeenth century' (Nikitin 1987: 33), but its greatness was somewhat diminished by the fact that it remained entirely unknown to the rest of the world for eighty-seven years. No word of it was published in or outside Russia and neither Moscow nor, later, St Petersburg, knew anything of it until Dezhnev's petitions for arrears of pay were unearthed in the archives at Yakutsk in August 1736. The discovery was made by Gerhard Friedrich Müller, historian of the so-called Second Kamchatka Expedition of 1734–9. One of the unfulfilled aims of this expedition was to sail round Chukotka from north to south: it failed where Dezhnev and his companions had succeeded.

Semen Ivanovich Dezhnev was born around 1605, perhaps at Pinega, certainly in Pomor'ye, and probably not in Velikiy Ust'yug, in spite of the statue of him in the town square there. In about 1630 he volunteered for military service with the Cossacks and was posted to the garrison at Tobol'sk and then to Yakutsk, where he joined yasak- or tribute-collecting detachments on the Lena, Yana and Indigirka Rivers. In the 1640s he was on the Kolyma with Mikhail Stadukhin and others, and was wounded twice in fights with the local Yukagirs, who resented his savage attempts, in the course of duty, to persuade them to pay yasak. From the Kolyma a group of promyshlenniks led by Isaya Ignat'yev sailed eastwards in 1646 along the coast as far as Chaunskaya guba, where they bartered a cargo of walrus ivory from the Chukchi and brought it back to the Kolyma. With a view to following this up by exploring as far as the River Anadyr', rumours of the fur wealth of which had already reached the Russians, an expedition was planned by a trader named Fedot Alekseyev, a native of Kholmogory on the Severnaya Dvina, who was acting as agent for the wealthy Moscow merchant Aleksey Usov. Applying to the local authorities for a military escort to accompany his expedition, Alekseyev obtained the services of Semen Dezhnev, but their attempt to sail east in 1647 from the Kolyma mouth failed because of impenetrable ice, blown tight against the shore by northerly and north-easterly winds. A more elaborate expedition with seven koches followed in 1648. Probably there was no single formally appointed leader. The expedition which set sail down the Kolyma on 20 June 1648 comprised three detachments. Alekseyev's group of some thirty traders and promyshlenniks was acting as private persons; with Alekseyev travelled his Yakut wife or mistress. Meanwhile, Dezhnev had hired and equipped some twenty promyshlenniks to accompany him as unofficial servicemen. He was under government orders to escort Alekseyev and to collect yasak from any natives they encountered. He had promised to collect 280 sable pelts for the government in this way. A third, entirely independent group, led by the Cossack Gerasim Ankudinov, had unofficially attached itself to the expedition. In the Arctic Ocean, storms seem to have been a more serious problem than ice. By the time the three koches carrying Dezhnev, Alekseyev and Ankudinov arrived at the entrance to Bering Strait, the other four ships had disappeared. Ankudinov's koch went down in a storm soon afterwards, though he and some of his crew were rescued. The fate of Alekseyev and his men is uncertain. There was a rumour that some of them reached Kamchatka and lived there for a time. Dezhnev and a handful of companions struggled ashore after their koch was wrecked, somewhere south of the Anadyr' mouth, wintered there, then moved upstream for a second overwintering. They were encountered on the river in 1650 by Mikhail Stadukhin and other Cossacks who had travelled there overland. These had tried, and failed, in the summer of 1649, to sail eastwards along the Arctic Ocean coast, just as Alekseyev and Dezhnev had done in 1648 (Samoylov 1945, Fisher 1981, Demin 1990). In retrospect, 1648 must have been a year of exceptionally favourable ice conditions in the East Siberian Sea.

THE NON-DISCOVERY OF BERING STRAIT

Tsar Peter I the Great (1692–1725) had always been fascinated by geographical problems, especially by the possibility of a Northern Sea Route along Russia's Arctic coast and the related question of whether there was a strait separating the continents of Asia and America. But he was always far too busy fighting his neighbours, Turkey and Sweden, founding St Petersburg, and modernizing and westernizing Russia, to pay much attention to the other end of his huge empire. Apparently unaware of the voyages of Cossacks and promyshlenniks, especially that of Alekseyev and Dezhnev, Peter instructed the military governor of Yakutsk in 1698 and 1700 to find out if it was possible to sail along the Siberian coast eastwards from the Lena. That official's answer to this question is not on record, though it lay hidden in his own archives! It was only at the end of his life, on 23 December 1724, that Tsar Peter, after finding that large parts of the shore of the Arctic Ocean were marked with a dotted line on the official maps of Siberia, issued a ukase or proclamation ordering the Admiralty, which he himself had founded in 1703, to organize an expedition to sail along the coast north from Kamchatka, and explore and map the area where that coast came nearest to America. A forty-four-year-old Dane, Vitus Jonassen Bering, who had served without distinction in the Imperial Navy since 1703, becoming a captain fourth rank in 1715, third rank in 1717, and captain first rank in 1720, was appointed to lead it. Bering's administrative skills enabled him to solve the logistical problems involved in transporting the First Kamchatka Expedition, complete with over thirty men and fifty waggons of baggage and equipment, overland for the mostly roadless 5,000 miles (8,000 km) from St Petersburg to the Sea of Okhotsk, and thence to the east coast of Kamchatka in three-and-a-half years (Gibson 1992: 90–9). The expedition's ship, the *Svyatoy Gavriil* (*St Gabriel*), was built on the Kamchatka River and sailed out of its mouth on 13 July 1728. The voyage to discover if there was a strait between Asia and America, which now followed, was completed in a mere fifty-one days, for the *Gabriel* was back in the mouth of the Kamchatka River on 2 September. The expedition had followed the coast north-eastwards as instructed, and had demonstrated good navigation by sailing in poor visibility precisely through the strait which James Cook charted fifty years later, and magnanimously named after Bering. The expedition then sailed north-east into the Chukchi Sea, but unaccountably turned back a little beyond 67° north latitude on 16 August. Again, Bering demonstrated his navigational skills by taking the *Gabriel* back through the strait on exactly the same route by which she had come. Because of fog, he contrived to sail both ways through it, without once seeing land in the direction of America, and only glimpsing Ratmanov or Big Diomede Island (Map 1) and Cape Dezhnev on the Asiatic side.

Bering had thus shown himself to be an able administrator and navigator, but a third-rate explorer, cautious and irresolute and so lacking in courage and determination as to be almost incapable of carrying out his instructions. What explorer worth his salt would not have sailed on until ice barred his way? Nor, surely, would a real explorer have returned the way he had come. If Bering had only turned to one side or the other on the return voyage he would have entirely carried out his brief, by either confirming that the north coast of Chukotka

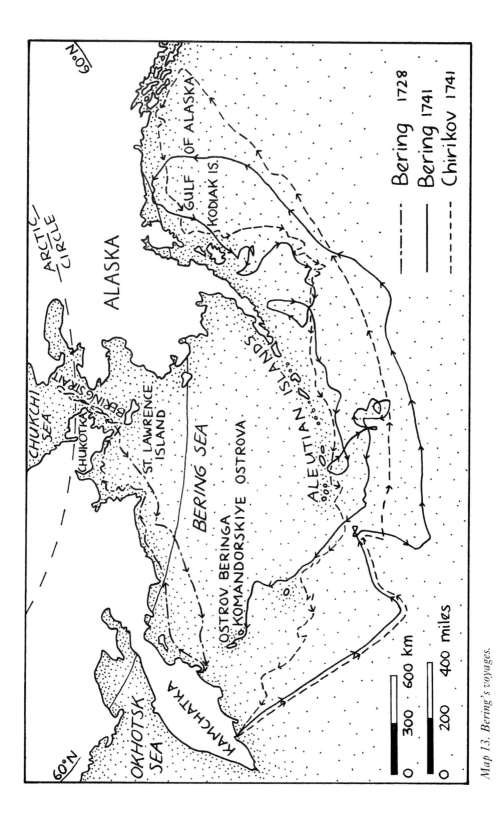

Map 13. Bering's voyages.

trended westwards, or by sighting Alaska. At the council of ship's officers called by Bering on 13 August when the *Gabriel* was in 65° 30' north latitude, one of his two lieutenants, the Dane Martin Spanberg, advised sailing north for a further three days and then turning back to winter in the Kamchatka River. Bering followed this fainthearted advice against the recommendation of the other lieutenant, Aleksey Chirikov (Fisher 1992, Divin 1993), who rightly claimed that they would be in breach of their instructions if they did not either proceed as far as the ice or make for the River Kolyma, and that in any event they ought to winter on the coast opposite the Chukchi Peninsula, namely in Alaska. The First Kamchatka Expedition could and should have discovered and mapped the strait separating Asia and America, but did not do so. No wonder Bering's reception on his return to St Petersburg was unenthusiastic. In the view of the Admiralty, Peter the Great had sent him to explore both shores of the strait and he had touched on neither. But he had discovered and named St Lawrence Island, and, as subsequent events showed, was not entirely discredited (Golder 1922, Fisher 1977, Pasetskiy 1982, Shumilov 1982, Armstrong 1983, Kushnarev 1990, Frost 1992).

A NORTHERN SEA ROUTE?

Soon after his return to St Petersburg Bering submitted two elaborate memoranda to the Admiralty. The first outlined in twenty-five points a programme for the general improvement of Siberia, including the construction of roads and ports, and schools for the Yakuts and other native peoples. The second proposed a new expedition, one of the most complex and grandiose ever conceived, to explore and chart the entire north coast of Siberia and to launch two separate voyages from Kamchatka, one to America, the other to Japan, in four ships to be built there. Ignoring Bering's proposed Siberian reforms, the government accepted his second proposal and promptly appointed him leader of the Second Kamchatka Expedition, with the rank of captain commander. The entire expedition was directed and staffed by the Imperial Russian Navy and was throughout under the direct orders of the Admiralty in St Petersburg. It comprised five separate detachments, which were later collectively called the Great Northern Expedition, to explore the whole of the Arctic coast of Russia; two detachments for the exploration of Japan and America; and, remarkably, a special scientific detachment of professors and adjuncts from Peter the Great's newly founded Academy of Sciences. Best known of these experts were the already mentioned Gerhard Müller (1986), official historian of the expedition and of Siberia, who unearthed the Dezhnev documents at Yakutsk, and naturalist Georg W. Steller (Ford 1966), who accompanied Bering on the ill-starred voyage to America in 1741. On that voyage Kodiak Island and some of the Aleutian Islands were discovered, but the captain commander and several crew members died during the return voyage on ostrov Beringa in the Commander Islands. Steller survived to give detailed scientific descriptions of the manatee or sea-cow named after him, and of the fur seals (*Callorhinus ursinus*), the meat of which helped to save the lives of the members of the expedition during their enforced stay on Bering Island. Bering's last voyage cannot, of course, form part of the history of the Arctic: its furthest point north was about 59° north latitude in the Gulf of Alaska (Golder 1922, 1925 prints the ships' logs and Steller's journal; see too Waxell 1952, Frost 1992).

Although the immediate aim of the five detachments forming the Great Northern Expedition was to explore and chart Russia's Arctic coast, the old idea of a Northern Sea Route certainly lay behind it. Fedor Stepanovich Saltykov, a close associate of Peter the Great, had suggested in 1713–14, in his *Concerning the Search for an Open Sea Route from the Dvina River to the Mouth of the Amur and to China* (Kushnarev 1990: 12), an investigation of the climate, animals, natural resources, anchorages, harbours and river mouths along the possible route. This now became the task of the Great Northern Expedition. But as soon as it started its work, the earlier Cossak voyages along parts of the route were seen to have taken advantage of favourable ice conditions that were certainly not present in most of the 1730s. Far from it. Even the relatively easy section from Arkhangel'sk on the Severnaya Dvina to the River Ob' was not completed in a single season. Lieutenants Stepan Voynovich Murav'yev and Mikhail Pavlov left Arkhangel'sk in July 1734 with two koches, the *Ekspeditsion* and the *Ob'*, but got no further than the Yamal Peninsula before bad weather and scurvy forced them to withdraw to the Pechora to winter near Pustozersk. Another attempt to round Yamal failed in 1735 and they returned again to the Pechora, whence Murav'yev informed the admiralty that it was impossible to sail from Arkhangel'sk to the Ob' in a single navigating season. The Admiralty was not impressed, and the apparently irresolute lieutenants were dismissed from their commands and court-martialled. In 1736 two more ships, *Nomer Pervyy* and *Nomer Vtoroy* (*Number One* and *Number Two*), were sent out from Arkhangel'sk, and Lieutenants Stepan Malygin and A. Skuratov were given the task of completing the work of the Dvina-Ob' division of the Great Northern Expedition. But they could do little better, in 1736, than their two disgraced predecessors, only sailing into the Gulf of the Ob', past the cape now named after Malygin, in 1737. Nor could Lieutenant Skuratov accomplish the return voyage, from Berezov on the Ob' to Arkhangel'sk, in a single season: he was forced to overwinter *en route* in the mouth of the Kara River in 1738–9. So a total of six navigating seasons had been required to sail to the Ob' and back. Perhaps Murav'yev had been right after all. But the principal aim of charting the coasts of the Yamal Peninsula and setting up navigation beacons had been achieved, much of it by geodesist Vasiliy Selifontov travelling overland with reindeer sleighs.

The Ob'-Yenisey detachment of the Great Northern Expedition, under Lieutenant Dmitriy L. Ovtsyn, found things no easier, though it had a shorter stretch of coastline to explore. The expedition ship *Tobol*, built at Tobol'sk under Ovtsyn's supervision, sailed northwards along the often fog-bound and stormy Gulf of the Ob' in the second half of June 1734, but had to return from 70° north in August after the flukes broke off two anchors and the ship lost her rudder in a storm. Nothing was achieved in the next season, 1735, because the gulf remained choked with the winter's ice until very late in the summer and scurvy struck the explorers, killing some. Nor was Ovtsyn's third attempt to get clear of the Gulf of the Ob' at its northern end and into the open sea any more successful than his first two: ice again barred the way. But if the Imperial Navy could not reach its

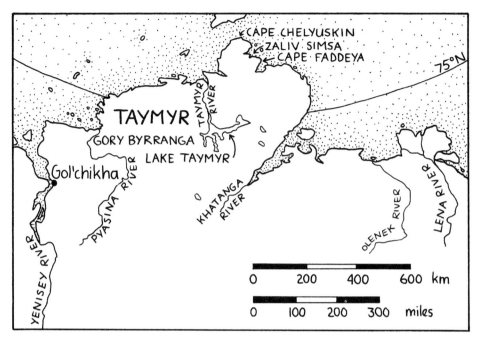

Map 14. Taymyr.

goal by sea it took to the land, and in February 1737 Ovtsyn sent an expedition with 120 reindeer and an escort of eight Cossacks to chart the coast between the Gulf of the Ob' and the Yenisey. Then, with an additional ship, the *Ob' Pochtal'yon* (*Ob' Postman*), the persevering lieutenant sailed north down the Gulf of the Ob' in the summer of 1737 for the fourth year in succession. He was at last successful in reaching the Yenisey and sailing up it, nearly as far as Turukhansk. Evidently ice conditions round the Yamal and Gyda Peninsulas, as elsewhere in the Arctic, varied a great deal from year to year and in 1737 they were so favourable that both the Dvina-Ob' and the Ob'-Yenisey detachments of the Great Northern Expedition could reach their goals by sea, the first rounding the northern tip of the Yamal, and the second that of the Gyda, Peninsula. Although perhaps the most effective of all the naval officers of the Great Northern Expedition, Ovtsyn was surely the least fortunate. In the autumn of 1738 he was arrested because of his friendship with the exiled prince Aleksey Dolgorukiy, demoted to the rank of able-seaman, and sent to Okhotsk to serve as such on Bering's voyage to America.

Beyond the Yenisey, between it and the Khatanga River, extended the huge expanse of the most northerly part of Siberia: the unknown, uncharted, almost uninhabited Taymyr Peninsula. The gigantic task of exploring this area was to be undertaken by two divisions of the Great Northern Expedition, one aiming eastward from the Yenisey, the other westward from the Lena. Fedor Minin was under orders to take the *Ob' Pochtal'yon* north and east from the Yenisey mouth in June 1738 and to sail right round the Taymyr Peninsula to the Khatanga. He got no further than 73° 14' north, somewhere near the mouth of the River Pyasina. Trying again in 1739, he started much too late and got nowhere. Then, in January 1740, Minin sent Dmitriy Sterlegov to sledge northwards by land, mapping the coast as he went. Travelling in an almost unceasing blizzard, and sleeping in a Nentsy tent or *chum*, Sterlegov managed to penetrate beyond the Pyasina mouth to 75° 29' north before returning to Gol'chikha at the end of April 1740. In his third attempt to sail round the Taymyr Peninsula from west to east, in the summer of 1740, Minin failed to push the *Ob' Pochtal'yon* through the ice as far as Sterlegov's furthest point on land. A further attempt in 1742 likewise failed. Minin subsequently had charges filed against him by subordinates and was reduced for two years to the rank of seaman. His efforts to circumnavigate Taymyr from the Yenisey had achieved only the mapping of the coast of west Taymyr to a little way north of the Pyasina River.

It was left to the fourth division of the Great Northern Expedition, travelling westward from the Lena Delta, to complete the exploration of the Taymyr coast. Just as Fedor Minin had failed to chart the west Taymyr coast by sea, so on the east Taymyr coast, this proved impossible. Lieutenant Vasiliy Pronchishchev, travelling with his wife Tat'yana (rather than Mariya as most authors have it, Kanevskiy 1989: 31–2), 'who had accompanied him on this voyage out of love' (Müller 1986: 83), took the double-sloop *Yakutsk* out of the Lena Delta in August 1735 under orders to sail her westward round the Taymyr Peninsula and into the Yenisey. After an unsuccessful attempt to make his way along the western branch of the Lena, he was forced to use an easterly branch, and then to double back westwards along the coast off the river's mouths. Because of this he had to interrupt his voyage for the winter in the mouth of the Olenek River, at present-day Ust'-Olenek, where several families of Russian promyshlenniks were living. In 1736 Pronchishchev, suffering from scurvy but hoping to recover on the voyage, and his able navigating officer, Semen Chelyuskin, took the *Yakutsk* north as far as, or slightly further than, Asia's most northerly point in a skilful and determined bid to round Cape Chelyuskin (then North-East Cape or mys Vostochnyy Severnyy). They did not succeed, and solid fields of ice, as well as Pronchishchev's failing health, forced them to turn back, many of the crew suffering from scurvy, to Ust'-Olenek. There Vasiliy Pronchishchev, who had died on board, was buried on 2 September. His wife followed him to the grave on 6 September. His detachment had mapped the Lena Delta and most of the east coast of Taymyr and, while new orders were awaited from the Admiralty, Bering having imposed a temporary halt on further northern exploration, the *Yakutsk* was taken back to Yakutsk to refit. It was only in May 1739 that she sailed again down the Lena with a new commander and most of the old crew, and with new instructions. The new commander, Lieutenant Khariton Prokop'yevich Laptev, aged thirty-nine, was to start out as soon as the ice broke up on the Lena. If he met with ice barring his way he was to sail round it to the north. If shallow water stopped him he was to wait for the tide. If he really was brought to a standstill by the ice he was to winter in the nearest possible place and not try to reach a settlement. And if he could not sail round Taymyr in one year, he was to try again the next year, and so on for up to four years. It went without saying that, if the ship was held up, no time was to be lost before sending out shore parties to explore the coast ahead. Laptev insisted on a well disciplined routine on the *Yakutsk*. Surgery was fixed at 9.30 a.m. and after it the doctor would visit those unable to attend. Crew members could take food to the galley to be cooked only from 6.30 to 10.00 a.m. and from 5.00 to 10.30 p.m.. The times of the watches were also laid down in detail.

The *Yakutsk* sailed off westwards from the Lena Delta on 22 July 1739 and reached Cape Faddeya in north-east Taymyr in the third week of August. It could get no further because of ice. The crew dug up a mammoth tusk and set it on end to serve as a navigation beacon, then returned south to the mouth of the River Khatanga, where they built a zimov'ye or winter house. During the winter scurvy was held at bay by Lieutenant Laptev's dietary prescriptions: raw fish, boiled barley water, and fresh reindeer meat (supplied by local promyshlenniks or natives) were compulsory items on the menu. In spring 1740 the geodesist Nikifor Chekin sledged overland with two dog teams from the Khatanga zimov'ye and followed the frozen River Taymyr down to the sea, while Laptev sent another expedition to lay down depots of provisions and dog food in central and western Taymyr. But his attempt to sail the *Yakutsk* round the peninsula, starting from the Khatanga zimov'ye in July 1740, ended in disaster in the third week of August when his ship was crushed and sunk by the ice in about 76° 26' north. He and his crew struggled back to the zimov'ye suffering from scurvy. He reported to the Admiralty that it was impossible to sail round the Taymyr Peninsula from Khatanga to the Pyasina mouth, and resolved to send an overland expedition to chart the coast which could not be charted by sea. This was partly accomplished in the spring of 1741 in three divisions: navigating officer Semen Chelyuskin sledged north from the Pyasina, mapping the coast as he went; geodesist Nikifor Chekin sledged north from the Khatanga estuary to map the east coast; and Laptev himself made for the mouth of the Taymyr, travelling inland, where he arrived on 7 May. Sledging first eastward from there along the coast, he failed to meet with Chekin. Turning back to the Taymyr mouth, Laptev then sledged westwards and soon joined forces with Chelyuskin. Both Chelyuskin's and Chekin's divisions had suffered from snow blindness, and Chekin had had to turn back from 76° 35' north. Thus the extreme northern section of the Taymyr coast was left unexplored in 1741. But this was brilliantly made good in 1742 when, in a remarkable sledge journey, Chelyuskin, using a supporting team to carry additional supplies part of the way and another to lay down a depot at the Taymyr mouth ahead of him, sledged mostly on sea ice right round the north-east shore of the peninsula from the Khatanga to the Taymyr mouth. He spent an hour on 9 May 1742 at Asia's most northerly point (77° 34' north latitude) and erected a cairn on what was then North-East Cape. It was renamed Cape Chelyuskin by the nineteenth-century explorer of the Taymyr, Alexander von Middendorff, who rightly regarded Semen Chelyuskin very highly: he was not only a meticulously accurate surveyor and navigator but an expert and determined sledger. Nonetheless, his survey of the north coast of Taymyr in 1742, involving a 4,000 km (2,500 mile) sledge journey, was necessarily cursory.

The most easterly of the Great Northern Expedition's five detachments had the longest stretch of coastline to explore, for it was supposed to sail down the

Lena and then eastwards round Chukotka, all the way to Kamchatka. The first attempt to do this was made in 1735 by Lieutenant Petr Lasinius in the *Irkutsk*, but only ten days after leaving the Lena ice induced him to go ashore to overwinter in an area where no fresh meat or other food was available. His crew mutinied, and he and many of his men died of scurvy. The new commander, Dmitriy Laptev, a cousin of Khariton Laptev, set sail in the *Irkutsk* in 1736, but ice prevented him rounding Cape Svyatoy Nos (Map 15 below). Returning to the Lena Delta to winter, D. Laptev entirely missed the favourable ice-year of 1737 by persuading Bering to call a halt to exploration while he travelled to St Petersburg to inform the Admiralty that it was impossible to sail round Svyatoy Nos because of ice. This was a story they had heard before, and June 1739 found him back again sailing down the Lena in the *Irkutsk* for another attempt. This time he rounded the cape easily and wintered at the mouth of the Indigirka River. In 1740 he took the ship as far as Nizhnekolymsk, where he wintered in 1740–1 before trying, without success, to sail eastwards out of the Kolyma mouth. Finally Dmitriy Laptev set out overland for Anadyr' with forty-five dog sledges and a hundred men. He arrived there in November 1741. Thus the Great Northern Expedition failed to navigate or chart the shore of the Arctic Ocean from a short distance east of the mouth of the Kolyma to Bering Strait.

The work of the five detachments of the Great Northen Expedition may be summarized as follows:

	Detachment	Commanders	Navigation seasons
1.	Dvina-Ob'	Murav'yev, Pavlov, Malygin, Skuratov	1734–9
2.	Ob'-Yenisey	Ovtsyn	1734–7
3.	Yenisey eastward	Minin	1738–42
4.	Lena westwards	Pronchishchev Kh. Laptev	1735–42
5.	Lena eastwards	Lasinius, D. Laptev	1735–41

The charting, or at least exploration, of Taymyr's 2,000 km (1,200 miles) of coastline was surely the greatest single achievement of the Great Northern Expedition. Its success was partly due to the help it received from native peoples as well as other local inhabitants, Russian promyshlenniks or Russianised Yakuts, who occupied winter houses here and there along the coast, for example at the mouths of the Pyasina, Taymyr and Khatanga Rivers. These men were invaluable as guides, and as purveyors of meat and fish they helped stave off that scourge of Arctic expeditions, the dreaded scurvy. Its success was also due to the determination and organizational skills of the Admiralty, which coordinated the various divisions of the expedition and communicated regularly each winter with their commanding officers. Above all it was due to the naval officers who led its different detachments, most of whom were trained at the School of Navigation in Moscow or at the Naval Academy in St Petersburg, both of them founded by Peter the Great. Indeed the Second Kamchatka Expedition, of which the Great Northern Expedition formed a part, was a monument to the reforming genius of that tsar and to the Imperial Russian Navy which he had virtually created. One cannot pretend that the role of Vitus Bering was anywhere decisive. When based at Yakutsk, purportedly to control and coordinate the different divisions of the expedition, Bering really only acted as a post office, and even then his superiors in St Petersburg and his subordinate commanders in the field preferred to communicate directly with one another. The Great Northern Expedition itself, which was active for an entire decade, 1733–42, was the most far-reaching, the most tenacious and the most meticulously planned of any Arctic expedition before or since. Its surveying was unequalled in those days. Every ship carried a qualified geodesist or surveyor, and the only stretch of coastline it failed to map was the north shore of the Chukchi Peninsula. The only reason it did not sail along the entire Russian and Siberian shore of the Arctic Ocean was because the ice conditions of the 1730s made this impossible for the ships of those days. As a lasting monument to the endeavours of its explorers, their names are to be found all over the map of the Russian Arctic: Sterlegov, Chelyuskin, Ovtsyn, Lasinius, Pronchishchev and others are all commemorated in this way. Not that they were conceited enough to name capes and islands and the rest after themselves; it was their subsequent admirers who raised these monuments to them. (This section is based on Golder 1914: 165–250, Belov 1956: 264–340, Pasetskiy 1982: 77–106, Armstrong 1983, Müller 1986: 81–8, Armstrong 1992a, and especially Glushankov 1980.)

ARCTIC ARCHIPELAGOS

By the end of the eighteenth century seafaring Russian promyshlenniks from Pomor'ye, roaming in search of furs and ivory, had discovered three of the six important archipelagos in the Arctic Ocean north of Eurasia, namely Spitsbergen, Novaya Zemlya, and the New Siberian Islands (Novosibirskiye ostrova). The other three, Franz Josef Land (Zemlya Frantsa Iosifa), Severnaya Zemlya and Wrangel Island (ostrov Vrangelya), with Herald Island (ostrov Geral'd), remained at that time undiscovered (Map 12). The arrival of the first Russian in Spitsbergen, called Grumant by the Russians, has been dated to 1557 by examining the tree-ring pattern of timbers from a ruined building (Gnilorybov 1988: 15), and other promyshlenniks probably went there in the seventeenth century. But the earliest detailed documentation of their activities in the Spitsbergen Archipelago dates from 1743, when four promyshlenniks from Pomor'ye, Ivan and his father Aleksey Khimkov, Stepan Sharapov and Fedor Verigin, went ashore on Edge Island (Edgeøya, Map 10), from a ship beset in the ice, found a hut they knew of in which to spend the night, and discovered to their horror next morning that their ship had disappeared. All they had with them was a gun with twelve rounds of ammunition, an axe, kettle and knife, a 20 lb sack of

Drawn by W. Livesay.

Plate 7. Remains of a promyshlennik's hut in the Spitsbergen Archipelago, with characteristic Russian crosses erected near it. Engraved in the nineteenth century from a sketch by W. Livesay, who accompanied British yachtsman James Lamont on his 1871 Spitsbergen voyage, the illustration is said to represent a cemetery. Such crosses, which made excellent navigation marks, were traditionally set up by Pomors, that is the inhabitants of Pomor'ye, the European Russian Arctic, at places where they safely made the shore after escaping the dangers of the sea, as well as to mark burials. These are said to have been at Keilhau Bay (Keilhaubukta) on the north shore of Tjuvfjorden, Edge Island. (From Lamont 1876: 342.)

flour, tinder and flints, and a pipe and tobacco. They shot twelve reindeer with their twelve bullets and fashioned primitive weapons out of the driftwood, some with nails in it, that they found on the shore. Their ship was never heard of again, and it was over six years before another arrived on 15 August 1749. The three surviving castaways were not too badly out with their reckoning of time: they had erroneously celebrated the feast of the Assumption of the Blessed Virgin Mary two days before. They had shot 250 reindeer with bows and arrows, trapped many Arctic foxes, and killed ten Polar bears with home-made lances. Ivan Khimkov, who had previously overwintered several times on the west coast of Spitsbergen, was able to tell them how to prevent scurvy: eat raw frozen meat, drink warm reindeer blood directly the animal was killed, eat scurvy-grass, and take as much exercise as possible. Fedor Verigin could not bring himself to drink reindeer blood and he died of scurvy in their fifth year. Their rescuers brought away with them the products of their hunting and trapping: some 900 kg (1,980 lb) of reindeer fat, and a quantity of reindeer skins and Arctic fox pelts (Vize 1933; see too Conway 1906: 234–7, Le Roy 1766, Le Roy 1774). The achievement of these castaways, surviving entirely on their own through six successive Spitsbergen winters in good health, and with no preparation whatsoever beforehand, has never been equalled in the annals of the Arctic. For at least a hundred years after they were rescued in 1749, Russian promyshlenniks repeatedly wintered on Spitsbergen, and sometimes came to grief there (Conway 1906, Jasinski 1991).

The early adventures of promyshlenniks in Novaya Zemlya, like those in the Spitsbergen Archipelago, have gone unrecorded. For example, almost nothing is known of Savva Loshkin's travels in Novaya Zemlya, except that he wintered twice on the east coast in the 1760s (Pasetskiy 1980: 41–2). Better known are the activities of the Yakutsk trader Ivan Lyakhov in the New Siberian Islands. While trapping Arctic foxes in March 1770 at Cape Svyatoy Nos, he saw a herd of wild reindeer coming in towards the land over the frozen sea. Following their tracks northwards on a sledge, Lyakhov discovered an island and, next day, still following the tracks, another island. The tracks still led north from this second island, but Lyakhov was not then equipped for a lengthy journey. However, in summer 1773 he sailed north from the second island to the southern shore of a much larger one, where the reindeer must have been grazing. In this way the New Siberian Islands became known, though Lyakhov's find of a copper kettle or cauldron (*kotel*) on the third island, which caused it later to be called ostrov Kotel'nyy, shows that others had been there before him. His first two islands are now named after him: ostrov Bol'shoy Lyakhovskiy and ostrov Malyy Lyakhovskiy. Not only were these islands rich in Arctic foxes; there were huge deposits of mammoth bones and tusks on them. To stay in the lead in the ivory rush that now developed, Lyakhov obtained a monopoly from Catherine the Great to collect ivory and trap Arctic foxes on his three islands, and on any others that might be discovered (Digby 1926: 144–65, Belov 1956: 403–7, Ivanov 1979: 12–13, and Pfizenmayer 1939).

These private activities of promyshlenniks were accompanied, in the second half of the eighteenth century, by official expeditions organized or supported by the Admiralty on Catherine the Great's behalf. The purpose of these voyages was the time-honoured one of searching for a route to Bering Strait round Russia's northern shores and, since the Great Northern Expedition had found the coastal route impracticable, they were aimed further north, where it was hoped an unfrozen open sea might be found. The greatest enthusiast for a Trans-Polar or more northerly Northern Sea Route in the eighteenth century was the polymath, poet, and St Petersburg academician, Mikhail Vasiliy Lomonosov (1711–65), inheritor of the ideas of Petrus Plancius. He came from Arkhangel'sk and is usually reckoned Russia's first scientist. He put forward a daring and imaginative proposal to explore the central parts of the Arctic Ocean and perhaps sail through them to Bering Strait from a base on Spitsbergen. He outlined a detailed programme of scientific research to be carried out by the expedition and persuaded the government to implement his plan. The proposed base was set up in August 1764 in Recherche Bay (Recherchefjord), on the south shore of Bell Sound (Bellsund; Map 10), by Lieutenant Mikhail Nemtinov, who sailed there from Arkhangel'sk with a squadron of six ships carrying prefabricated store-

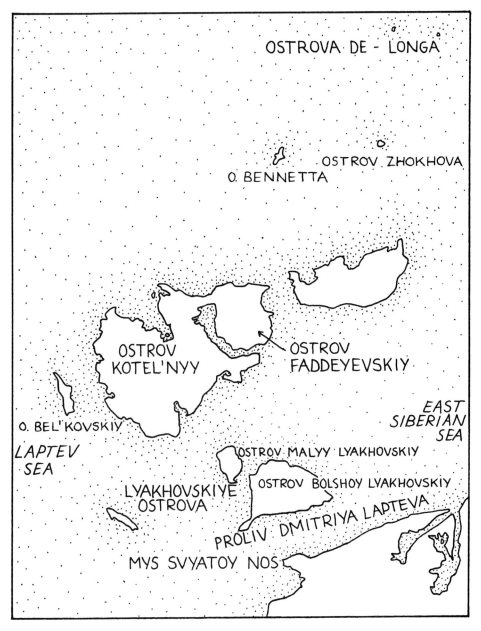

Map 15. The New Siberian Islands.

sheds, living accommodation, a bath-house, part of the provisions required for the expedition, and an eleven-man wintering party. Lomonosov died just as this first Russian high latitude Arctic expedition was setting out. It comprised three specially built warships provisioned for three years and was commanded by Captain First Rank Vasiliy Yakovlevich Chichagov, who was optimistically instructed to proceed northwards between Spitsbergen and Greenland and then head across the centre of the Arctic Ocean for Bering Strait. On 29 July 1765 Chichagov turned back after reaching a point furthest north of 80° 26' on 23 July, convinced that there was absolutely no way through the ice. Instead of making use of his carefully prepared Spitsbergen base to overwinter, his squadron sailed straight back to Arkhangel'sk. Meanwhile, the wintering party narrowly escaped death from scurvy or starvation when its supply ship was prevented by ice from reaching it in the late summer of 1765. The Admiralty, understandably annoyed, ordered Chichagov to try again. But his second attempt in 1766 likewise failed, the same three ships with the same commander getting no further north than 80° 30', no further than Dutch and other whalers regularly voyaged. After calling at the Recherche Bay base and remaining there a month in August-September, Chichagov abandoned the place and sailed back to Arkhangel'sk, attributing the failure of both his expeditions to the impenetrable barrier of ice north of Spitsbergen. There were no further high-latitude expeditions for the time being (Conway 1906: 263–5, Laktionov 1955: 42–52, Belov 1956: 360–81, Nulin 1982).

Soon after the failure of Captain Chichagov's attempt to penetrate the Arctic Ocean and reach Bering Strait, the governor of Arkhangel'sk, E. Golovtsyn, helped launch an expedition with the modest aim of trying for a more northerly route between Arkhangel'sk and the Ob'. In 1768 Fedor Rozmyslov was instructed to sail to Novaya Zemlya, explore and chart the narrow strait Matochkin Shar, which divides it into two islands, sail through it and, if the Kara Sea was free of ice, sail across it to the Gulf of the Ob' (Belov 1956: 384–90; Pasetskiy 1980: 42–5). After overwintering, Rozmyslov sailed along the east coast of Novaya Zemlya as far as 73° 41' north, but, as usual, the Kara Sea was *not* free of ice: there *was* no practicable northerly route to the Ob'. Everywhere in the eighteenth century, the Russians, both explorers and promyshlenniks, had found their way barred by ice, but they tried and tried again and their efforts ensured that by 1800, theirs was by far and away the best-known part of the Arctic.

SIX

The Hudson's Bay Company and the Royal Greenland Trade

The chartered company was a favourite way of promoting trade and colonization in early modern times, and in particular of obtaining and marketing furs and ivory. The Arctic whale oil rush had been greatly facilitated in England by the monopoly granted by royal charter to the Muscovy Company (1555) and in Holland by the State's General's charter to the Noordsche Compagnie (1614). The fur trade was fostered in a similar way in North America by Charles II's grant of a charter in 1670 to the 'Governor and Company of Adventurers of England tradeing into Hudson's Bay' (Newman 1985: 321), and by the trading monopoly granted in 1799 by Tsar Paul I to the Russian-American Company, which operated in Alaska and the Aleutians (Alekseyev 1982: 102–28, Alekseev 1990). These were private companies given public duties like defence and jurisdiction which amounted almost to outright ownership, or sovereignty, over the territories covered by their monopolies. Different from them in one important respect was the Royal Greenland Trading Company set up in 1774, for it was virtually a department of the Danish government. Leaving whaling on one side, the history of the exploitation of furs and other animal products in the non-Russian Arctic is mainly the history of the Hudson's Bay Company and the Royal Greenland Trading Company. The Russian-American Company never penetrated the Arctic because the furs it traded for, those of the fur seal and sea otter in particular, came from the Bering Sea, which is not in the Arctic. It is true that much of the Hudson's Bay Company's territory was not really in the Arctic either, and the furs it sought were mostly of animals like the beaver, which were denizens of the sub-Arctic taiga or northern coniferous forests rather than the Arctic tundra. But the company did penetrate significantly into the Arctic, and its general history cannot be entirely excluded from a history of the area.

THE HUDSON'S BAY COMPANY'S FUR EMPIRE

French cod-fishers initiated the import of North American furs to Europe in the sixteenth century. Bartered in the St Lawrence River basin from Algonquin and Montagnais Indians, the pelts, mostly beaver skins, were processed in Paris and other French centres into felt, which was used to make the beaver hats which became fashionable around 1600. This trade was handled in the first half of the seventeenth century by a series of companies chartered by the French crown, the last of which was Richelieu's Compagnie de la Nouvelle France of 1628. Independent operators known as *coureurs de bois*, 'woodsmen' or 'wood-runners', took over the trade after the mid-century collapse of the companies. It was the arrival of two of these woodsmen in London in 1665, with proposals for developing a lucrative fur trade based on Hudson Bay and its extensive hinterlands, inhabited mainly by Cree Indians, that prompted a group of British courtiers, businessmen and scientists to found the Hudson's Bay Company in 1670. The Frenchmen's names were Médard Chouart, sieur de Groseilliers, called 'Mr Gooseberry' in English sources, and his brother-in-law, Pierre Esprit Radisson, but the real originators of the company were King Charles II's cousin, Prince Rupert of the Rhine, dashing leader of the Royalist cavalry in the Civil War, and his secretary James Hayes. Rupert was appointed the company's first governor, and its enormous territories, defined in the charter as all lands 'upon the Coastes and Confynes of the Seas Streightes Bayes Lakes Rivers Creekes and Soundes' which 'lye within the entrance of the Streightes commonly called Hudsons Streightes' (Newman 1985: 320), were to be called Rupert's Land. The governor of the company and his successors were to be 'the true and absolute Lordes and Proprietors' of this territory. The initial capital was £10,500, put up by the eighteen 'Adventurers' mentioned in the charter. They had to wait fourteen years for their first dividend, which was a generous 50 per cent.

During the first century of its existence the Hudson's Bay Company changed but little. It was a stable, bureaucratic, money-making concern run from London by a governor, deputy governor and seven-man committee of principal investors called directors. Ignoring alike the possibilities of exploration, conversion of the natives to Christianity, and of settlement, this governing body concentrated its attention on the fitting out of two or three company ships each year. These carried trade goods such as knives, axes, blankets and tobacco, and supplies for the shore establishments on the bay, and returned with cargoes of beaver pelts and other furs. The other principal concern of the London Committeemen was the sale of the furs in London. Around the shores of Hudson Bay the company maintained a handful of trading posts or depots, usually called forts or factories – Albany Fort, Moose Fort and Charles Fort on the Rupert River round the 'Bottom of the Bay', that is in James Bay; York Fort or Port Nelson on the Hayes River; and Prince of Wales Fort at modern Churchill, on the west coast of the bay. All these posts and others established later were together manned by a couple of hundred personnel, chief factors, chief traders, clerks and others, most of whom came from Scotland or the Scottish Isles. Resident Indian hunters helped provision the personnel. It was to these posts that the Indians flocked every summer, bringing the pelts of the animals they had trapped during the winter

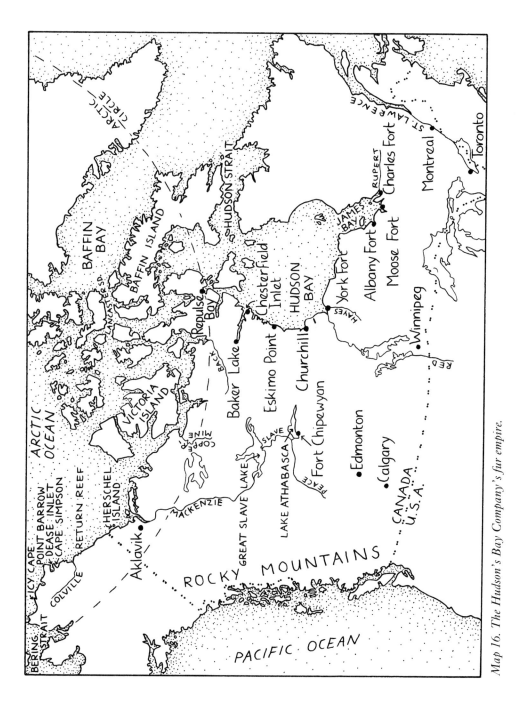

Map 16. *The Hudson's Bay Company's fur empire.*

Plate 8. A Hudson's Bay Company field officer travelling in winter by cariole or dog-drawn toboggan. From a drawing by R.M. Ballantyne (1857: 160), who describes the cariole as 'very narrow, just broad enough to admit one person. It is a wooden frame covered with deer-skin parchment, painted gaudily, and is generally drawn by four Esquimaux dogs'.

downriver in their canoes, to barter for European manufactured goods. The Indian, who might bring upwards of a hundred beaver pelts, first handed them over in bundles and received in exchange a piece of wood, a quill or a stick as a token for each beaver pelt or its equivalent. These equivalents were called 'Made-Beavers'. He took his tokens to the store, where he was free to select from the coats, knives, blankets, powder-horns, flints and so on, each of which was priced in Made-Beavers, until his supply of tokens was exhausted.

In the second century of its existence the Hudson's Bay Company, now boasting some 250 shareholders receiving an annual dividend of around 10 per cent, was forced by competition from Canadian-Scottish fur traders based in Montreal, loosely organized into the North West Company (Davidson 1918, Campbell 1957, Rumilly 1980), to expand westwards inland from Hudson Bay until its territories extended to the Pacific. After some years of virtual warfare between the two rival organizations, the Hudson's Bay Company swallowed up the North West Company in 1821 and the famous governor-in-chief of its now huge North American territories, George Simpson, known as 'the Little Emperor' (Chalmers 1960, Galbraith 1976), presided over the golden age of the company between 1820 and 1860. But in the decade thereafter it lost much of its land and its fur-trading monopoly. The land was purchased by the newly founded Dominion of Canada, which granted the company several million acres of fertile prairie in part return, and it was transformed, during the third century of its existence (1870–1970), into a chain of four hundred department stores known for short as 'The Bay', with headquarters in Toronto in place of London (see Innis

1956, Stefansson 1960, Morton 1973, and Rich 1967 in general; and Mackay 1937, Rich 1958, Rich 1959, Newman 1985, Newman 1987, Newman 1989, Newman 1991, for the Hudson's Bay Company).

THE FUR COMPANIES REACH THE ARCTIC OCEAN SHORE

In the second half of the eighteenth century hopes and dreams of the discovery of the long searched for North-West Passage led both North American fur companies, the Hudson's Bay and the North West, to organize exploring expeditions to the Arctic, thus beginning the laborious business of mapping the hitherto unknown northern shores of the North American continent. The first of these expeditions was sent off by the Hudson's Bay Company from Fort Prince of Wales (Churchill) on 6 November 1769 with a seven-gun salute. It was led by a young seaman called Samuel Hearne who had served in the Royal Navy and on the company's ships. He was accompanied by two white men, two Cree Indian hunters from the fort, and an Indian guide with his companions. Hearne was instructed to report on the copper deposits said to exist somewhere far to the north, to take possession of any Arctic rivers he discovered 'on behalf of the Honourable Hudson's Bay Company', and to throw as much light as possible on the whereabouts, if it existed, of the North-West Passage. This first attempt of Hearne's was a failure. Barely 200 miles (320 km) out from the fort his Indian guides deserted him, and he was lucky to get back alive, if half-starved, on 11 December. But the determined young man was off again, with other Indian guides and purposely without European companions, on 23 February 1770. This time Hearne was in the field for nine months, before the breakage of his quadrant and the realization that his guides had no idea of the whereabouts of the copper deposits near the Coppermine River, brought him back again to Fort Prince of Wales on 25 November. But he only stayed there twelve days before setting out on a third-time-lucky journey. Now he was guided across the Barren Lands or tundra by a mixed-blood Chipewyan/Cree Indian leader called Matonabbee, who in his youth had lived for several years at Prince of Wales Fort, having been born there. He was 'the most sociable, kind, and sensible Indian' Hearne had ever met with (Glover 1958: 35–6). Matonabbee knew the Coppermine River country at first hand, and his five to eight wives would make good what was lacking on Hearne's first two expeditions, namely women, for he had taken none with him. Matonabbee explained to Hearne the difficulties of travelling without them (Glover 1958: 35):

'Women', added he, 'were made for labour; one of them can carry, or haul, as much as two men can do. They also pitch our tents, make and mend our clothing, keep us warm at night; and, in fact, there is no such thing as travelling any considerable distance, or for any length of time, in this country, without their assistance. Women,' said he again, 'though they can do every thing, are maintained at a trifling expence; for as they always stand cook, the very licking of their fingers in scarce times, is sufficient for their subsistence'.

With the help of Matonabbee and his wives, 'most of whom would for size have made good grenadiers' (Glover 1958: 56), Hearne completed the 1,250 miles (2,000 km) round trip to the mouth of the Coppermine River in Coronation Gulf, in latitude 67° 49' north, and back to Prince of Wales Fort, in eighteen months on foot. Though he made a serious error in placing the river's mouth some 200 miles (320 km) north of its true position, Hearne was successful in establishing that the native copper found near the Coppermine River was not readily exploitable, though he collected a four-pound lump of it which eventually found its way to the British Museum. He also showed that any North-West Passage that might exist was much too far north to be navigable the year round. Hearne was the first white man to see the northern shore of the North American continent. He described his expedition in what soon became, and has ever since remained, a classic of Arctic travel literature: *A Journey from Prince of Wales's Fort, in Hudson's Bay, to the Northern Ocean undertaken by order of the Hudson's Bay Company, for the Discovery of Copper Mines, a North West Passage, etc.*, published in 1795. Hearne's graphic and informative narrative includes admirable descriptions of the Chipewyan Indians and of birds and animals. The habits of the beaver and musk ox were described by him for the first time in accurate detail. Best known among the incidents he recorded was the savage butchery by his Indian companions of an unfortunate party of Eskimo men, women and children asleep in their tents by the Coppermine River on 17 July 1771; but his account of this has recently been called in question (MacLaren 1993. On Hearne, besides Glover 1958, see Brebner 1933: 389–98, Speck 1963, Stone 1986).

Twenty years after the Hudson's Bay Company had sent Samuel Hearne off to the Arctic Ocean shore, the rival North West Company sent Alexander Mackenzie 'in search of a Passage by Water through the N.W. Continent of America from [Lake] Athabasca to the Pacific Ocean' (Lamb 1970: 163). Embarking in birch-bark canoes at the original Fort Chipewyan, on the south shore of Lake Athabasca, on 3 June 1789, Mackenzie's expedition comprised, besides himself, four French-Canadian *voyageurs* or boatmen, two of them accompanied by their wives, an unidentified German, and a Chipewyan 'who had acquired the title English Chief'. This Indian, who had been a follower of Hearne's friend and guide Matonabbee, was accompanied by his two wives and two Indian youths. The canoeists spent a week negotiating the Slave River, with its numerous rapids, between Lake Athabasca and the Great Slave Lake, and took a further nineteen days to make their way across the half-frozen waters of the Great Slave Lake before they entered the Mackenzie and began to descend it. Some time in the first half of July Mackenzie realized that the majestic waterway down which his men were paddling at a rate of 75 miles (120 km) taking him to the Northern or Arctic Ocean and not to the Pacific, as he and the North West Company had hoped. He carried on nonetheless to the spot where the river discharged into the sea 'as it would satisfy People's Curiosity tho' not their Intentions' (Lamb 1970: 17). The 1,500 mile downstream journey took forty days and ended when Mackenzie camped on Garry Island off the Mackenzie Delta in 69° north latitude. Fog and ice prevented him and his men from seeing the sea, but the rise and fall of the water proved that it was tidal. The return voyage upstream was narrowly accomplished before ice closed the route: the expedition was back at Fort Chipewyan on 12 September 1789, 102 days after it had left there, having reached a point on the Arctic Ocean shore some 800 km (500 miles) as the crow flies west of the point reached by Hearne. Four years later, in 1793, Mackenzie set out from a camp on the Peace River and made his way across the Rocky Mountains to the Pacific Ocean (Daniells 1969, Lamb 1970).

THE ADMIRALTY AND THE COMPANY

It was not until after the merging of the North West and Hudson's Bay Companies in 1821 that the fur traders again became involved in Arctic exploration. Now, it was a question of surveying the mainland coast of the North American continent in conjunction at first with the British Admiralty, in order to facilitate the renewed search for the North-West Passage. The company could do little to help Lieutenant John Franklin and Dr John Richardson on their first overland expedition between 1819 and 1822 (Franklin 1824) because it was still at odds with the North West Company. Though he returned to a hero's welcome in England, being promoted to captain by the Admiralty and elected a member of the Royal Society, Franklin had led several of his men to their deaths and the rest to the brink of disaster by starvation. To the Hudson's Bay Company, as evidenced by the future governor of its overseas territories, George Simpson, the naval officers were inexperienced amateurs. 'Lt. Franklin, the officer who commands the party, has not the physical power required. He must have three meals per diem. Tea is indispensable, and with the utmost exertion he cannot walk above eight miles in one day' (Newman 1985: 294). On their next expedition in 1824–7 (Franklin 1828), Franklin and Richardson received valuable aid from the company, which, among other things, seconded chief factor Peter Warren Dease to the expedition. He helped to organize provisions and other supplies, obtain Indian auxiliaries, and build accommodation. This increasing role of the Hudson's Bay Company in Arctic exploration was a result of George Simpson's rise to power; in 1825 he ordered that demands for supplies made by the Franklin expedition 'must be met whatever inconvenience the Service may experience.' (Mackay 1937: 213. On this and the two following sections see Wallace 1980.)

Cooperation between the Admiralty and the company was taken a stage further in 1833, when Captain George Back RN, who had been with Franklin on his two overland expeditions, volunteered to lead a third overland expedition, partly to search for John Ross and his companions, who had entered Lancaster Sound in 1829 in the paddle steamer *Victory* and had not been heard of since. Back, accompanied by an enthusiastic young volunteer called Richard King in the capacity of surgeon-naturalist, was to descend the Great Fish, or as it is now called, Back, River and travel by small boat northwards from its mouth looking for Ross. A second purpose was to map the unexplored section of the Arctic Ocean shore from Point Turnagain eastwards to Fury and Hecla Strait. In the event, Ross and his men were rescued by a whaler, and Back travelled no further than the mouth of the river. This was almost a company expedition: both the governor (John Henry Pelly) and the deputy governor (Nicholas Garry) were members of the expedition's Standing Committee, and the Admiralty 'required and directed' Back to undertake the expedition 'placing yourself for the purpose at the disposition of the Governor and Committee of the Hudson's Bay Company, who have undertaken to furnish you with the requisite resources and supplies' (Back 1836: 18–19). The company ordered its officers to render all possible assistance to Back and put at his disposal 120 ninety-pound bags of pemmican, two boats and two fine canoes. George Simpson even sent Back a letter from himself addressed to 'four of the Commissioned Gentlemen of the North', requiring one or other of them to 'place his services at the command of the expedition'. Soon afterwards the explorers met with Alexander R. M'Leod, the first of the four company officers to whom Simpson's letter was addressed. Although he was on his way home with his family to recuperate from a spell of poor health, he turned back at once together with his wife, three children and servant and joined the expedition. He proved invaluable in assembling stores and equipment, in erecting buildings for winter quarters, in route-finding and in dealings with the Indians, but did not accompany the expedition to the mouth of the Back River (Back 1836, King 1836).

DEASE AND SIMPSON

Determined to complete the delineation of the continent's Arctic shore, begun for the Admiralty by Franklin, Richardson and Back, the Hudson's Bay Company, in the shape of George Simpson, now launched a series of expeditions carried out by its own personnel, using their own travel techniques. The simple equipment, small but well-provisioned parties, swift movement, and ability to live off the land of the company's experienced officers on the spot now replaced the clumsy, heavy-weight expeditions of novices to the north hitherto sent out from England. An ideal mix of two leaders was hit on by governor George Simpson for the first of these expeditions, the instructions for which he himself drew up. The experienced Peter W. Dease, who had participated in Franklin's second overland expedition, was to be accompanied by his own cousin, an impetuous, energetic, brilliant (if arrogant and ambitious) Scot still in his twenties, Thomas Simpson. Dease and Simpson set out from Fort Chipewyan on Lake Athabasca on 1 June 1837 with twelve or fourteen men. Simpson's skill and determination as an Arctic traveller had been demonstrated that winter, when he sledged and snow-shoed the 1,277 miles (2,043 km) from Red River south of Winnipeg to join Dease at Fort Chipewyan in forty-six days, making a daily average of 28 miles (44 km) (Simpson, A. 1845: 214). The expedition made its way down the Mackenzie in two boats and a canoe and explored the coast westwards from that river's delta, following in the footsteps of Franklin's first expedition as far as Return Reef, but continuing beyond Franklin's furthest to Point Barrow, which Simpson and five others reached on foot and in a borrowed Eskimo umiak on 4 August 1837, having left Dease some days' march behind with the expedition's boats. The two wrote their own and their friends' names on the map all along the western Arctic coast. Between Return Reef and Point Barrow at least seventeen Hudson's Bay Company men were commemorated, for example Dease Inlet, Cape Simpson (named after the governor George Simpson), and the Colville River (named after London committee man Andrew Colvile; Map 16). Thus in 1837 Dease and Simpson had completed the charting of the Arctic Ocean shore from its western end as far east as the mouth of the Coppermine. (In 1826 a party from HMS *Blossom*, Captain F.W. Beechey, had followed the coast from Icy Cape to Point Barrow, and Richardson in the same year had mapped the coast from the Mackenzie Delta to the mouth of the Coppermine.) The party spent the winter of 1837/8 on the Great Bear Lake (Map 36). Though they were initially on short rations, by midwinter Simpson, who, as he tells us, 'highly relished the animation of the chase' (1843: 206), was providing his companions with caribou meat and fish on an unbelievably lavish scale (Simpson 1843: 218).

> . . . The daily ration served out to each man was increased from eight to ten, and to some individuals twelve pounds of venison; or, when they could be got, four or five white-fish weighing from fifteen to twenty pounds. This quantity of solid food, immoderate as it may appear, does not exceed the average standard of the country; and ought certainly to appease even the inordinate appetite of a French Canadian.

In 1838 Dease and Simpson travelled down the Coppermine River to the Arctic shore and explored eastwards along the south shore of Dease Strait. Disappointingly, they could get only about 60 miles (96 km) beyond Franklin's expedition of 1821, namely Point Turnagain. From Cape Alexander on the Kent Peninsula, looking across Dease Strait, Simpson saw and named Victoria Island after his new queen. In 1839, again with a twelve-man party, Simpson and Dease repeated the 1838 voyage. This time Coronation Gulf was nearly free of ice before the end of July, and it was possible to map the northern coast of the continent as far as the mouth of the Great Fish or Back River (Map 16) and even some way beyond, proving *en route* the insularity of King William Island and making 'by far the longest voyage ever performed in boats on the Polar Sea' (Simpson, T. 1843: 388). On his three celebrated journeys with Dease, Simpson seems to have done the surveying, drawn the maps, and to have provided the audacity and persistence which ensured success, often travelling ahead of his companion, who acted more as organizer and wise man. Simpson's considerable literary skills are apparent in his well-written *Narrative of the discoveries on the north coast of America effected by the officers of the Hudson's Bay Company during the years 1836–1839* (Simpson, T. 1843). The Hudson's Bay Company now approved his proposed solo expedition, in which he hoped 'to bear the Honourable Company's flag fairly through and out of the Polar Sea' (Mackay 1937: 265), but Thomas Simpson was killed in a fracas with the métis he was travelling with in the summer of 1840 (Stefansson 1939: 48–101, Simpson, A. 1845: 352–73, and Ballantyne 1857).

Map 17. *Canada's mainland Arctic coast.*

JOHN RAE

It was not until 1844 that George Simpson found a successor for Dease and Simpson to chart the still unexplored eastern section of the Arctic shore which included Boothia, still thought by some to be an island, and the Gulf of Boothia. That successor was a thirty-two-year-old Edinburgh-trained doctor from Orkney who had served as Hudson's Bay Company surgeon at Moose Factory in James Bay (Map 16) for ten years and was not only 'very good-looking' but could 'walk 100 miles easily in 2 days' (Rich 1953: xviii; on Rae, see Richards 1985). According to R.M. Ballantyne (1857: 226), who served in the Hudson's Bay Company in the 1840s before becoming a writer of boys' adventure stories, Rae was 'well accustomed to the life he will have to lead, and enters upon it not with the vague and uncertain notions of Back and Franklin, but with a pretty correct apprehension of the probable routine of procedure, and the experience of a great many years spent in the service of the Hudson's Bay Company'.

Rae's first Arctic expedition (Rae 1850), which was planned in the first place by George Simpson, started from York Factory on 13 June 1846 and returned there on 6 September 1847. It was a turning point in the history of Arctic exploration. Rae took two boats specially built for the expedition at York Factory, each about 22 ft (7 m) long and 7½ ft (2.5 m) broad, and twelve men: four Orkneymen, a Shetlander, one man from Ross-shire, two French-Canadians, a

Plate 9. John Rae, medical doctor, chief factor of the Hudson's Bay Company and arguably the greatest British Arctic explorer in the nineteenth century. It was he who first discovered the fate of John Franklin and his men. He was an Orkney man, born 1813, died in London in 1893. The portrait shown here is by courtesy of the National Portrait Gallery.

métis, an Indian hunter, and two Eskimo interpreters picked up at Churchill. He was successful in mapping another 960 km (600 miles) of hitherto unexplored coast on either shore of the Gulf of Boothia, from Lord Mayor Bay on the west, to just south of Cape Englefield on the east coast, and in confirming that Boothia was not an island but a peninsula. This exploration was based at a stone house he had built at the head of Repulse Bay, where he spent the winter of 1846/7. Rae was an excellent shot and he and his companions found game plentiful enough. In September 1846 their bag was 63 reindeer, 5 hares, 1 seal, 172 partridges and 116 salmon and trout. The house was still standing in 1927 (Hunter 1983: 48) but has since been destroyed by vandals. Although Rae's Arctic travels were in the tradition of those of his immediate predecessors in the Hudson's Bay Company, Dease and Simpson, he made at least two significant innovations, in 1846–7, which gave him a unique standing among Arctic explorers of his day. First, his expedition was almost entirely self-sufficient in food and fuel; he and his men even returned home with eight bags of pemmican and four of flour, unused, out of their original supplies. Second, instead of returning to winter quarters within the forest where log cabins could be constructed, Rae wintered successfully on the Arctic shore far beyond the forest, where winter would cause the minimum interruption to the work of exploring. This was resumed, after the winter, on 5 April 1847. Rae's success was due partly to his adoption of Eskimo travelling techniques, especially the snow house, which he and his men learned to construct and made much use of.

Rae's work of Arctic exploration and coastal surveying for the Hudson's Bay Company was interrupted in 1847–8 and 1850–1 when he was employed by the admiralty in the search for the missing Franklin expedition (see Chapter 7), but he was still intent on completing the mapping of the Arctic shore of continental north America for the Hudson's Bay Company, the more so because the Admiralty had refused to accept his discovery of the peninsularity of Boothia. His proposals were accepted by the company, and he duly began to chart the so far unexplored west coast of Boothia Peninsula in 1854. But he was forced by bad weather and soft snow to turn back some distance short of the western end of Bellot Strait, leaving at least 240 km (150 miles) of Boothia's west coast unexplored. As a consolation prize he obtained information about Franklin's fate from some Eskimos he met with, and this was soon reinforced by pieces of silver plate stamped with Franklin's and his officers' names and initials, and other articles which had been recovered from corpses of white men. Thus at the end of October 1854 Rae arrived in London as the discoverer of the fate of Franklin. When he retired from the Hudson's Bay Company soon afterwards, he wrote that he had devoted 'eight summers and four winters' to 'Arctic survey and research', had 'seen more of the Arctic coast of America than any man living', and had 'individually traced as much new coast as Dease and Simpson did jointly' (Rich 1953: 293). Although some of Rae's work was done on behalf of the Admiralty, the Hudson's Bay Company could nonetheless rightly boast that, in the first half of the nineteenth century, it had made a more substantial contribution than the Royal Navy to the exploration and mapping of the north American continental coast.

THE BAY IN THE TWENTIETH CENTURY

After 1869, when it lost its fur-trading monopoly, the Hudson's Bay Company diversified its activities while shifting many of them northwards into the Arctic. In the early twentieth century its fortunes rose as it sold hundreds of thousands of acres of land to farm purchasers in the Canadian West and to urban settlers in newly emerging cities like Edmonton and Calgary, and used the proceeds to build large, modern department stores in these and other cities. Later, smaller shops were opened in almost every Arctic settlement. In 1920, the Canadian Arctic explorer Vilhjalmur Stefansson launched a scheme for the domestication of reindeer in the eastern Canadian Arctic which was modelled on the United States' government's efforts to make some of the Alaskan Inuit into reindeer herders. These efforts had begun in 1891 and were still continuing, with some success (Andrews 1939). Now Stefansson, having obtained a lease of 295,077 sq km (113,900 square miles) in south-west Baffin Island from the Canadian government, persuaded the Hudson's Bay Company in London to set up a Canadian subsidiary called the Hudson's Bay Reindeer Company which would import reindeer and their herders from Norway in the hope of establishing a herd in southern Baffin Island. In the summer of 1921, 687 reindeer were purchased in Norway, six Sami families were signed on as herders, and in November that year the deer and the Sami were disembarked in Baffin Island. But the project failed lamentably, partly because of insufficient good reindeer pasturage in the area. By June 1922 only 210 deer remained alive, scattered and ever dwindling in number. By 1935 the Hudson's Bay Reindeer Company's capital was exhausted and the company's shares had become worthless: a year later it was defunct (Diubaldo 1978: 147–60).

Meanwhile, the fur trade had been aggressively pushed by the Hudson's Bay Company further north in eastern Baffin Island and along the western Arctic coast, fuelled by the hunt for the Arctic fox in place of the beaver, and using Inuit in place of Indian trappers (Godsell 1951: 273, Zaslow 1981: 69–73). Trading posts opened at Chesterfield Inlet, Repulse Bay, Baker Lake and Eskimo Point between 1912 and 1924, at Aklavik in the Mackenzie Delta shortly before the First World War, at Lake Harbour, Cape Dorset and Frobisher Bay, now Iqaluit, between 1911 and 1914, and at Pond Inlet and Arctic Bay in 1921 and 1926. This penetration into the eastern Arctic was converted into a monopoly when, mainly in the 1920s, other firms trading in the area were bought up, principal among them H.T. Munn, which had trapping stations at Pangnirtung and Pond Inlet, Robert Kinnes of Dundee, the Moravian Mission which traded in Labrador, and Paris-based Revillon Frères (Munn 1932). In the western Arctic the Hudson's Bay Company had to compete with other firms like the Canalaska Trading Company, with five posts between Herschel Island and Gjøa Haven; and Kris Klengenberg, trading at Rymer Point in south-west Victoria Island and elsewhere (MacInnes 1932). This lasted until the Hudson's Bay Company purchased their assets in the 1920s and 1930s. In the 1930s the company was contracted by the Canadian government to transport the Eastern Arctic Patrol on the annual supply ship to its eastern Arctic posts. This was the *Nascopie*, which left Montreal every year on a three-month voyage. In 1937 the RMS *Nascopie* met another company

Plate 10. Lake Harbour, Baffin Island, photographed shortly before the outbreak of the Second World War in 1939, showing the Hudson's Bay Company compound and buildings. This post was founded in 1911. The company's thousand-ton supply ship and icebreaker, the RMS Nascopie, *is at anchor in the harbour. (From Finnie 1944: 144–5.)*

ship, the *Aklavik*, which had sailed from the western Canadian Arctic, on 1 September at Bellot Strait. It was on this occasion that a new company post, to be called Fort Ross, was established on Bellot Strait: within a week a dwelling house had been erected, the company flag was flying, the chimney smoking, and stores deposited in the warehouse (Anderson 1961). An optimistic historian has asserted that this event inaugurated 'the commercial use of the North-West Passage' (Cooke 1981: 56). Since the Second World War the Hudson's Bay Company has contrived to survive the decline and collapse of the fur trade, once its *raison d'être*. In 1991 it even ceased altogether to sell furs in its four hundred department stores.

EARLY TRADING IN GREENLAND

The earliest-recorded contacts between Greenlanders and Europeans in modern times, as opposed to contacts with Norse settlers in medieval times, took place somewhere near present-day Nuuk on 29 and 30 July 1585 during the Devonshire seaman John Davis's first voyage in search of the North-West Passage (Markham 1880: 8–9; see also Chapter 3 above). The Greenlanders were not prepared for bartering: they traded the weapons, kayaks and sealskin and birdskin clothing they were using or wearing at the time in return for anything Davis and his men gave them. But a quarter of a century later, on 28 May 1612, in the same place, the Greenlanders who paddled out to James Hall's ships were intent on barter. They brought with them 'pieces of unicorn horn, with other trifles which they did barter with us for old iron' (Markham 1881: 13). By 1656 this bartering was well developed. In that year a ship fitted out at Vlissingen in Zeeland, skippered, according to the French source, by Nicholas 'Tunes', who may have been a Dane called Tønnes or a Dutchman called Theunisz, visited the Nuuk area to trade with the natives and brought back a precious cargo: several narwhal tusks of great value, nine hundred large seal skins, bundles of whalebone (baleen), Inuit fur clothing, implements and weapons, as well as kayaks and an umiak (Gad 1970: 256, de Jong 1978: 185–6). Until the beginning of the eighteenth century sporadic trading voyages to west Greenland were made by Dutch and Danish ships, but by the time the mayor of Hamburg, Johann Anderson, compiled his *Reports from Iceland, Greenland and Davis Strait* from information supplied by Dutch and other skippers in 1746 (Anderson 1756: 225), these voyages had become annual and were being reinforced by the permanent Norwegian-Danish presence in west Greenland, from 1721 onwards, of Hans Egede and other missionaries. Although Anderson supposed that the Greenlanders had no trade among themselves, they had in fact developed a thriving exchange economy, based on a network of bartering (or *aasivik*) places up and down the coast, where soapstone lamps and pots made in the Nuuk area, baleen, fox skins and other commodities, were exchanged. This trading system was in part disrupted by the arrival of European traders (Gulløv 1987). According to Anderson, these procured train oil, whalebone, narwhal tusks and skins of seals, foxes and reindeer from the Greenlanders in exchange for wool and linen cloth, Icelandic socks and gloves, copper and tin kettles, knives, scissors, needles and some iron and wood.

THE ROYAL GREENLAND TRADE

As early as 1703 a detailed proposal was submitted to the Danish king by the Icelander Arngrimur Thorkelsson Vídalín for the resumption of connections between the Danish-Norwegian crown and Greenland: a royal chartered company was to be founded with permission to establish a colony of five hundred families there. The 'lost' Norse colony was to be searched for, trade with the Greenlanders was to be organized using mirrors, needles, knives, scissors, bells 'and other trifles which dazzle the eyes', as well as mead or brandy, and they were to be converted to Christianity (Gad 1973: 1–5). These ideas found fruit in a series of short-lived trading companies, all of them chartered by the Danish crown: the Bergen Greenland Company of 1723, based in Bergen, Norway; the Copenhagen merchant Jacob Severin's Greenland Trading Company of 1734; and the General Trading Company of 1747, to which the Greenland trade was transferred in 1749–50. Finally, when the General Trading Company was abolished in 1774, it was replaced by the Royal Greenland Trading Company (Den kongelige grønlandske Handel or KGH) or Royal Greenland Trade for short, which has survived in altered form to the present day (Bobé 1929, Krabbe 1930, Gad 1973, Gad 1982, Gad 1984, Tejsen 1977, Sørensen 1983).

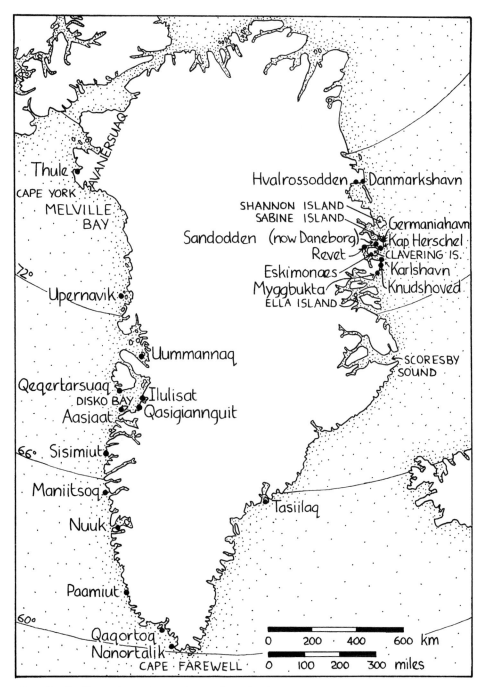

Map 18. Trading and trapping stations in Greenland.

The Royal Greenland Trading Company, later called the Royal Greenland Trade Department, differed in important respects from the Hudson's Bay Company. The Greenland company was entirely controlled and owned by the state, and was based from the first on the conversion of the Greenlanders to Christianity. Both companies depended on a network of trading stations. While the Hudson's Bay Company's posts were visited once or twice annually by Indians merely for the purpose of trading, only a few of whom, the so-called 'Home Guard', actually lived in them, in Greenland the trading stations, often coinciding with missions and later called colonies, functioned as residential centres for the Greenlanders, whose former nomadic way of life was exchanged for a sedentary one. As Table 2 shows, most of the present-day municipalities of west Greenland derive from colonies founded in the eighteenth century, several of them by Jacob Severin. Unlike the Hudson's Bay Company, which concentrated mainly on furs, the Greenland Company traded for a wider range of products, all of them truly Arctic. Although both companies depended for their success on a monopoly protected by the government, that of the Greenland Company was the more effective and enduring because it was state-owned. A series of Danish royal proclamations during the eighteenth century, supported by other measures, gradually squeezed out the Dutch traders, who were especially active in west Greenland in the first half of the century (Bobé 1915, Dekker 1975), by closing the coast and inshore waters to them but permitting offshore whaling. These royal proclamations climaxed in the decree of 1776 which gave the Royal Greenland Trade exclusive rights of trading 'with the colonies and trading posts that are already established or that may hereafter be established in Greenland and the adjacent islands in Davis Strait and Disko Bay' (Gad 1973: 382; see also Isachsen 1925: 185–6). Another way in which the Greenland Company differed from that of Hudson's Bay was that, unlike the Hudson's Bay Company, it was not in essence a profit-making organization, though until 1950 Greenland was expected to pay for itself. This meant that the cost of maintaining missionaries and all other expenses had to be met by the company from the sale of its Greenlandic products.

Danish name	Greenlandic name	Date of foundation	Population 1991
Godthåb	Nuuk	1728	12,657
Christianshåb	Qasigiannguit	1734	1,730
Jakobshavn	Ilulissat	1741	4,519
Frederikshåb	Paamiut	1742	2,499
Sukkertoppen	Maniitsoq	1755	4,120
Egedesminde	Aasiaat	1759	3,567
Umanak	Uummannaq	1763	2,611
Holsteinsborg	Sisimiut	1764	5,172
Upernavik	Upernavik	1769	2,445
Godhavn	Qeqertarsuaq	1773	1,160
Julianehåb	Qaqortoq	1775	3,565
Nanortalik	Nanortalik	1797	2,661

Table 2.   Some modern west Greenland municipalities founded as colonies before 1800, based on Stefansson 1943: 176, Grønland 1990. Statistisk Årbog 1991: 338, Tejsen 1977.

As with the Hudson's Bay Company, the Royal Greenland Trade's entire structure was based on the trader, the official effectively in charge of each colony and trading post. The detailed instructions regulating his behaviour and activities, issued on 19 April 1782, which remained in force for almost a century, give an idea of the principles, some enlightened, some now seeming prudish or puritanical, which governed the directors' notions of the correct colonial administration of Greenland. They also underline the many skills required by an effective trader. Historian Louis Bobé summarized these instructions as follows (1929: 133–5; see too Gad 1982: 22–8 and Lidegaard 1991: 113–15):

The trader was earnestly instructed to associate with the Greenlanders in a sensible and careful manner, to distribute them among the best sealing grounds, to encourage them to diligence, economy and the trades which, according to the season, must be considered most profitable, to instruct them in fishing and the right manner of intercourse, to exhort them to enter into partnership or reasonable contracts with the Danish whalers, when and where it was required by circumstances; in short, to attend to their interests in all matters. Without offending the inhabitants or depriving them of necessities, the trader should purchase betimes and send home by the first vessel all products available within his district. Further he should, to the best of his ability, oppose illicit trading and, therefore, desist from all private trade whether with Europeans or with Greenlanders, his own people or foreigners. Finally he should keep regular accounts and a daily journal. . . .

In order to prevent immoral intercourse between the Greenlanders and sailors spending the winter in Greenland, and other Europeans, the trader, together with the missionary, should select elderly women to attend to their wants. These were to be needy widows and wives of poor breadwinners, whereas especially young Greenland women should, if possible, be exempt from accompanying Europeans on their voyages, so as not to be led into temptation. Under pain of the most severe punishment it was forbidden to make the inhabitants drunk with beer and spirits; also, to treat them freely to coffee, tea and other European articles, as such things would impair their health, spoil their manner of living and incline them to spend their days in the houses of the Europeans. It was forbidden to give the Greenlanders gin, the penalty for this being 10 rigsdaler or corporal punishment. The crews were not allowed to while away their time in the houses of the Greenlanders, nor to appear there at suspicious hours – late at night or early in the morning, or when the husbands were out sealing or fishing – but only in their lawful business and with the permission of the trader. Anyone who was found guilty of immoral conduct and, due warning being given, persevered therein, should be sent home by the first vessel. The father of illegitimate children should, until such children had completed their twelfth year, pay six rigsdaler a year for their maintenance, and was not permitted to leave the service of the trading company until the sum was paid in full. If the paternity were not established until later, the father should, wherever he was found, by legal prosecution be made to pay the whole sum or work it off.

The instructions, further, contain a provision on the preservation of the eiderduck which is in itself very interesting. When collecting down, care should be taken not to frighten away the birds or to chase them from the places where they were still to be found. The trader should, in a kind and sensible manner, persuade the Greenlanders not to ill-treat the young of these birds or take away their eggs without any reason, as frequently happened. Danes were not allowed to collect eiderdown, as this was reserved for the Greenlanders; neither were they, in the brooding period, allowed to destroy or chase away the birds by firing at them, to kill their young or to take away their eggs. Infringements of these regulations were punished with fines of 2–10 rigsdaler.

A hundred years after the foundation of the royal trading monopoly in Greenland, the leading nineteenth-century Danish administrator in Greenland, Henrik Rink, was enthusiastic about the benefits it brought to the Greenlanders. He saw it as a means of protecting them from the exploitation which he thought would inevitably occur in an open market. He reckoned that the Greenlanders were paid between a fifth and a quarter of the value of their products in the European market, and were charged only 20 per cent above cost price for goods sold to them. For example, in 1870–4 goods to the value of £23,844 per annum were sold to the Greenlanders in return for Greenlandic products worth £45,600. The company's transport costs amounted to £8,879 p.a., so the annual revenue available for all other expenses was £12,859. Transport costs included the fleet of nine ships travelling between Denmark and Greenland, and along the west coast of Greenland between the principal stations and their satellite outposts, as well as the cost of maintaining the Greenlandic postal service. In winter letters were delivered in the north by dog sledge, otherwise by kayak post (Rink 1877: 287):

> Between the extreme points Julianehaab [Qaqortoq] and Umanak [Uummannaq], express posts may be sent in summer for any distance required. The whole route, under favourable circumstances, would take about five weeks, and the expense amount to about £16. No postage at all is paid for private letters sent by mails of the Royal Trade. The kayakers generally are rather proud of being trusted with the conveyance of letters. To avoid mischief by accidents, two kayakers are generally employed at the same time. Post-kayakers may be recognized at a great distance by their rowing closely abreast of each other, neither deviating from their course nor throwing their javelin, as the kayakers have the habit of doing merely as a pastime. When these kayakers are perceived, it is directly announced by shouting *paortut* [paartoq], and the people shout louder than usual when the postmen, raising their paddles, indicate that they bring tidings of a ship having arrived from abroad.

As director of the Royal Greenland Trade from 1871 to 1882 Rink was virtual governor of Greenland, for he and his staff managed the civil government of the country along with its trade. The two senior officials under the governor, the inspectors, one in charge of the northern part of west Greenland, the other the southern, also acted as magistrates. Something over two hundred personnel in all represented the company's staff in Greenland. There were eleven agents – sometimes called governors – in charge of the chief stations, aided by eighteen clerks, as well as 182 traders in charge of the outposts, not to mention boatswains, craftsmen, sailors and labourers, including apprentices (Rink 1877: 282). Rink lists the average annual exports from Greenland in the period 1853–72 as follows (pp. 312–13):

train oil	1,185	barrels
seal skins	35,439	
fox skins	1,436	
bear skins	41	
waterproof jackets	811	
waterproof trousers	1,003	
raw eiderdown	3,533	lb
feathers	6,900	lb
whalebone	2,300	lb
dried codfish	22,500	lb
narwhal tusks	500	lb
walrus tusks	87	lb
reindeer skins	1,817	

Just as the Hudson's Bay Company, faced with the far-reaching changes which began in the 1850s and brought modern Canada into existence, refused to die but chose to transform itself, so the Royal Greenland Trade has survived in present-day Greenland in a different form. Shorn of its general administrative functions in the early twentieth century, like the Hudson's Bay Company it replaced its trading posts with retail shops and opened up many new lines of business. As early as 1906 it introduced sheep into south Greenland from Iceland. From 1933 onwards it pioneered the prawn and shrimp fisheries at Sisimiut and in Disko Bay. In 1952 it took a leaf out of the Hudson's Bay Company's notebook and opened a reindeer breeding station near Nuuk, which was later taken over by private reindeer herders. More recently, often under the brand name Royal Greenland, frozen salmon, halibut, cod fillets, prawns and other Greenlandic fishery products have been exported world-wide, while narwhal skin or *mattak*, whalemeat, and other products of northern hunting have been marketed in the growing towns of south-west Greenland. In the early 1970s a new product was introduced called Ice Cap Rocks, which were soon being sold in supermarkets all over the world. These small lumps of ice for use in cocktails and other drinks are quarried at Ilulissat 'Icy Mountains' (formerly Jakobshavn), on Greenland's west coast. A booklet produced by the company explains their origins (Christiansen 1973: 29):

Here . . . nature has created the largest iceworks in the world. A glacier spews out more than 20 million tons of Ice Cap into the sea every 24 hours. Majestic icebergs sail on the water and calve with a thunderous crash. This is where the Royal Greenland Trade Department obtains its 'Ice Cap Rocks'. Enormous blocks of it are taken into tow at the glacier face and brought to the processing plant in Jakobshavn. Here they are rinsed in crystal clear water, crushed, packaged ready for the consumer, and sent in refrigerated ships to Denmark for export far and wide.

The little lumps of ice actually consist of snow which fell on the Greenland Ice Cap millenniums ago. Snow from the times of Alexander the Great has undergone a lot of change in the milling process in the glacier, to emerge as sparkling icebergs. It has been under enormous pressure and transformed into the hardest of ice imaginable, with tiny bubbles of air imprisoned in it and set free in the drink to an audible splutter and fizz. . . .

Because of its hardness, this ice melts very much slower than ordinary ice cubes do, and therefore cools off a drink without watering it down. It will retain its shape in the ice bucket without melting together into an unmanageable mass.

Although officially in 1950 the Royal Greenland Trade's 'monopoly was abolished and Greenland was opened up for free intercourse with the rest of the world' (Petersen and Staffeldt 1978), in practice private enterprise and investment was slow to come, even from Danes and Greenlanders, and there was virtually none from other countries. The company, or department, retained, and for the most part still retains, full control of maritime communications between Greenland and Denmark, the Greenland postal services, the monetary system, savings banks, and the airport and hotel at Søndre Strømfjord (now Kangerlussuaq; Map 30 below). Later in the 1950s it was granted the sole right to import spirits, wine, cigarettes and sweets from Denmark into Greenland and paid and passed on the government duty on them in so doing. The privatization, or taking over by individual Danes or Greenlanders, of the retail trade in Greenland, proceeded slowly: in 1954 the company still owned 90 per cent of this trade; in 1960, 80 per cent; but in the 1970s more and more shops were opened by Greenlandic co-operatives and by 1974, for example, all the bakeries were managed by Greenlanders (Tejsen 1977). Meanwhile, the company was increasingly staffed by Greenlanders rather than Danes. By 1976, 92 per cent of its 4,483 staff were Greenlanders (Petersen and Staffeldt 1978: 264), and in 1985–6 the Royal Greenland Trade Department was handed over in its entirety to the government of Greenland, known to Danes as the Greenland Home Rule Authorities or Administration. As from 1 January 1986 the Royal Trade had a new Greenlandic name, Kalaallit Niuerfiat, 'Greenland Trade', and was based at Nuuk in Greenland instead of in Copenhagen. It continues to play a significant role in the Greenlandic economy, controlling about half the country's retail trade, a larger slice of the wholesale trade, and still retaining shipping, postal services, and the monopoly of imported alcoholic beverages, tobacco and sweets. As to the products of the hunt, once the lifeblood of the Royal Greenland Trade, these are now handled by the Greenland government's processing division. In 1990 this agency exported 53,465 seal skins, valued at nearly 15 million Danish crowns, 289 Arctic fox skins worth 43,000 crowns, and 92 Polar bear skins worth over half a million crowns (Grønland 1990 Statistisk Årbog 1991: 117–20, 129–33, 393–4).

BEYOND THE MONOPOLY IN NORTH AND EAST GREENLAND

Although the monopoly enjoyed by the Royal Greenland Trade endured for nearly a century after the Hudson's Bay Company's had been abolished, it covered a much more restricted area, being limited to the strip of land along Greenland's west coast as far north as Melville Bay. As long ago as 1863 the Danish government granted to Englishman Joseph W. Tayler, representing Anthony Gibbs and Sons of London, a thirty-year monopoly in the whole of east Greenland to hunt, fish, mine and trade with natives. The East Greenland Trade minted its own coins and adopted its own flag, but ice prevented its ships from ever reaching east Greenland (Sømod 1991). In the twentieth century, furs and ivory were obtained in two parts of Greenland, namely Avanersuaq in the north-west, formerly called the Thule District, and in north-east Greenland – in neither case by the Royal Greenland Trade.

Avanersuaq, or north-west Greenland, was not formally annexed by Denmark until 1937. Until then it was a traders' no-man's-land, first exploited in the 1890s when Scottish whaling captains and American explorers Robert Peary and Frederick Cook bartered pipes, tobacco, knives, rifles and ammunition and other manufactured articles, as well as wood for kayaks and sledges, with the 250 or so local Inuhuit Eskimos in exchange for bear and Arctic fox skins, and walrus and narwhal tusks (Vaughan 1987). This flourishing trade was developed and regularized by Danish explorers Knud Rasmussen and Peter Freuchen, who in 1910 opened their own private trading post which they called the Cape York Thule Station. It was a few hundred metres from the Inuhuit settlement of Uummannaq near the south shore of Wolstenholme Fjord and some 130 km (80 miles) round the coast northwards from Cape York. During the next two decades, boom years for the Inuhuit's principal trading commodity, Arctic fox furs, the station made substantial profits which helped to fund Rasmussen's five famous 'Thule' Expeditions. It purchased two ships for his trading company, and provided the Inuhuit with medical services. By the time the Danish state took over Avanersuaq, and the Royal Greenland Trade took over the Thule Trading Station, in 1937, the Inuhuit's lifestyle had been transformed by the introduction of commercially produced foods, a money economy, Christianity, European clothing and laws, and a written language (West Greenlandic) (Vaughan 1991).

In 1894 a Danish colony was established in the only area then inhabited by Greenlanders on the east coast of Greenland, at Ammassalik, now Tasiilaq, and the Royal Greenland Trading Monopoly was extended to cover trade with the east Greenlanders living there. But most of the east Greenland coast was uninhabited, and from the beginning of the twentieth century until the outbreak of the Second World War in 1939 both Danish and Norwegian private trappers operated there, especially between Scoresby Sound (70° north latitude) and Germania Land (78° north). A 1924 treaty between Denmark and Norway (Lauritsen 1984: 19–21) permitted the Norwegians to continue these trapping activities for the next twenty years. In an exchange of notes accompanying the treaty, the Danes claimed sovereignty over the area, while the Norwegians insisted that it was *terra nullius* – a no-man's-land (Skeie 1931: 50–1). In spite of this treaty, a serious dispute between Denmark and Norway developed in the 1920s over the sovereignty of Greenland

and came to a head in 1930–2. The Norwegian government claimed on 10 July 1931 to have occupied and placed under its own sovereignty a large slice of north-east Greenland north of Scoresby Sound, to be called Eirik the Red's Land, and on 12 July 1932 similarly claimed the coastal area of south-east Greenland from 60° 30' north to 63° 40', that is most of the coast between Cape Farewell and Tasiilaq. The Danes countered by despatching to the disputed area north of Scoresby Sound what was described in 1934 as 'the greatest scientific expedition that has ever wintered in either the Arctic or Antarctic' (Hayes 1937: 191). The Norwegians may be forgiven for likening it to a military expedition; it was active from 1930 to 1934 and was credited with three ships, twelve motorboats, two seaplanes and over a hundred staff. The dispute, which was settled in 1933 in Denmark's favour by a judgement of the Permanent Court of International Justice in The Hague, seems not at all to have bothered the trappers themselves, who had more important problems to attend to than the largely theoretical one of the sovereignty of the remote areas of Greenland in which they were struggling to earn a living (Skeie 1931, Smedal 1931, Berlin 1932, Horn 1939).

The Norwegian and Danish trappers in east Greenland built huts of wood, stone or turves at widely scattered points, using larger ones as winter homes and as bases for their trapping activities, and smaller ones as refuges while travelling by dog sledge to visit traps. They hunted bears with rifles and trapped Arctic foxes with steel or other traps sometimes buried in the snow, usually near a cache of walrus or bear meat put down beforehand as bait. These traps would be set out at intervals over a distance of 100 km (62 miles) or more and had to be visited regularly. In a good winter a good catch could amount to four hundred fox skins. Overwintering Norwegian trappers had been doing this since the 1820s on Spitsbergen (Lønø 1972, 1976), where they inherited the traditional way of life of the promyshlenniks from Pomory'e. These Russians wintered and trapped there from around 1700 until the disastrous winter of 1851/2, when eleven of eighteen Russian trappers died of scurvy in Raudfjord (Red Bay; Map 10) (Conway 1906: 275–6). Norwegians first overwintered ashore in east Greenland in 1908/9 and 1909/10, and, after a pause, resumed annual overwinterings in 1922, when they built a radio station at Myggbukta (Map 18) where several trappers wintered that year. In 1923, when the *Conrad Holmboe* became beset in the ice and could not relieve them, these men started home in the *Anni*, but she and her passengers and crew were lost in the ice without trace (Rodahl 1946: 97). In the same disastrous autumn the twenty-one Danes aboard the *Teddy* were fortunate to escape with their lives to Tasiilaq after their ship had drifted helplessly in the ice for 710 miles (1,140 km) in seventy-one days and then had to be abandoned in a sinking condition (Dahl 1925, Hayes 1937: 193–201). Quite apart from the fact that drifting ice made east Greenland's inshore waters among the most dangerous and difficult to access in the world, the winter life of these hardy trappers was lonely and fraught with danger. At the isolated trapping station called Revet, on the mainland opposite Clavering Island, the renowned Norwegian trapper Gerhard Antonsen earned the sobriquet 'King of Revet' by living there alone during seven winters in succession from 1932 (Rodahl 1946: 33). Another well-known Norwegian trapper, Hallvard Devold (1940), almost lost his life in curious

Plate 11. The winter's catch of white and blue Arctic fox pelts at a Norwegian trapping station in east Greenland in the 1920s. The trapper's station is visible on the left behind the line of suspended furs. Around him in the snow he has arranged some white wolf skins. (From Drastrup 1932: 89.)

circumstances in 1929. He was leading a ten-man expedition for the firm Arktisk Næringsdrift A/S, and using the then unoccupied Danish trapping station at Karlshavn as a refuge hut while inspecting his line of fox traps north of Myggbukta. On one midwinter visit, arriving in a snowstorm in the dark, he was amazed to find that it had gone. When he had left it a month before a fire had still been burning in the stove, and a spark must somehow have ignited the gunpowder which the Danes had stored in the loft with other supplies. Devold only just managed to make the long journey back that night to the next hut south (Drastrup 1932: 30–1, Rogne 1981: 66). The Danish trapper who reported this incident, Elmar Drastrup, has described his visit to the trapping station at Cape Herschel in 1931 which was occupied by two Norwegians, Herman Andresen and Knut Røbekk. (What follows is translated by the author from Drastrup 1932: 20; see too Rogne 1981: 108.)

> Andresen and Røbekk were great hunters and tough customers. They talked much about foxes and bears, fur prices and trapping. And they rolled a cigarette and baked bread as only a veteran trapper could, for they had both lived a long time where cigarettes and bread were life's keenest pleasures. . . . They had the

country's swiftest and strongest dogs, the best sledges, the longest whip and the biggest catch. They knew bears, and cold, and storm, and the darkness. Their hair was blond and their eyes blue. They had long legs and big lungs, and a day's march of 100 km [62 miles] was simply nothing. They said so themselves.

A few months later tragedy overtook one of these fine fellows. When Andresen got back to Cape Herschel for Christmas from a trapping trip to the north there was no sign of his companion, the seventeen-year-old Røbekk, who should have arrived there from Eskimonaes. He feared the worst, but searched in vain until the spring of 1932, when he eventually found Røbekk's body, those of his dogs, and his sledge, frozen in ice offshore. He chopped Røbekk's body out of the ice and took it back to Cape Herschel for burial. Going through new ice in the winter darkness was an almost routine accident.

By 1939 there were fifteen Norwegian trapping stations along the east Greenland coast between 71° 30' and 77° 30' north latitude, and 128 refuge huts spaced out between them, 10–30 km (6–18 miles) apart. Danish trapping in the area (Lauritsen 1984) started in 1919 when Hans Ludwig Jensen, who had been a member of the famous *Danmark* Expedition to north-east Greenland in 1906–8, founded the East Greenland Company, which sent out an annual vessel for several years after 1919. The loss of the company ship *Teddy* in 1923, following the loss of its first ship, the *Dagny*, in 1920, brought about its liquidation in 1924. It had built trapping stations at Danmarkshavn, Hvalrossodden, Germaniahavn, Sandodden and Karlshavn (Map 18). In 1929 another Danish company, the East Greenland Nanok Company (Østgrønlandsk Fangstkompagni Nanok A/S) (*nanok* or *nanoq* is the Greenlandic word for the Polar bear), started operations and took over its predecessor's trapping stations, except for Karlshavn which, as related above, had inadvertently been burnt down. The Nanok Company replaced it in 1930 with a new station called Knudshoved, and built more than fifty new huts and trapping stations during the 1930s. It introduced conservation measures, laying down close seasons for bear shooting (except in emergencies) and fox trapping, prohibiting the use of poison, and insisting that traps be visited daily. Walrus were not to be shot within a kilometre (two-thirds of a mile) of their hauling-out places and eider ducks were not to be shot at their breeding places. Dogs should, if possible, be fed on seal, walrus or bear meat and not on musk-ox meat, unless no other meat was obtainable. The company issued its trappers with an inventory of essential items they would have to buy for their annual outfit – three woollen blankets, two anoraks, two English woollen sweaters, twelve pairs of woollen socks, and, of course, rifle, compass and notebook for the journal. The list included 110 pieces of soap, 15 boxes of matches, 10 rolls of toilet paper and a calendar. The year's ration was fixed at 800 kg (1,764 lb) in all. The day's ration was made up of flour, groats, peas or beans, sugar, fat or bacon, milk, tinned food, tea and coffee to a total of 600 gm (21 oz), as well as 650 gm (23 oz) of fresh onions, potatoes and lemons. For the year, the trapper was recommended to take 7½ kg (16½ lb) butter, 25 kg (55 lb) margarine, a kilo of cocoa and 15 kg (33 lb) of salt (Lauritsen 1984: 146–9). The Nanok Company ceased operations in the 1950s, since when the whole of north-east Greenland has become an uninhabited national park. Would-be visitors must obtain written permission from the government of Greenland in Nuuk, and may not hunt, trap, collect birds' eggs, or take souvenirs from the old trappers' cabins.

Danish and Norwegian trapping in east Greenland was carried out by a handful of men who risked death and endured discomfort not so much to make money, and not because they wished to wave their country's flag in remote places (though they willingly did this when required by their government), but because they craved adventure and solitude and, above all, because they fell under the spell of the Arctic and learned to love it (Dahl 1925, Smedal 1931: 103–12, Drastrup 1932, Hayes 1937: 193–201, Ingstad 1937, Rodahl 1946, Giæver 1956).

The busy traders and lonely trappers who have figured in this chapter learned to live in, survive, and enjoy the Arctic, but, unlike the Inuit and other Arctic peoples, they did so only on a temporary basis. They depended on the outside world, which in Arctic America came to be called 'the outside', for everything of importance to them. Few of them lived in the Arctic for as long as a year without contacts and supplies from the outside. After their years of Arctic service, they retired to their home countries. Both in North America and in west Greenland they often enjoyed the sexual partnership of natives, but these partners, and especially their children, were considered to be of low status. In North America such alliances were called 'country' marriages. It was only from the mid-nineteenth century onwards that traders began to bring out European, or, later, Canadian, wives to live with them for a time in the Arctic. None of these people were real settlers, but the Danes in west Greenland came nearer to this than any of the other traders and trappers of European origin mentioned in this chapter.

SEVEN

The Arctic Defeats the Royal Navy

'A NORTHERN COMMUNICATION BETWEEN THE ATLANTIC AND PACIFIC OCEANS'

Second Secretary John Barrow of the British Admiralty used these words in 1818. The search for a passage 'round North America', so far unsuccessful, should, he insisted, be resumed now that the Napoleonic Wars had been brought to a successful conclusion. In this he was flying in the face of experience (Barrow 1818: 364). A long series of attempts to find this passage, many of them described in Chapter 3 above, had ended in failure, balked by barriers of ice. On the other hand armchair geographers, especially the Dutchman Petrus Plancius (died 1662) and the Russian Mikhail Lomonosov (died 1765), had firmly insisted that the continuous daylight and frequent sunlight of the summer months would ensure that there could be no impenetrable barrier of ice north of 80° north latitude. There must be, they argued, an unfrozen or 'Open' Polar Sea. Their ideas had been taken up in France by explorer Louis-Antoine de Bougainville in 1772, and expounded at length in a book by Swiss geographer Samuel Engel published in a new edition in 1772. They were reiterated in England by the naturalist-lawyer Daines Barrington, author of papers published in 1775 and 1776 urging the practicability of finding a connection between the Atlantic and Pacific Oceans in very high northern latitudes (Barrington 1818). Early in 1773 Barrington's detailed proposals to the Royal Society to search for this were passed by that august body to the Admiralty, and a British naval expedition was sent to Spitsbergen waters later that year 'to try how far navigation was practicable towards the North Pole' (Phipps 1774: 10). The enthusiasm of the Royal Society and the Admiralty for such an expedition had been fired by two recent events. In 1771 Lieutenant James Cook RN had returned triumphantly from his first circumnavigation of the globe with a team of naturalists led by Joseph Banks. The voyage, which inaugurated the blend of scientific investigation and geographical exploration that characterized all subsequent naval expeditions, had been organized jointly by the Royal Society and the Admiralty. Then, in 1772, Samuel

Hearne, who had seen active service as a seaman in the Royal Navy during the Seven Years War with France between 1757 and 1763, returned from his overland expedition from the shore of Hudson Bay to the shore of the Arctic Ocean at the mouth of the Coppermine River (Glover 1958). He found the Arctic Ocean still frozen over in July, which would make a North-West Passage along its southern shore all but impossible, and his journey also virtually ruled out the possibility of a North-West Passage via Hudson Strait. In future the North-West Passage had to be looked for in more northerly latitudes. The Russians had already come to this conclusion as regards the North-East Passage, after their Great Northern Expedition (1733–42) had repeatedly been foiled by ice: in 1765 and 1766 Captain Vasiliy Chichagov had tried in vain to sail across the central Arctic Ocean to Bering Strait from a base on Spitsbergen (see Chapter 5 above).

The royal naval expedition of 1773 was indeed a repeat of the imperial naval expeditions of the previous decade, but the British Admiralty cautiously instructed the 1773 expedition to proceed only as far as the North Pole. In command was Captain Constantine John Phipps. The ships, HMS *Racehorse* and *Carcass*, were men-of-war called 'bombs', the strongest vessels available. Even so, the Admiralty took the precaution of strengthening their bows and bottoms against ice. It also issued the crews with special Arctic clothing: flannel jackets, lined waistcoats, fearnaught trousers, and woollen mittens and stockings. This outfit, however, would have been woefully inadequate had the ships been beset in the ice – which they very nearly were – and their crews forced to overwinter. Nor did they carry adequate provisions for such a contingency. The expedition did, however, take an array of chronometers and other scientific instruments, an astronomer named Israel Lyon, and a distillery allegedly invented by Dr Charles Irving, the expedition's surgeon, for obtaining fresh water from salt water. This yielded 34–40 gallons daily of excellent drinking water and usefully supplemented traditional supplies obtained from freshwater pools on the sea ice and meltwater streams ashore. By the time the *Racehorse* and *Carcass* reached the mouth of Magdalenefjorden (Map 10) at the north-west corner of Spitsbergen early in July, fifteen Dutch and British whaleships were in sight. On 5 July the naval explorers were in ice and fog. The ice cracked with a noise like thunder and the crews staved it off with ice poles. When the fog came down they fired guns, tolled bells and beat drums so that the two ships could keep in touch with one another. After being repeatedly stopped by ice at 80° 30' north latitude or a few minutes north of it, the ships were beset by ice at the end of July. At first the crews amused themselves playing leapfrog on the ice, but by 6 August they had put four large ship's boats out on the ice, with provisions stowed in them, and were preparing to abandon ship. They were saved by a lucky change in the weather: a strong easterly breeze blew the ice away towards the north-west, and they were able to break free. The expedition's achievements were modest. It had got no further north than either the Russians in 1765–6 or the whalers, who sailed to Spitsbergen seas every year. It had discovered nothing. It had, however, permitted the fourteen-year-old Horatio Nelson to begin his career as a British naval hero by nearly getting himself killed by a Polar bear during a midnight escapade on the ice (Phipps 1774, Markham 1879: 81–228 (*Journal of Midshipman Thomas Floyd*), Barrow 1818: 303–11, Savours 1984).

The Royal Navy was not at all deterred by the failure of Phipps's expedition to force its way through the ice further than 80° 37' north. In 1776 parliament amended the existing legislation of 1745, which had offered a £20,000 reward for the first successful voyage through the North-West Passage by a British subject, but had limited it to non-naval vessels and to ships starting from Hudson Bay. Now, the reward was made available to naval vessels as well, and to the discoverer of 'any northern passage' by sea anywhere between the Atlantic and Pacific Oceans. Moreover, an additional £5,000 reward was offered to any ship that approached within one degree of the North Pole (89° north latitude) (Barrow 1818: 312). The new legislation might have been specially designed for James Cook, now a captain, who left Plymouth Sound in the *Resolution* on 12 July 1776 bound for the Cape of Good Hope, various points in the southern hemisphere, and Bering Strait (Beaglehole 1967). He was instructed to sail through the strait and then eastwards along the North American shore and thus make his way home through the North-West Passage or, as he put it himself, 'make my passage home by the North Pole' (Stamp and Stamp 1978: 107). On 9 August 1779 the 'immortal navigator' (as La Pérouse called him, Victor 1964: 94) finally entered Bering Strait, but ice barred his way eastwards along the North American coast and at the end of August he withdrew southwards to winter in the Hawaiian Islands, where he met his death at the hands of natives. Cook's successor as commander of the expedition, Captain Charles Clerke, was also stopped by ice when, in 1780, he tried to sail eastwards from the northern entrance to Bering Strait. Meanwhile, the Admiralty had sent an armed brig, the *Lion*, in 1776 to reconnoitre the approaches to the North-West Passage in Baffin Bay, and again in 1777, in the hopes of meeting with Cook emerging from it there. But neither Lieutenant Richard Pickersgill in 1776 nor Lieutenant Walter Young in 1777 came anywhere near exploring the northern or western shores of Baffin Bay. Young's instructions explicitly ordered him to explore the western shore and any inlets that might afford a passage into the Pacific Ocean, and, if he found any, to attempt the passage, but he ignored them (Barrow 1818: 311–28; and, on Cook, Stamp and Stamp 1978, Brosse 1983: 35–74. For this and what follows see Kirwan 1962, Owen 1978, Cameron 1980, Savours 1987, Berton 1988 and Levere 1993).

NAVAL OFFICERS ONLY

After the final defeat of Napoleon in 1815, the resumption of British Arctic exploration was almost a foregone conclusion. Although French sea power had suffered an irretrievable reverse in the Napoleonic Wars, Russian imperial expansion in the North Pacific was now seen by the British as a threat to her North American interests. Not only were the Russians colonizing the Aleutian Islands and Alaska in the 1780s and 1790s, but in 1816 Lieutenant Otto von Kotzebue, in the course of the second Russian circumnavigation of the globe, sailed north through Bering Strait in search of the North-West Passage, and discovered Kotzebue Sound (Map 1). John Barrow had no intention of allowing England to stand quietly aside and suffer 'another nation to accomplish almost the only interesting discovery that remains to be made in geography', namely the North-West Passage (Barrow 1818: 365, and Gough 1986. On Barrow, see Lloyd 1970). He was also determined that British Arctic exploration should remain a monopoly of the Royal Navy, even though the most experienced navigators in Arctic waters were the whaling captains. In 1773 at least three of them had sailed further north in the Greenland Sea than Captain Phipps. John Clarke in the *Sea Horse* reached 81° 30' north, Thomas Robinson in the *St George*, 81° 16' north, and Captain Bateson in the *Whale* attained 82° 15' north latitude (Barrington 1818: 59, 18, 64). But the naval establishment disdained these so-called 'Greenland Masters' and would only employ them for Arctic exploration in a subordinate capacity. In 1817, when the famous Whitby whaling captain William Scoresby reported the east Greenland coast free of ice between 74° and 80° north latitude for the first time in his experience, he offered his services, and those of his own ship, for an exploring expedition in northern waters, or he said he would accept any position in a government expedition 'which a gentleman could hold' (Ross 1819: x). The upshot of an unsatisfactory interview he had with John Barrow in London was that he would only be employed as a pilot, 'subject to the direction of the naval captain' (Stamp and Stamp 1976: 68). He did not pursue the matter any further.

THE EXPEDITIONS OF 1818

Even before Scoresby's interview at the Admiralty, plans had been made for a two-pronged naval assault on the Arctic to be launched in the summer of 1818 using four ice-strengthened ships, commanded by four respected naval officers. Commander John Ross and Lieutenant Edward Parry, in the *Isabella* and *Alexander*, were to try for the North-West Passage, their instructions being similar to those of Lieutenant Walter Young in 1777. Captain David Buchan and Lieutenant John Franklin, in the *Dorothea* and *Trent*, were to try for the Trans-Polar Passage, repeating Captain Phipps's attempt to sail northwards from Spitsbergen. The whalers were represented by two 'Greenland Pilots' on each ship, namely 'a master and a mate of whale-fishing vessels' (Ross 1819: 2), whose status is reflected in their salary: they were paid £4 or £5 monthly, while a lieutenant received £18.8.0, the carpenter £6, the cook £4 and able seamen £3 each (Ross 1819: xiv–xv).

Parliament demonstrated its appreciation of the efforts to be made by the expeditions of 1818 by revising the act of 1776 offering rewards for polar discoveries. Now it permitted the Board of Longitude to offer a graduated scale of awards so that, while £20,000 was still on offer for a voyage through the North-West Passage to the Pacific Ocean, £15,000 was offered for sailing as far as 150° west, £10,000 for reaching 130° west, and £5,000 for sailing to 110° west longitude, within the Arctic Circle. As to discovery towards the North Pole, the full reward of £5,000 was still on offer for sailing to 89° north, but £1,000 was now offered for reaching 83° north, £2,000 for reaching 85° north, £3,000 for 87° north and £4,000 for 88° north (Scoresby 1820a: 53).

The Admiralty took great care to provision and prepare ships and crews adequately against the rigours of the Arctic, and this elaborate outfitting became

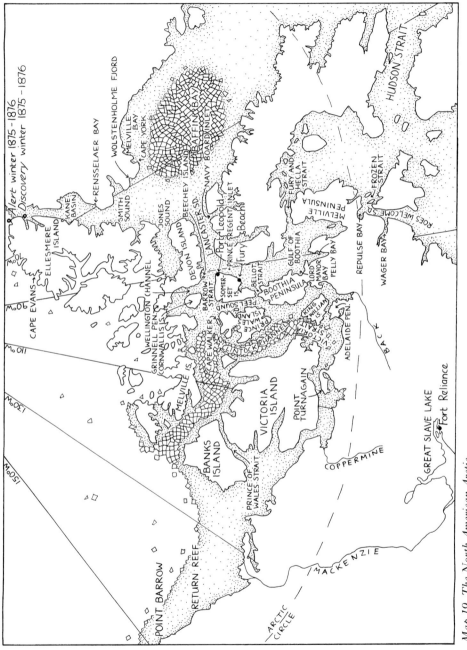

Map 19. The North American Arctic.

standard on all subsequent expeditions. The complete suit of 'warm clothing' issued in 1818 to each man comprised a Flushing jacket of rough, thick, wool; a monkey jacket, short and close fitting; a red shirt, pair of Flushing trousers, a pair of swan-skin drawers, a woollen hose, a scarlet and fawn cap, mitts, a fur cap, worsted wrist cuffs, and a pair of shoes (Ross 1819: xx). According to the *Alexander*'s surgeon, Alexander Fisher, the antiscorbutics taken were 'a plentiful supply of Donkin's preserved meats and soups, sourcrout, essence of malt and hops, and several tons of potatoes and other vegetables' (Fisher 1819: v), but all four ships, which were provisioned for twenty-six months, took supplies of lemon juice as well, sufficient for 28 g (1oz) daily for everyone on board, and also essence of spruce. The daily allowance per head of beef and pork was over half a pound (250 g); of tobacco just over an ounce (28 g); and the ships were stocked with enough spirits to provide each man with more than a quarter of a pint (162 ml) daily (see the tables in Ross 1819: xxix–xxx). All four Arctic naval vessels of 1818 were strengthened outside with oak planks 3 in (7.5 cm) thick. Iron plates were fitted on their bows.

The Admiralty's instructions for the two expeditions, in view of the many previous attempts that had all failed, were sublimely optimistic. After negotiating the North-West Passage and making the best of his way through Bering Strait to the Pacific, Ross was to sail to Kamchatka and hand over duplicates of the ships' journals to the Russian governor there for forwarding to St Petersburg and London, before continuing southward to winter in the Hawaiian Islands or elsewhere in the Pacific. He was given leave to return either by the same route or via Cape Horn. Before leaving British waters he was to fix a rendezvous with Buchan in the Pacific and, should the *Dorothea* and *Trent*, or either of them, join him there, he was to take overall command of the squadron. As it happened, both 1818 expeditions were dismal failures and neither came near winning a parliamentary reward. Ross merely repeated the 1616 voyage of William Baffin when he sailed round the shores of the bay named after him. Ross sailed past Baffin's three sounds, all of them possible entrances to the North-West Passage, without exploring them. He even insisted, against the views of some of his officers, that Lancaster Sound was a mere inlet, its head blocked by a massive range of mountains which he named the Croker Mountains after John W. Croker, the First Secretary of the Admiralty. They later proved to be non-existent. On the credit side, Ross was the first white man to be seen by the Inuhuit Eskimo inhabitants of north-west Greenland or Avanersuaq and, with the help of his Greenlandic interpreter John Sacheuse, he was able to provide a fascinating account of them (Ross 1819, Vaughan 1991). Buchan took the *Dorothea* and *Trent* into the ice-choked Spitsbergen seas but could get no further north than Phipps had done in 1773, his furthest point being 80° 34' (Ross 1819, Fisher 1819, Beechey 1843, Barrow 1846).

THE ADMIRALTY PERSISTS, 1818–37

In the course of ten years starting in 1818 the Admiralty sent no fewer than twelve exploring expeditions to the Arctic, and another followed in 1837. In terms of destination, equipment, provisioning and organization the two of 1818 were models for all the others. Some details of these expeditions are set out in Table 3. The aim

Date & Refs	Commanders	Purpose	Means of Transport	Achievement
1818 (Ross 1819, Fisher 1819)	John Ross W.E. Parry	To find the North-West Passage	HMSs *Alexander* & *Isabella*	Sailed round Baffin Bay
1818 (Beechey 1843)	David Buchan John Franklin	To sail to North Pole & beyond to Bering Strait	HMSs *Dorothea* & *Trent*	Reached 80° 34' N latitude north of west Spitsbergen
1819–22 (Franklin 1824)	John Franklin John Richardson	To survey mainland coast eastward from Coppermine	On foot and by canoe	Traced coastline from Coppermine to Point Turnagain
1819–20 (Parry 1821, Fisher 1821)	W.E. Parry Matthew Liddon	To find the North-West Passage	HMSs *Hecla* & *Griper*	Reached 110°W longitude at Melville Island
1821–3 (Parry 1824, Lyon 1824)	W.E. Parry G.F. Lyon	To find the North-West Passage via Hudson Strait	HMSs *Fury* & *Hecla*	Reached Fury and Hecla Strait
1823 (Clavering 1830)	D.C. Clavering	To measure swing of pendulum in different latitudes (E. Sabine)	HMS *Griper*	Reached 80° 20' N north of Spitsbergen Discovered Shannon Is, Greenland in 75° N
1824 (Lyon 1825)	G.F. Lyon	To survey mainland coast from west shore of Melville Peninsula to Pt. Turnagain	HMS *Griper*	Turned back in Roe's Welcome Sound
1824–5 (Parry 1826)	W.E. Parry H.P. Hoppner	To find the North-West Passage via Prince Regent Inlet	HMSs *Hecla* & *Fury*	Entered Prince Regent Inlet
1825–7 (Franklin 1828)	John Franklin John Richardson	To survey mainland coast east and west from Mackenzie	On foot & by boat	Traced coast from Return Reef to Coppermine
1826–8 (Beechey 1831, Huish 1836, Gough 1973)	F.W. Beechey	To be in Bering Strait in summer 1826 & 1827 to meet Franklin	HMS *Blossom*	Explored coast from Kotzebue Sound to Point Barrow
1827 (Parry 1828)	W.E. Parry	To reach North Pole with 2 sledge-boats from Spits-bergen	HMS *Hecla*	Reached 82° 45' north lat.
1836–7 (Back 1838)	George Back	To survey mainland coast from Wager or Repulse Bay north to Fury & Hecla Strait and west to Point Turnagain	HMS *Terror*	Beset in Frozen Strait; no surveying accomplished

Table 3.   The Royal Navy's exploring expeditions, 1818–37, from Barrow 1846, Simmons 1852, Cooke and Holland 1978.

of two of them was to reach the North Pole via Spitsbergen; both failed. The aim of another four, all of which likewise failed, was to find the North-West Passage. Four other expeditions were sent to survey the northern mainland coast of North America. Of these four, the two that travelled overland were in large measure successful (Franklin and Richardson), while the two undertaken by sea were failures (Lyon, Back). The remaining two expeditions, of HMS *Blossom* to Bering Strait and HMS *Griper* to measure the swing of the pendulum in Spitsbergen and Greenland, were wholly successful. The same officers and men served repeatedly on these expeditions, and the most popular hero of them all was William Edward Parry. His first voyage in 1819–20 went some way towards finding the North-West Passage. He sailed through Lancaster Sound and named its continuation, which at first promised to be the North-West Passage, Barrow's Strait. A bay on the northern shore of Lancaster Sound was named Croker's Inlet (now Croker Bay), as some compensation, a wag maintained, 'for having transformed . . . the magnificent and insuperable range of mountains which a former expedition had assigned to one secretary of the admiralty, into a broad and uninterrupted passage, bearing the name of the other secretary' (Barrow 1846: 66). Parry thus continued John Ross's practice of naming capes and bays after fellow-officers or naval bigwigs. At the end of his first winter in the Arctic he began the tradition of making exploratory sledge journeys from the ship. He wintered successfully on four occasions in the Arctic without appreciable loss of life. This was achieved partly through discipline and the maintenance of morale. Officers entertained the men with theatrical performances (see Claustre 1982), 'school', and weekly newspapers. But the success of Parry, Ross and others in overwintering was even more a result of daily contact with visiting Inuit who 'afforded, both to officers and men, a fund of constant variety and never-failing amusement, which no resources of our own could possibly have furnished' (Parry 1824: 378). They also supplied the explorers with quantities of fresh meat and fish, thus helping to stave off scurvy, and drew charts for them which proved remarkably accurate.

A perusal of the pages of the *North Georgia Gazette and Winter Chronicle*, the newspaper on Parry's first expedition, shows how morale was sustained with the aid of some good-natured humour. On 21 February 1820 the editor, Captain Edward Sabine of the Royal Artillery, the expedition's 'astronomer' or scientist, printed the following letter (Parry 1821: Appendix, pp. 63–4):

Sir,
The melancholy event which happened on Friday on board the Hecla, I mean the non-cookery of our pies in proper time for dinner, has given rise to some reflections, which, as the matter concerns us all alike, may not be uninteresting to your readers.

It was truly distressing to see the long and wo-begone faces to which this unusual and unexpected occurrence gave rise. One member had just warmed and rubbed his hands, and then declared that he was 'quite ready', when it was announced on authority that could not be disputed, that the pies were not quite so ready; in short, that a whole hour at least must elapse before the said pies, or any substitute for them, could possibly be brought to table. . . .

I doubt whether history can produce another such instance as this of cheerful resignation, and heroic fortitude! Amidst all the hardships which we have been called upon to suffer, none, Mr Editor, has equalled this. And how did our gallant comrades conduct themselves under this affliction? Let it ever be recorded to their immortal renown, that they patiently bowed down their heads under the stroke, and instead of murmurs and complaints, nothing but – snores were heard till dinner arrived.

Little do they think at home, Mr Editor, what we have been, and are still, undergoing for our country's sake! Little do they think that we have only as much to eat as we can conveniently stuff into our maws, and that as one of your early correspondents remarks, we can only 'snatch our ten hours' rest at night!' How would their hearts sink within them, could they be told, that once in nine months we have been reduced to the heart-breaking alternative of going without our dinner, or of roughing it upon half a pound of fresh meat, ditto bread, with all the little supplementary *etceteras* of cheese, brandy, lemon-juice and wine, with which his Majesty has been graciously pleased to supply us!

Each of Parry's North-West Passage expeditions was less successful than its predecessor. The first (1819–20), in which he was to carry out the instructions which Ross, either 'from misapprehension, indifference, or incapacity' (Barrow 1846: 62), had failed to carry out in the previous year, won for himself and his crews the £5,000 reward offered by parliament for reaching 110° west longitude within the Arctic Circle. On the third voyage (1824–5), one of Parry's two ships, HMS *Fury*, had to be abandoned after her stores had been dumped ashore nearby. The plan of the fourth expedition (1827), originally proposed by John Franklin, was to drag two specially built sledge-boats over the ice to the North Pole from the most northerly point that could be reached in the *Hecla*. This was work which John Barrow thought an 'unusual kind of disgusting and unseaman-like labour' which 'is not precisely such as would be relished by the men, and it may be said, is not exactly fitted for a British man-of-war's man . . . ' (Barrow 1846: 217). The attempt was abandoned when the ice was found to be extremely bumpy and uneven, and to be drifting the sledge-boats southwards faster than they could be manhandled northwards. A contemporary correctly stated that 'Not a single discovery was made worthy of any notice' and added that the expedition met with 'general ridicule and censure' (Huish 1835: 101–2). William Scoresby, who had always believed the North Pole was attainable by travelling over the ice, commended Parry's efforts in an 1828 article but pointed out that his sledge-boats were far too heavy. Scoresby advised the use of light-weight Eskimo umiaks or dog sledges instead. Already in 1815 and 1820 he had drawn attention to the remarkable journey the Cossack Aleksey Markov made over the ice north of the Yana Delta in 1714, with sledges drawn by dogs: he had covered some 1,280 km (800 miles) in twenty-four days. Scoresby thought the journey from Spitsbergen to the North Pole could be made in the same way (Scoresby 1815: 286–7, 334; 1820a: 59–61). He also pointed out quite rightly that Parry started out much too late in the season in 1827, when the ice was already thawing, and referred to his

Plate 12. Landing stores from HMS Fury *in August 1825. On W.E. Parry's third voyage in search of the North-West Passage one of his two ships was so badly damaged by ice that her stores had to be landed and, soon afterwards, she had to be abandoned. The depot thus formed ashore at Fury Beach continued to provide edible provisions for naval parties at least until the close of the Franklin search (M'Clintock 1859: 242–4). The crew of the* Victory *lived off these stores through their fourth winter (1832/3) in the Arctic, jocularly referring to the place as the North Pole Victualling Yard. (Parry 1826: facing p. 119.)*

1815 paper *On the Greenland or Polar Ice* (p. 331) in which he had argued that a start would have to be made in April or the beginning of May. His excellent advice had been ignored by the Admiralty.

In spite of his failures, and this criticism, Parry was treated in England like a conquering hero. In December 1820 he was unanimously voted the Bedfordian Gold Medal of the Bath and West of England Society for the Encouragement of the Arts, Manufactures and Commerce. Soon afterwards, the sum of 500 guineas was subscribed in order to present to the 'Explorer of the Polar Sea' a silver vase 'highly embellished with devices emblematic of the arctic voyages'. He was also given the freedom of the cities of Bath and Winchester and of the borough of King's Lynn (Simmonds 1852: 154). After his north polar expedition of 1827 Parry was knighted. Thereafter he retired from active service at sea. The Parry era of Arctic exploration was over (on Parry, see Parry, E. 1858, Parry, A. 1963).

JOHN ROSS PERSISTS, 1829–33

The Royal Navy's voyages of Arctic exploration, resulting largely from John Barrow's polar enthusiasm, were often carbon copies of each other, sent to the same areas with similar instructions. They were ponderous expeditions using large ships with large crews. HMS *Griper* was one of the smallest, but even she weighed 180 tons and was crewed by thirty-five to forty men. After Parry's failure to reach the North Pole in 1827 the series was interrupted by an expedition which, though its aim was the traditional one of finding the North-West Passage via Prince Regent Inlet, was novel in important ways. After he failed to penetrate Lancaster Sound on his 1818 voyage because of the imaginary Croker Mountains, and after he became involved in an intense personal dispute with Edward Sabine, John Barrow and others (Jones 1992: 219–28), John Ross had not again been selected by the Admiralty to command an Arctic expedition, though he had been promoted to captain on his return. 'In the thermometer of public estimation the gallant captain stood, like his thermometer in Lancaster Sound, twenty degrees below zero', wrote a contemporary wit (Huish 1835: 103). To restore this damaged reputation, Ross proposed to lead a new North-West Passage expedition using one of the newly-invented steamships, but was turned down by the Admiralty in 1827 and 1828, being informed that no further North-West Passage attempts were planned. However, he was at liberty, though still a captain in the Royal Navy, to launch a private expedition of his own, and he found a wealthy patron in the shape of Felix Booth, distiller of gin and recently sheriff of London. At first Booth was unwilling to finance Ross, for fear he might be accused of doing this merely in the hope of being more than recouped for his outlay from the £20,000 reward money offered by parliament to the discoverer of the North-West Passage. But in 1828, when the Board of Longitude was abolished, the parliamentary rewards for Arctic discovery were also abolished and, his scruples now removed, Booth put up the necessary £17–18,000 for Ross's expedition. Later, he had the satisfaction of having the land discovered by Ross named Boothia Felix (now Boothia Peninsula) after him, as well as the Gulf of Boothia, and Sheriff Harbour and Felix Harbour in Lord Mayor Bay. Ross set out in the *Victory* in 1829, and successfully penetrated further south down Prince Regent Inlet than Parry had done on two previous occasions. He wintered in his ship in Lord Mayor Bay in the Gulf of Boothia in 1829/30 and perforce again in 1830/1 and 1831/2, for in neither the summer of 1830 nor in that of 1831 did the break-up of the ice permit any significant movement of the imprisoned *Victory*. In the spring of 1832 the *Victory* was abandoned and the ship's boats were dragged on sledges northwards to the beach called Fury Beach, where the *Fury*'s stores had been unloaded by Parry in 1825. An expedition in the boats to the northern end of Prince Regent Inlet in August 1832 was foiled by solid ice in Barrow Strait and Lancaster Sound, and a fourth winter, that of 1832/3, had to be spent at Fury Beach, where a substantial building was erected and the *Fury*'s stores put to good use, nearly all the foodstuffs being as good in 1832 as they had been when orignally packaged for Parry in 1824. In the summer of 1833 Ross and his men set out for Lancaster Sound once more in their boats, and were finally picked up on 26 August by the Hull whaler *Isabella* – the very ship Ross had commanded in 1818 (Ross 1835, Huish 1835, Dodge 1973, Holland and Savelle 1987, Ross and Savelle 1992).

Plate 13. The Victory'*s crew saved by the* Isabella, *26 August 1833. After John Ross took the* Victory *into Lancaster Sound in 1829 to search for the North-West Passage nothing more had been heard of him and anxiety was mounting in the summer of 1833 when he and his crew, nineteen persons in all, made their way in ship's boats to Lancaster Sound. There he was rescued by a whaler, the* Isabella *of Hull, the mate of which assured Captain Ross that 'he had been dead two years' (Ross 1833: 720). Ross had himself commanded the* Isabella *in 1818. (Ross 1833: facing p. 720.)*

John Ross's expedition of 1829–33 in which his nephew, Commander James Clark Ross, was an able second-in-command in spite of disputes between the two of them, was outstanding in many ways. Even allowing for his good fortune in being able to use the *Fury*'s stores, jocularly called by the *Victory*'s crew the 'North Pole Victualling Yard' (Huish 1835: 128), Ross did well to bring back nineteen men out of twenty-two after four Arctic winters. Their survival in reasonable health was largely due to the Netsilik Eskimos, who not only supplied them with salmon, seal meat and other edibles, but helped them in other ways. For his sledging expeditions from the ship, in which he surveyed Lord Mayor Bay (Ross and Savelle 1990: 66–79) and reached as far west as the northern tip of King William Island, James Ross used the expedition's six dogs as well as Inuit guides, and learned to sleep in an Inuit snow house. But these attempts at utilizing Eskimo travelling methods did not enable the explorers to dispense with man-hauling the sledges. Ross's pioneering use of steam was an attempt to put into practice his visionary *Treatise on Navigation by Steam*, published in 1828. It was not a success. The *Victory*'s paddle wheels worked only slowly and fitfully, often one at a time, and seldom propelled the ship faster than 1 mile per hour. They were jettisoned in disgust after her arrival in Prince Regent Inlet. As to geographical discoveries, it was claimed that Ross had failed to find the North-West Passage but had determined where it was *not* to be found, namely via Prince Regent Inlet. But this was not actually the case, because the expedition failed to notice Bellot Strait connecting Prince Regent Inlet and Peel Sound, though it did ascertain the peninsularity of Boothia. Its chief claim to fame at the time was James Ross's visit to the North Magnetic Pole of which, together with the 'adjoining territory', he took possession 'in the name of Great Britain and King William the Fourth' (Ross 1835: 557). On his return, the College of Arms presented him with a fanciful addition to the Ross coat-of-arms representing 'the flag flying on the Magnetic Pole, with additional crest, "on a rock, a flag-staff erect, thereon hoisted the Union-Jack, inscribed with the date, 1st June 1831"' (Barrow 1846: 227). Honours perhaps in excess of Parry's were heaped on John Ross in consequence of his Arctic expeditions, and Barrow sarcastically enumerated some of them: Knight Second Class of the Order of St Anne of Prussia, of the Legion of Honour, of the Red Eagle of Prussia, of Leopold of Belgium; gold medals from the Geographical Society of London, the Geographical Institute of Paris and the Royal Societies of Sweden, Austria and Denmark; freedom of the city from London, Liverpool, Bristol and Hull; six gold snuff boxes from Russia, Holland, Denmark, Austria, London and Baden; and swords from the Patriotic Fund and the king of Sweden (Barrow 1846: 355). On 24 December 1835 John Ross was knighted and made a Companion of the Order of the Bath (Dodge 1973: 163).

John Barrow at the Admiralty dismissed the Ross's expedition as 'a private speculation, not authorized by any branch of the government' and professed amazement at 'the real object that could have induced a captain of the navy to take the command of a merchant ship, without a commission, without official instructions, and without any authority but such as is given to the skipper of a trading vessel . . . ' (Barrow 1846: 344, 345). Not surprisingly, the Admiralty was unwilling to mount an official expedition to go to the rescue of an unofficial one, so Back and King undertook the unofficial relief expedition overland via the Back River (described in Chapter 6) which Ross's rescue by the *Isabella* rendered unnecessary.

THE SEARCH FOR FRANKLIN

In September 1843 James Clark Ross returned triumphantly with HM Ships *Erebus* and *Terror* from a brilliant three-year voyage of exploration in Antarctic seas, during which the Ross Sea and the Ross Ice Shelf were discovered and named. Their arrival offered John Barrow a last opportunity, before his retirement in 1845 aged eighty, to mount yet another expedition to find the North-West Passage (Cyriax 1939, Wright 1959, Owen 1978). In what would virtually be a repeat of Parry's three unsuccessful expeditions, he urged that the *Erebus* and *Terror* should sail through Lancaster Sound and Barrow Strait as far as Cape Walker and then head south-westwards through what he hoped would be 'sailing ice' to Bering Strait. Both the Royal Society and the Arctic veterans of the day supported the general idea of yet another large-ship deep-sea naval attempt on the North-West Passage but added to the expedition's instructions a clause allowing its commander to try the route northwards up Wellington Channel, should ice bar the south-west route (Cyriax 1945). His return home was optimistically laid down via Hawaii and Cape Horn. This time steam would be used, and both ships were fitted with railway engines and screw propellers. No one opposed the appointment of John Franklin to command the expedition after James Ross declined on the grounds that, at forty-five, he was too old, even though Franklin was fifty-eight and had never served on a naval vessel in the North American Arctic. Richard King and John Ross opposed the planned voyage. King told John Barrow he was sending Franklin to the Arctic 'to form the nucleus of an iceberg' (Wallace 1980: 54) and urged a two-pronged land expedition via the Coppermine and Back Rivers instead of the proposed voyage (King 1855). Ross thought the ships were too big and was convinced the expedition would fail; he urged Franklin to leave ship's boats and depots behind him to cover his retreat, and to place a note in a cairn at his first wintering place outlining his proposed route thereafter (Dodge 1973: 223–4). Ross also promised to lead a search party to look for him if he was not heard of by February 1847. No one, least of all Franklin himself, listened to Ross, not even when, in February 1847, no word had come of the *Erebus* and *Terror*. They had last been seen by Robert Martin, in command of the Peterhead whaler *Enterprise*, at the end of July 1845 in Melville Bay (Simmonds 1852: 394–6).

True to his word, on 9 February 1847, Ross arrived at the Admiralty to offer his services as commander of an expedition to search for Franklin, but was dismissed out of hand. He was told that Barrow, Parry, James C. Ross, Sabine, Richardson and others had all been consulted and 'were of the unanimous opinion that it was unnecessary to send out a relief expedition that year' (Dodge 1973: 225). In April 1847 Frederick W. Beechey submitted a comprehensive relief plan to the Admiralty, which might well have saved the lives of some members of the Franklin party, but it was ignored. It was only in the summer of 1848 that the Admiralty's first Franklin search expeditions got under way and, as time went by and still no news came, private individuals joined in the search, too (Wallace 1985). Many suggestions were made. W. Parker Snow, who sailed on Jane Frankin's behalf (Stone 1993) in the *Prince Albert* in 1850 to help search for Franklin, proposed that the government should 'employ picked men from convicted criminals' in the search, as they are 'possessed of almost inexhaustible mental resources' (Simmonds 1852: 244). The German geographer August Petermann proposed in 1852 that a search expedition should be sent northwards through 'the wide opening' between Spitsbergen and Novaya Zemlya which 'probably offers the easiest and most advantageous entrance into the open, navigable Polar Sea, and perhaps the best route for the search after Sir John Franklin' (Brown 1858: 241). Lieutenant Bedford Pim RN proposed to lead a dog-sledge expedition north across the ice from the north Siberian coast; he got no further than St Petersburg (Barr 1992). For the discovery and rescue of her husband, Jane Franklin offered £5,000 in reward; and in March 1850 the British government offered a £20,000 reward to anyone who 'shall discover and effectively relieve the crew of HM Ships *Erebus* and *Terror*'. (Simmonds 1852: 251.) The most important of the Franklin search expeditions are listed in Table 4.

Date and references	Commanders	Means of transport	Comments
1848–9	J.C. Ross E.J. Bird	HMSs *Enterprise* & *Investigator*	Wintered at Port Leopold; explored w. and e. shores of Somerset Island
1848–55 (Hooper 1853, Seemann 1853, Pullen 1979, Bockstoce 1988)	T.E.L. Moore H. Kellett	HMSs *Plover* & *Herald*	Wintered in Alaska with supplies for Franklin; searched n. Alaska coast
1848–9 (Richardson 1851)	John Richardson assisted by J. Rae	Small boats	Searched coast from Mackenzie to Coppermine mouth
1849–50	J. Saunders	HMS *North Star*	Wintered Wolstenholme Fjord; landed stores for Franklin at Navy Board Inlet
1850–5 (Osborn 1856, Armstrong 1857, Neatby 1967, Collinson 1889)	R. Collinson, R.J. M'Clure	HMSs *Enterprise* & *Investigator*	Explored shores of Banks Island, Prince of Wales Strait and western and southern shores of Victoria Island
1850–1 (Osborn 1865)	H.T. Austin E. Ommanney	HMSs *Resolute, Assistance, Pioneer Intrepid*	Found Franklin's 1845/6 winter quarters on Beechey Island and Cape Riley. Explored e. and w. shores of Prince of Wales Is. and s. shore of Melville Is. from Cape Walker
1850–1	John Ross	*Felix, Mary*	Ross's own private expedition
1850-1 (Sutherland 1852)	W. Penny A. Stewart	HMSs *Lady Franklin, Sophia*	Two whalers in naval service
1850 (Snow 1851)	C.C. Forsyth	*Prince Albert*	Private expedition of Jane Franklin
1850–1 (Kane 1856c)	E.J. de Haven	USSs *Advance* & *Rescue*	Private expedition funded by Henry Grinnell
1850-1	John Rae	On foot and by boat	Explored s. coast of Victoria Island
1851–2 (Kennedy 1853, Bellot 1854)	W. Kennedy J.R. Bellot	*Prince Albert*	Discovered Bellot Strait. A private expedition of Jane Franklin
1852 (Inglefield 1853)	E.A. Inglefield	*Isabel*	Private expedition of Jane Franklin
1852–4 (Belcher 1855, M'Dougall 1857, de Bray 1992)	E. Belcher H. Kellett	HMSs *Assistance, Resolute, Pioneer, Intrepid, North Star*	Rescued M'Clure and his men from HMS *Investigator*; Belcher abandons HMSs *Resolute, Intrepid, Assistance* & *Pioneer*
1853–5 (Kane 1856a &b)	E.K. Kane	USS *Advance*	Private expedition funded by H. Grinnell; wintered at Rensselaer Bay, n.w. Greenland
1855 (Anderson 1940–1)	James Anderson	By canoe and on foot	A Hudson's Bay Company expedition. Found relics of Franklin expedition on Montreal Island
1857–9 (M'Clintock 1859, Petersen 1860)	F.L. M'Clintock	*Fox*	Private expedition of Jane Franklin; searched King William Is. shores, found the record of the Franklin Expedition

Table 4.   Principal Franklin search and relief expeditions, 1848–59. Compiled from Simmonds 1852, King 1855, Richardson 1861: 172–4, Nourse 1884: 35–7, Wordie 1945, Wright 1959, Neatby 1970, Cook and Holland 1978, Wallace 1980, 1985, Ross 1985, Berton 1988.

Plate 14. HM ships Assistance *and* Pioneer, *which took part under Sir Edward Belcher in the Franklin search, wintering off the Grinnell Peninsula, Devon Island, 30 November 1852. This sketch by Lieutenant Walter W. May shows a very fine display of paraselenae, or bright spots on lunar haloes, which Belcher described as follows:*

> *This beautiful phenomenon was represented by two concentric halos, incomplete near the horizon, accompanied by two strong crucial rays, vertical and horizontal, having the moon for their centre, the moon at this moment being four days past the full. It was also accompanied by arcs of other eccentric circles, having their common centre at a point within the zenith. The greater of these intersected the moon and outer halos, forming, at their contacts, luminous spots. So nearly did this represent the rectangular crucial form at the moon, that it was only by following the lower rays of the greater eccentric halo that they could be traced to be really a segment of a great circle. At the points of intersection of these halos, bright paraselenae, forming five on the lower and two on the upper arcs, presented themselves; the moon and the intersections by the vertical ray, exhibiting the most luminous.*

(Belcher 1855a: facing p. 169.)

The lengthy and exhaustive search for Franklin (King 1855, Brown 1858) which was also a search for the North-West Passage, altered over the years into a search to discover his fate. But results were meagre. The two most penetrating and protracted of these searches were the voyages of M'Clure and Collinson in the *Investigator* and *Enterprise*. They entered the Canadian Arctic Archipelago from the west, that is via Bering Strait, near the start of the Franklin search, and were heard from again only near its end. In August 1854 Richard Collinson finally extricated his ship the *Enterprise* from the narrow ice-filled straits of the western Arctic coast south of Banks and Victoria Islands. He had wintered there

Plate 15. Departure of sledge parties from HM ships Resolute *and* Intrepid, *4 April 1853, on the south coast of Melville Island. These ships, under the command of Captain Henry Kellett, formed part of Sir Edward Belcher's squadron. It was a sledging party from HMS* Resolute *under Lieutenant Bedford Pim which returned shortly after this scene was depicted having contacted and rescued M'Clure and his men from HMS* Investigator, *beset on the north coast of Banks Island. (M'Dougall 1857: facing p. 210.)*

three times in succession and approached nearer to the scene of the Franklin tragedy than any other searcher. M'Clure and his scurvy-ridden crew were rescued from the *Investigator*, which remained beset on the north coast of Banks Island, by a sledge party led by Bedford Pim, which arrived over the ice from the east from one of Belcher's ships. Neither Collinson nor M'Clure had found traces of Franklin but both had made important geographical discoveries. During all the years of searching, from 1848 to 1854, only one significant discovery relating to the Franklin expedition was made: in the last few days of August 1850 at and near Beechey Island, off the south-west coast of Devon Island, at least five of the searching vessels, commanded by De Haven, Ross, Penny, and others, found the first season's winter quarters of the Franklin expedition, which it had occupied in 1845–6. Besides all kinds of bric-à-brac, there were over six hundred empty tins that had once held preserved meat, and three graves – of W. Braine, John Hartnell and John Torrington (Kane 1856c: 161–7, Osborn 1865: 87–93). But there was no message, and no indication whatsoever of the direction taken by the expedition when the *Erebus* and *Terror* left Beechey Island, presumably in the summer of 1846. Apart from two pieces of wood now believed to be from the *Erebus* or *Terror*, picked up by Rae on the south-west shore of Victoria Island on 21 August 1851 (which he took to London in March 1852, but which the Admiralty failed properly to identify) (Rich 1953: lxvii–lxxi, Richards 1985: 81), no further traces of the Franklin expedition were found. After seven years of effort, after the removal of the names of Franklin and his officers from the Navy List, and after Edward Belcher had abandoned an entire squadron of Her Majesty's ships in and around Lancaster Sound, the Admiralty, now embroiled in the Crimean War, finally abandoned the search. Then on 22 October 1854, John Rae, exploring for the Hudson's Bay Company, arrived in London with a description obtained from Eskimos he had met in the Pelly Bay and Repulse Bay area of a large party of white men. They had been seen struggling southward along the shore of King William Island in the spring of 1850, in starving condition, dragging a boat with them, and heading for the Back River. In confirmation of his story, Rae brought back some things that the Eskimos had collected from or near corpses of the white men they had later found in the same general area. These Rae had purchased from them. They included 'a small silver plate with "Sir John Franklin K.C.B." engraved upon it' and spoons and forks with the initials of several officers of the lost expedition on them (Richards 1985: 107).

Although the Admiralty asked the Hudson's Bay Company to send a small expedition down the Back River in 1855 to search for relics of the Franklin expedition (Anderson 1940–1), the government had evidently decided that Rae had satisfactorily cleared the matter up, and it now washed its hands of the Franklin affair. But Jane Franklin was unremitting in her efforts to elucidate further the fate of her husband and his 129 companions. In 1857–9 she despatched a final expedition in her own 177 ton screw-propeller steam yacht *Fox*, commanded by Captain F.L. M'Clintock (1859, 1869; Petersen 1860). She instructed him to search for any possible living survivors and to recover 'the unspeakably precious documents of the expedition, public and private, and the personal relics of my dear husband and his companions' (M'Clintock 1859: 13). M'Clintock had made sledging expeditions in search of Franklin with J.C. Ross in 1848–9, under Austin in 1850–1, and under Belcher and Kellett in 1852–4 (Wordie 1945: 188). After being delayed a whole year in the Baffin Bay pack ice, he took the *Fox* as near as he could get to King William Island, which was the eastern entrance to Bellot Strait, and wintered there in 1858–9. Then, early in 1859, his sledging parties, though suffering badly from scurvy, explored the entire coast of King William Island and parts of the mainland coast to the south. Remains of the Franklin expedition were found scattered all along the western shore of the island, from Victory Point in the north to its southern tip, and beyond that to Montreal Island, in the mouth of the Back River. A large sledge-boat contained two skeletons, several watches, five or six books, all of them devotional except for Oliver Goldsmith's *Vicar of Wakefield*, a great deal of clothing, twenty-six silver spoons and forks bearing initials and crests of Franklin and other officers, and all kinds of other articles. Of food, there was only a little chocolate and 18 kg (40 lb) of tea. At last the long-sought written record of the expedition was found, in a cairn at Victory Point. This showed that, after sailing north up Wellington Channel and south down the west side of Cornwallis Island, the expedition had wintered at Beechey Island in 1845–6. Then the *Erebus* and *Terror* had sailed south, probably through Peel Sound, to the entrance to Victoria

Strait, and had become beset there on 12 September 1846 in the stream of heavy
ice moving south down M'Clintock Channel. In May 1847 Lieutenant Gore led a
small party ashore to King William Island. On 11 June 1847 John Franklin died
and Captain F.R.M. Crozier took command of the expedition, which remained on
the ships through the winter of 1847/8, still beset in the ice and drifting slowly
further into Victoria Strait. By the time the ships were deserted on 22 April 1848,
only 105 officers and men were still alive to attempt the long and difficult journey
on 26 April southwards to the Back River, where game might be found. Thus far
the expedition's written record. Inuit testimony collected subsequently
(Woodman 1991), as well as other evidence, points to the probability that some of
the 105 subsequently returned to one of the ships, which perhaps eventually sank
separately at different times and in different circumstances, one of them perhaps
south of King William Island, off the west coast of the Adelaide Peninsula.
Survivors may have lived on until 1849 or 1850 or possibly even later, before
eventually succumbing to scurvy, starvation, exposure, or some other fate. When
M'Clintock and his men scoured the King William Island shores in 1859, picking
up hundreds of relics from near the abandoned boat – skeletons, clothes, and
miscellaneous belongings that littered the beaches – they assumed that scurvy had
struck down most of the struggling survivors in that spring and summer of 1848
on a final, fatal, march. What exactly did happen may never be ascertained, but
the search for Franklin relics and for further elucidation of the mystery that still
surrounds the expedition's fate is certainly not over.

The Franklin search was by no means futile, though it had failed to rescue
Franklin, and not one of its ships had sailed through the North-West Passage. It
did achieve the detailed exploration of the involuted coastlines of dozens of ice-
bound islands. And this was done by Royal Naval parties using a combination of
dog and man-hauled sledges, which, according to M'Clintock, covered nearly
43,000 miles (70,000 km) in all (Nourse 1879: xxxiv). The Canadian Arctic
Archipelago was still largely unknown when Franklin and his men penetrated into
it in 1845. In 1860 many of its main waterways and islands had been mapped,
especially Banks Island, Victoria Island and King William Island, not to mention
a large area north and west of Barrow Strait. After the return of the *Fox* the
public, the Admiralty and the Royal Geographical Society lost interest in the
North American Arctic and the search for the North-West Passage, which had
occupied them for some forty years, and turned instead to Australia and Africa.

CAUSES OF THE FRANKLIN TRAGEDY

Many explanations have been advanced for the loss of Franklin and his men since
Vilhjalmur Stefansson in 1939 included the tragedy in his book, *Unsolved
Mysteries of the Arctic*. To judge from Inuit evidence, the historical record, and
modern analysis of bones, scurvy was the main cause of death of expedition
members. This dreaded disease haunted every British naval expedition and killed
members of almost every wintering party. It could not be prevented by the
standard antiscorbutics of the day, namely cranberries, pickles, vinegar, spruce
beer and lime or lemon juice, because most of these quickly lost their efficacy. In

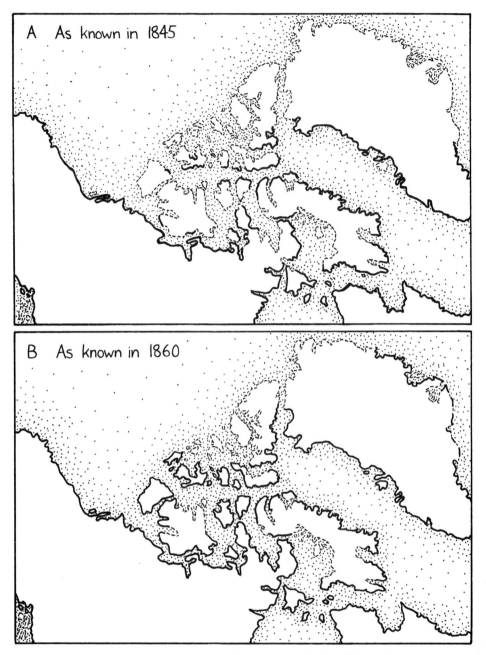

Map 20. The Canadian Arctic Archipelago before and after the Franklin search.

default of quantities of fresh vegetables, fresh meat was absolutely essential to provide sufficient vitamin C (Rodahl 1949, Carpenter 1986). There was enough game in many parts of the Arctic to ward off scurvy among a small group of skilled hunters, but not to keep a large group of people in one place in good health. W.E. Parry helped to prevent scurvy in his ninety-four-strong party which spent nearly a year at Winter Harbour on the south coast of Melville Island in 1819–20 by ordering the men 'to gather daily a prescribed quantity' of sorrel in the summer months, and by organizing shooting parties which killed sufficient musk oxen, caribou, hares, ptarmigan, geese and ducks to provide each man with about 20 kg (40 lb) of fresh meat (Parry 1821: 227, 221n). John Ross and his men escaped scurvy during four successive winters by obtaining supplies of meat and fish from Eskimos and because they numbered only twenty-three persons in all. Franklin and his officers, like Back in 1836–7, were evidently unable to provide enough fresh meat for their men. How could a hundred-strong party hope to live off the land on the King William Island tundra and its barren shores, where only tiny scattered groups of Netsilik Inuit could survive on a strictly seasonal hunt, especially when Royal Navy personnel did not normally eat the meat of bears, foxes, wolves and seals (M'Clintock 1869: 282), and the seal formed the staple diet of the Netsilik? Franklin's officers apparently made things more difficult by concentrating their men on a single escape route instead of scattering them in several directions, and by failing to insist that the men travelled as lightly as possible. In the boat he discovered on King William Island in 1859, M'Clintock (1859: 296) was astonished to find ' a quantity of articles of one description and another . . . such as, for the most part, modern sledge-travellers in these regions would consider a mere accumulation of dead weight, but slightly useful, and very likely to break down the strength of the sledge-crews'. Furthermore, Franklin committed the blunder of quitting his Beechey Island winter quarters in the spring of 1846 without leaving messages behind in cairns indicating his future plans, and of not marking his route with a series of cairns, as Parry and Ross had done. The Admiralty blundered, too. Its Arctic veterans, who became institutionalized during the search in the form of the Arctic Council, were too complacent, too slow in organizing relief and rescue expeditions, and too obtuse to send one to the area around and north of the mouth of the Back River, where many of Franklin's men in fact met their death, and where Richard King had repeatedly urged them to search. For the most part the search expeditions were directed to the north and west of Barrow Strait rather than to the south-west, 'the course that Franklin had been expressly enjoined to take' (Markham 1891: 253).

All kinds of less specific explanations have been advanced for the loss of Franklin and his men. One of many contemporary ballads underscores the failure of his and similar expeditions to adapt to the Arctic environment (Simmonds 1852: 278):

> O, whither sail you, brave Englishman?
>   Cried the little Esquimaux.
> Between your land and the polar star
>   My goodly vessels go.

> Come down if you would journey there,
>   The little Indian said;
> And change your cloth for fur clothing,
>   Your vessel for a sled.
>
> But lightly laughed the stout Sir John,
>   And the crew laughed with him too;
> A sailor to change from ship to sled,
>   I ween, were something new!

The naval explorers often failed to learn from experience. Franklin had faced starvation on his first overland voyage, but a few years later set out on a second very similar one, which, though better supplied by the Hudson's Bay Company, still had to go on short rations for a time. Off Spitsbergen in 1818, when the *Dorothea* was reduced to a sinking condition by the ice and his own ship the *Trent* was badly damaged, Lieutenant Franklin proposed carrying on alone. This Captain David Buchan would not allow, wisely resolving to return home with the two stricken ships in company (Beechey 1843: 130–1). In spite of this experience, Franklin was credited with planning, in 1845 'to put his ships into the drift ice at the western end of Melville Island' (Simmonds 1852: 212). The vagaries of the Arctic climate may have contributed to the Franklin disaster: during the years 1845–60 Peel Sound and Victoria Strait may have been blocked with perennial ice in four years out of five (Alt *et al.* 1985). The hypothesis has recently been proposed, but by no means generally accepted, that lead poisoning from the soldering of tins of preserved meat may have been disastrous to the expedition (Kowal *et al.* 1989, Beattie and Geiger 1989, but see Fordham 1991, Powell 1992, Savours 1992). In fact, though high levels of lead were found in the remains of all three Franklin expedition members buried on Beechey Island, autopsies showed that in each case the most likely cause of death was pneumonia complicated by tuberculosis (Trafton 1989). Behind all the long history of Royal Naval expeditions in the Canadian Arctic and behind the Franklin tragedy, too, is the John-Bull-like figure of 'Mr Barrow of the Admiralty', who despatched his cumbersome ships in pairs, apparently unaware that these floating citadels were far too big to scrape through shallow Arctic channels, carried unnecessarily large crews, and were extremely vulnerable to destruction or immobilization by the ice. It was like repeatedly firing off projectiles at an invisible target while blindfolded.

Later, long after the British Admiralty had forgotten about the North-West Passage, men navigating tiny ships and using dog sledges were to feel their way through the maze of icy channels and triumphantly complete the exploration of the Canadian Arctic Archipelago. The North-West Passage was first navigated from east to west by Norwegian explorer Roald Amundsen in his 47 ton motor yacht *Gjøa* between 1903 and 1906, with a crew of four Norwegians and a Dane. The route (Map 28) was via Peel Sound and the east side of King William Island, and the explorers overwintered three times (Amundsen 1908). The first navigation from west to east was by Norwegian-born Sergeant Henry Larsen of the Royal Canadian Mounted Police in the 80 ton *St Roch* in 1940–2 (Tranter 1944, Larsen 1967).

THE NAVY GOES FOR THE POLE

In 1845, the very year when John Franklin sailed to his doom with the *Erebus* and *Terror*, Parry assured John Barrow that he now believed a repetition of his 1827 attempt on the North Pole might well succeed if only the expedition wintered in the extreme north of Spitsbergen so that a start could be made in April when the ice was hard, and the thaw had not yet allowed it to begin drifting. Barrow, who called the Pole 'the most remarkable spot on the earth's surface' (1846: 221), waxed enthusiastic about the scientific benefits to be gained by visiting it. So did Russian explorer F.P. Vrangel', at a meeting of the Russian Geographical Society on 29 November 1846. But he criticized Parry's revised plan, suggesting instead that a party using dog sledges should set out for the Pole from northern Greenland after wintering there (Laktionov 1955: 60–2). Nearly twenty years later, in 1865, a veteran of the Franklin search, Captain Sherard Osborn, read a paper to the Royal Geographical Society 'On the exploration of the North Polar region' urging the use of a ship or ships to sail through Smith Sound as far as possible northwards up the coast of Ellesmere Island, and dog sledges to reach the Pole over the ice from there (Cameron 1980: 111). The American explorers E.K. Kane and I.I. Hayes had already followed this route, unsuccessfully as far as the Pole was concerned, before Osborn spoke (see Chapter 8 below). In 1861 the Swede Otto Torell had tried to repeat Parry's attempt on the Pole via Spitsbergen. Arriving there too late in the season to make a start, he had to be content with a tasty meal of roast meat embedded in jelly and fat, found in a hermetically sealed tin in one of Parry's depots (Leslie 1879: 47–103, Thorén 1978: 11–36). Another Swedish attempt on the Pole from Spitsbergen, led by A.E. Nordenskiöld in 1872–3, this time with reindeer sledges, likewise failed to get under way, though four Sami, forty reindeer and a cargo of reindeer moss were transported as far as Spitsbergen (Leslie 1879: 176–277, Kish 1973: 94–104). In 1866 August Petermann had appealed to his countrymen for a German programme of Arctic exploration. This resulted in two expeditions commanded by Karl Koldewey in 1868 and 1869–70 to explore the region around the North Pole. Neither came near success. The second twice attempted to sail and sledge northwards up the east coast of Greenland but reached only 77° north. One of the expedition ships, the *Hansa*, was lost in the ice: her fourteen-strong crew camped on a drifting ice floe from October 1869 until they got ashore in south Greenland on 4 June 1870 (Koldewey 1874, Lindeman and Finsch 1875, Venzke 1990, Reinke-Kunze 1992: 18–47). Hard on the heels of the Germans went the Austro-Hungarians, led at sea by Lieutenant Karl Weyprecht of the Imperial Navy, and ashore by First Lieutenant Julius Payer of the Imperial Army, who had distinguished himself as leader of the sledge parties on the 1869–70 German expedition. The aim of the Austro-Hungarian North Polar Expedition of 1872–4, which, after its ship the *Admiral Tegetthof* became beset in the ice, accidentally discovered Franz Josef Land (Zemlya Frantsa Iosifa), was not to attain the North

Pole itself but to explore the seas or lands north-east of Novaya Zemlya. It, like the German expeditions before it, was inspired by August Petermann's belief in an Open Polar Sea. In the event Julius Payer, commander of the expedition on shore, explored the central parts of the Franz Josef Land Archipelago with sledges as far north as Crown Prince Rudolf's Land (now ostrov Rudol'fa or Rudolf Island), and discovered and named many of the islands. Then, when lack of provisions for a third winter forced the expedition to retreat south in open boats, Karl Weyprecht led it skilfully and resolutely to Novaya Zemlya (Payer 1876).

It was thus in the context of increasing activities in the Arctic by other European powers, as well as by American explorer C.F. Hall, whose ship the *Polaris* had achieved a record northerly point of 82° 11' north via Smith Sound in 1871, that in June 1873 the Arctic Committee of the Royal Geographical Society proposed a renewal of British royal naval Arctic exploration almost in the form suggested by Osborn in 1865. Two moderate-sized steamships, one to winter not far beyond the entrance to Smith Sound, the other to winter as far as possible to the northward, would be employed to launch sledge parties in the early spring to travel over the ice to the Pole (Markham 1875: 286–307). The committee insisted, rather ironically in view of Franklin's fate, that 'all British Arctic authorities' were agreed that such expeditions must be 'under naval control and discipline', because, that way, 'the safety of an expedition is comparatively guaranteed' (p. 303). Not surprisingly, the 1875–6 British Arctic Expedition under Captain George Nares turned out, in most important respects, to be a copy of earlier naval expeditions, including Franklin's. The ships were bigger than ever: the *Alert* was a steam sloop of 751 tons and the *Discovery* a former whaler of 556 tons (Pullen 1981: 155), and the combined crews numbered 120 men. The fact that the only Franklin search voyage to achieve its goal was M'Clintock's 1857–9 expedition in the *Fox*, a small ship (177 tons) with a small crew of twenty-four men, was apparently forgotten. Even though the *Alert* and *Discovery* wintered over 80 km (50 miles) apart (Map 19), sufficient game could never have been obtained to supply regular fresh meat for all, especially as shooting expeditions ashore were for officers only. No notice was taken of the techniques of Arctic exploration developed by the Hudson's Bay Company's men in the 1830s and 1840s. The eight-man heavy duty naval sledges of 1875 were designed by the great M'Clintock himself, 'who is the highest living authority on Arctic sledge travelling' (Markham 1878: 262), but were far too large and cumbersome. Fifty-five Eskimo dogs were obtained in Greenland but ineffectively used, and not at all for the exploring parties to the north (Markham 1891: 295). The wrong type of snow shoe was taken, though one officer, advised by John Rae to take a pair of Canadian snow shoes, found them invaluable (Richards 1985: 154). Tents were used instead of snow houses. The rations were virtually the same as those taken on the Franklin search expeditions and indeed on all earlier expeditions going back at least to 1818. Sledge-hauling was still accompanied by a daily allowance of grog, even though John Rae had found alcohol to be unnecessary in the Arctic and thought it might even be harmful. The only difference between the 1875–6 expedition and many earlier ones was the elaborate insistence in its official instructions on the need to leave depots behind and to raise cairns on every headland to indicate its route. In his 1873 book, *The Threshold of the Unknown Region*, the secretary and later president of the Royal Geographical Society, Clements R. Markham, cousin of Albert Markham, was enthusiastic about the planned expedition: the naval sledgers of the 1850s had already accomplished the necessary distances, and scurvy was no longer a serious danger. 'Now then, is the time for old England to take her place once more in the van of Arctic discovery' he exclaimed at the end of his book (p. 319).

In 1872–4 Captain George Nares RN (Deacon and Savours 1976) was recalled from Hong Kong, where he was commanding HMS *Challenger* on one of the most important voyages of scientific investigation made in the nineteenth century (Linklater 1972), and sent to the Arctic to command an expedition of a totally different character, the scientific programme of which had been pushed into the background. Nares did have experience of sledging in the Arctic, having served under Henry Kellett on HMS *Resolute* between 1852 and 1854 along with F.L.M. M'Clintock, B.C.T. Pim, and G.F. Mecham, during the Franklin search. His sailing orders of 1875 stated that the 'primary object' of the expedition was 'to attain the highest northern latitude, and, if possible, to reach the North Pole' (Nares 1878a: xi). The expedition left Portsmouth Harbour on 29 May 1875 amid a surge of patriotic Arctic enthusiasm and with the approbation of Prime Minister Benjamin Disraeli and the blessing of Queen Victoria. At first everything went like clockwork. Winter berths for the two ships were easily found. That of the *Alert* in 82° 24' north latitude was the furthest north a ship had ever penetrated up to that time. The winter passed uneventfully but then, soon after the all-important spring sledge expeditions got under way on 3 April 1876 (in point of fact a month too late to reach the Pole and back in safety before the spring thaw), scurvy struck down the men and was soon also affecting those who had remained on board ship. Though Commander Albert H. Markham took his sledge party to a heroic furthest north 'ever reached by man' of 83° 20' 26" on 12 May, his men were already suffering from scurvy. By 27 May the returning party had been reduced to a critical condition (Markham 1878: 357):

. . . five men were in a very precarious condition, utterly unable to move, and consequently had to be carried on the sledges; five others nearly as bad, but who nobly persisted in hobbling after the sledges, which they could just manage to accomplish, for, as the sledges had to be advanced one by one, it gave them plenty of time to perform the distance; while three others exhibited all the premonitory scorbutic symptoms. Thus only the two officers and two men could be considered as effective!

One man died on 8 June. Rescue came on 9 June. On 25 June another sledge party under Lieutenant Pelham Aldrich reached the *Alert*: four men were on their feet, four others were being carried on the sledges. Aldrich and his group had explored the north coast of Ellesmere Island to a little beyond Cape Evans. Lieutenant Lewis A. Beaumont had sledged eastwards along the north Greenland coast, but at the expense of two deaths from scurvy. At the end of June, Nares, with only nine entirely scurvy-free men on the *Alert* out of fifty-three, decided to terminate the expedition and sail for home, thus narrowly averting a repetition of the Franklin disaster. Although the North Pole had eluded them, Nares's sledging parties had explored about 480 km (300 miles) of the coastlines of northern Ellesmere Island and northern Greenland, hitherto unexplored by white men, and, instead of discovering an open Polar Sea they had found a frozen Arctic Ocean (Nares 1876, Markham 1878, Moss 1878, Nares 1878, Rink 1878: 82–100, Hattersley-Smith 1976, Lidegaard 1985: 176–206, Levere 1993: 264–306). *En route* for England, Nares telegraphed home the laconic and categorical but erroneous message: 'The North Pole impracticable!' (Laktionov 1955: 91; compare Nares 1878a: 326).

Although it can be argued that overmanning, ineffective use of dog sledges, and poor equipment contributed to the British Arctic Expedition's lack of success, it was the outbreak of scurvy that caused its leader to abort it. The committee of three admirals and two doctors appointed after the expedition's return to enquire into the causes of this outbreak blamed the absence of lime juice from the diet of the sledging parties. M'Clintock, Clements Markham and George Nares refused to accept this. In giving evidence to the committee John Rae claimed that fresh meat and fish were the only effective antiscorbutics in the absence of fresh vegetables; of lime juice and its effects he had no first-hand experience. Clements Markham (1877) analysed the occurrence of scurvy among the *Alert* and *Discovery* crew members and showed that 'at least nine men contracted scurvy even though they had been taking lime juice regularly for some time before they fell ill' (Savours and Deacon 1981: 153, see too Nares 1878a: 256–61, Richards 1985: 156–8, Carpenter 1986: 139–45). Had the expedition been supplied with fresh lemons, or lemon juice rather than lime juice, scurvy might have been prevented; of course, vitamin C had not yet been discovered. Fresh meat, demanding a small exploring party, was the only effective prophylactic available to nineteenth-century Arctic explorers. Nares did have two West Greenlanders with him and one of them at least, Hans Hendrik or Suersaq, provided fresh meat for some of those stricken with scurvy, which certainly assisted their recovery (Rink 1878: 97, Lidegaard 1985: 203–4). The Royal Navy, in yet another remarkable manifestation of heroism, had once more demonstrated its inability to adapt to the demands of the Arctic environment. The next victims of this mindless gallantry would be Robert F. Scott and his companions at the South Pole.

EIGHT

America and the Arctic in the Nineteenth Century

The United States had begun explorations in the Antarctic before the Arctic, but the naval expedition under Lieutenant Charles Wilkes, the United States Exploring Expedition of 1838–42 (Wilkes 1845), which established the existence of a single large Antarctic continent, was not immediately followed up in either the Antarctic or the Arctic. Then, in July 1848, an adventurous whaling captain, Thomas Roys, sailing from Sag Harbour, Long Island, in the bark *Superior*, penetrated north through Bering Strait into the Arctic Ocean and took eleven bowhead whales in the Chukchi Sea. His 1,600 barrels of train oil started an oil rush which quickly made whaling in the western Arctic a pre-eminent commercial concern of the United States and, in contributing to the purchase of Alaska by the United States in 1867, gave her an important political stake in the western Arctic as well (Nourse 1884, Bruun 1902, Caswell 1956, Neatby 1966).

THE UNITED STATES JOINS THE SEARCH FOR FRANKLIN

Whalers apart, it was the Franklin search that took the United States into the Arctic. On 4 April 1849 Jane Franklin wrote to President Zachary Taylor appealing for his help in searching for, and hopefully rescuing, her missing husband and his men, but to little or no effect. In a second letter of 11 December 1849, pointing out that the missing explorers had now entered on their 'fifth winter in the dark and dreary solitudes', she again implored the president to act (Simmonds 1852: 325–7, 329–31). Eventually, in January 1850, President Taylor did ask Congress for an appropriation to fit out an expedition, but a private citizen, Henry Grinnell, a successful New York businessman who had made a fortune in the whaling trade, now took the initiative (Kane 1856c, Corner 1972, Cruwys 1990, Cruwys 1991, Cruwys 1992). Between March and May 1850, while corresponding directly with Jane Franklin, Grinnell bought two suitable ships, the *Rescue* and *Advance*, persuaded Congress to place them under naval orders, and arranged for Lieutenant Edwin J. De Haven to command them. A much-travelled naval surgeon, Elisha Kent Kane, volunteered for the expedition and served with De Haven in the *Advance*. Thus it was that the United States Navy

Plate 16. *Famous nineteenth-century Arctic personalities illustrated in a popular twentieth-century history of Arctic exploration (Miller 1928: 138). Henry Grinnell (above, centre), New York shipping tycoon and first president of the American Geographical Society of New York, funded Arctic expeditions led by Americans C.F. Hall (lower left) and E.K. Kane (upper right). G.W. De Long (below, centre) was likewise American. John Franklin (upper left) and George Nares (lower right) were British Royal Naval explorers, while Julius Payer (centre) was a lieutenant in the Imperial Austro-Hungarian Army and co-leader with Karl Weyprecht of the Austro-Hungarian North Polar Expedition of 1872–4 which discovered Franz Josef Land (see Chapter 7).*

joined the Royal Navy and other British searching expeditions in Lancaster Sound in August 1850 and took part in the discovery of Franklin's Beechey Island winter quarters of 1845–6 (Map 19). W. Parker Snow, purser and surgeon on Jane Franklin's search ship the *Prince Albert*, which was also in Lancaster Sound in August 1850, met and admired both De Haven and Kane. He has this to say of the *Advance* (Snow 1851: 300–1):

> If ever a vessel and her officers were capable of going through an undertaking in which more than ordinary difficulties had to be encountered, I had no doubt it would be the American; and this was evinced to me, even while we were on board, by the apparently reckless way in which they dashed through the streams of heavy ice running off from Leopold Island. I happened to go on deck when they were thus engaged, and was delighted to witness how gallantly they put aside every impediment in their way. An officer was standing on the heel of the bowsprit, conning the ship and issuing his orders to the man at the wheel in that short, decisive, yet *clear* manner, which the helmsman at once well understood and promptly obeyed. There was not a rag of canvass taken in, nor a moment's hesitation. The way was before them: the stream of ice had to be either gone through boldly or a long *detour* made; and, despite the heaviness of the stream, *they pushed the vessel through in her proper course.* Two or three shocks as she came in contact with some large pieces, were unheeded; and the moment the last block was past the bow, the officer sung out, 'So: steady as she goes on her course;' and came aft as if nothing more than ordinary sailing had been going on. I observed our own little barky nobly following in the American's wake; and, as I afterwards learned, she got through it pretty well, though not without much doubt of the propriety of keeping on in such procedure after the 'mad Yankee,' as he was called by the mate.

Many of the expeditions purporting to search for Franklin in fact combined this intent with the continuing search for the North-West Passage. Elisha Kent Kane, after his return in 1851 from the United States Grinnell Expedition in search of Sir John Franklin, immediately proposed, in a series of successful public lectures, a second Grinnell Expedition in search of Sir John Franklin. The real aim of this projected expedition, mounted partly in response to a personal appeal to Kane from Jane Franklin, but only thinly disguised as a Franklin search, was the exploration of the region around the North Pole. For Kane, apparently influenced by the subsequently famous American oceanographer Lieutenant Matthew F. Maury, was inclined to believe in the existence of a gigantic permanent polynya around the North Pole, the so-called Open Polar Sea, which he might hope to reach by sailing northwards through Smith Sound. The tenuous link with Franklin was the hypothesis that, since no traces of his expedition had been found south of Lancaster Sound, he must have travelled northwards through Wellington Channel (Map 19) after wintering near its southern end in 1845/6, and might be trapped somewhere on the shores of the Polar Sea. Congress would make no appropriation for the proposed expedition, but Kane was able to enlist the financial support of Henry Grinnell, the London-based American financier

Map 21. Americans in the Eastern Arctic.

George Peabody, the Geographical Society of New York, the Smithsonian Institution in Washington, and the American Philosophical Society. He was much encouraged and assisted by Secretary of the Navy John Pendleton Kennedy, who seconded ten non-commissioned naval personnel to the expedition and placed Kane on special duty on his full surgeon's pay. He set out from New York on 30 May 1853 in the *Advance*, which Grinnell had made available to him, with a crew of seventeen persons serving under himself as captain. He planned 'to pass up Baffin's Bay . . . to its most northern attainable point; and thence, pressing on toward the Pole as far as boats or sledges could carry us, examine the coast-lines for vestiges of the lost [Franklin] party' (Kane 1856a: 18).

In September 1853 Kane took the *Advance* boldly northwards until she was beset in a bay he named Rensselaer Harbour after the maiden name of his grandmother, van Rensselaer, who was of Dutch ancestry. It was on the Inglefield Land coast, some 16 km (10 miles) further north than Edward A. Inglefield (1853) had taken the *Isabel* the year before (Table 4). The ice around the *Advance* held her fast all through the summer of 1854, when travelling parties discovered the Humboldt Glacier, and explored Kane Basin and parts of the Washington Land and Ellesmere Island coasts as far as the mouth of Kennedy Channel, but not quite as far as Kane made out (Corner 1972: 258–63). William Morton, travelling with the expedition's Greenlandic interpreter and guide, Hans Hendrik or Suersaq, even thought they had discovered the Open Polar Sea, 'a boundless waste of water, stretching away toward the Pole' (Godfrey 1857: 156) to the north of Kennedy Channel. On these expeditions on foot Eskimo (in this case Inuhuit) means of transport were indispensable: Kane (1856b: 307) stated in his report to the secretary of the navy that 1,100 of 3,000 miles (1,800 of 4,800 km) of travel accomplished in spring and summer 1854 were made by dog sledge and that he himself in the winter of 1854/5 travelled 1,400 miles (2,250 km) by dog sledge. At the end of August 1854, when it became clear that the explorers faced another long, dark Polar winter, seven of them left the *Advance* under the leadership of the surgeon Isaac I. Hayes. They hoped to make their way south some 1,600 km (1,000 miles) to the Danish colonies in west Greenland in two open boats. Whether this exodus represented what amounted to a mutiny, or whether Kane gave anyone who wished to leave full permission to do so because of the likely shortage of provisions and outbreak of scurvy in the cramped quarters of the *Advance* during the ensuing winter, remains uncertain. In the outcome, this withdrawal party was lucky to struggle back to the *Advance* in December 1854 after travelling only about 300 km (200 miles) to the south. Its members were worn out, and owed their lives to the local Inuhuit Eskimos, who had supplied them with fresh meat and transported them back to the *Advance* with their dog sledges. Kane all but scared the Inuhuit away from the *Advance* by locking up one of their number for allegedly damaging a rubber boat, and holding two women to ransom who had purloined a dog, cooking pot, some buffalo-skin robes and other things. Nevertheless, by a clever combination of threats and gifts, he persuaded them to assist his hunting parties in obtaining fresh meat, and to supply him and his men with walrus, seal, and other fresh meat during the difficult second winter. Without the Inuhuit, Kane's expedition would surely have ended in disaster. As it was, in May 1855 he extricated his fourteen men remaining of the original eighteen, and skilfully led them safely to Upernavik, using sledges and open boats. Thence they travelled in a Danish ship to Godhavn (now Qeqertarsuaq) where they were picked up by a relief expedition sent rather tardily to their rescue by the United States Navy. It had left New York on 31 May 1855, just two years after the *Advance* had sailed, under the command of Lieutenant Henry J. Hartstene, who wrote to the secretary of the navy as he set out: 'To avoid further risk of human life in a search so extremely hazardous, I would suggest the impropriety of making any efforts to relieve us if we should not return' (Elder 1858: 214).

Kane and his men suffered the usual tribulations of wintering in the Arctic, but, besides the cold and darkness, and the inevitable outbreaks of scurvy, they experienced a plague of rats. Having failed to smoke them out with 'the vilest imaginable compound of vapours – brimstone, burnt leather, and arsenic' while the crew bivouacked on deck, Kane decided to fumigate them with carbon dioxide, lighting fires and burning charcoal below decks to this end. Though fourteen rats died, this dangerous experiment was nearly disastrous. When the French chef, Pierre Schubert, 'stole below to season a soup', he collapsed asphyxiated and was narrowly hauled out alive. Then the ship caught fire and Kane himself passed out temporarily. Fortunately a fire hole had been kept open through the 36 cm (14 in) thick ice by the ship, and the blaze was quickly extinguished (Kane 1856a: 118–21, Godfrey 1857: 110–11). Crew member William Godfrey reported that 'the rats . . . in spite of Dr Kane's grand fumigation, continued to be very numerous and troublesome'. An Arctic fox he had trapped alive and called Jack, 'killed more of the long-tailed rascals in half an hour than the fumigation aforesaid did in two days'. Monsieur Schubert, who 'boasted his ability to prepare exquisite dishes . . . actually prepared a rat fricassée' which some of the officers found excellent. Few of the men 'could be persuaded to touch this mess', in spite of Schubert's assertions that 'similar preparations were often served up at some of the most fashionable restaurants of Paris', and that 'among French gourmands, if a dish was found to be palatable, no idle curiosity was ever manifested with regard to its composition' (Godfrey 1857: 116–17). During the second winter the rats were just as numerous and troublesome, gnawing into and destroying furs, woollens, shoes and specimens of natural history. Kane wisely desisted from the risky methods of pest control employed in the previous winter. Instead the Greenlander Suersaq stalked and shot the rats with a bow and arrow, and Kane attributed his 'comparative immunity from scurvy' that winter to the meat soup made from them which he relished, but most of his companions spurned (Kane 1856a: 393–5).

At least five narratives by members of Kane's 1853–5 expedition have been published and together they portray the man and his qualities in vivid and contrasting colours. The Dane, Carl Petersen, who was signed on in Greenland as dog driver and Eskimo interpreter, makes disparaging remarks about Kane's inexperienced crew, his rashness, his lack of nautical expertise, his boasting, and his belief in an Open Polar Sea (Petersen 1857, Villarejo 1965). William Godfrey (1857), a volunteer seaman, was a troublemaker who quarrelled with Kane repeatedly and, treated by Kane as a deserter, was on one occasion shot at by him. But Godfrey's narrative is by no means entirely unfavourable to Kane. The expedition's surgeon, Isaac I. Hayes (1860), who led the withdrawal party, confines his narrative to it, and insists that his party left, and returned to, the *Advance*, on cordial terms with Kane. A fourth account of the expedition was put together from the oral reminiscences of its Greenlandic member, Suersaq (Rink 1878: 21–35, Lidegaard 1985: 13–43), who praises Kane for 'not despising native food' (Rink 1878: 30) but criticizes him for behaving haughtily towards his crew. Suersaq's desertion early in 1855 was caused either by a romantic attachment to an Inuhuit girl, or by fear and mistrust of Kane, or more probably by a combination of both. Kane's own two-volume *Arctic Explorations* is an enduring classic which sold 65,000 copies in the first year after its publication and is said to have received over a thousand reviews (Elder 1858: 257). Within a year of its publication in 1856 its author died, aged only thirty-seven (biographies by Elder, Mirsky, Corner).

CHARLES FRANCIS HALL AND THE INUIT

While Charles Francis Hall was pursuing a successful career as a seal-engraver and newspaper proprietor in Cincinnati, Ohio, during the 1850s he developed an increasing obsession with the Arctic (biography: Loomis 1972). Specifically, he was concerned about the failure of the Franklin search expeditions to explain adequately the disappearance of the 105 men who, it became known in 1859 on M'Clintock's return in the *Fox*, were still alive when they left their ships to attempt to reach the mouth of the Back River (Map 19). Hall entertained the not entirely lunatic idea that some of them might still be alive ten years later, perhaps living with the Inuit, and appealed to his Cincinnati fellow citizens in February 1860 to assist him in fitting out an expedition 'in search of survivors of Sir John Franklin's exploring party' and in 'satisfactorily settling and completing' its history (Nourse 1879: xxiv). Hall was encouraged by a letter from Thomas Hickey, who had served as a seaman on Kane's expedition. He wrote that the 'many severe trials' they experienced were mostly due to their 'mode of living'. 'When we lived as Esquimaux, we immediately recovered and enjoyed our usual health' (Hall 1865: xxi–ii). In March 1860 Hall announced his plan: 'to acquire personal knowledge of the language and life of the Esquimaux, with a view thereafter to visit the lands of King William, Boothia and Victoria [Map 19]; then endeavour, by personal investigation, to determine more satisfactorily the fate of the 105 companions of Sir John Franklin now known to have been living' on 25 April 1848 (pp. xxiii–iv). An Inuit interpreter would be taken on the expedition, and Inuit guides employed. No problem was experienced in raising the $980 required: fourteen Cincinnati citizens subscribed $30 each; Hall's wife donated $27; and when this amount, added to other donations, fell short of $980, Henry Grinnell, who shared Hall's belief in the possibility of living survivors of the Franklin expedition and did much to encourage him, made up the difference, to the tune of $343 (Hall 1865: 586). The outfit itself was modest in the extreme (Hall 1865: 30):

The [whale-]boat, already described; 1 sledge; ½ ton of pemmican; 200 lb. Borden's meat biscuit; 20 lb. 'Cincinnati cracklings' – *pork scraps*; 1 lb. preserved quince; 1 lb. preserved peaches; 250 lb. powder; a quantity of ball, shot, and percussion caps; 1 rifle; 6 double-barreled guns, covers, and extra fittings; one Colt's revolver complete; glass beads, a quantity of needles, etc., for presents to the natives; 2 dozen pocket knives and choppers; some tin-ware, 1 axe, 2 picks, files, etc.; a good supply of tobacco and pipes; wearing apparel for self, and red shirts for presents; a supply of stationery and journal books, etc.; 1 common watch; 1 opera-glass; 1 spy-glass; 1 common sextant and 1 pocket sextant; 1 artificial horizon, with extra glass and mercury; 1 azimuth compass; 1 common compass; 2 pocket compasses; 3 ordinary thermometers and two self-registering ones. Some navigation books and several arctic works, with my Bible and a few other volumes, formed my library.

In the summer of 1860 the New London, Connecticut, whaler *George Henry*, Captain S.O. Budington, landed Hall near Frobisher Bay in Baffin Island, but his plans were overturned a few days later when a storm wrecked his whale boat. Instead of travelling to Igloolik and beyond, he perforce remained in the Frobisher Bay area. Instead of discovering relics and recording oral traditions of Franklin, he found traces of Frobisher's voyages of 1576–8 and, most importantly, learned that the local Inuit had preserved a remarkably full and accurate oral tradition of Frobisher's Baffin Island activities (see Chapter 3). Hall's many months living with the Inuit between 1860 and 1862 enabled him to learn something of their language. When the *George Henry* took him home at the end of the summer of 1862 he had with him two Inuit he had befriended, Adlala or Ebierbing and his wife Tookoolitoo, known as Joe and Hannah, who had been taken to England by a whaler in 1853, lived there for a time, and been presented to Queen Victoria. They were to accompany Hall on the next expedition, on which he was more than ever determined, especially now that he was able, he maintained, to speak with the Inuit, live among them, and support himself in the same way as they did. He was convinced, since the Inuit traditions of Frobisher 'were so clear . . . that among them may be sought, by one competent, with every chance of complete success, the sad history of Sir John Franklin's men' (Hall 1865: iii–iv). This was too optimistic.

Hall's second Arctic expedition was delayed because both Henry Grinnell and American whaling interests in general suffered severe financial losses in the Civil War (1861–5). Grinnell, still an enthusiastic supporter of Hall, could not this time finance him, but he did help launch a public appeal which brought in enough for a limited outfit, and the whaleship owners of New London, Williams and Haven, gave Hall free passage to and fro and some supplies. He left New London on 1 July 1864 on the whaler *Monticello*, which landed him in Roe's Welcome Sound. Here he spent the winter of 1864/5 before moving to Repulse Bay. It was only in August 1869, after sledging over 4,000 miles (6,500 km) in all, that he finally left Repulse Bay for home on the whaler *Ansell Gibbs*. He had lived off the land like an Eskimo, with his two Eskimo companions, Joe Ebierbing and his wife Tookoolitoo, and sometimes with a few American whaling hands. He had travelled widely from his Repulse Bay base, though he was only briefly able to reach the south-eastern shore of King William Island in May 1869 when the relics of Franklin's men were mostly concealed under a blanket of snow. His many conversations about the Franklin expedition with the Inuit, in which he relied on Tookoolitoo's skill as an interpreter, yielded innumerable jig-saw puzzle pieces of information, often self-contradictory, often fanciful, which neither he nor anyone since has been able to put together into a meaningful picture. Inevitably there was a strong tendency for the Inuit he questioned, not to mention his interpreter Tookoolitoo, to tell Hall what he wanted to hear, and an equallly strong predisposition for Hall to hear what he wanted to hear. Thus on 6 December 1864 at Repulse Bay a story he was told via Tookoolitoo by some visiting Inuit caused him to write in large letters in the margin of his journal: 'FOUR SOULS OF SIR JOHN FRANKLIN'S EXPEDITION HEARD FROM – ONE OF THESE F.R.M. CROZIER: THREE OF THESE MAY YET BE ALIVE' (Loomis 1972: 190). His account of the conversation shows that he accepted quite uncritically that Crozier, who took over command of the *Erebus* and *Terror* after Franklin's death on 11 June 1847, had been correctly identified, though this is by no means certain; that Crozier's men had been eating the flesh of Koblunas or white men, that is of their deceased companions; and that the two ships mentioned were indeed the *Erebus* and *Terror*. Neitchille appears to refer to the hunting grounds of the Netsilik in and around present-day Spence Bay. Crozier, then a midshipman, was with Parry and Lyon at Igloolik in 1822–3. Here is the passage in question (Nourse 1879: 589):

> I had not got two words out before Too-koo-li-too signaled to me by a motion of her hand to keep silent. She then said, 'They are saying something that I will like much to hear.' Of course I waited with great solicitude. Too-koo-li-too's face soon glowed with delight as she said; 'That same man, Crozier, who was at Igloo-lik when Parry and Lyon were there, was Esh-e-mut-ta (meaning captain in this case, the literal chief) of the two ships lost in the ice at Neitchille. Crozier was the only man that would not eat any of the meat of the Koblunas as the others all did. Crozier and the three men with him were very hungry, but Crozier, though nearly starved and very thin, would not eat a bit of the Koblunas, – he waited till an Innuit who was with him and the three men caught a seal, and then Crozier only ate one mouthful, – one little bit first time. Next time, Crozier ate of the seal he took a little larger piece, though that was a little bit too. One man of the whole number four died because he was sick. The others all lived and grew fat, and finally Crozier got one Innuit with his kiak to accompany him and the two men in trying to get to the Koblunar country by traveling to the southward. The Innuits here think these two men and Crozier are alive yet; think they may have returned to Neitchille, if they found they could not get home to the Koblunar country, and lived again with the Innuits.

Hall's initial enthusiasm soon evaporated and he learned to treat Inuit tales with caution, especially after his experience with the elderly woman Erktua, who claimed that at Igloolik in 1822–3 she became the mistress of both Parry and

Lyon. Some months later Hall was irritated to discover that she had been spreading rumours about him, 'saying that he had tried to solicit her through the offices of Tookoolito' (Loomis 1972: 189). By the end of his five-year quest for Franklin survivors, Hall was a disappointed man. He had indeed collected some bones and a skull on King William Island which later proved to be those of Lieutenant Le Vesconte of the *Erebus*, and buried other bones, and he had obtained a number of indisputable Franklin relics, weighing in all 125 lb (57 kg), from the Inuit, but he found no trace of living survivors. He returned home resenting the fact that the Inuit had for the most part refused to go to the aid of Franklin's exhausted men, either by feeding or guiding them, and that they had removed everything of value to themselves, even plundering corpses and dismantling cairns. Hall had learnt to live like an Eskimo, but not to think and behave like one (the narratives of Hall's first two expeditions are in Hall 1865 and Nourse 1879).

SCHWATKA'S SEARCH

Not only had Hall been unable to search King William Island thoroughly for Franklin relics, but he had died in 1871, and the narrative of his 1864–9 expedition was not published until 1879. Not surprisingly therefore, in the 1870s there was still considerable interest in a further investigation which would repeat, though at greater length and at a favourable time of year when the snow had melted, the one and only at all systematic search so far made of the King William Island shores – that of M'Clintock in 1859. It was partly to this end, and partly in an attempt to sail through the North-West Passage via Peel Sound in Franklin's footsteps as it were, that Allen Young took the *Pandora* into Lancaster Sound in the summer of 1875. His unsuccessful voyage was financed in part by James Gordon Bennett jun. (Riffenburgh 1991), then chief executive officer of his father's New York *Herald*. *Herald* correspondent Januarius A. MacGahan described the voyage in a series of spirited articles put together in his *Under the Northern Lights* (Beynen 1876, MacGahan 1876, Lillingston 1876, Young 1879). Bennett's interest in the Franklin relics was further aroused by Inuit stories of a cache of documents placed in a cairn by a 'great white man', which whaling captain Thomas Barry had heard while wintering in Repulse Bay as mate of the *Glacier* between 1871 and 1873. When he returned in 1877 from wintering at Marble Island, Barry reported that an Inuk had told him that the 'great white man' kept a log book just like his, and another Inuk had given him a spoon engraved with the name 'Franklin'. These stories were the subject of articles in Bennett's newspaper and in 1878 he enlisted the aid of the American Geographical Society and a New York whaling firm to launch an expedition to find the cairn and other Franklin records and relics. Lieutenant Frederick Schwatka of the Third United States Cavalry, of Polish origin but born in America, volunteered to lead it. Another of Bennett's reporters, William H. Gilder, was appointed second-in-command, and Joe Ebierbing was hired as Inuit interpreter and hunter. Two volunteers joined the group: Heinrich W. Klutschak from Prague, who acted as artist and surveyor, and Frank F. Melms, an exwhaleman. Schwatka's party was landed by Captain Thomas Barry from the whaler *Eothen,* a little north of the mouth of Chesterfield Inlet. After wintering there, the party travelled by dog sledge overland with Inuit guides more or less directly to King William Island, and spent 26 May–30 September 1879 searching the Adelaide Peninsula and the west coast of King William Island between Montreal Island and Cape Felix, splitting as required, before returning to the Hudson Bay coast during the winter of 1879/80. Schwatka and his group had covered 3,251 miles (5,230 km) in less than a year without any losses or even injuries, having killed and eaten 522 reindeer. Schwatka had proved an outstanding leader, in dealing both with the expedition members and with the Inuit travelling with them. On one occasion he covered 75 miles (120 km) on foot, nonstop, without food, accompanied by an Inuk, in twenty-three hours. But the expedition's success perhaps depended even more on the survival skills of the Inuk Tulugaq (Raven). It was his energy and drive that enabled the group to use Inuit travel techniques as effectively as had John Rae and Charles Hall. The expedition's aims were entirely accomplished: for the first time a systematic search for Franklin relics was made and this proved that 'time, climatic conditions, and the natives have eliminated any hope of finding' any other significant relics (Klutschak 1987: 135). Moreover, every bone discovered had been given a decent burial, except those of Lieutenant John Irving, which were removed for burial in England. Finally, the expedition had recorded a fund of Inuit testimony about the Franklin expedition which supplemented the mass of material gathered by Hall, though it was equally inconclusive.

Considering the ground it covered, Schwatka's search was a bargain, costing under $5,000. Donations helped. Wilson and Co. of Chicago gave 200 lb (90 kg) 'of their famous corned beef'; the Wilson bakery in New York donated 500 lb (225 kg)of hardtack and 400 lb (180 kg)of margarine. Other gifts were two magazine rifles from Winchester and Co., two army rifles from Remington and Co., 'one fine Treadmere target rifle worth $115 with 1,000 shells and 1,000 extra bullets ready moulded and with all the accessories for Joe, our Inuit interpreter' from Whitney and Co., 'from the Merwin Co. one Evans 26-shot magazine rifle with 500 shells and accessories for special testing by Lieutenant Schwatka', and two Russian army revolvers with 500 shells. 'The commissariat of the Weapons Administration of the Militia of the State of New York' donated twenty muzzle-loading rifles – but these were for trade with the natives (Klutschak 1987: 15–16; the sources for Schwatka's search are Gilder 1881, Stackpole 1965, Klutschak 1987).

WHALING IN ALASKAN WATERS

Thomas Roys had made his historic whaling voyage through Bering Strait in 1848, the year before Jane Franklin's appeal to the American president. In 1849, forty-six American whaleships sailed north through Bering Strait and over a hundred did so annually between 1850 and 1853. Thereafter, numbers were smaller, seldom rising above forty but not dropping below about twenty per annum, until the end of the century. Then, between 1900 and 1914 the Beaufort Sea Whale fishery (Bockstoce 1986) drew to its close. By the 1890s, as mineral oil

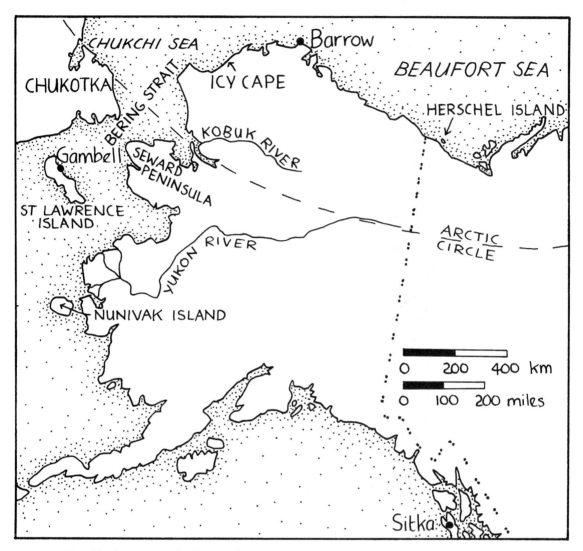

Map 22. Americans in the Western Arctic.

replaced whale oil, blubber was hardly worth trying out because the oil fetched so little. In 1907 the market for whalebone collapsed. By this time, in any case, there were scarcely any bowheads left. The life of the fishery had been extended by technical and other innovations: from the late 1860s walrus hunting became a profitable sideline; overwintering, first on the Chukotka coast and then in the 1890s and later at Herschel Island and elsewhere (Cook 1926), extended the whale catching season; shore whaling stations were established in the 1880s to the same end; steamships increasingly replaced sail after 1879 (Bockstoce 1977); and voyages were substantially shortened from the 1880s, when San Francisco took over from New Bedford as the American whalers' headquarters.

Like other whale fisheries (see Chapter 4), the Chukchi and Beaufort Sea fishery suffered some spectacular disasters. In 1865, after its formal close, the American Civil War reached Bering Strait in the form of the Confederate cruiser *Shenandoah*, which, a steamship among sailers, torched a score of Arctic whalers between 22 and 28 June that year. In 1871 the Arctic ice took its toll: thirty-two ships, out of a total Arctic whaling fleet of forty, were beset along the coast north of Icy Cape and many were smashed to pieces as a south-west wind drove the pack ice against the shore in August and September. All the ships had to be abandoned. The crews, with some woman and child passengers, made their way in open boats to the remaining seven ships of the fleet, which awaited them south of the ice. These seven took 1,219 persons safely to Honolulu, Hawaii. Not a life was lost. In 1876 both ships and lives were lost. Ten ships which drifted, locked in the ice, east from Point Barrow late in the season, were abandoned by their captains and most of their crews. Of the fifty or more men who chose to remain on the ships, only five struggled ashore to reach Barrow, and only three of these lived.

After further shipwrecks in subsequent years, a United States government rescue station was built at Barrow in 1889 but ceased to function a few years later, and was sold at the end of 1896. Less than a year afterwards its absence was sorely felt by the 275 or so men from that season's eight wrecked or beset whaleships on the north Alaskan coast. About a hundred of them were cared for, fed, and housed at Barrow through the winter of 1897/8, largely by the efforts of a single private citizen, Charles D. Brower, part-owner of the Cape Smyth Trading and Whaling Company, which he had helped set up at Barrow in 1893. Brower also helped supply the whalemen who remained on, or camped out near, their ships along the coast, and obtained fresh meat for them by enlisting the aid of local Inupiat Eskimos to go hunting inland. When news of ships trapped or lost in the ice, with possibly starving crewmen, reached San Francisco with the first returning whaler in November 1897, the United States federal government took action and sent the revenue cutter *Bear* to the rescue. Heavy ice barred her way to the Seward Peninsula and the projected overland expedition had to be disembarked further south than was planned, on the mainland opposite Nunivak Island. First Lieutenant David H. Jarvis, of the United States Revenue Cutter Service, organized and led the overland relief expedition with daring and skill and complete success. It was undertaken in winter, from December to March, but Jarvis's travels continued to and fro between Barrow and the beset ships still occupied by their crews along the coast, until the *Bear* eventually reached Barrow on 28 July 1898. He travelled in all some 2,500 miles (4,000 km) by dog sledge, and on his way to Barrow drove 448 domestic reindeer about 700 miles (1,100 km) from the Seward Peninsula to the tundra just south of Barrow. It may be true, as Brower relates, that these deer were reduced to skin and bone on arrival and were unfit to eat. If so, they must have recovered quickly. According to Jarvis, the animals provided 12,481 lb (5,661 kg) of fresh meat for the castaways. The loss was made good by the birth of 190 healthy fawns to the herd while it grazed the tundra near Barrow that summer. The deer were subsequently returned to their owners. But Jarvis did not rest content with supplementing the castaways' diet with this supply of fresh meat. He organized better living quarters for them, saw that those needing it received medical treatment from his colleague of the Revenue Cutter Service, Surgeon S.J. Call, enforced much-needed discipline, improved cooking facilities and clothing, and insisted on regular hygiene and exercise. All 275 castaways survived the ordeal, some hundred of them being taken home on the *Bear*, and the rest on their own ships after these were freed from the ice (Jarvis 1899, Cook 1926: 123–5, Brower 1950).

The catastrophic impact of the Chukchi and Beaufort Seas whale fishery on the Eskimos living on the shores of these seas is described in Chapter 12. As to the bowheads, no one knows how many were left in 1914 after the whalers had killed an estimated 18,650 in all (Bockstoce 1986: 345), but it must have been the merest remnant. In the 1990s it seems likely that this population of bowheads, which migrates every spring through Bering Strait and spreads in summer through the Chukchi and Beaufort Seas, just as it did before 1848, numbers fewer than 10,000 animals and possibly fewer than 5,000 (Moore and Clarke 1991, Moore 1992). Since the end of commercial whaling in Alaskan waters, Inuit subsistence whaling at a dozen coastal villages between Gambell on St Lawrence Island and Barrow has continued, and is generally regarded as a vital element in Inuit social life (Donovan 1982: 35–48). Between 1910 and 1969 only about a dozen whales were taken annually by these Eskimos, but since 1970 the harvest has increased to thirty or forty or more and it is now strictly controlled by the Alaska Eskimo Whaling Commission (Huntington 1992a, 1992b). By contrast, the estimated average annual catch in the years 1850–99, by commercial as opposed to subsistence whalers, was 307 (Bockstoce 1986: 346–7).

RUSSIAN AMERICA BECOMES ALASKA

The sale of Russian America to the United States of America in 1867 (Farrar 1937, Tomkins 1945: 170–90, Gruening 1954: 23–9, Jensen 1975, Alekseev 1990 and especially Bolkhovitinov 1990), without any reference whatsoever to its native inhabitants, or to the Russian-American Company, made America an Arctic power overnight. Only the northern one-third of the territory concerned (which Senator Charles Sumner named Alaska, from the Aleut word for 'mainland') is north of the Arctic Circle and only a relatively narrow strip of terrain, Alaska's Arctic or North Slope, is tundra. Moreover, Russia's colonies in America, which were governed from the Russian-American Company's Far Eastern headquarters at Novoarkhangel'sk, now to be renamed Sitka, were all south of the Arctic. There were no Russian settlements north of Bering Strait, where American whalers and traders had been busy doing whatever they pleased since 1848. In 1855 a detachment of the United States North Pacific Surveying Expedition of 1853–6, consisting of the USS *Vincennes*, under Commander John Rodgers, sailed north through Bering Strait to survey and reconnoitre this area. Behind the despatch of this first American federal ship to the Arctic Ocean was the enthusiasm and drive of Kane's staunch supporter, Secretary of the Navy J.P. Kennedy, who believed it should be the aim of the Navy Department to employ ships and men in discovery, in opening up new fields for trade, and in enlarging the boundaries of knowledge.

A party from the *Vincennes* made the first recorded landing on Herald Island (ostrov Geral'd) in August 1855, but fog prevented any exploration of Wrangel Island (ostrov Vrangelya) (Map 23), nor did the *Vincennes* visit the north coast of Alaska (Nourse 1884: 110, 116–29, Caswell 1956: 185–8). Americans did begin the exploration of Alaska while it was still Russian America, for the Western Union Telegraph Expedition was busy surveying in the Yukon Valley and the Seward Peninsula in 1865–7 under Robert Kennicott and, after his untimely death perhaps by his own hand when only thirty-one, under William Healey Dall (1870). These men were making daring and prolonged dog-sledge journeys in Russian America, as were their colleagues, George Kennan (1870) (who wrote a most entertaining account of his experiences) and Richard J. Bush (1872), in the Anadyr' region of Siberia (Map 12). One of their most notable dog-sledge journeys was made by Richard Lewis, a young telegraph operator with no experience of wilderness travel and no knowledge of Russian. He was credited by Kennan (1910: 390–1) with accomplishing the 1,200 mile (1,900 km) trip from Petropavlovsk in Kamchatka to Gizhiga in November-December 1866 in forty-two days, thus averaging 29 miles (47 km) a day. To their great disappointment, the work of the Telegraph Men was brought to an abrupt end when it was only half finished by the laying of a telegraph cable under the Atlantic in 1866, which caused the Western Union Telegraph Company to cancel its planned cable from America to Siberia. It had completed a section of the line in British Columbia, surveyed nearly the whole of it, and the Asiatic division 'had cut and prepared fifteen or twenty thousand telegraph poles' (Kennan 1910: 411). All this to no purpose (Sherwood 1965: 15–35, Neering 1989).

By the middle years of the nineteenth century the Russian government had perfectly valid reasons for selling Russian America to the United States. Particularly compelling were its great distance from Russian administrative centres, the very small population of Russian settlers there (only 672 in 1863), and the belief that it would fall to the United States in any case. There was reason to believe that the Americans would be glad to purchase Alaska: they had made the Louisiana purchase from France in 1803 for fifteen million dollars, and bought Florida from Spain for five million dollars, not to mention Texas and California. To add to these inducements for a sale, the Russian-American Company's chronic administrative and financial problems came to a head between 1860 and 1865, when the question of extending its monopoly, which ran out in 1862, was hotly debated. In 1866 the company was in debt to the tune of a million roubles and was receiving an annual subsidy from the government of nearly two million roubles. At the very time when the Russian hold on America was becoming increasingly difficult to maintain, the 1860 Treaty of Beijing gave Russia trading rights in China, control of the Amur Valley, and a new territory on the Pacific east of the Ussuri River, with the magnificent harbour of Vladivostok ('Master of the East'). This formed a much better base for Russia's Pacific interests than Russian America.

In 1853 the Russian-American Company, fearful of an Anglo-French naval attack on the eve of the Crimean War, actually discussed the possibility of a fictitious transfer or sale of all its properties and privileges for three years to a San Francisco Company, confusingly called the American-Russian Commercial

Company, which had contracted to deliver basic supplies to Russian America and in return was granted the monopoly of coal and lake-ice exports to California from there (Busch 1985: 102–03). In the following year, 1854, the United States government informally asked the Russians if they might be willing to sell Russian America. Though the reply was a firm negative, Grand Duke Constantine Nikolayevich, Tsar Alexander II's brother, suggested in 1857 to the Russian foreign minister that, in view of the financial problems caused by the Crimean War 'we would do well to take advantage of the excess of money at the present time in the treasury of the United States of America and sell them our North American colonies' (Jensen 1975: 10). By the end of the 1850s the Russian minister in Washington, Edouard de Stoeckl, the governor-general of Siberia, Nikolay N. Murav'yev, and Rear-Admiral Andrei Alexandrovich Popov, commander of the Pacific Fleet, were all pressing for the sale. Although the American Civil War delayed things, it brought Russia and America closer together because Russia alone supported the Union or North, while Britain and France appeared to incline toward the Confederacy or South. In 1863, fearing a war with England and France, Russia sent her fleets to New York and San Francisco to avoid having them blockaded in their home ports, as they had been during the Crimean War. This move substantially reinforced the growing *entente* between Russia and America, who now regarded themselves as allies against England and France. The crunch finally came in 1866, when the Russian-American Company rejected a proposed charter renewing its monopoly offered by the imperial government, which could not afford, or did not wish, to take the administration of Russian America into its own hands. It preferred to sell it to the United States of America, rather than leave Russian power in America to crumble, which would invite other countries, especially Britain, to intervene. The decision to sell was made in St Petersburg in December 1866 by Tsar Alexander II, his brother Grand Duke Constantine, the ministers of finance, foreign affairs and the marine, and the tsar's representative in Washington, Edouard de Stoeckl.

Secretary of State William H. Seward, who had always been enthusiastic, was ably assisted by de Stoeckl, and had little difficulty in persuading congress to agree to the purchase of Russian America for $7,200,000. Only about $7,000,000 actually reached the Russian government; the remainder was distributed among congressmen and others by de Stoeckl. Many Russians were not entirely happy about the sale, and one or two sarcastic newspaper articles appeared before the government censorship committee swung into action. One Russian paper professed not to believe that American businessmen would pay seven million dollars 'for the metropolis of Sitka, consisting of several barbaric country houses and the residence of the colonial governor, and also for several half-century-old windjammers and steamships' (Jensen 1975: 96–7). Another facetiously wondered if they might soon be hearing of the sale of the Crimea, Transcaucasia or the Baltic provinces. In the present century Soviet writers have voiced their disapproval of the sale. A.I. Alekseyev, the noted historian of Russian America, called it 'this shameful deal', and 'the saddest fact in the history of the formation of the Russian state in the Far East, a fact which illustrates the depravity of the rotten tsarist regime in Russia' (Alekseev 1990: 290). As to the Americans, though a knowledgeable minority at the time drew attention to the enormous value of Alaska's natural resources, far exceeding the purchase price, opponents of the sale were the more vociferous, dubbing Alaska 'Walrussia', 'Icebergia' or 'Seward's Icebox'. The minority report of the House of Representatives Committee on Foreign Relations concluded that Alaska would be of no value to the United States and 'that the right to govern a nation . . . of savages in a climate unfit for the habitation of civilized men was not worthy of purchase'. One member of the house sarcastically suggested that Greenland and Iceland might soon be on the market (Gruening 1954: 28).

Once named and purchased, Alaska was forgotten by the United States government (Gruening 1954: 33–43; see also Tomkins 1945: 191–212). In the seventeen years 1867–84 it received no appropriation of federal funds and was given no government. Only two legislative acts concerning Alaska passed through congress in these years. First, it was made a customs district of the United States and the sale of liquor to natives was forbidden. Subsequently, attempts were made to enforce this law by US revenue cutters sent regularly to Alaskan waters from 1879. The second of the two acts made the Pribilof Islands (which are not in the Arctic, being on the same latitude as Aberdeen) a reservation for the fur seals that bred there in large numbers, and granted the Alaska Commercial Company of San Francisco monopoly control of the herd, with the right to kill 100,000 animals per annum, for twenty years starting in 1870 (Busch 1985: 95–122). By the time Alaska was given a governor and made a District, in 1884, explorations inland were beginning to supplement the coastal patrols of the US revenue cutters *William Rush*, *Corwin* and *Bear* along Alaska's Arctic coast. In 1883 Lieutenant Frederick Schwatka led a small US army expedition down the Yukon River, and in 1884 and 1885 Lieutenants George M. Stoney of the US Navy and John C. Cantwell of the Revenue Marine Service explored the hitherto unexplored Kobuk River, which was indubitably Arctic (Sherwood 1965: 98–102, 119–32, Cantwell 1889). By this time Alaska was progressing from ex-governor Ernest Gruening's 'era of total neglect (1867–84)' to his 'era of flagrant neglect (1884–98)'. Only in the dawn of the new century would 'the era of mild but unenlightened interest (1898–1912)' of the United States in Alaska begin (Gruening 1954). On 3 January 1959 Alaska was finally admitted to the Union as the forty-ninth state.

THE NORTH POLE AND THE OPEN POLAR SEA

When in 1853 Elisha Kent Kane sailed north in Smith Sound with the aim of pushing the *Advance* through the ice into a supposed unfrozen polar sea, he had talked about finding Franklin there. The surgeon of his expedition, Isaac Israel Hayes, led an exploring expedition of his own through Smith Sound in 1860 in the 133 ton schooner *United States*. This was in many respects a mere repeat of Kane's expedition, but Franklin was now forgotten and instead the North Pole figured prominently in the expedition's plans. 'My object', wrote Hayes, 'was to complete the survey of the north coasts of Greenland and Grinnell Land [Ellesmere Island], and to make such explorations as I might find practicable in the direction of the North Pole' (Hayes 1867: 1; for what follows on expeditions to the North Pole, Bryce 1910, Laktionov 1955 and Hassert 1956 are still perhaps the best guides). Hayes called at Prøven (now Kangersuatsiaq, see Map 21), and Upernavik, on the west coast of Greenland, to pick up thirty-six dogs, two Danish dog drivers, Peter Jensen and Carl Christian Petersen, and three Greenlandic hunters. He stopped again at Cape York to take on board the Greenlandic hunter who had deserted from Kane's expedition to marry an Inuhuit girl, Hans Hendrik or Suersaq, together with his wife and child. Hayes did not succeed in navigating the *United States* as far north as Kane had the *Advance*, for he was compelled to take his ship into winter quarters on the south side of Foulke Fjord, opposite Iita (Map 21), some eighty miles along the coast south-west of Rensselaer Harbour. But in the spring of 1860 he did take a sledging party further north along the Ellesmere Island coast than he had travelled during Kane's expedition in 1854. From his furthest point north, about half-way through Kennedy Channel on the Ellesmere Island shore, which he reached on 18 May 1861, Hayes was convinced he could see stretching away northward the long-sought-after Open Polar Sea. He returned to Boston in 1861, after what he optimistically regarded as a successful expedition. Although he lost all his west Greenlandic dogs to an epidemic in December, he was able to acquire seventeen more from the Inuhuit. His Danish dog drivers had put the dogs to excellent effect, though they were not employed for Hayes's brief excursion on the Inland Ice – one of the first recorded. He had lost two men. A Greenlander,

Plate 17. *'The shores of the Polar Sea' from a sketch by Isaac I. Hayes, looking north along the Ellesmere Island coast from near the northern end of Kennedy Channel, May 1861 (Hayes 1867: 346). Here, thought Hayes, he was standing 'upon the shores of the Polar Basin', and he supposed that within a month the entire sea would be free of ice (pp. 349–50). This was Hayes's furthest north, and he unfurled two United States flags, two Masonic flags 'and our Expedition signal-flag, bearing the Expedition emblem, the Pole Star – a crimson star, on a white field . . . ' (p. 351).*

Peter, had deserted and was later found dead; and the expedition's scientist and second-in-command, August Sonntag, died after breaking through thin ice. Hayes prided himself on 'bringing my party through without sickness', but the expedition probably escaped scurvy because it spent only one winter in the Arctic, rather than because of Hayes's good management. He planned to return with a steamer in the following year to found a colony-cum-trading post at Port Foulke, as he called his winter harbour, and 'with a corps of scientific associates, to make that the centre of a widely extended system of exploration' (Hayes 1867: 452). The American Civil War interrupted and, as it turned out, postponed for ever Hayes's future Arctic plans. His trading post cum exploring centre was set up in 1910 at Uummannaq (Map 21), further south in Avanersuaq, by Knud Rasmussen and Peter Freuchen (Vaughan 1991; see also Chapter 10).

When Charles Francis Hall returned from his five-year stay among the Inuit of the Repulse Bay area in the autumn of 1869, his obsession with the fate of the Franklin expedition had been replaced by a passion for the North Pole, which he had first entertained as early as 1863 (Davis 1876: 17). He reinforced his new-found fame with lecture tours, and his Arctic experiences were described in numerous newspaper articles. In Washington that winter he persuaded senators and congressmen among his aquaintance to support his proposed United States North Polar Expedition, and won over President Ulysses S. Grant. In June 1871 he sailed from New York in the US steamer *Polaris*, funded to the extent of around $100,000 by congress, and instructed by Secretary of the Navy George M. Robeson after crossing Melville Bay to 'make all possible progress, with vessels, boats, and sledges, toward the North Pole' (Davis 1876: 31). This was to be virtually a repeat of the Hayes expedition of 1860. Besides a rather motley crew, which was half American and half German, Hall took with him a small Inuit colony: his old friends Ebierbing and Tookoolitoo and a child of theirs, and the now indispensable Suersaq, with his wife and children. After starting brilliantly, when the *Polaris* was iced in on the coast of Hall Land (Map 21) further north than any ship had so far wintered (81° 37'), having first penetrated to 82° 11' north, the expeditions suffered disaster. Its respected and much-liked commander, Charles Hall, was taken ill and died on board ship on 8 November 1871; the *Polaris* was badly damaged by ice during the winter; and, deprived of its commander, the expedition's members foolishly attempted to proceed northwards in open boats, instead of with sledges. They also fell out among themselves and discipline nearly broke down. But the worst was yet to come. In October 1872, while the *Polaris* was drifting south in heavy ice through Smith Sound, a storm swept the ice against the ship, which seemed about to sink. Provisions, boats and other gear were thrown out onto the floe. But then, when nineteen men, women and children had moved onto the ice and fourteen men were still aboard the *Polaris*, she broke free of the ice and drifted rapidly away. Those on the floe, fortunately including the Inuit members of the expedition, drifted at least 3,000 km (2,000 miles) south-south-east on the ice for 197 days through the polar winter before they were rescued off the Labrador coast (Map 9) by the steam sealer *Tigress*, captained by Isaac Bartlett, on 30 April 1873. They had with them at the start only 11½ bags of bread, 14 45-pound tins of pemmican, 14 small hams,

120 1- and 2-lb tins of meat and soup, a 22-lb tin of dried apples, and 'about 20 lb of chocolate and sugar mixed' (Blake 1874: 211), but their Eskimo companions kept them alive when these provisions were exhausted by killing seals. Those remaining on the *Polaris* managed to get ashore, wintered on the Greenland coast just north of Foulke Fjord in a house built with timber from the *Polaris*, and made their way south in two boats likewise constructed with wood from the *Polaris*. They were picked up by a Scottish whaler, the *Ravenscraig* of Kirkcaldy, at the northern end of Melville Bay, on 23 June 1873.

The expedition had achieved very little. Its furthest norths on land and sea were soon afterwards bettered by the British Arctic Expedition of 1875–6. Only one life was lost, that of Hall. The expedition's chief scientific officer, Emil Bessels, who had read medicine at the University of Heidelberg and zoology at those of Jena and Stuttgart, was a man of wide interests and admirable powers of observation. He wrote an excellent account of the expedition which has never been translated into English (Bessels 1879). He found no evidence for an Open Polar Sea, but correctly surmised that the interplay of currents, tides and winds produced local polynyas or leads, and patches of open water here and there. He also published detailed and valuable ornithological records made during the expedition (Bessels 1879: 311–12, Bessels 1875) and the first scientific account of Inuhuit ethnology, in the preparation of which he measured a hundred Inuhuit craniums (Bessels 1879: 350–73, Bessels 1884). In a solitary excursion, Bessels walked 27 miles (43 km) onto the Inland Ice, reaching an altitude of 3,181 ft (970 m) above sea level, and found a crevasse which was over 5 ft (1½ m) wide and 570 ft (174 m) deep (Bessels 1879: 401).

The puzzle of Hall's death has never been solved in spite of the exhumation carried out by his biographer Chauncey C. Loomis in 1968 and the autopsy performed on his body at that time. While the official Board of Inquiry concluded that he died of 'natural causes, viz, apoplexy', the autopsy revealed that Hall had 'received toxic amounts of arsenic during the last two weeks of his life' (Loomis 1972: 345). This finding was based on the arsenic content of hair and fingernail fragments; the internal organs had disintegrated. Who administered the arsenic which killed Hall? Suicide is inconceivable. The possibility that Hall was murdered by Emil Bessels seems equally remote. More likely, he inadvertently gave himself overdoses of arsenious acid, a commonly used medicine of the day. If this was indeed the case, history repeated itself in the Arctic some thirty years later when Hermann Walther, surgeon of the Russian Polar Expedition of 1900–3 (Barr 1981), seems to have killed himself with an overdose of digitalis, self-administered in an attempt to improve his heart condition (Toll 1909: 457–60. On Hall's last expedition see especially Blake 1874, Davis 1876, Bessels 1879, Loomis 1972: 228–354).

The notion of an Open Polar Sea died hard. It still played a role in the disastrous voyage of the *Jeannette*, formerly Allen Young's *Pandora*, which was initiated and funded by James Gordon Bennett of the New York *Herald*, led by Lieutenant George Washington De Long, US Navy, and organized as a United States naval expedition (Newcomb 1882, E. De Long 1884, 1883, Gilder 1883, Melville 1896 and Riffenburgh 1991). But the ideas behind her projected cruise through Bering

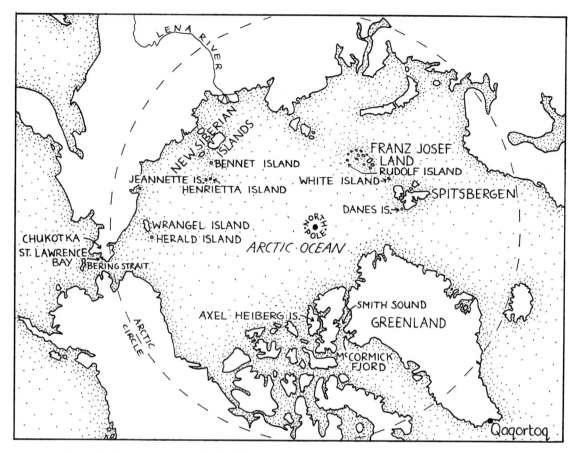

Map 23. Approaches to the North Pole.

Strait towards the North Pole came from Gustave Lambert, who had planned a French expedition into the Polar Sea via Bering Strait in 1867–8 (Beaujeu-Garnier 1990), and above all from August Petermann. This German geographer, based at Gotha, had acquired an international reputation through his famous *Geographische Mitteilungen*, though he had no first-hand knowledge of the Arctic. His hare-brained ideas about the central Arctic basin had already caused a succession of polar disasters, one of which was the misconceived German North Polar Expedition of 1869–70. Then, Petermann had proposed voyaging to the North Pole via the east Greenland coast; now, in 1878, just months before his suicide, Petermann advised Bennett that the high road to the North Pole led through Bering Strait. He still insisted that 'The central area of the Polar regions is more or less free from ice' (Guttridge 1988: 40), while not ruling out the possibility of land stretching some way between Wrangel Island and Greenland. De Long took the *Jeannette* into the ice north of Herald Island in September 1879, and she drifted to and fro, not, as had been hoped, on a course for the North Pole, but mainly north-westwards. Eventually her crew sighted two small, isolated islands which De Long named

Jeannette Island (ostrov Zhannetty) and Henrietta Island (ostrov Genriyetty). He contrived to send a landing party under Chief Engineer George Melville to Henrietta Island (named after Bennett's mother) and claim it for the United States as the ship drifted past, locked in the ice. In 1937, personnel of the Soviet Polar station on Henrietta Island found De Long's record almost rotted away, in the cairn in which Melville had placed it (Belov 1977: 123). The *Jeannette* was crushed and sank on 13 June 1881, and her crew made their laborious way over the ice via Bennett Island and the New Siberian Islands, heading for the Lena Delta. While crossing the unfrozen sea between the New Siberian Islands and the Lena Delta in September 1881, their three open boats were separated. One was lost and no trace of it has ever been found. Another, De Long's, reached the shore, but De Long and all but two of the crew died of starvation before they could be rescued. George W. Melville got his boat safely ashore and soon made contact with natives. The expedition had confirmed that there was no Open Polar Sea, and severely restricted the size of any possible North Polar continent. It occasioned the despatch of three unsuccessful relief expeditions. The USS *Rodgers*, Lieutenant Robert M. Berry commanding, charted the coast of Wrangel Island but was destroyed by fire in her St Lawrence Bay (zaliv Lavrentiya) winter quarters, the USS *Alliance* cruised to Spitsbergen, and the US Revenue Marine Steamer *Corwin* searched the northern Chukotka coast in 1881.

THE UNITED STATES AND THE INTERNATIONAL POLAR YEAR

Not long after the return of the Austro-Hungarian North Polar Expedition in 1874, Lieutenant Karl Weyprecht, of the Imperial Austro-Hungarian navy, one of the leaders of that expedition, proposed a concerted international one-year programme in the Arctic which might, but did not, replace the current nationalistic free-for-all of North Pole expeditions. An International Polar Commission was set up and a dozen countries agreed to man stations in 1882–3, carrying out a stipulated programme of meteorological, auroral and geomagnetic studies. The twelve stations manned in the Arctic are listed in Table 5.

For the most part the International Polar Year expeditions were uneventful, and the overwintering by a dozen different parties in as many different parts of the Arctic went off without a hitch. But two expeditions met with serious difficulties. The Dutch expedition ship *Varna* became beset in ice in the Kara Sea on 16 September 1882, before she could land the staff of the planned scientific station on Dikson Island. She sank on 17 July 1883, but the crew made a successful sledge and boat journey to the mainland (Snellen 1886).

The other expedition that came to grief was that of the United States to Lady Franklin Bay, near the northern tip of Ellesmere Island (see Map 21). First Lieutenant Adolphus Washington Greely set up a US Army signal station here which began observations under the International Polar Year programme on 18 August 1881 and continued them successfully for two complete years (Greely 1886, Schley and Soley 1889, Brainard 1929, Powell 1961). The station, called Fort Conger after a senator who had concerned himself with the expedition, was on the shore of Discovery Bay, where HMS *Discovery* had wintered in 1875/6.

Country	Leader and no. of personnel	Location	°N. Lat	Comments
USA	A.W. Greely + 21	Lady Franklin Bay, Ellesmere Island	81	US army. Only 6 survivors
USA	P.H. Ray + 9 (Ray 1885)	Barrow, Alaska	71	US army
Britain	H.P. Dawson + 3	Fort Rae, Great Slave Lake	62	British Army
Germany	W. Giese + 12	Shilmilik Bay, Baffin Island	67	–
Denmark	A. Paulsen + 5	Nuuk, Greenland	64	–
Austria-Hungary	E. von Wohlgemuth + 13	Jan Mayen	71	Austro-Hungarian Imperial Navy
Sweden	N. Ekholm + 12	Kapp Thordsen, Spitsbergen	80	–
Norway	A. Steen + 4	Alta (Bossekop), Finnmark	70	–
Finland	E. Biese + 4	Sodankylä, Finland	67	–
The Netherlands	M. Snellen + 9	[Ostrov Dikson] Kara Sea	[73]	–
Russia	N. Jürgens + 6	Ostrov Sagastyr', Lena Delta	73	organized by Imperial Russian Geographical Society
Russia	K.P. Andreyev + 8	Malyye Karmakuly, Novaya Zemlya	72	organized by Imperial Russian Geographical Society

Table 5.   Arctic stations manned during the First International Polar Year, 1882–3. Compiled from Nourse 1884: 531–2, Bruun 1902: 283, Greely 1929: 174–82, Vize 1932, Baker 1982, Barr 1985.

Besides the completion of the programme of observations at the International Polar Year's most northerly station, Greely and his men undertook important explorations with dog sledges, both in the interior of Ellesmere Island, where they discovered Lake Hazen and Greely Fjord, and along the north coast of Greenland, where on 15 May 1882 Lieutenant James Booth Lockwood reached a furthest north at Lockwood Island of 83° 24', just beating Markham's 1876 record (Lanman 1885). Meanwhile, efforts to support and relieve Greely were going sadly awry. While the *Proteus*, taking Greely north in 1881, like HMS *Discovery* in 1875, had sailed without serious hindrance from ice all the way to Lady Franklin Bay, the *Neptune* in 1882 could get no further north than Cape Sabine, where she left a diminutive depot of 250 rations: ten days' supply for the expedition's twenty-five men. A similar depot was left at Littleton Island on the wrong side of Smith Sound, and, for some extraordinary reason, 'the remainder of the stores carried by the *Neptune*, amounting to at least 2,000 rations, or a full supply for three months, had been safely brought back to St John's from the perils of the Arctic' (Schley and Soley 1889). Worse still, in 1883 the *Proteus* was wrecked by the ice near Cape Sabine, and her crew left only a few additional provisions for Greely before escaping south in open boats. Meanwhile, Greely, following his instructions, had retreated with his men south from Lady Franklin Bay, where the plentiful musk oxen had kept them free of scurvy during two winters. He set up camp near Cape Sabine, on the north shore of Pim Island, in October 1883 to

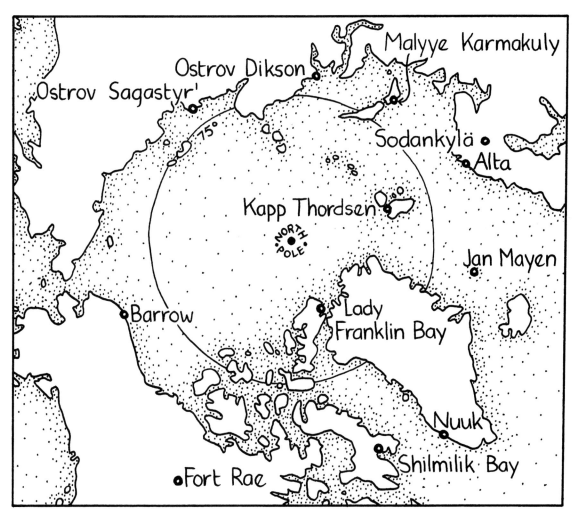

Map 24. Arctic stations planned for the First International Polar Year, 1882–3.

await relief and, as it turned out, to spend the winter with very inadequate supplies of food in an area with little or no game. When relief and rescue finally did come, in June 1884 with the arrival of the *Thetis*, Commander Winfield S. Schley, at Pim Island (Schley 1887), only Greely and five others were still alive, to be rescued from starvation in the nick of time. The disaster was partly due to the vagaries of the Arctic climate, still not fully understood today, which filled Kane Basin with ice in 1882 and 1883. It was also in part due to Greely's instructions to retreat south from Fort Conger in 1883 if he was not relieved. This should have been left to his discretion, for if the party had remained at Fort Conger for another winter a disaster would probably have been averted. In part, too, Greely bears some responsibility for what happened: he should have tried much harder to cross to Greenland, where Inuhuit help might have been secured. But the main reason why seventeen out of Greely's twenty-two–man party died of starvation was the ineptitude of the relief measures taken by the United States authorities. On 9 October 1883 Sergeant George W. Rice found a message which had been left for Greely at Cape Sabine by Lieutenant Ernest A. Garlington, a cavalry officer of no Arctic experience who had been given command of the 1883 relief expedition. Written on 24 July 1883, it stated that 'everything within the power of man will be done to rescue the brave men at Fort Conger from their perilous position' (Greely 1886b: 164). Greely himself, and many others, believed that by no means everything possible was done to rescue them.

It is hardly surprising that a pause of ten years now ensued in American Arctic exploration. Kane had lost the *Advance*, both Hall and De Long had lost their lives and ships, and now came the Greely disaster.

THE NORTH POLE OVER THE ICE

Of the expeditions which set out almost every year between 1893 and 1909 to attempt to reach the North Pole, eight were American, one Norwegian, one Swedish and one Italian. Norwegian participation in at least six of the American expeditions should not be overlooked. The disastrous *Jeannette* expedition had finally exploded the myth of an unfrozen Polar Sea. It had shown that the Arctic Ocean was covered with pack ice, firmer in winter, looser and softer in summer. It also produced evidence pointing to something now known to be a fact (Sugden 1982: 130–1; see also Chapter 9), namely that this enormous sheet of ice was slowly spinning round the pole in a clockwise direction, for the *Jeannette* had drifted from Wrangel Island nearly to the New Siberian Islands in two years. After a further three years, a pair of oilskin trousers belonging to expedition member Louis Noros, along with other articles which must have come from the sinking *Jeannette*, were discovered on the drifting ice off Qaqortoq (Julianehåb) in south-west Greenland (Nansen 1893a, 1897a: 17–18). They had been taken out of the Arctic Basin on the stream of ice that flows south through the Greenland Sea and Denmark Strait, and then swings round Cape Farewell, northwards up the west Greenland coast. It was this drift of Arctic Ocean ice westwards or north-westwards north of Siberia (see Map 27) which inspired Norwegian explorer Fridtjof Nansen to build a ship specially designed with rounded sides, like the Russian koch, to withstand or escape the pressure of the ice, and to drive her into the ice north of ostrov Kotel'nyy (Map 15) in the New Siberian Islands. Nansen thought that his ship, the *Fram* (*Forward*), might drift across the North Pole. Failing that, he planned to leave the ship when it was near the pole and to travel from ship to pole by kayak and dog sledge. In the event, he and Hjalmar Johansen (1898) attained a furthest north of 86° 14' and the *Fram* drifted to 85° 57' north; neither man nor ship had ever been so far north (Nansen 1897, Laktionov 1955: 109–33, Bang 1981). The explorers were exceedingly fortunate to escape from this daring but rash enterprise with their lives. They were saved by a chance encounter with English explorer Frederick Jackson, who happened, unbeknown to Nansen, to be in Franz Josef Land (Zemlya Frantsa Iosifa) at the time. Jackson correctly thought that Nansen was extremely lucky to have hit on a wintering place in northern Franz Josef Land where game was

Plate 18. Norwegian explorer Fridtjof Nansen photographed at Cape Flora, Franz Josef Land, by English explorer Frederick G. Jackson on 17 June 1896 (Nansen 1897b: 466). Nansen had reached Cape Flora that day after kayaking and sledging with Hjalmar Johansen from the Fram *toward the North Pole and then south to Franz Josef Land, where they had wintered in a makeshift shelter. No wonder, after 477 days living off the land in the far north, Nansen looked, as he described it himself, 'a wild man, clad in dirty rags, black with oil and soot, with long uncombed hair and shaggy beard, black with smoke, with a face in which the natural fair complexion could not possibly be discerned through the thick layer of fat and soot' he had been unable to remove during the winter (p. 461). 'Aren't you Nansen?' enquired Jackson after they had greeted each other and shaken hands. 'Yes I am', replied Nansen. 'By Jove, I'm d–d glad to see you!' exclaimed Jackson, adding: 'I congratulate you most heartily; you have made a deuced good trip of it, and I'm awfully glad to be the first person to congratulate you.' (Jackson 1899: 507–8 and Nansen 1897b: 461–3.)*

plentiful, and even luckier to have made contact with him. Nansen and Johansen were able to go home on Jackson's ship, the *Windward*, in August 1896, reaching Norway just as the *Fram* arrived there after emerging from the ice north of Spitsbergen. Jackson added: 'I only trust that Dr Nansen's extraordinary immunity from penalty will not lead the inexperienced to suppose that they may go larking about within the polar circle with merely a dog and a gun, and that all things will be well with them.' (Jackson 1899: 516–17.)

If the North Pole could not be reached on the ice of the Arctic Ocean, perhaps it could be reached by air. Already in 1879 Commander John P. Cheyne RN had proposed using balloons for Polar exploration (Stefansson 1935). In 1896, when the *Fram* called at Spitsbergen after escaping from the ice at the end of her drift, her crew found Swedish engineer Salomon August Andrée about to set out from Danes Island (Danskøya) in his balloon *Ornen* (*Eagle*) for the North Pole. It was the world's biggest balloon to date. The attempt was aborted because of unfavourable winds. In 1897 Andrée and two companions tried again on 11 July, and the balloon was soon lost to sight over the northern horizon. Their fate remained a mystery for thirty-three years, a famous unsolved riddle of the Arctic. Then, in the summer of 1930, a Norwegian expedition to Franz Josef Land, consisting of sealers and scientists in the *Bratvaag*, followed by a Swedish journalist in another Norwegian sealer, the *Isbjörn*, landed on isolated White Island (Kvitøya). They found the remains of Andrée's last camp, the bodies of the three explorers, and Andrée's diary. The balloon had come down on the ice and the explorers had struggled over the ice to White Island, where they died. The body of Nils Strindberg, nephew of dramatist August Strindberg, had been interred some distance from the camp: he must have died first. Andrée's and Knut Fraenkel's remains were found among camp bric-à-brac: cooking utensils, a primus stove, clothing and so on. The puzzle of what happened to Andrée's 1897 Polar expedition was solved, but the puzzle of exactly how the three explorers died has never been solved. Suggestions include suffocation by a fall of snow, carbon monoxide poisoning from a malfunctioning primus, and trichinosis from Polar bear meat they had perhaps not cooked thoroughly enough. The three men were entirely without experience of survival and travel in the Arctic. Andrée's expedition may not have been the 'mad escapade' it has been called (Victor 1964: 175), but it surely was unbelievably foolhardy. On the other hand, its historical significance overshadows most of the other expeditions mentioned in this chapter: three daring pioneers had undertaken the first-ever flight over the Arctic (Lachambre and Machuron 1898, Putnam 1930, Adams-Ray 1931, Stefansson 1939: 185–294, La Croix 1954: 65–126, Thorén 1979: 207–28, Liljeqvist 1987).

American journalist Walter Wellman (1911) had already in 1894 made one unsuccessful attempt to reach the North Pole over the pack ice, starting from the north of Spitsbergen and using dog sledges and an aluminium boat. In 1895 he was in Paris, toying with the idea of a North Pole balloon expedition, but changed his mind at the last moment. In 1898 he organized another attempt on the North Pole, this time from Franz Josef Land, again, as he had in 1894, making use of a Norwegian ship. As in 1894, most of the expedition members were Norwegian. But Wellman's second attempt likewise failed. Setting out over the ice after

Plate 19. Andrée's balloon the Eagle *on the ice. Photograph taken by Nils Strindberg showing Salomon Andrée and Knut Fraenkel by the balloon* Ornen *soon after it had come down on the pack ice on 14 July 1897 some 200 miles north of White Island, from a film developed in Stockholm in 1930 (Adams-Ray 1931: 128). The car is lying on its side to windward of the balloon, which is still half filled with gas.*

wintering in the south of the archipelago, he had travelled no further north than Rudolf Island (ostrov Rudol'fa) when an injury to his leg, and an ice-quake which caused the loss of most of his equipment and many of his dogs, forced him and his companions to retreat (Wellman 1899). A sledge party, however, did much to complete the mapping of the archipelago. In particular it discovered and explored Franz Josef Land's most easterly island, Graham Bell Land (now ostrov Greem Bell). This was named after one of the expedition's leading supporters, Alexander Graham Bell, then president of the National Geographic Society. As their ship the *Capella* left Franz Josef Land to take them home, Wellman and his companions were able to greet the incoming North Polar expedition of Luigi Amedeo of Savoy, Duke of the Abruzzi, alias HRH Lieutenant Louis of Savoy, in the converted Norwegian whaler *Jason*, renamed *Stella Polare*. This expedition comprised four officers of the Royal Italian Navy aged between twenty-six and thirty-six, four Alpine guides from the Val d'Aosta, two Italian sailors, an Italian cook, and a Norwegian captain and crew. The *Stella Polare* reached almost as far north as Wellman had sledged, namely Rudolf Island, in August 1899. There, on the last night of the century, 31 December 1899, the Polar darkness was illuminated by bonfires steeped in petrol, and an elaborate firework display of rockets and fiery fountains lit up the expedition's winter quarters. The following spring, Captain Umberto Cagni attained a furthest north over the ice with dog sledges of 86° 34' on 25 April 1900, narrowly beating Nansen's record of 1895 (Savoia 1903, Zavatti 1981: 135–49), and making the longest-ever sledge journey over the Arctic Ocean ice before that claimed by Frederick Cook. Cagni and his three companions nearly lost their lives because of the westerly drift of the ice they were on, and one of his supporting parties was lost without trace, probably because of this same drift. Determined as ever, between 1906 and 1909 Wellman made a third attempt to reach the North Pole, this time from Andrée's starting point, Danes Island, Spitsbergen, in the airship *America*. But the *America* failed even to get properly started in August 1909 and, when Wellman heard the news soon afterwards of Robert Peary's attainment of the Pole, he turned his attention instead to crossing the Atlantic.

Robert Peary (Green 1926, Hobbs 1936, Weems 1967) had begun his serious Arctic explorations in 1891–2 in north-west Greenland, when he sledged diagonally across the Inland Ice to the head of Independence Fjord and back with the Norwegian Eivind Astrup (1898), after wintering in McCormick Fjord (Map 30). It was not until 1898–1902 that he made his first attempts to reach the North Pole from Ellesmere Island using the steamer *Windward*, which was given to him by the founder of the London *Daily Mail*, Alfred Harmsworth (later Lord Northcliffe). While Peary was working almost on his own, with limited resources, the American baking-powder millionaire William Ziegler financed two successive expeditions, both aiming to reach the North Pole from Franz Josef Land. Though they were mere repeats of the Duke of the Abruzzi's expedition, neither was as successful. The first, led in 1901–2 by Evelyn Briggs Baldwin, was aborted after disputes between the members, who were partly American and partly Norwegian. The second, led by Anthony Fiala, could only reach 82° north. The main expedition ship was the Dundee whaler *Esquimaux*, renamed the *America*, which was lost in the ice during the second expedition (Fiala 1906, Friis 1976).

At the time Fiala and his companions were being brought back from Franz Josef Land in August 1905, Peary was voyaging north through Smith Sound in a new, specially built steamship, the *Roosevelt*, named after Theodore Roosevelt, the president of the day. With the patriotism characteristic of the Arctic explorers of his time, Peary proudly explained that 'the *Roosevelt* was built of American timber in an American shipyard, engined by an American firm with American metal, and constructed on American designs. Even the most trivial items of supply were of American manufacture' (Peary 1910:19). Peary was intent on reaching the North Pole by dog sledge, after wintering as far north as he could push the *Roosevelt* through the ice. He had already earned acclaim as an explorer by attaining 83° 50' north latitude in May 1900 from the northern tip of Greenland, and 84° 17' 27" north on 21 April 1902 from the northern tip of Ellesmere Island. When Peary was introduced to the Royal Geographical Society in London in December 1897, Clements Markham presented him as 'without exception, the greatest glacial traveller in the world. He is also far and away the greatest dog-sledge traveller in the world as regards rapidity and distance' (Hobbs 1936: 112). Markham forgot the Eskimos. The comment referred to Peary's journey across the Inland Ice with Eivind Astrup in 1892, accomplished without any assistance from the Inuhuit

Eskimos, which demonstrated in particular his superb navigational skill (Vaughan 1991: 37). At his next appearance before the Royal Geographical Society, in 1903, Peary was introduced by Lewis A. Beaumont, who had been a member of the British Arctic Expedition of 1875–6. He pointed out that Peary had sledged further north than other members of that expedition and further round the north Greenland coast, and had done so from a starting point 640 km (400 miles) further south (Hobbs 1936: 248–9). In 1905 Peary took the *Roosevelt* to about the same northerly starting point as reached by the *Alert* in 1875 (Map 19), and sledged over the pack ice with Inuhuit assistance to a claimed 87° 6' north on 21 April 1906 (Peary 1907). Then, in 1908–9, he made his final assault on the pole. That he reached 87° 47' north was attested by Robert A. Bartlett, skipper of the *Roosevelt*, who accompanied him that far, and this has been generally accepted (Horwood 1977: 87–91). From the point where Bartlett left him, Peary pressed on toward the pole, 139 miles (222 km) away, accompanied by his life-long black servant and associate Matthew A. Henson and four Inuhuit assistants: Ukkujaaq, Oodaaq, Iggiannguaq and Silluk. As to whether or not he actually reached the Pole, a persistent lobby has variously maintained that Peary was a fraud who failed to reach the Pole but pretended that he had done so; that he thought he had attained the Pole but was mistaken; that he simply could not have got there because the required day's marches were too long; or even that he was too ill to have reached the Pole (Hall 1917, Hayes 1929, Lewin 1935, Rawlins 1973, Herbert 1989, Bonga 1992). In spite of these hypotheses, and in spite of the absence of proven facts, it seems likely that Peary did reach the North Pole or its immediate vicinity on 6 April 1909 with Matt Henson and the above-named four Inuhuit (Molett 1989, Davies 1990). The Inuhuit (Ulloriaq 1984, and see Peter Freuchen's testimony in Hunt 1981: 265–6) remembered in particular the good weather, smooth ice and excellent condition of the dogs, from which the party benefited both on the dash to the Pole and on the first few days of the return journey. Some of the doubt surrounding Peary's achievement was removed in 1986 when the American Will Steger and his companions re-enacted Peary's 1909 journey. They proved that the North Pole could be pinpointed with only a sextant, as Peary had claimed, and that Peary's sledging rate in the vicinity of the pole of 35 miles (56 km) to 50 miles (80 km) per day, was not impossible, or even improbable (Steger and Schurke 1987: 272). Besides the Inuhuit members of Peary's 1909 expedition, his American colleagues unanimously believed that he did indeed reach the pole (Bartlett 1928, Borup 1911, Goodsell 1983, Henson 1912, MacMillan 1934; see also Peary 1910). Peary's success as an Arctic explorer was due to his dogged determination; his fund-raising skills, which gave rise to the Peary Arctic Club; his technical innovations and skill as a navigator; his perfection of the sledging system using supporting parties, which predecessors like Cagni and Fiala had developed; and above all, his Inuhuit assistants. These Eskimos from north-west Greenland were consummate Arctic travellers. Peary's close relationship with them and the leadership he exercised over them enabled him to marshall all their skills in the interests of reaching the North Pole. Without them he could never have succeeded. Peary's mastery of Arctic travel techniques and his powers of leadership are forcibly demonstrated by the way he won the admiration and developed the sledging skills of two young men he took with him on his last expedition: George Borup (1911) and Donald MacMillan (1934). Both were new to the Arctic, yet in spring 1909 they made record-breaking sledge journeys along the northern shores of Greenland and Ellesmere Island, marching eight to eighteen hours to average 48 km (30 miles) per day or more, always, however, with Inuhuit assistance. MacMillan went on to lead the Crocker Land Expedition to north-west Greenland between 1914 and 1918 (MacMillan 1918), and others subsequently. Borup died in a drowning accident in Long Island Sound in 1912, before he was thirty.

As Peary was returning from his last North Pole expedition in the late summer of 1909, his erstwhile colleague of the North Greenland Expedition of 1891–2, Frederick Albert Cook, likewise American, was on his way home from Greenland via Copenhagen. Cook claimed to have reached the North Pole via the northern tip of Axel Heiberg Island with two young Inuhuit companions on 21 April 1908 – a year before Peary. While at first expert and public opinion were divided (Riffenburgh 1993: 165–90), both soon swung toward Peary, so that history has accepted Peary as the discoverer of the North Pole and forgotten Cook, though Cook still retains some loyal supporters (Cook 1911, Cook 1953, Freeman 1961, Weems 1961, Wright 1970, Eames 1973, Hunt 1981, Osczevski 1990). More importantly, the effect of Cook and Peary's North Pole expeditions, combined soon afterwards with that of Roald Amundsen's attainment of the South Pole on 14 December 1911, was to extinguish the Polar enthusiasm which had aroused the exploring efforts of so many governments and individuals since the middle of the nineteenth century. The very fact that the long succession of North Polar expeditions ceased abruptly in 1909 reflects the verdict of history, that Peary had made it. Apart from the hurriedly fitted-out expedition of the endearingly eccentric Russian Lieutenant, Georgiy Yaklovich Sedov, who died from scurvy in 1914 while attempting to sledge to the Pole from Franz Josef Land, almost sixty years were to elapse after Peary's return before the next surface attempt to reach the North Pole.

NINE

The Northern Sea Route

The nineteenth century was the heroic age of Arctic exploration. First, the British dominated the scene, then the Americans. The more various and widespread Arctic operations of the twentieth century form the subject of Chapter 10, but the development by the Russians of the former North-East Passage into a modern Northern Sea Route (*Severnyy morskoy put'*) is unique, and demands a chapter to itself. Other aspects of the modern Russian or (from 1917 to 1991) Soviet Arctic, especially mineral exploitation and the treatment of Arctic peoples, are considered in relevant sections in the last three chapters of this book. (On what follows here see Taracouzio 1938, Armstrong 1952, Krypton 1956, Belov 1959, Pinkhenson 1962, Belov 1969, Chubakov 1979, Armstrong 1980, Chubakov *et al.* 1982, Arikaynen 1984, Horensma 1991 and Armstrong 1992b.)

THE TSARS AND THE SOVIETS

Although in the pages of world history the Union of Soviet Socialist Republics will inevitably and rightly continue to receive separate treatment, in terms of the development of Eurasia's northern seaway there was little change in policies or activities after the disruptions of the 1917 Revolution and the civil war that followed it. But the speed of development greatly increased. This was partly due to a warming climate, which produced a high proportion of favourable ice years along the route. Furthermore, the Bolsheviks were constrained by foreign hostility to make the utmost possible use of domestic raw materials, many of which were in the north. They were likewise persuaded to place a new emphasis on northern development by the need to strengthen the national economy in order to raise the standard of living. But almost every Soviet initiative had a tsarist precedent. Thus the world's first seagoing Polar icebreaker, the *Yermak*, built in Newcastle in 1898, was the brainchild of Vice-Admiral Stepan Osipovich Makarov of the Imperial Russian Navy. He had hoped to break through the ice to the North Pole, and did take the *Yermak* as far as 81° 28' north in Spitsbergen waters on her maiden Arctic voyage in 1899, and to Novaya Zemlya and Franz Josef Land in 1901. The world's first permanent Arctic radio station came into service on Dikson Island (ostrov Dikson) on 25 August 1915 (Belov 1977: 29–30), and three others had been established before 1917. Polar stations, combining weather-reporting and radio communications, and icebreakers, were both essential ingredients of the Northern Sea Route as created by the Soviets; a third

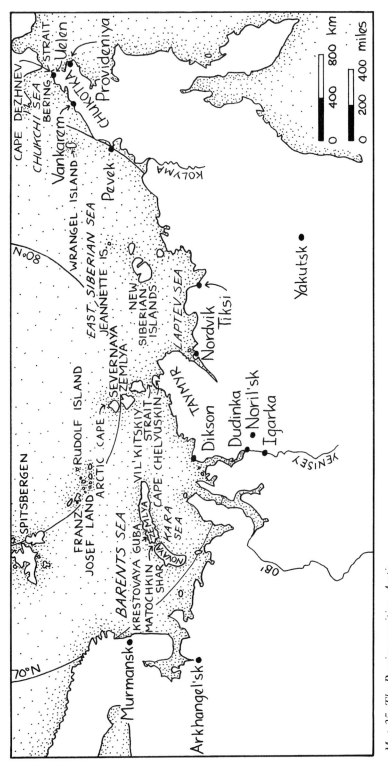

Map 25. The Russian maritime Arctic.

was aircraft. Here, too, tsarist governments showed the way. In August 1914 Russian army pilot Jan Nagursky (1888–1976), a Pole, made the first flights ever in the Arctic, along the west or Barents Sea coast of the northern island of Novaya Zemlya, searching in vain for Georgiy Sedov's missing expedition. Nagursky's French-built Farman seaplane was shipped in dismantled parts to Krestovaya Bay (Krestovaya guba) and there, on the open shore, in fog, snow, rain and sleet, Nagursky and his mechanic E. Kuznetsov had to assemble it. On 8 August, after two trial flights, they flew north as far as the Barents Islands (ostrova Barentsa), a distance of some 300 km (200 miles), in a flight lasting four hours twenty minutes. Other flights followed (Vodopyanov no date: 83–6). Long before the Soviets arrived on the scene the sections at either end of the Northern Sea Route had been brought into use for regular annual voyages; namely the Kara Sea route from ports in the west to the Ob' and Yenisey (Lied 1945), and the seaway around Cape Dezhnev, from Vladivostok to the Kolyma. It was under the tsars, too, that in 1916 the port of Romanov-na-Murmane was built, which later, as Murmansk, became the western terminus of the Northern Sea Route.

The need for renewed and much more systematic activity to develop the Northern Sea Route had been impressed on the imperial government by its disastrous defeat in the Russo-Japanese War of 1904–5, when the Baltic Fleet had to sail 20,000 km (12,000 miles) to Japanese waters via the Indian Ocean, instead of the 10,000 km (6,000 miles) along the Northern Sea Route. This was the main motive for the Arctic Ocean Hydrographic Expedition of 1910–15, during which two specially built icebreaking survey ships, the *Taymyr* and *Vaygach*, undertook a methodical investigation of the entire seaway. They made a series of voyages culminating in 1915, when they completed the transit from Vladivostok to Arkhangel'sk after wintering *en route* (Transehe 1925, Barr 1975a, Starokadomskiy 1976). The expedition's leader, Boris A. Vil'kitskiy, and one of its commanders, Aleksandr V. Kolchak, opposed the Soviets. Vil'kitskiy fled to London and Brussels after the Revolution. Kolchak led the White forces in Siberia against the Soviets, until a firing squad ended his life in January 1920. The expedition's most important geographical discovery was what later turned out to be the southern island of the archipelago of Severnaya Zemlya. A landing party promptly ran up the Russian flag ashore and annexed the new territory under the name of Emperor Nicholas II Land. Nor was that tsar's government slow in laying yet another foundation stone of the Northern Sea Route: it announced in 1916, after reference to this discovery, that 'The Imperial Russian Government has the honour herewith to inform the governments of allied and friendly powers that these lands have been incorporated in the territory of the Russian Empire', and that the New Siberian Islands, Wrangel Island, and other islands in the Arctic Ocean likewise formed 'an integral part of the Empire' (Stefansson 1925: 395–6, Krypton 1956: 18–19, n.15).

Although post-revolutionary Russians were immensely proud of their achievements under the Soviets, they did not necessarily decry those of their predecessors under the tsars. This continuity is especially apparent in the Arctic. There is a striking difference too, between the attitudes of zealous first-generation communists like Ivan Dimitriyevich Papanin (see below) and those of subsequent generations. Papanin hung a portrait of Stalin on the wall of his tent at the North Pole in May 1937 (Brontman 1938: 148). His motives may not have been purely ideological; Stalin returned the compliment by appointing Papanin head of Glavsevmorput in 1939. On the other hand, on 1 June 1979, when Dmitriy Shparo and six other Young Communist Leaguers or members of Komsomol arrived on skis at the North Pole, three portraits were displayed there, those of E.V. Toll, V.A. Rusanov and G. Sedov, all of whom had died before the Russian Revolution in the midst of their Arctic explorations (Sklokin 1982).

ADMINISTRATION

As early as 1920 the Siberian Revolutionary Committee set up a government agency to administer the Northern Sea Route. *Komseveroput'*, or the Northern Sea Route Committee (*Komitet Severnogo morskogo puti*), was charged with 'the all-round equipment, improvement, and study of the Northern Sea Route with the object of turning it into a permanent and practical communications artery' (Armstrong 1980: 97). In 1932 *Komseveroput'* was replaced by a much more powerful and comprehensive agency directly under the control of the Council or Soviet of People's Commissars of the Soviet Union, called *Glavsevmorput'* or the Chief Administration of the Northern Sea Route. With the senior editor of the *Great Soviet Encyclopedia*, bearded academician Otto Yul'yevich Shmidt (1891–1956), as its first head, Glavsevmorput became for a time a veritable Arctic empire or state within the state, in control of economic development in Siberia north of 62° north, as well as of the Northern Sea Route. It took over various Arctic enterprises such as Arktikugol, which mined coal in Spitsbergen (see Chapter 11), the Reindeer-breeding Trust, the Taymyr Trust (which was responsible for developing river transport, ports and industry in Taymyr), and the administration of the Arctic islands. Its central office was soon divided into separate departments, and seven territorial headquarters were established in Leningrad, Murmansk, Arkhangel'sk, Yakutsk and elsewhere. It was Glavsevmorput, in the 1930s, which used forced labour to mine apatite at Kirovsk in the Kola Peninsula (Map 34), and to build Noril'sk. Glavsevmorput was also busy increasing the annual catch of the state fisheries in the Barents Sea, exporting timber from Igarka, and controlling the sea-mammal hunt in the White Sea (Webster 1950). But such a bureaucratic monster could not long survive the disastrous Arctic shipping season of 1937, a very bad ice year (Vodopyanov, no date: 290, Smolka 1937: 140), when no fewer than twenty-six ships were beset in the ice and forced to overwinter, among them seven of the eight icebreakers or icebreaking ships Glavsevmorput had in service at the time. Its influential chief, Otto Shmidt, resigning in 1939, avoided a worse fate by deploying his very substantial scientific talents as director of the Soviet Academy of Science's new Institute of Theoretical Geophysics (Levin 1982). Soon, enterprises not directly concerned with the administration of the Northern Sea Route were withdrawn from Glavsevmorput. In 1953 it became merely the Arctic shipping division of the Ministry of the Merchant Fleet. Early in the 1960s the Ministry of Civil Aviation took over aviation along the route, the hydrology and meteorology committee of the Council of Ministers of the USSR took over the Polar stations, and Glavsevmorput itself was liquidated in 1964. At the end of 1970 it reappeared as a department of the Ministry of Merchant Marine, with the more modest title 'the Administration of the Northern Sea Route' instead of 'the Chief Administration of the Northern Sea Route'. The ships themselves had, in 1957, been transferred to two shipping companies, the Murmansk Shipping Company and the Far Eastern Shipping Company, based at Vladivostok. After the dismantling of the Soviet Union in 1991 the Administration of the Northern Sea Route became a department of the Ministry of Transport of the Russian Federation.

EXPLORATION AND SOVIET SOVEREIGNTY

Two important tasks confronted the Soviet government in the 1920s as, under pressure from V.I. Lenin, it began work on the Northern Sea Route. One was a question of sovereignty, related chiefly to Wrangel Island (ostrov Vrangelya), which between 1921 and 1924 was occupied by an expedition originally sent there by the Stefansson Arctic Exploration and Development Company based in Vancouver. The other was a question of exploration, and concerned chiefly Severnaya Zemlya. This was still almost entirely unexplored, though its exploration was urgently required for the better understanding of ice conditions in Vil'kitskiy Strait (proliv Vil'kitskogo), which lay between it and Cape Chelyuskin (mys Chelyuskina), forming the most northerly and probably the most hazardous section of the Northern Sea Route.

Neither the Canadian, nor the British, nor the American government was prepared to claim sovereignty over Wrangel Island, in spite of Vilhjalmur Stefansson's persuasion and his private occupation of the island (Stefansson 1925, Diubaldo 1978: 161–86). No one was surprised, and no one complained, when, on 18 August 1924, the armed icebreaking ship *Krasnyy Oktyabr* (*Red October*), commanded by the distinguished naval hydrographer Boris Vladimirovich Davydov, commander of the *Taymyr* in 1910–12, arrived in Rodgers Bay (bukhta Rodzhersa), Wrangel Island. Soon the Soviet flag was flying from an 11 metre (36 ft) tall flagpole. A metal board at its foot, inscribed in Russian and English, read 'Proletarians of every country, unite! Far Eastern Hydrographic Expedition 19 August 1924' (Belov 1977: 103). On the following day Wrangel Island was formally and ceremonially incorporated into the territory of the Soviet state. The single American and thirteen Eskimos the Russians found there were taken off (Shentalinskiy 1980) and replaced in 1926 by a party of some sixty Chukchi and Eskimo settlers, led by Amur Cossack and former Red Army officer Georgiy Alekseyevich Ushakov (1901–63), who lived there with his family for three years (Ushakov 1972, Kanevskiy 1979: 37–8). His success established his reputation as one of the leading Soviet *polyarniks*, a word then coming into vogue for members of Polar expeditions and the staff of Polar stations (Kanevskiy 1989: 130). For his work on the island Ushakov was awarded the Order of the Red Banner of Labour (Ushakov 1953: 8).

Georgiy Ushakov was an obvious choice to lead what was the last, and perhaps greatest of historic Arctic exploring expeditions by dog sledge. His brief was to survey the land whose name was changed on 11 January 1926 by the Presidium of the Central Executive Committee of the Soviet Union from Nicholas II Land to Severnaya Zemlya ('North Land'). It had remained unexplored in spite of repeated attempts from 1919 on to send expeditions there. Ushakov had to ascertain 'whether this was one huge island that would, as many then thought, obstruct navigation along the Northern Sea Route, or several islands with straits perhaps wide enough to allow ships to pass through them'. He carried with him the following credentials (Gvozdetsky 1974: 27–8 and Ushakov 1953: 15):

> The bearer of this, Deputy Director of the Arctic Institute Georgiy Alekseyevich Ushakov, is dispatched to Severnaya Zemlya as leader of the Severnaya Zemlya Detachment of the government Arctic Expedition. Comrade Ushakov and his party are charged with the exploration of Severnaya Zemlya. In the event of ships failing to reach Severnaya Zemlya in the next two navigation seasons or owing to any other conditions developing during the period of work in Severnaya Zemlya, Comrade Ushakov and his people should cross Vil'kitskiy Strait by dog sledge, make their way through the Taymyr Peninsula to inhabited places, and thence proceed to Leningrad.

Ushakov and his companions, in the full knowledge that they might well have to get back to civilization on their own, disembarked on 30 August 1930 from the icebreaker *Georgiy Sedov* with forty-three dogs, a prefabricated house and three years' supplies, including five tons of dog pemmican, at their future base. This turned out to be an offshore island which they named ostrov Domashniy or Home Island. This base, which now became a Polar station, was manned by eighteen-year-old radio operator Vasiliy Vasil'yevich Khodov. Ushakov, with his companions, dog-team driver and professional hunter-trapper Sergey Prokop'yevich Zhuravlev (Bolotnikov 1980), and the veteran Arctic explorer and geologist Nikolay Nikolayevich Urvantsev, perhaps formed the strongest team ever launched on Arctic exploration. All of them were experienced Arctic overwinterers. Urvantsev, who had discovered the mineral wealth of Noril'sk (see Chapter 11) and had led expeditions in Taymyr more than ten years before, subsequently fell foul of the Soviet authorities and was nearly wiped altogether off the historical record before being rehabilitated. In the 1953 edition of Ushakov's four-hundred-page book *Po nekhozhenoy zemle* (*On untrodden land*), Urvantsev's name does not appear on the title page, nor is he mentioned anywhere in the text, although the book describes the Severnaya Zemlya Expedition. In the 1959 edition, however, he reappears as Ushakov's respected colleague and his name occurs on almost every page. It may be relevant that, unlike Ushakov, Urvantsev was not a member of the Communist Party. Still, his own book on the Severnaya Zemlya Expedition (Urvantsev 1935; see also Urvantsev 1933) went through at least two editions. Ushakov's political affiliations are only too apparent from his naming of the geographical features he discovered in Severnaya Zemlya: Cape Hammer and Sickle, Sovetskaya Bay, Red Army Strait, October Revolution Island, Komsomolets or Young Communist Leaguer Island, Bolshevik Island, and the like. At least this was a change from

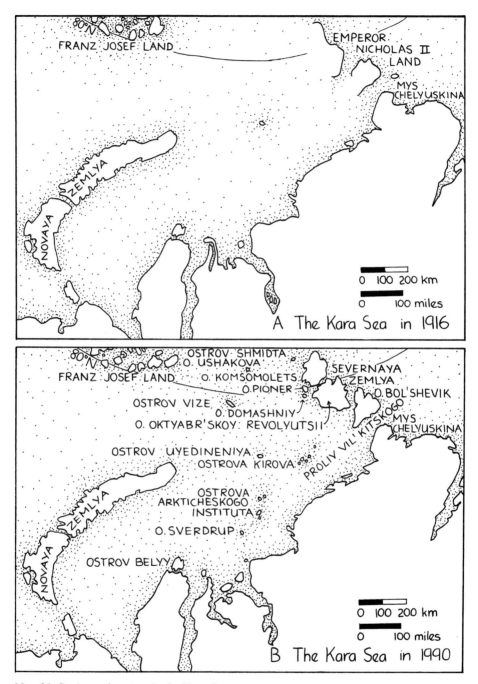

Map 26. Soviet explorations in the Kara Sea.

British admirals and American businessmen! In two years of almost ceaseless dog sledging the party travelled just over 3,000 km (2,000 miles) at a rate of 15 to 20 km (9–12 miles) per day and was able for the first time to produce an accurate map of Severnaya Zemlya. This turned out to consist of five large islands covered with dome-shaped glaciers, two of them over 160 km (100 miles) long (Gvozdetsky 1974: 24–34). The expedition was brought home in the summer of 1932 by the icebreaking ship *Rusanov*. This time Ushakov was rewarded for his efforts with the more prestigious Order of Lenin. He had not omitted, on 5 October 1930, to raise the Soviet flag and, in the presence of Urvantsev and Zhuravlev, to declare Severnaya Zemlya to be annexed to the Soviet Union (Ushakov 1953: 94). The same had been done by Otto Shmidt on 29 August 1929 for Franz Josef Land (Kanevskiy 1977: 31–2, Belov 1977: 64).

Ushakov's Severnaya Zemlya Expedition had been organized by the Arctic Institute in what was then Leningrad, before the creation of Glavsevmorput, which was soon vying with the Geological Committee of the Soviet Union and the Soviet Academy of Sciences in organizing expeditions of its own along the Northern Sea Route. For example, the construction of the Polar station at Cape Chelyuskin in 1933 was followed in 1940–1 by the detailed mapping of the coast of north-eastern Taymyr by a thirty-eight-man expedition led by A.I. Kosoy (Gvozdetsky 1974: 71–6).

TRANSITS OR THROUGH VOYAGES

In the 1930s, the rapidly increasing commercial use of both ends of the Northern Sea Route, that is the Kara Sea and Vladivostok-Kolyma routes, though of the utmost significance for the Soviet economy, was pedestrian, even monotonous. Instead, public interest and government attention was focused by Otto Yul'yevich Shmidt on the excitingly spectacular prospect of a single-season transit; that is, of sailing from one end to the other in a single summer or shipping season. So far this had never been done, and the Soviets were determined to do it. The attempts they made, in 1932–3, the first successful, the second unsuccessful, were among the twenty-seven maritime expeditions agreed in advance as part of the massive Soviet contribution to the Second International Polar Year of 1932–3 (Suzyumov 1982; see also Vize 1932).

On 28 July 1932 the ex-Newfoundland sealer *Aleksandr Sibiryakov*, captained by Vladimir Ivanovich Voronin and built in Glasgow in 1909, left Arkhangel'sk with a scientific expedition led by Otto Shmidt on board (Barr 1978, Limcher 1982). Neither of the icebreakers, the *Malygin* and the *Sedov*, were in commission at the time, or one of them would doubtless have been used. After calling at ostrov Domashniy to pick up a copy of Urvantsev and Ushakov's newly made map of Severnaya Zemlya, Captain Voronin used it to make the *Sibiryakov* the first ship to sail round the northern tip of that archipelago. Though ice conditions that year were favourable, heavy ice off the north coast of Chukotka smashed the *Sibiryakov*'s propellers. She only struggled into Bering Strait on 1 October 1932 with the help of jury-rigged sails made from tarpaulin hatch covers. Thereafter she was taken in tow by a trawler. The *Sibiryakov*'s historic first through passage of the Northern Sea Route pointed, distantly as soon emerged, to the possibility of ordinary ships rather than icebreakers being able to use this northern seaway as an effective short cut from the Atlantic to the Pacific. Indeed many optimistic Soviet writers, polyarniks among them, considered the *Sibiryakov*'s voyage to mark the opening of the Northern Sea Route as a regular sea lane. This was even asserted by a post-war head of Glavsevmorput, V.F. Burkhanov (Kanaki 1974: 5).

In high hopes of a similar success, Otto Shmidt led the second International Polar Year expedition through the Northern Sea Route in 1933. In default again of an icebreaker, the ship made available was an ordinary freighter, unstrengthened for cruising in ice, and built for the Soviet Union in Denmark. Captain Voronin had serious doubts about her (Kanevskiy 1989: 64–5). The *Chelyuskin* left Murmansk on 10 August. She was one of eleven ships that successfully passed through Vil'kitskiy Strait and rounded Cape Chelyuskin, the Northern Sea Route's half–way mark, in 1933. But the Chukchi Sea ice, which had all but wrecked the *Sibiryakov* the year before, closed round the *Chelyuskin*. Tightly beset, she drifted into Bering Strait and then out again before being crushed and sunk on 13 February 1934. Only one life was lost, and 104 men, women and children set up Camp Shmidt on the ice 130 km (80 miles) north-east

Plate 20. Camp Shmidt – the first day on the ice, 14 February 1934. Before she sank, the ropes securing the Chelyuskin's *deck cargo were cut, and much of the first day camping on the ice was spent rescuing this, mainly timber and fuel, from the hole in the ice where the ship went down. The temporary tents in the foreground were soon replaced by tents with wooden frames and floors. (Brown 1935: 120.)*

of Vankarem and patiently awaited rescue by air, while the *Chelyuskin*'s radio
operator, Ernst Teodorovich Krenkel', maintained communications with the new
Polar station at Uelen (Map 25; Brown 1935). There one of the first of many
polyarnitsas, or women polyarniks, Lyudmila Nikolayevna Shrader, was the radio
operator. She found herself handling the entire rescue operation, sleeping by her
transmitter and earning high praise from the Chelyuskinites, who called her
familiarly 'our Lyudochka' (Kanevskiy 1979: 113–14; see also Kanevskiy 1989:
65–78).

It was two months before the last of the Chelyuskinites was flown out of Camp
Shmidt. Life there was reasonably comfortable because ample provisions, tents,
warm clothing, timber and fuel had been unloaded from the ship before it went
down, or were recovered afterwards. Shmidt, a member of the Communist Party
since 1918, was the life and soul of the camp. Besides leading a two-hour seminar
every other day on dialectical materialism, he presided over the systematic
proselytizing and indoctrination of non-party members among the crew and
passengers by the communists. As one of these wrote (Brown 1935: 177):

> Our party work became an organic part of the whole life of Schmidt Camp,
> became a most important constituent part of life there – the part which shaped,
> formed, directed the whole. Party work went on all the time and everywhere: in
> the tents, at work, while hunting, in the queue at the cookhouse. Only of course
> it had not got a label stuck on it, none of that 'watch me, I'm doing party work,
> according to such-and-such a resolution' sort of thing.
>
> But, concretely, in what did that work consist, what was the technique of this
> 'party work'? Here again I must refer to Otto Schmidt. At the first meeting of
> the party bureau on the ice he said, 'From now on every gesture of a
> communist, every movement he makes, every word he utters, in whatever
> conversation with a non-party comrade – in rest moments, at work, at tea in his
> tent, in chance passing talk – must be uninterrupted political work'.

The scope of Shmidt's intellectual activities on the ice seemed boundless. On
28 March 1934 the Moscow zoologist Vladimir Stakhanov made the following
entry in his diary (Brown 1935: 185–6):

> It is now seven o'clock by Moscow time, that is, seven in the morning, while
> here it is four of the afternoon. Ernest is taking down Tass Agency reports
> from Cape North [now Cape Schmidt or mys Shmidta]. Schmidt is lolling
> back busy with some mathematical calculations in his notebook. Bobrov is
> reading an English novel, going into raptures about a certain Emmie and
> cursing a scoundrel named Arthur. The fuel jet in the stove is sputtering and
> every now and then throws out a ring of paraffin vapour and smuts. Outside,
> by the stores (opposite us), Kantzyn is cutting up bear carcasses. The flag of
> the Chief Administration of the Northern Sea Route, which flies from our
> tent, shows a faint west wind. . . . Here are all the talks led in our tent by
> Comrade Schmidt.
>
> February 14–March 6: On Comrade Schmidt's expedition to the Pamirs for

mountain research; on future socialist society; on the history of South America; on Scandinavian mythology; on the lines of development of the Soviet North and the tasks of the Northern Route Administration; on Freud's theory of psychoanalysis; on the present state of biological work in the Arctic; on aeroplane reconnoitring of wild creatures in the Choukchi Peninsula; on contemporary Soviet poetry; on the theory of determinants; on contemporary science and scientists; on the Lithuanians, their civilization and history; on socialism, the dictatorship of the proletariat, and the state. . . . Reading in German – Heine's poems. On the creative work of Heine and his life. On formal logic. On the fascist theory of the white race. On an atlas of the world.

March 6–22. The history of German imperialism and the Hohenzollern dynasty; on music and composers; the history of the House of Romanov; the commencement of the imperialist war; Schmidt's story of how he became encyclopaedist; Schmidt's idea of creating a scientific research institute in the USSR for the study of various theoretical scientific problems outside dependence on or service to any particular branch of science; on the activity of the Administration of the Northern Sea Route and its tasks; on the theory of evolution; on the history of the Netherlands; of the inception of Italian fascism; of the recording of the life of the Arctic and of Antarctic regions and the organization of a regular system of this in the Administration of the Northern Sea Route; of the conception of nations and nationalism.

Through transits of the Northern Sea Route continued, in spite of the loss of the *Chelyuskin*, which had caused the soul of the Soviet Union to be laid bare on the ice of the Chukchi Sea and emphasized the Communist Party's role in the opening up of the Soviet Arctic. In 1934 the icebreaker *Litke*, which had failed to help the *Chelyuskin* out of the ice in 1933, made the first single-season transit from east to west; in 1935 two cargo ships steamed right through in either direction; and in 1936 the first Soviet-built icebreaker, the *Iosif Stalin*, made a double transit, sailing both ways in a single season. Since the 1930s through traffic on the Northern Sea Route has continued, but has remained limited. For the most part, the ships have been Russian, but in 1940 the German raider *Komet* was helped through from west to east in record time by the Russian icebreakers *Stalin* and *Kaganovich* (Armstrong 1958: 80–9), and in 1991 the French expedition ship *L'Astrolabe* sailed from Murmansk to Provideniya with Russian help, using satellite images of the ice cover. The Soviet offer in 1967 to open the Northern Sea Route to foreign ships was not taken seriously, and was perhaps not meant to be so taken, but in 1990–2 there were clear indications of progress in this direction, though there was little sign of the route becoming a regular international shipping lane (Brigham 1991, Simonsen 1992, Armstrong and Brigham 1993, Brigham 1993).

LIFE AT A POLAR STATION

A glimpse of life at the oldest and most important of the Northern Sea Route's Polar stations, situated on Dikson Island off the port of Dikson, during the heady early years of Glavsevmorput, was given by a perhaps rather impressionable correspondent of the New York *Herald Tribune*, Ruth Gruber, who was there briefly in the summer of 1935 (Gruber 1939: 275–6, 277–8).

Perhaps the only way to describe the warmth on the enchanted island is to tell you how its inhabitants and visitors spent this ordinary working day. Remember there wasn't a native among them. They were all Russians, born in ordinary beds under ordinary temperate conditions. Most of them knew only what they had studied about the Arctic. They had come up here on a two-year contract with Goose M.P. [Glavsevmorput], equipped with microscopes, Diesel motors, tons of canned foods, and loads of enthusiasm.

Everyone shared the work and everything was communal and free. Kopeks were as common as a palm tree. When I offered to pay for a fur-lined coat, they stared at me first in amazement and then in pity. To change the subject, one of the men asked me to show him a rouble. He had forgotten, he said, what money looked like. Food was free, cigarettes were free, clothing was free, housing was free, entertainment was free, transportation from Leningrad and back was free – and besides that, salaries were doubled and trebled. After two years, the colonists returned to the Arctic Institute in Leningrad where they received from two to five thousand roubles. They were 'Soviet millionaires' and they lived that way. They rode down to the Crimea first-class, spent two months lolling in the sun on the Black Sea, bought new clothes, books, fancy perfume and even Soviet Fords. After their fling, they returned to work at the Arctic Institute or at Goose M.P. in Moscow for a year and then begged to be sent back to live and die in the Arctic. . . .

Work began officially at ten. There were crews, of course, like the wireless operators, who worked in three shifts for twenty-four hours. But the scientific and industrial work, such as building the wharf and making charts, was limited to eight hours in the summer and to five or six hours in the winter, when huge unshaded electric street lights, which burned constantly from November to February, made the Polar station look like Broadway on a Saturday night.

Now, after breakfast, you suddenly found yourself in a gigantic laboratory. Dickson had split its scientific work among seven crews. The two meteorologists, a thinnish man and a very large woman, went off to their small white wooden closets outdoors to check up on their self-recording thermograph and hygrograph. The hydrologists sailed out on a small picturesque motorboat for the sea, where they were studying the depth of the water. The aerologist sent a pilot balloon into the air; the hydrographer pulled out his latest chart of the coast and sea; the actinometrist adjusted his instruments for measuring the intensity of the sun's rays; the two magnetologists fixed their compasses to study some new phenomenon of the magnetic qualities of the earth; the scientists working on radioactivity left for their laboratory while you remembered poignantly that they were carrying on Marie Curie's work.

AVIATION

The need for ice reconnaissance made aviation an essential feature of the Northern Sea Route. Ten years after Nagursky had flown the first aeroplane in the Arctic, Soviet army pilot Boris Grigoryevich Chukhnovskiy (1898–1975) made several flights in 1924 over the Kara and Barents Seas at either end of Matochkin Shar Strait, Novaya Zemlya, as a member of the Northern Hydrographic Expedition. In the following year, 1925, the expedition used two aircraft, piloted by Chukhnovskiy and the Finn Otto Kalvits. Their flights from Matochkin Shar out over the Kara Sea showed that there was no ice for upwards of 150 km (80–90 miles) east of the strait. The ships waiting at the mouth of the Ob' to sail west through the Kara Sea were consequently advised to take that route and on 16 September they reached the strait accompanied by the icebreaker *Malygin* without encountering any ice (Vodopyanov, no date: 88–90). From then on ice patrols by aircraft became increasingly commonplace along the entire length of the Northern Sea Route. Soon after its creation in 1932, Glavsevmorput had five aircraft in its Polar Air Service (*Polyarniya aviyatsiya*), founded in 1933, which were engaged on ice reconnaissance and piloting ships (Vodopyanov, no date: 180). By 1955, twenty-two aircraft were in service on these patrols.

The sinking of the *Chelyuskin*, leaving 104 persons stranded on the ice in a remote part of the Arctic on 13 February 1934, was turned into a triumph by Soviet fliers assembled from far and wide, and the rescue underlined the vital role of aviation on the Northern Sea Route. After many difficulties, the only plane available in Chukotka was flown to Camp Shmidt on 5 March to rescue the women and children, but it was afterwards irreparably damaged when it crash-landed on the ice. It was only in April, after an airstrip had been cleared at Vankarem and other aircraft, some rushed from Alaska, had arrived, that the remaining Chelyuskinites could be rescued. The seven pilots involved had to make a total of twenty-five separate flights to Camp Shmidt, carrying fewer than half-a-dozen persons each time. They were the first of thousands to receive a new distinction, the Gold Star of Hero of the Soviet Union.

In the summer of 1937 a series of spectacular long-distance flights over the Arctic by Russian pilots in Russian aircraft, organized by a special government commission, earned world renown for Soviet aviation but ended in disaster. In May, P.G. Golovin flew to the North Pole and back from Rudolf Island, the most northerly island of the Franz Josef Land archipelago. In June, a three-man crew led by chief pilot Valeriy Chkalov (Tschkalow 1939) flew non-stop from Moscow to just north of Portland, Oregon, crossing the Arctic Ocean near the North Pole (Baidukov 1938). In July, Mikhail Gromov (1939) repeated Chkalov's flight but passed over the Pole and continued further south down the Pacific coast of North America to near San Jacinto, California, 100 km (60 miles) south-west of Los Angeles. But when, in August, ace pilot Sigizmund Levanevskiy tried to take a large four-engined plane, capable of carrying passengers or freight, from Moscow to Los Angeles over the same route, he and his five-man crew were lost without trace somewhere in the Arctic Ocean. An extensive and prolonged international search never found any sign of them or their plane (Stefansson 1939: 295–336). Golovin's flight on 5 May 1937 had been merely a preliminary reconnaissance for

Plate 21. Stores ready to load for the first drifting ice station, April 1937. The four-engined heavy-weight plane, capable of carrying over two tons of freight, is parked on the airstrip laid out on the dome-shaped icecap of Rudolf Island (ostrov Rudol'fa), about 275 m (900 ft) above sea level. (Brontman 1938: 120.)

a squadron of four bright orange, four-engined planes based on Rudolf Island, where an airstrip and Polar station had been set up by ship in the previous autumn. These planes arrived one after another at the North Pole between 21 May and 5 June to unload equipment for a scientific station, which was set up on the ice. On 6 June they took off from the ice, and all four were safely back on Rudolf Island on 6 June. This North Pole expedition, led in person by Shmidt, was a triumph for him and Glavsevmorput (participants' accounts include Brontman 1938, Vodopyanov, no date: 187–261, Stromilov 1977, Shevelev 1979. See also Laktionov 1955: 224–56, Simmons 1965, and Lebedev and Mazuruk 1991). Another success was the evacuation of some five hundred persons from ships beset in the ice along the Northern Sea Route in the winter of 1937/8, all by air.

The Soviet aviators did not rest on their laurels. In December 1940 pilot Ivan Ivanovich Cherevichnyy and auspiciously named navigator Valentin Akkuratov, who were normally employed on ice reconnaissance along the Northern Sea Route, went to the Arctic Institute, at that time administered by Glavsevmorput in what was then Leningrad, with a proposal. They would take a group of scientists on three separate flights to the region of the so-called Pole of Relative Inaccessibility (the region most difficult to reach), each time landing on a floe and remaining encamped there for some days while scientific observations were made. The projected flights were successfully carried out from Wrangel Island in April 1941, and a bonus was that ice conditions along nearly the whole of the Northern Sea Route were reconnoitred both on the outward and return flights (Armstrong 1958: 51–66, Akkuratov 1981). On their outward flight in March Cherevichnyy and Akkuratov noticed a gigantic tabular iceberg with rivers on it and surf breaking along the shore (Laktionov 1955: 343 n.1, Akkuratov 1981). Something similar was seen in 1946 during a routine ice patrol by I.S. Kotov; 'a large, hilly "island" about 400 or 500 square km in area, rising above the drift ice north-east of Wrangel Island' (Gvozdetsky 1974: 45). Subsequently more 'islands', which are really only huge ice floes, have been discovered and called ice islands. Many are thought to be detached fragments of the ice shelf along the coast of northern Ellesmere Island and Greenland; others may have originated as unusually large and stable floes building up over many years in shallow Siberian seas. The presence of these ice islands drifting around the Arctic Ocean may explain the mythical lands reported to exist by Arctic explorers, such as Giles or Gillis Land (1707), Andreyev Land (1764), Sannikov Land (1806) and Crocker Land (1906). Flights over the Arctic Ocean were resumed after the Great Patriotic War. In 1945 M.A. Titlov flew to the North Pole. In 1948 a series of annual high-latitude air expeditions called North (Sever) 1, North 2, and so on, up to North 38 in 1986 and beyond, began. Each continued for several weeks or months and involved several planes and landings on the ice. One of their main tasks after 1950 was the establishment, supply and evacuation of drifting ice stations and, later, the servicing of twenty or more automatic weather stations scattered over the Arctic Ocean pack ice (Kanaki 1974: 90–4). In the early post-war years these operations were carried out by Glavsevmorput's Polar Air Service.

DRIFTING ICE STATIONS

The Polar stations set up by the Soviets in 1937 and from 1950 onwards on drifting ice floes in the Arctic Ocean, complemented the network of Polar stations they had already created on the mainland and islands throughout their part of the Arctic. As long before as 1918, Stefansson's colleague Storker T. Storkerson (1922), with four companions, had made observations for six months from a drifting ice floe in the Beaufort Sea. Otto Shmidt had considered the possibility of setting up scientific observatories on the ice, even right up to the North Pole, in 1930, and his colleague Vladimir Yul'yevich Vize, prolific author of books on Soviet Arctic exploration, had written about it in 1931. But Shmidt's ideas, which originated in a proposal of Nansen's, seem to have taken concrete form only after the *Chelyuskin* affair had shown that camping out on the Arctic Ocean pack ice, even though it was always in movement, was perfectly feasible; and, more importantly, that such a drifting encampment could be set up, supplied and evacuated by air. The navigational problems encountered by shipping on the Northern Sea Route, caused by ice in the Kara, Laptev, East Siberian and Chukchi Seas, had quickly convinced Shmidt of the need to study ice drift in the Arctic Ocean as a whole, of which these seas were mere large shallow bays, open towards the north. It was wholly logical, then, for him to fly four of Glavsevmorput's most experienced polyarniks to the North Pole, and to leave them encamped on an ice floe to make the first serious study of the hydrography and ice circulaton of the Arctic Ocean since the drift of the *Fram*.

On 6 June 1937, after the Soviet flag had been ceremonially hoisted, the *International* sung, and salutes and cheers given for the Soviet Union and Comrade Stalin, the four aircraft whose flight to the North Pole is described above left a fully equipped Polar station on a 3 m (10 ft) thick ice floe some 20 km (12 miles) from the pole. Its four-man staff was headed by the tubby, jovial, secret policeman Ivan Dmitriyevich Papanin (1894–1986), former head of the Cape Chelyuskin Polar station and the only non-scientist in the party. His companions were the already mentioned Ernst Teodorovich Krenkel' (1903–71), wireless expert and participant in the 1931 *Graf Zeppelin* flight (Chapter 10), and in the voyages of the *Sibiryakov* and *Chelyuskin*; geophysicist Evgeniy Constantinovich Fedorov, a twenty-seven-year-old protegé of Papanin's who had worked in polar stations with him between 1932 and 1935; and Arctic marine scientist Petr Petrovich Shirshov, who had also been on the *Sibiryakov* and *Chelyuskin*. Their station was generously equipped and provisioned. Its main structure was a rectangular black marquee, 3.7 m (12 ft) long, 2.5 m (8 ft) broad and 2 m (6½ ft) high, of tarpaulin padded with eiderdown over a Duralumin tube frame. It bore the Hammer and Sickle and Red Star at one end, and along its length were the letters USSR, with the inscription 'Glavsevmorput Drifting Expedition 1937'. The deerskin-covered plywood floor was laid on rubber cushions which, when inflated, could serve as a raft for the tent. Next to the marquee a kitchen was built of snow blocks, with cupboards in the walls and aluminium crockery arranged on shelves. Here weekly menus, devised in Moscow with the help of the Institute of Public Nutrition, were posted up. Two days' meals give a sufficient idea of the polyarniks' fare (Brontman 1938: 160):

Plate 22. Ivan Papanin's drifting ice station set up 12 miles from the North Pole at the end of May 1937. The main living tent, nicknamed 'Government House', coloured dark to absorb heat from the sun, displays the letters CCCP, for USSR, and a Red Star. (Brontman 1938: 140.)

First day: Breakfast: coffee, caviare, omelette *nature*, white meat biscuits. Lunch: borsch soup with smoked pork, meat cutlets with peas, stewed fruit, rye rusks. Tea: tea with vitamin sweetmeats, bacon, meat biscuits. Supper: *bœuf Stroganov* with potatoes, rice pudding, chocolate, meat biscuits.
Second day: Breakfast: cheese, butter, potted meat, chocolate, meat biscuits. Lunch: barley soup, smoked pork with potato *purée*, bilberry jelly, rye biscuits. Tea: rice pudding with stewed fruit, coffee and biscuits. Supper: caviare, goulash with potatoes, tea and biscuits.

These menus were produced from five tons of dehydrated foods, designed to last eighteen months (Brontman 1938: 40–1).

All products were saturated with vitamins and in addition tablets of the anti-scurvy Vitamin C were packed in each can. The usual hard biscuits were replaced by white rusks made of milk, eggs and butter, and containing 35 per cent meat. All food was packed in air-tight metal boxes each containing food rations for twenty-five days. Each box contained forty different products. Had Papanin wished, he might have opened quite a good *delicatessen* shop at the North Pole. In addition to the products mentioned above and all sorts of condiments such as salt, pepper, mustard, bay leaves, vinegar, horse-radish sauce, onions and garlic, he has fruit, chocolate, caviare, cheese, sausage, stewed fruit, jellies, cocoa, coffee, tea, egg-powder, milk-powder, bacon, ham, and even pelmeni (a kind of miniature Cornish pasty). The only thing that is scarce is liquor. The group on the ice has a very small stock of high-grade brandy and nothing else.

Neither starvation nor scurvy was likely to trouble these new-style Arctic explorers, who were also equipped with four sledges, a collapsible boat, ten pairs of skis, a portable typewriter, fifty notebooks and, at Papanin's insistence, a rubber stamp. They also had all sorts of scientific instruments: plankton nets, microscopes, a hydrological windlass with 5,000 m (16,000 ft) of cable, and so on. In all, their outfit weighed over 10 tons. Arctic clothing in wool, silk, wolfskin, sealskin, reindeer fur, fox fur, leather and canvas was supplied. They slept in silk pyjamas, in wolf-fur sleeping bags lined with silk and eiderdown.
    A fifth member of the North Pole ice-floe expedition was the dog Vesyoly 'Happy', a black husky who proved his worth as a Polar bear alarm and whose popularity with the public led to his subsequent presentation to Moscow Zoo. He was installed there in a refrigerated kennel and provided with an air-cooled swimming tank (Segal 1939: 167–8).
    The world's first drifting ice station was entirely successful. Starting on 21 May near the North Pole, it drifted on a zig-zag course steadily southward. By December 1937 it was moving southward in the Greenland Sea between Greenland and Spitsbergen. Thereafter the speed of its drift increased as it neared the coast of Greenland. Finally, battered by storms and blizzards and threatened with the thawing and disintegration of their floe, the four Papaninites, as they were called in Russia, were taken off the ice by the icebreaking steamers

Taymyr and *Murman* on 19 February 1938, not far north of the mouth of Scoresby Sound. For the last ten days they had had the Greenland coast in sight. Their station had been able to provide valuable weather information for the trans-Arctic flights in the summer of 1937. Thereafter it continued to send weather reports four times daily to Moscow. The Papaninites also measured the depth of the ocean and the temperature at different depths, sampled the sediments at the bottom, and indeed successfully carried out their very full scientific programme. Naturally Papanin and his three companions were created Heroes of the Soviet Union; they were also appointed members of the Supreme Soviet of the USSR. Over two thousand books and articles about their exploits appeared in the Soviet Union, quite a few by Papanin himself (see especially in English Brontman 1938, Segal 1939: 133–68, Papanin 1939, Krenkel 1939; and, in Russian, Laktionov 1955: 257–81, Tikhomirov 1980).

After an interruption caused by the Second World War, the Soviet drifting ice station programme was resumed in 1950. It had the advantage over the high latitude air expeditions, which were confined to the summer months, of providing year-round meteorological and other observations. The second drifting ice station was set down by air in April 1950 some 500 km (300 miles) north of Wrangel Island. Its sixteen-man staff, led by Mikhail Mikhaylovich Somov, subsequently leader of the First Soviet Antarctic Expedition between 1955 and 1957, was taken off 376 days later, in April 1951. From 1954 onwards, two new stations were set up each year and they were now given the name 'North Pole' (*Severnyy Polyus*, shortened to SP) and a serial number. The two 1954 stations were SP3, which started near the North Pole, and SP4, which was set up north of Wrangel Island. By 1980 the pace had slackened to one new station per year or less, but many of them remained in service for several years, their staffs renewed annually. SP30 was established north of Wrangel Island in the autumn of 1987 by the research ship *Vitus Bering* and the icebreaker *Yermak* (*Soviet Weekly*, 31 October 1987). Longest-lasting of all these stations has been SP22. Set up on a 10 sq km (4 square miles) ice island, on ice 30 m (100 ft) thick, on 13 September 1973, it was evacuated after a drift of more than 16,000 km (10,000 miles) in April 1982, when it was some 400 km (250 miles) off the Greenland coast (*Soviet Weekly*, 24 April 1982).

A typical drifting ice station was staffed by fifteen to thirty men whose tour of duty lasted a year, beginning in the spring. The weight of material needed for a single station far exceeded Papanin's ten tons, some of the later ones requiring several hundred tons in all. Requirements naturally became increasingly elaborate. Dominoes and chess, as well as a bath-house and a dog or two, were standard. They were soon supplemented by a piano. Accommodation was improved: the KAPSH-1 and KAPSH-2 Arctic frame tents designed for SP2 by engineer Shaposhnikov were replaced on SP4 in 1954 with the heated Shaposhnikov Prefabricated House. This was a roomy 4.6 m (15 ft) by 2.7 m (9 ft) in size and had a lobby, two-burner gas cooker, living room, two bunks, small window and table. Shaposhnikov actually flew out to the station to see how his houses were appreciated. When everyone complained of the lack of ventilation, he easily resolved things by boring a hole in the wall of a house, using a cork to close

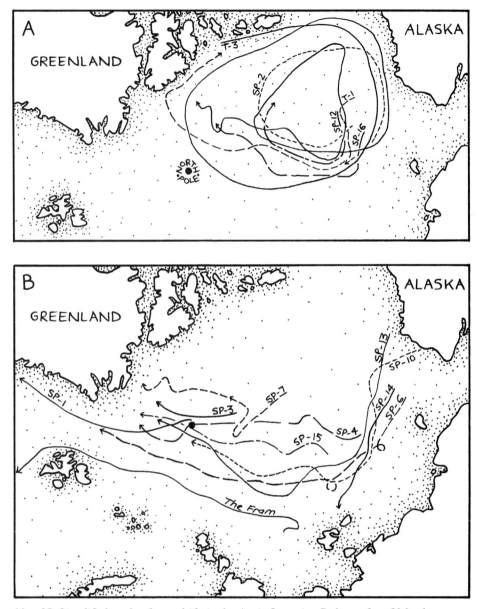

Map 27. Simplified tracks of some drifts in the Arctic Ocean ice. Redrawn from Yakovlev 1975: 200, 202. (a) Drifts in the Beaufort Gyre circulating clockwise north of the Beaufort Sea. T-1 and T-3 are US stations on ice islands. (b) Drifts in the Polar Drift Stream from Wrangel Island to Greenland.

or open this primitive ventilation shaft. Methods of transport were improved, too. In 1950 SP2 was supplied with a dog team and sledges and a snowmobile; later stations were equipped with tractors and helicopters. Much ingenuity was shown in technological improvements. Already on SP2, mechanic M.S. Komarov made an improved auger for boring holes in the ice, and also invented a driftometer to measure its drift, which might vary in speed from 3 km (2 miles) per day in the morning to 20 km (12 miles) per day in the evening, if a strong north wind got up. It was hard to say if life on a drifting station was less unpleasant in winter or summer. Winter was the time of storms, blizzards, and temperatures down to -30°C (-22°F). The summer thaw caused two serious problems: the station might be flooded by water, which could not always easily be drained by digging canals or boring holes in the ice; and the station buildings and tents, by preventing the ice below them melting, soon became raised above ground level on pedestals of ice. These could be up to 3 m (10 ft) high, necessitating the use of ladders for entry and egress. Naturally the splitting or disintegration of the station's ice floe was an ever-present danger, often requiring evacuation to another floe; and the size of the floe normally diminished substantially during the life of a station. In 1966, SP14 collided with Henrietta Island (ostrov Genriyetty) and broke up, and its fifteen-man staff had to be evacuated by air in the dead of winter. The most important scientific work of the drifting stations has been to explain in detail the way that the floating ice cover of the Arctic Ocean circulates, to map the relief of the ocean floor, and to provide much information on the composition of its water. The Arctic Ocean has been found to be roughly divided in two by the 1,800 km (1,100 mile) long Lomonosov Ridge (khrebet Lomonosova) which, extending from the New Siberian Islands past the North Pole to Ellesmere Island, effectively separates inflowing Atlantic water from water deriving from the Pacific (Armstrong 1958: 67–79, Gvozdetsky 1974: 44–65 in English; Kanaki 1974, Yakovlev 1975 in Russian).

SHIPPING AND NAVIGATION

Long before scientific work from drifting ice stations began, Glavsevmorput had organized annual ship-borne expeditions to study the hydrography, meteorology, and ice conditions along the Northern Sea Route, as well as to call at the Polar stations. In the poor ice year of 1937 the icebreaking ship *Georgiy Sedov*, on such a mission, was beset in the Laptev Sea and drifted in the ice from there to the Greenland Sea between October 1937 and January 1940, when she was extricated by the new icebreaker *Iosif Stalin*. She thus involuntarily repeated the drift of the *Fram*, and on a rather similar course (Armstrong 1958: 17–50). Naturally, the main role of icebreakers and icebreaking ships is to escort cargo ships through icy seas and, if necessary, to break a passage for them through the ice. The Russian icebreaker fleet has always been the world's largest. It first made headlines in 1928 when the *Krasin* rescued survivors of Umberto Nobile's airship *Italia* north of Spitsbergen (see Chapter 10). She had been built on Tyneside, launched in 1916 as the *Svyatogor*, and renamed *Krasin* in 1927 after Soviet diplomat Leonid B. Krasin, who had died in 1926. The fleet, which comprised some fifteen ships in the late 1940s, was doubled in size in the next thirty years. These icebreakers, which were built in Finland and the Soviet Union, became ever larger and more powerful, culminating in the *Lenin*, the world's first nuclear-powered surface ship, in 1959, the even more powerful nuclear-powered *Arktika* (renamed *Leonid Brezhnev* for a time), and *Sibir'* in 1975–7, and the *Rossiya* in 1985. Besides their routine work of leading cargo ships through the Northern Sea Route, these nuclear-powered icebreakers made some remarkable experimental voyages to test the feasibility of a more northerly Northern Sea Route; to try out the capabilities of the world's most powerful icebreakers; and to discover if a cargo ship could be successfully escorted through very thick ice. In the summer of 1977 the *Arktika* voyaged across the Barents Sea from Murmansk, rounded mys Zhelaniya (Cape Desire), the northern tip of Novaya Zemlya, and then headed through Vil'kitskiy Strait and out into the Laptev Sea (Map 25). There she altered course for the North Pole, which she became the first surface ship to reach, on 18 August 1977 (Spichkin and Shamont'yev 1979). In the following year, Captain Vladimir Konstantinovich Kochetkov took her sister ship, the *Sibir'*, out of Murmansk on 26 May and headed north-east for mys Zhelaniya. *En route* the *Sibir'* was joined by the cargo ship *Kapitan Myshevskiy*, which the *Sibir'* then escorted through thick ice across the northern part of the Kara Sea and past Arctic Cape (mys Arkticheskiy), the northern tip of Severnaya Zemlya. Then the two ships turned south-east to follow the eastern section of the Northern Sea Route nearly to Bering Strait, where they separated. While the *Kapitan Myshevskiy* proceeded south with her 6,000 tons of cargo to Magadan, the *Sibir'* returned along the Northern Sea Route to mys Shelagskiy near Pevek, and then headed north across the East Siberian Sea through multi-year ice famous hitherto for its impenetrability. Its crew then set up drifting station SP24 not far east of Jeannette Island (ostrov Zhannetty) in 77° north latitude (Map 25). Thence she returned to the Kara Sea via Arctic Cape for routine ice-breaking duties (Tyutenkov 1979, Kochetkov 1980). In 1987 it was the *Sibir'*'s turn to smash her way through the ice to the North Pole (Frolov 1991).

In spite of a crisis in 1983, when many ships were caught in the ice, the shipping season along the Northern Sea Route continues to be extended with the help of icebreakers and, perhaps, an ameliorating climate. Already nearly year-round navigation has been achieved on the Kara Sea Route from Murmansk to Dudinka on the Yenisey, the port for Noril'sk (Brigham 1991).

Although it seems that, in the fifty years between 1940 and 1990, no non-Russian ships transited the Northern Sea Route, many used the Kara Sea Route. American icebreakers, as well as nuclear submarines (Lyon 1987, McLaren 1987), cruised on several occasions in seas north of Russia between 1958, when the nuclear submarine *Skate* passed within 160 km (100 miles) of the New Siberian Islands (Calvert 1963: 193), and 1967, when the US Coast Guard icebreakers *Edisto* and *Eastwind*, failing to round the northern point of Severnaya Zemlya because of heavy ice, had to turn back when the Soviet authorities refused their request to pass through Vil'kitskiy Strait. In 1965 the US icebreaker *Northwind*, cruising to and fro in the Kara Sea, collected water samples for oceanographic purposes at 160 different points, but did not cruise eastwards beyond Severnaya Zemlya for fear of encounters with Soviet warships (Petrow 1967).

Navigation along the Northern Sea Route has been greatly facilitated since the early twentieth century by the construction of lighthouses, ports and Polar stations. By 1935 there were seventy-two Polar stations in the Soviet Arctic, twenty-nine of them run by Glavsevmorput (Taracouzio 1938: 497–9), and it was claimed that in 1984 there were over a hundred Polar stations operating along the Northern Sea Route. The seaway's most important ports, several of which were built with forced labour, are Murmansk (1916), Igarka (1929) and Dudinka on the Yenisey, Dikson, Tiksi and Pevek (1942–6) (Map 25). Above all, Russia's northern seaway is a product of the special skills of the highly trained men and women who operate it: seamen, meteorologists, ice forecasters and many others.

THE FUTURE

The creation of the Northern Sea Route was no grandiose Stalinesque propaganda contrivance. It is geography that dictates its existence. The Arctic Ocean is Russia's Mediterranean. Her northern shores curve round the Arctic Basin in a huge arc, embracing almost half of it. Her majestic north-flowing rivers, traffic highways in winter and summer, enter the Arctic Ocean at intervals along the shore and these, together with the Northern Sea Route, form the indispensable arteries through which the economic life-blood of northern Eurasia is bound to flow. Even if the Russian Federation were to be dismantled into separate units, the Arctic historian of a century hence will surely require a chapter for the Northern Sea Route.

TEN

The Arctic in the Twentieth Century

At the beginning of the twentieth century the Arctic was dominated by a handful of illustrious Scandinavian explorers. They were individualists and all-rounders, but their days were numbered, and they soon gave way, first to specialization, which produced a new breed of explorer scientists, and then to the teamwork of expeditions which, though having leaders, were almost groups of equals. Three new inventions transformed Arctic activities of all kinds during the twentieth century: the wireless, the aeroplane, and the motorized sledge. When war came to the Arctic, between 1940 and 1945, these were all put to use. Since then scientific research has continued apace, but has been largely institutionalized and professionalized. The lone adventurer still has his or her place in the Arctic at the end of the twentieth century, but in terms of sport rather than exploration (Hayes 1937, Hassert 1956, Victor 1964).

THE LAST EXPLORERS

The Swede, Adolf Erik Nordenskiöld (Kish 1973, Brusewitz 1991), born in 1832 in Helsinki, was a worthy successor of earlier Scandinavian Arctic explorers like Eirik the Red, Jens Munk and Vitus Bering. Three Norwegians, all of whom were in their prime when Norway gained her independence from Sweden in 1905, followed in his footsteps: Otto Sverdrup (Fairley 1959), born in 1854; Fridtjof Nansen (Reynolds 1949, Shackleton 1959, Greve 1973, Greve 1974, Pasetskiy 1987), born in 1861; and Roald Amundsen (Amundsen 1927, Arnesen 1929, Turley 1935), born in 1872. Only one other Arctic explorer of the period can compare with these in achievements – the American Robert Edwin Peary (see Chapter 8). All five were talented leaders, had technical and navigational skills, were determined to succeed, and shared a passion for the Arctic and for their respective countries. All of them described their explorations in their own words, in books which soon became established classics (Nordenskiöld 1881, Nordenskiöld 1885; Sverdrup 1904; Peary 1898, Peary 1907, Peary 1910; Nansen 1890, Nansen 1897; Amundsen 1908, Amundsen 1921. Riffenburgh 1993 discusses them all).

Adolf Nordenskiöld was a trained mineralogist, and his explorations were scientifically motivated and scientifically productive (Leslie 1970, Thorén 1979). He was intrigued by problems that demanded solutions. He and the initiator of Sweden's Golden Age of Arctic exploration, Otto Torell, had already toyed with the idea of solving the so-called 'Polar question' in 1861 by voyaging north from Spitsbergen. But Nordenskiöld's furthest north by sea in the *Sofia* in 1868 was only 81° 42', barely exceeding William Scoresby Senior's 81° 30' in the *Whitby* in 1806. Discouraged, Nordenskiöld next tried for a furthest north with reindeer sledges, in 1872–3, but the reindeer never even reached the expedition's proposed starting point for the northward sledge journey, and difficult ice conditions, storms, scurvy and accidents all conspired to prevent the expedition fulfilling its northern goal. Instead, Nordenskiöld and Louis Palander made the first crossing of the North East Land (Nordaustlandet) ice cap. In Greenland, Nordenskiöld, after Torell's 1859 reconnaisance, was fascinated by the Inland Ice, but neither in 1870, nor in 1883 (Nordenskiöld 1885; Map 30), did he succeed in finding the ice-free ground he thought might exist inland, nor could he substantiate his idea that the greyish powder he found on the surface of the Inland Ice was cosmic dust. By 1875 Nordenskiöld had become intrigued by a quite different Arctic problem: was the Kara Sea really an impenetrable ice cellar, as Karl Ernst von Baer, visiting Novaya Zemlya in 1837, had claimed (Map 12)? Or did recent Norwegian sealing expeditions into the Kara Sea, culminating in Edvard H. Johannesen's circumnavigation of Novaya Zemlya in 1870 (Bruun 1902: 322–3), prove otherwise? In 1874, an English merchant navy captain, Joseph Wiggins (Johnson 1907), clinched the matter by chartering the small steamer *Diana* from James Lamont and taking her from Dundee to the mouth of the Ob' and back in less than four months. Wiggins's voyage was promptly followed up by Nordenskiöld in 1875 and 1876, when he made two summer cruises up the River Yenisey. These proved to be mere trial runs for his voyage through the North-East Passage, which he all but succeeded in accomplishing in a single navigation season. Leaving Tromsø on 21 July 1878, the steam whaler *Vega* passed Cape Chelyuskin (mys Chelyuskina; Map 14), the most northerly point of the Eurasian mainland, on 19 August, but on 26 September, just beyond Kolyuchin Bay (Kolyuchinskaya guba), she was beset by ice and forced to winter, only 210 km (130 miles) short of Bering Strait. Freed from the ice on 18 July 1879, two days later the *Vega* rounded Cape Dezhnev (mys Dezhneva) into Bering Strait (Map 1). While Nordenskiöld's role as leader of the expedition was of the first importance, the man who actually navigated the *Vega* through the North-East Passage was its able commander, Lieutenant Louis Palander of the Royal Swedish Navy. Nor should the Russian contribution to the *Vega* expedition, comprising encouragement and a substantial cash donation from businessman Aleksandr Mikhaylovich Sibiryakov, as well as navigational aids, be forgotten. (Belov 1977: 26–8; besides Nordenskiöld 1881 see also Hovgaard 1882, Garting 1979, Nordqvist 1983.)

Fridtjof Nansen has been accurately and tersely described as 'a man who in daring, in endurance, and in intellectual stature is supreme among Arctic explorers' (Kirwan 1962: 215). Sverdrup's judgement of him, that he was great as a Polar explorer, still greater as a scientist, and greatest of all as a man, is well known (Kanevskiy 1979: 91). At the age of eighteen he broke the world skating record for the mile, and then won the Norwegian national cross-country ski race in twelve separate years. In 1882 Nansen's first Arctic voyage on the sealer *Viking* took him to Jan Mayen and east Greenland (Nansen 1925); while on it, he was appointed curator of the Zoological Museum in Bergen. Inspired by Nordenskiöld's venture on skis on the Inland Ice of Greenland in 1883, and prompted further by Peary's exploit there with the Dane, Christian Maigaard, in 1886, Nansen conceived the idea of ski-ing across Greenland from east to west. Many thought the plan crazy. A Bergen newspaper carried the satirical announcement: 'In the month of June next, Curator Nansen will give a ski-ing display, with long jumps, on the Inland Ice of Greenland. Reserved seats in the crevasses. Return ticket unnecessary' (quoted in Reynolds 1949: 41). But Maigaard, whom Nansen met in Copenhagen, was encouraging, and the feat was accomplished successfully between 15 August and 24 September 1888 (Map 30) (Nansen 1890). Descending from the Inland Ice at the head of Ameralik Fjord, Nansen and Otto Sverdrup constructed a boat from tent material and willow branches and rowed triumphantly to Godthåb (now Nuuk) (Map 5a). Nansen was surprised and amused when he was congratulated by the

Plate 23. *Fridtjof Nansen and his five companions skiing across the Inland Ice of Greenland, 1888. The Norwegians, Nansen, Otto Sverdrup, Oluf Christian Dietrichson and Kristian Kristiansen are followed by the two Sami, Samuel Balto and Ole Ravna. (From Nansen 1890: 468.)*

first Dane he met in Nuuk, not for crossing the Inland Ice, but on the award of his doctorate. The party was too late for the last ship back to Denmark, but its leader took advantage of his enforced winter among the West Greenlanders to gather material for his book *Eskimo Life*, published in 1893. Some account of the famous drift of the *Fram* between 1893 and 1896, of Nansen and Johansen's attempt to reach the North Pole, and of their subsequent rescue by Frederick Jackson in Franz Josef Land, has already been given in Chapter 8. The *Fram* expedition made the first serious investigation of the Central Arctic Basin, and its scientific results, like those of Nordenskiöld's *Vega* expedition, were fully published in a series of large-format volumes.

Otto Sverdrup, a former merchant marine captain who had volunteered to ski across Greenland with Nansen in 1888, commanded the *Fram* for him between 1893 and 1896, demonstrating exceptional skill in ice navigation. Within a few days of his return with the *Fram*, Sverdrup was asked by Nansen if he would lead a new Norwegian Polar expedition, to be financed by Axel Heiberg and Messrs. Ringnes the brewers, who had been among the patrons of Nansen's expedition. The delighted Sverdrup borrowed the *Fram* from the Norwegian government and set off on the famous four-year expedition (1898–1902), during which he surveyed and mapped the north-western section of the Canadian Arctic Archipelago, namely most of the hitherto unexplored west coast of Ellesmere Island and the three large islands he named after his expedition's patrons: Axel Heiberg, Ellef Ringnes and Amund Ringnes. He brilliantly achieved his aim of filling in a large white space on the map, but, in spite of repeated efforts, failed to persuade his own government to make any sort of effective claim to these islands. Only in 1925 did the Norwegian consul in Montreal make Norway's first official contact with Canada about the Sverdrup Islands, enquiring on 12 March 'how far Canada regards the areas discovered during the 1898–1902 expedition as Canadian, and on what the Canadian Government bases its claims' (Fairley 1959: 279). No reply was ever forthcoming. At the end of his life, despairing of the Norwegian claim to sovereignty, Sverdrup sent Canadian Prime Minister Mackenzie King 'an invoice for work done' in discovering and charting a large part of Canada, and eventually received $67,000 from the Canadian government. In 1914, Sverdrup, commanding a former Dundee whaler, the *Eclipse*, joined in the search for no fewer than three Russian Polar expeditions missing in the Kara Sea: those of Georgiy Sedov in the *Svyatoy Foka*, Georgiy L. Brusilov in the *Svyataya Anna* (La Croix 1954: 129–57), and V.A. Rusanov in the *Herkules* (Rabo and Vittenburg 1924, Barr 1984). Sverdrup used his ship's radio telegraph, then a new invention, to intercept and relay Russian messages, and organized a dog sledge party led by himself on skis to help extricate thirty-nine Russians trapped by the ice (Barr 1991b). Again in 1920, when he earned the title 'king of ice navigation' from the *Daily Telegraph*, and in 1921, Sverdrup commanded ships in Russian Arctic waters.

Roald Amundsen was perhaps the most versatile and successful of all Polar explorers, for the discoverer of the South Pole also voyaged through both the North-West and North-East Passages, and was a pioneer of Arctic aviation. He was the first to navigate the North-West Passage (1903–6) (Map 28), which he combined with a full year of scientific observations near the North Magnetic Pole, overwintering twice for this purpose. In 1909, when he was preparing to lead another *Fram* expedition toward the North Pole, this time starting from Bering Strait, news of Peary's attainment of the North Pole caused Amundsen to change his mind and go for the South Pole instead. In the years thereafter he was described as 'A remarkable-looking fellow with thin long nose like the beak of a hawk, his weather-beaten face of the texture of pigskin' (Lied 1945: 174). It was only between 1918 and 1921 that he finally got round to taking his own ship, the *Maud*, her hull built like an egg halved along its length, along the Arctic coast of Russia. But in spite of overwintering three times, dense summer ice repeatedly foiled his plans to force the *Maud* into the pack and drift like the *Fram* towards the North Pole. By the time the *Maud* reached Seattle in August 1921 to refit, Amundsen, ever an adventurer, had developed a passion for aviation. Leaving the *Maud*, commanded by Oscar Wisting, to enter the pack near Herald Island (Map 23) in August 1922, drift in the ice to the northern tip of the New Siberian Islands and then, using motor and sail, return again to Bering Strait in 1925 (Sverdrup 1926), Amundsen went off to New York to buy an aircraft with a view to flying from Alaska to Spitsbergen. He was in the north of Alaska in 1922 with two aircraft, but weather made flying impossible; instead, he found himself walking a claimed 800 km (500 miles) in ten days from Barrow to Kotzebue. In 1923 Amundsen was at Wainwright again preparing for his flight over the Arctic Ocean. Realizing that he carried insufficient fuel to reach Spitsbergen from Barrow, he planned to take a sledge and kayak with him. But his Junker aircraft crashed on its first trial landing, and he had to cancel the arrangements that had been made for his relief and reception in Spitsbergen. These included the supremely optimistic plan of leaving a depot of supplies on the pack ice where Amundsen was expected to land, and to meet or search for him in a Junker seaplane piloted by A. Neumann from Hamburg. News of Amundsen's misfortune in Alaska only reached this relief expedition after it had crossed the Arctic Circle. It continued nonetheless and, during flights over Spitsbergen, Lieutenant Walter Mittelholzer of the Swiss Air Force took a splendid series of air photographs of the Spitsbergen Archipelago (Mittelholtzer 1925). It was not until 1925, after his meeting with the son of an American financier, Lincoln Ellsworth (whose father reluctantly lent him $85,000 to help finance the expedition), that Amundsen and Ellsworth made their historic but unsuccessful first polar flight. Taking off in two Dornier flying boats, N24 (Ellsworth) and N25 (Amundsen), from King's Bay (Kongsfjorden), Spitsbergen, they flew toward the North Pole, where they planned to transfer to a single plane and carry on to Alaska. But they were forced down on the ice in about 88° north latitude. One aircraft was wrecked, but eventually, after nearly a month on the ice making a runway for the other to take off, the whole party returned safely to King's Bay (Amundsen 1925, Amundsen and Ellsworth 1925, 1926, Ellsworth 1938). The real hero of the venture was the aviator First Lieutenant Hjalmar Riiser-Larsen of the Royal Norwegian Navy; Amundsen and Ellsworth were officially co-leaders, and Amundsen also navigated. No wonder, after this adventure, that they turned to another type of flying machine for their Arctic explorations – the airship.

Robert Edwin Peary seems to have been inspired by Nordenskiöld in his early Inland Ice explorations in Greenland, as well as in his interest in meteorites. He was a man of wide interests whose expeditions carried out valuable scientific research in Greenland, especially in glaciology and ethnology (Vaughan 1991). After 1898 he concentrated exclusively on reaching the North Pole by dog sledge over the pack ice with the help of the Inuhuit Eskimos, whom he had known well since he wintered on McCormick Fjord (Map 30) in 1891–2. Once that object was attained, his interest in the Arctic gave way to a growing interest in aviation. In 1910 he made a triumphant tour of Europe, accepting invitations to lecture before eleven different geographical societies, and receiving gold medals from many of them. In 1917 he published an interesting and cogent book on his methods of Polar travel. He died in 1920 at the age of sixty-three.

EXPLORER SCIENTISTS

The five great men so far discussed earned world renown as adventurers and explorers. Their achievements were undeniable, but only three of them made significant new discoveries. Nansen had revealed the nature and extent of the Inland Ice in Greenland; he and Peary had shown that most of the Arctic Basin was an ocean covered with a layer of pack ice; and Peary and Sverdrup between them had explored and mapped the ice-bound shores of north Greenland and the northernmost part of Canada's Arctic Archipelago. The Icelandic-Canadian-American explorer Vilhjalmur Stefansson has been credited with discovering between 1914 and 1918 'some of the world's last major land masses' (Diubaldo 1978: 2, 127), but these only amounted to the outlying Brock, Borden, Meighen and Lougheed Islands, the biggest of which, Borden Island, is only 80 km (50 miles) long. This is not to deny that Stefansson was one of the greatest Arctic travellers of all time, but his controversial personality, his inability to lead a large and complex expedition, his failure effectively to pursue his anthropological interests, and his occasional grave errors of judgement, conspired to undermine his popularity in Canada and took the edge off his renown as an explorer. All this was in spite of numerous admirable qualities, which included imagination, literary talent, and a flair for publicity. These made him the best-known Arctic expert of his day (accounts of explorations: Stefansson 1919, 1922, Noice 1924; autobiography: Stefansson 1964; biography: Hunt 1986; see also Neatby 1966: 365–408).

In the early twentieth century the time had come for the truly scientific explorer to make his mark on Arctic history; it was the age of specialists in those sciences most relevant to the Arctic, namely anthropology, glaciology, geophysics and geology. The Norwegians had had their turn, and now it was the Danes who came to the forefront. Naturally their activities were concentrated on Greenland. The anthropologist Knud Rasmussen (1879–1933) began his career in 1910 by founding the Thule Trading Station, near the former Inuhuit settlement of Uummannaq, in Avanersuaq, north-west Greenland (Map 30), with Peter Freuchen's help (Vaughan 1991). The station did such profitable business with the local Inuhuit Eskimos, by obtaining Arctic fox furs from them in exchange for rifles, ammunition, tea, sugar and the like, that Rasmussen was able to organize

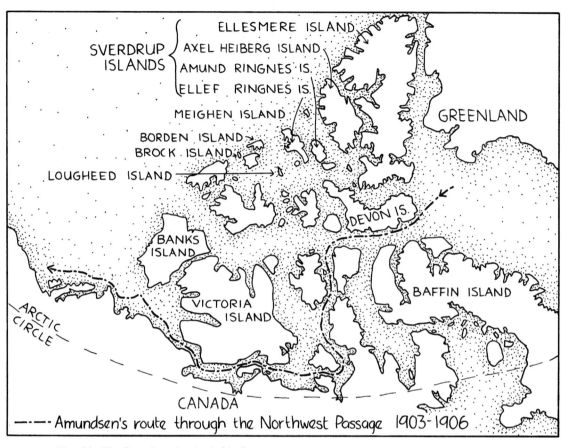

SVERDRUP ISLANDS
ELLESMERE ISLAND
AXEL HEIBERG ISLAND
AMUND RINGNES IS.
ELLEF RINGNES IS.
MEIGHEN ISLAND
GREENLAND
BORDEN ISLAND
BROCK ISLAND
LOUGHEED ISLAND
DEVON IS.
BANKS ISLAND
BAFFIN ISLAND
VICTORIA ISLAND
ARCTIC CIRCLE
CANADA
———·—·· Amundsen's route through the Northwest Passage 1903-1906

Map 28. The Canadian Arctic Archipelago.

and finance two expeditions of geographical discovery across the Inland Ice to north-east Greenland (Map 30), as well as anthropological expeditions to study the East Greenlanders and, between 1921 and 1924, nearly all the Inuit groups of North America. This last was the famous Fifth Thule Expedition, an anthropological *tour de force*, accomplished by Rasmussen as leader, aided by cartographer-naturalist Peter Freuchen, archaeologist Therkel Mathiassen and ethnologist Kaj Birket-Smith, all Danes, and a varying group of Inuit assistants, some with their wives (Rasmussen 1933). Meanwhile, Rasmussen had introduced the twenty-one-year-old student Lauge Koch (1892–1964) to the Arctic in 1916 by giving him a place on his Second Thule Expedition to north-east Greenland. Lauge Koch was a nephew of the explorer J.P. Koch, who had played a leading role in the ill-fated *Danmark* expedition to north-east Greenland of 1906–8. He was an outstanding geologist and cartographer; but also a controversial figure who seems to have lacked the human touch (Malaurie 1990: 261–8) and whose publications and scientific method were also called in question. Between 1913 and 1959 Lauge Koch led over twenty expeditions to north and east Greenland and spent thirty-four summers and six winters there. Starting with dog sledges and ending with aeroplanes, he mapped the coastal regions of north-west, north, and much of east Greenland (Dawes 1992, Odsbjerg 1992). While he was still at work, two Danish archaeologists began their revolutionary studies of Inuit prehistory in Greenland, Erik Holtved (1942) from 1935 on in the north-west, and Eigil Knuth (1967) from 1945 in Peary Land and the north-east.

But Greenland was by no means a Danish preserve. In terms of the history of world science, the pre-eminent Greenland explorer of the early twentieth century was the German Alfred Lothar Wegener (1880–1930). As a member of the *Danmark* expedition, he carried out meteorological, glaciological and cartographical work in north-east Greenland, then crossed the Inland Ice from Danmarkshavn to near Kangersuatsiaq in 1912–13 with J.P. Koch and others: the first party to overwinter on the ice. Soon afterwards Wegener came up with the apparently crazy idea that Greenland was drifting slowly westwards at the rate of 1½ m (5 ft) per annum, but few then accepted Wegener's theory of continental drift. After a reconnaissance trip in 1929, he led a German expedition to the Inland Ice in 1930. Using propeller-driven motorized sledges to transport stores and equipment to the expedition's station about half-way across the Inland Ice, at 2,957 m (9,700 ft) above sea level, three expedition members successfully overwintered there. But Alfred Wegener and the Greenlander accompanying him died in unknown circumstances while travelling between Mid-Ice or *Eismitte* and the expedition's headquarters on the western margin of the Inland Ice above Uummannaq (Georgi 1934, Wegener 1939, Reinke-Kunze 1992: 48–76). Wegener's work was taken up after the Second World War by French explorer Paul-Emile Victor, who, encouraged by Jean Charcot, had led an ethnographical expedition to east Greenland in 1934–5, crossed the Inland Ice from west to east in the summer of 1936 with two French colleagues and the Dane Eigil Knuth, and spent a year living with East Greenlanders in 1936–7 (Victor 1939). Then, from 1948 to 1953 and subsequently, Victor led a series of expeditions starting from near Ilulissat on the west coast to investigate the Inland Ice using ex-US army Weasels with caterpillar tracks. As near as possible to the site of Mid-Ice, he established Station Centrale (Bouché 1952), which was occupied for two consecutive winters while Victor and his colleagues of the Expéditions Polaires Françaises, 'blazed 10,000 miles of trail across Greenland' with their Weasels (Victor 1956: 147; see too Victor 1964: 260–2). At twenty-six years of age Jean Malaurie joined Victor's expedition as geographer, then spent the winter of 1950/1 living with the Inuhuit Eskimos of north-west Greenland, while he studied them with an anthropologist's eye and made the first maps of Inglefield Land (Map 30). The discerning book he wrote soon afterwards describing his experiences was called *The Last Kings of Thule* (1956, 1982), after Rasmussen's trading station of that name founded in 1910 (now no longer in existence). The 'last kings of Thule' are the Inuhuit Eskimos of Avanersuaq. In the second half of the twentieth century Malaurie, as writer, organizer of conferences, film maker, and expert on Arctic peoples, has remained France's premier Arctic scientist (Malaurie 1990).

In Russia the age of the lone scientific explorer was over by the time of Stefansson, Rasmussen and Koch. Teamwork, naturally enough, was the hallmark of Soviet Arctic research. Men like Lieutenants F.P. Vrangel' (alias Ferdinand von Wrangell) and P.F. Anzhu (alias Anjou) of the Imperial Navy, who explored the north Siberian coast and some of its islands between 1820 and 1824 (von Wrangell 1844), as well as von Toll (Toll 1909), Georgiy Sedov and Georgiy Ushakov, were explorers of the traditional dog-sledging type. Toll died in 1902 searching for the mythical Sannikov Land. Ushakov's career and activities have already been mentioned in Chapter 9. Two great specialist Arctic explorers active in Russia and Siberia in the nineteenth century, both of foreign origin (like Wrangell and Toll), were outstanding scientific pioneers: the Finnish linguist and ethnologist Mathias Alexander Castren (1813–52), and the naturalist-traveller A.T. von Middendorff (alias Aleksandr Fedorovich Middendorf, 1815–94), who was of Baltic German extraction. Castren, born at Rovaniemi (Map 12) on the Arctic Circle, travelled between 1842 and 1847 through the tundra on either side of the Arctic Circle, visiting Mezen (Map 38), Pustozersk, Obdorsk (now Salekhard), Turukhansk and Dudinka (Map 12), often in winter, to study the languages and peoples of Finno-Ugric origin, especially the Sami and the Nentsy. His *Northern Journeys and Researches* were published in German in eleven volumes. This great scholar and intrepid explorer has been sadly forgotten by twentieth-century historians of Arctic exploration (Hartwig 1874: 171–86). Middendorf's fame has been less dimmed by neglect: his detailed investigation of the plants and animals of Taymyr in the summer of 1843 was an important pioneering effort (Barr 1991a).

AIRSHIP TRIUMPHS AND TRAGEDIES

Within days of their narrow escape from disaster in the N24 and N25, Amundsen and Ellsworth had decided to repeat their attempted crossing of the Arctic Ocean from Spitsbergen to Alaska in an airship (for Arctic aviation see Clarke 1964, Grierson 1964, Simmons 1965; Soviet Arctic aviation has already been considered in Chapter 9). On 25 July 1925 they and Hjalmar Riiser-Larsen met in Oslo with a representative of the Aero Club of Norway and Colonel Umberto Nobile, who had been designing and building airships in Rome for the Italian and other governments. (For what follows on Nobile, see Dr Gertrude Nobile's bibliography, Stolp 1984, which lists all the many published eye-witness accounts and other studies; Ferrante 1985 and Broude 1992 are biographies of Nobile; for Nobile's accounts of his own exploits, see especially Nobile 1928, Nobile 1961.) The airship N1 was duly bought for the expedition, rechristened the *Norge*, and Nobile was appointed commander. Ellsworth provided the funds, and Amundsen was the expedition's leader, but on the flight Nobile piloted the craft, assisted by a crew of Italians and Norwegians. The aim of flying right across the Pole to Alaska was brilliantly accomplished on 11–13 May 1926. The airship landed at Teller (Map 1) after a nonstop flight of 70 hours and 40 minutes, having travelled 5,100 km (3,180 miles). But this success was marred by acrimony. Italian public opinion and Fascist propaganda – Benito Mussolini was consolidating his power just at this time – led to the flight of the *Norge* being treated as an Italian national triumph, and Nobile became an Italian national hero. The *Corriere della Sera* headline read 'Umberto Nobile describes his flight over the Pole'. Amundsen was irritated, and took his feelings out on Nobile, who was probably more interested in his little dog Titina, who shared all his flights with him, than in Il Duce. Not only did Amundsen attack Nobile fiercely in the press, accusing him of bad judgement, of being a poor airship pilot, and of gesturing with his hands while giving orders, but he devoted ninety-five pages of his autobiographical work *My Life as an Explorer*, published in 1927, to vilifying Nobile. He complained that Nobile had dropped a much larger Italian flag at the North Pole than his and Ellsworth's Norwegian and American flags. He was furious when Nobile turned up for a reception in Seattle in the resplendent dress uniform of a colonel in the Italian army. He accused Nobile, when in the United States, of 'travelling all over the country telling false things about the expedition and dragging the name of Norway in the dirt' (Amundsen 1927: 220). And, insisting that Nobile was a mere skipper, Amundsen argued that he was certainly no leader, and was not a member of 'the most exclusive club in the world', founded on 17 December 1926 by himself and Ellsworth, namely the Polar Legion. Membership was only open to leaders of expeditions which had reached either Pole. The only members were Amundsen, Bird, Ellsworth and the deceased Scott and Peary (Amundsen 1927: 222).

Nobile's triumph was followed by a tragedy. He attempted another flight over the North Pole from Spitsbergen in May 1928 in a new airship, the *Italia*, this time without Norwegian or American help. The *Italia* reached the Pole successfully, but crashed in poor weather conditions on 25 May near the end of her return flight to Spitsbergen. Nobile and others in the airship's cabin survived on the ice in a tent which they tried to colour red to make more conspicuous, but six men with the main part of the airship, still airborne, drifted away and were never seen again. Of the nine living survivors, two, one of them Nobile, were injured. Eight were taken off the ice by aircraft and ship after a monumental international search and rescue operation. The last five survivors were finally taken aboard the Soviet icebreaker *Leonid Krasin* on 12 July, after it had smashed its way through ice up to 3 m (10 ft) thick. The flight, which was more of a stunt then an exploring expedition, did little or nothing to enhance Nobile's reputation, and seriously undermined the national prestige of Italy. The rescue was undertaken in the main by Norwegians, Swedes and Russians. What the Italians themselves did was too little and too late. Nobile was blamed for allowing himself to be rescued first, by Swedish flier Einar Lundborg, though he was wounded. Italian naval officers Filippo Zappi and Adalberto Mariano were blamed for abandoning their starving companion, the Swede Finn Malmgren, to die on the ice, though he had insisted they should go on without him. The captain of the Italian support ship *Città di Milano*, Giuseppe Romagna Manoja, was accused of ineptitude and inefficiency, and he and others were blamed for failing to search for the other six crewmen missing with the airship's hull. Of all the Italians caught up in the disaster, only radio operator Giuseppe Biagi seems to have won universal acclaim. With a small transmitter, he was tireless in sending messages from the Red Tent. On the *Città di Milano* his transmissions were not even listened for, it being assumed that everyone on the *Italia* was dead. But eventually a Russian radio ham near Arkhangel'sk picked up one of Biagi's messages, and for

Plate 24. Umberto Nobile's Red Tent on the ice off North East Land (Nordaustlandet), Spitsbergen Archipelago. Photographed from the Russian icebreaker Krasin *on 12 July 1928 by Russian flier Boris Chukhnovskiy. To the left of the tent is Swedish pilot Lieutenant Einar Lundborg's crashed Fokker aircraft, from which he escaped unhurt some time after rescuing Nobile. In the right foreground two of the survivors, probably Lieutenant Alfredo Viglieri followed by the Czech scientist Franz Behounek, approach the* Krasin. *(From van Dongen 1929: 176.)*

the first time in Arctic history lives were saved by wireless telegraphy. Among other heroes of the occasion were Amundsen, who took off from Tromsø on 18 June in a flying boat to search for Nobile, and his French pilot René Guilbaut, who were never heard of again, and Professor Rudol'f Samoylovich and the Soviet icebreaker fleet, comprising the *Malygin*, *Krasin*, *Sedov* (all British-built) and others, with their aircraft.

In 1931 a successful Polar flight was made by a much larger airship, the *Graf Zeppelin*, which had proved its mettle in 1929 by flying round the world. Count Ferdinand von Zeppelin had personally visited Spitsbergen in 1910 and planned airship flights from there (Miethe and Hergesell 1911), but the First World War intervened. Then, in 1925, Aeroarctic, the International Association for the Exploration of the Arctic with Aircraft, was founded with Fridtjof Nansen as president. The great explorer, then aged sixty-nine, was planning to fly over the North Pole in the *Graf Zeppelin* in 1930 when death cut short his hopes. Aeroarctic went ahead with its *Graf Zeppelin* Arctic expedition in the last week of July 1931, when the 13,200 km (8,200 mile) flight from Friedrichshafen over Franz Josef Land, the Taymyr Peninsula and Novaya Zemlya went without a hitch. Overall leader of the expedition was Hugo Eckener. In the fifteen-strong

Soviet detachment was Nobile's principal rescuer, Rudol'f Samoylovich, scientific leader of the expedition, the stratosphere researcher and inventor of the radiosonde Pavel Aleksandrovich Molchanov, and radio expert Ernst Teodorovich Krenkel'. The airship flew much of the time at a height of 200–300 m (1,000 ft) above sea level and a speed of around 100 km (60 miles) per hour. Forgoing a flight over the North Pole, the *Graf Zeppelin*'s only stunt was briefly to land on the sea in Franz Josef Land and exchange mail with the Soviet icebreaker *Malygin*. Unlike the *Italia*, the *Graf Zeppelin* experienced good weather throughout the trip, though it was prepared for the worst. Stowed away on board just in case were twelve four-person red tents with sewn-in groundsheets, a reindeer-fur sleeping bag apiece for passengers and crew, twenty-three Nansen sledges, five twelve-person boats and 115 24 kg (53 lb) waterproof sacks of pemmican and other provisions arranged in one-day, four-person rations. Besides scrapping a couple of islands from the map of Franz Josef Land and adding some new ones, the expedition used a massive nine-lens panoramic camera invented by C. Aschenbrenner for systematic aerial photography, and added substantially to knowledge of the sea ice in the Barents and Kara Seas (Kohl-Larsen 1931, Ellsworth and Smith 1932, Seidenfaden 1939: 75–6). In spite of this triumph, the future of Arctic flying lay with the aeroplane. Already in April 1928 the Australian-born explorer Hubert Wilkins (1928) and US Army pilot Lieutenant Carl Ben Eielsen had flown across the Arctic Ocean from Barrow to Spitsbergen in a Lockheed Vega monoplane, and aeroplane flights in the Arctic soon became commonplace.

WAR AND STRATEGY

Already in the Crimean War a military confrontation between European powers – England and France against Russia – had led to warfare in the Arctic. In 1854 a British naval squadron set fire to the famous Solovetskiy monastery on the Solovetskiye Islands in the White Sea with pre-heated shot. It then sailed up the Kola River to bombard the town of Kola (Stone 1983). During the Second World War military activities, including actual fighting, took place in the Arctic because vital supply routes to Britain and the Soviet Union passed through the Arctic and both naval and air operations depended on reports from weather stations in Greenland, Spitsbergen and elsewhere in the North Atlantic. Fair weather was required to find and attack the enemy, foul weather was needed for evasion. The war of the weather stations began as soon as Hitler invaded and conquered Denmark and Norway in April 1940, leaving their overseas possessions, Iceland, Greenland and Spitsbergen, open to attack or occupation (Blyth 1951, Liversidge 1960, Steen 1960, Schwerdtfeger and Selinger 1982, Selinger and Glen 1983, Schofield and Nesbit 1987). It was a war of isolated posts held by handfuls of men and fought between tiny patrols, often in extremely harsh weather conditions. After the fall of Norway the four Norwegian weathermen on Jan Mayen risked their lives by sending their weather reports to Britain instead of Norway. A fishery protection ship, the *Fridtjof Nansen*, commanded by Captain Ernst Ullring of the Royal Norwegian Navy, which had escaped from Tromsø to Britain

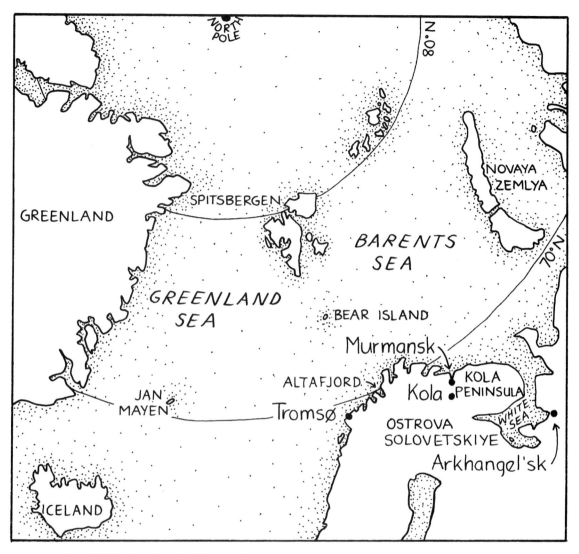

Map 29. The Greenland and Barents Seas.

in May, had spent the summer dismantling four German-controlled Danish weather stations in east Greenland. Then she voyaged with reinforcements and supplies to Jan Mayen, but was wrecked and sunk after hitting a reef there in rough seas before she could be unloaded (on wartime Jan Mayen, see Richter 1946, Elbo 1953).

The islands of the Spitsbergen Archipelago offered much better opportunities for operating a clandestine weather station than Jan Mayen. No sooner had the Allies successfully evacuated two thousand Russian coalminers to Arkhangel'sk and nearly a thousand Norwegian miners to Britain in August–September 1941, and put the Spitsbergen coal mines out of commission, than the Germans flew in a small meteorological party which set up weather stations in Advent Valley (Adventdalen) and in an inlet at the head of Cross Fjord (Krossfjorden; see Map 32) called Signehamn. In spite of the establishment by the British of a Norwegian garrison based on Longyearbyen from 1942 onwards, the Germans were still able to maintain weather stations on the archipelago. They were set up and supplied by U-boats. The six-man station at Signehamn in Cross Fjord operated for almost eighteen months before the Norwegians found it. What might be called the battle of Signehamn was typical of the weather war (Fjærli 1979: 101–4). On 18 June 1943 Ernst Ullring, whose legendary wartime feats included hunting U-boats with a rowing boat and a tin opener, set out from Barentsburg in a motorboat with three officers, a sergeant, and five men to search for the German radio station known by the British Admiralty to be somewhere in or near Cross Fjord. As he approached Signehamn he spotted rowing boats, a hut, and a radio mast. Stealing up to the hut, his party found it unoccupied but containing provisions and equipment. Mindful of the possibility of a large German force in the neighbourhood, Ullring left Lieutenant Augesen and four men at Signehamn to keep watch for the Germans, while he returned to Barentsburg for reinforcements. Just as members of Augesen's party were concealing themselves some way from the hut, a man came walking toward them. It was Heinz Köhler, second in command of the German weather station, returning from photographing the bird life in a neighbouring marsh. As soon as he came within earshot, the Norwegians shouted to him to put his hands up and surrender. But Köhler turned and ran off, zig-zagging and firing a pistol at the pursuing Norwegians, who returned fire with their rifles. Then he disappeared, and later the Norwegians heard a single shot. After waiting an hour, two of them warily approached, covered by the others. They found that Köhler had crouched behind a rock, pointed his pistol at his temple, and shot himself. Meanwhile some of Köhler's companions, arriving unseen by the Norwegians, withdrew. They informed Tromsø and Kiel by radio of events and asked for the relieving U-boat they expected on 23 June to be sent to a point further along the coast. On 22 June Ullring was back again with eight men, an officer, and machine guns. On 23 June the U-boat duly took off the five remaining Germans as arranged. Thinking that Köhler had been shot by the Norwegians, the U-boat commander decided to take reprisals. His coded message telling Kiel of his intentions was intercepted by the British Admiralty and passed on to Ullring, but it was too late for evasive action because Ullring's men were already out searching for the Germans and Ullring himself could abandon neither his men nor his boat. In the afternoon of 23 June the silver-grey U-boat, moving slowly and quietly on the surface through the ice floes into Signehamn, suddenly opened fire on the Norwegian motorboat. The three men on it dived into the water. Two got behind an ice floe and swam safely ashore; the third was hit by a bullet and killed. After firing some salvoes at the Norwegian tents, the U-boat headed for the mouth of the fjord and dived. Ullring's appeal for help to Barentsburg was passed on to the Admiralty in London, and he and his remaining men were rescued and taken back there by a British submarine. One man had been killed on either side: 'An eye for an eye, a tooth for a tooth' was a Norwegian's comment. Later that year, on 8 September

1943, a German fleet comprising the battleship *Tirpitz*, the battle cruiser *Scharnhorst*, and nine destroyers, arrived in Ice Fjord (Isfjorden) and, after shelling the Norwegian positions at Barentsburg and Longyearbyen, landed troops to attack the 152-man Norwegian garrison. The defenders had forty-one men captured and six killed; the remainder withdrew into the mountains. Both Barentsburg and Longyearbyen were virtually demolished. The German fleet left at once and was back in its Altafjord base in north Norway on 9 September before it could be intercepted by the British Home Fleet, which had been ordered to head for Spitsbergen. Three other German weather stations operated in the Spitsbergen Archipelago between 1942 and 1945. Two of them remained in operation until evacuated by Norwegian sealers in August–September 1945, months after the end of the war (Aasgaard 1946, Elbo 1952, Fjærli 1979; for the last operational German weather station in the archipelago, see Barr 1986).

On the other side of the Greenland Sea to Spitsbergen the fjord-cut, uninhabited coast of north-east Greenland offered excellent possibilities for the Germans to set up hidden weather stations. Even before the United States was formally at war with Germany, in September 1941, the US Coast Guard ship *Northland* intercepted and captured a Norwegian trawler, the *Busko*, and destroyed the German weather station it had just set up ashore. At the same time, Danish governor Eske Brun, in conjunction with the American authorities, organized the North-east Greenland Sledge Patrol, with headquarters at Scoresby Sound (now Ittoqqortoormiit) and bases at Ella Island (Ella Ø), and Eskimonæs on the south shore of Clavering Island (Map 18). To make sure the patrol's members were not treated as civilians and executed on capture, Brun founded the Greenland Army and, deciding not to have any private soldiers in it, he appointed Ib Poulsen captain, another Dane sergeant, and the other European patrol members corporals. This patrol of fifteen volunteers, Danes, Norwegians and non-combatant Greenlanders, patrolled up and down the coast through the winter months with dog sledges to defend the Allied weather stations at Eskimonæs and elsewhere, and to search out and if possible destroy any stations established by the Germans (Bjerre 1980). In this extraordinary war two battles were fought. On 23 March 1943, Austrian-born Lieutenant Hermann Ritter, commanding a German weather station that had been operating on Sabine Island (Sabine Ø) since the previous autumn, led an attack on Eskimonæs. Ib Poulsen and the other occupants managed to escape. On 25 March, after waiting in vain for their return, the Germans burned down the weather station buildings and started back to Sabine Island. While they were preparing to put up for the night at Sandodden a solitary man approached with sledge and dogteam. It was Corporal Eli Knudsen, and, when he ignored Ritter's signal to halt, the Germans shot him dead, though Ritter had ordered them to fire only at his dogs. Later they captured Knudsen's two companions. One of these escaped; the other, Corporal Marius Jensen, managed to turn the tables on his captor, Lieutenant Ritter, took him prisoner, and marched him off to Scoresby Sound (Howarth 1957). The other battle was fought on Shannon Island, where the Germans operated a weather station from autumn 1943. Here they had dug themselves caves and tunnels in which to live in a massive snowdrift, so that their station was virtually invisible. Nonetheless, the Sledge Patrol found them, and on 22 August 1944 Captain Niels Jensen led a six-man attack on the snowdrift bunkers. Going ahead to reconnoitre, Jensen was suddenly confronted with a German officer, Lieutenant Gerhard Zacher, the weather station's military commander. Surprised by Jensen's peremptory command to lay down his arms, which was backed by a submachine gun he was pointing directly at Zacher, the German obeyed, dropping his gun in the snow. But his reaction to being asked to put his hands up and follow Jensen was to pull a revolver out of his pocket and fire at Jensen from a range of 3 m (10 ft). He missed; Jensen meanwhile had shot him dead. The Danish patrol, outnumbered by the Germans, managed to withdraw under fire without any casualties, thanks to a fog bank which unexpectedly enveloped the area (Olsen 1965). The demoralized Germans were subsequently evacuated by a German plane. The last German weather station in east Greenland was captured intact with its personnel just after it had been landed on North Little Koldewey Island, across the strait from Danmarkshavn, on 4 October 1944. It was taken by an American force that had been landed by the big new icebreaker, *Eastwind*.

The weather stations were essential to the Allied supply routes that were developed from 1941 onwards (Carlson 1962). The Americans were permitted by the Danes in Greenland, led by Eske Brun, to build bases there. Their airfields at Narsarsuaq (Ancker 1993) and Søndre Strømfjord (now Kangerlussuaq) (Map 30) were used as staging posts from April 1942 onwards to fly hundreds of warplanes over the Inland Ice to beleaguered Britain (Balchen *et al*. 1945). After the Soviet Union was attacked by Hitler in June 1941, convoys carrying every kind of military and other supplies from Britain and the United States sailed through Arctic waters north of Norway and even Bear Island to Murmansk and Arkhangel'sk. The Barents Sea became the scene of intense fighting and heavy casualties, especially among Allied merchant shipping, as German aircraft and heavy naval units like the *Tirpitz*, based in north Norway, wreaked havoc among them. Shipwrecked crews were stranded on the frozen shores of Spitsbergen and Novaya Zemlya (Schofield 1964, Blond 1965, Smith 1975). Another Arctic supply route, based on the construction of the Alaska Highway and a chain of airfields, using fuel piped from Norman Wells on the Mackenzie (the Canol Project; Barry 1992), enabled some seven thousand warplanes to be flown to Russia by Russian pilots from Ladd Field, Fairbanks, Alaska, via Nome (Map 31) to Siberia. When, from 1947 onwards, the war between the Allies and Hitler's Germany was replaced by the confrontation between the former wartime Allies and the Soviet Union, the Arctic became the scene of intense and wide-ranging military preparations. The Kola Peninsula became a huge fortress and missile base, and a line of radar warning stations was stretched across Greenland and the north American Arctic (Fletcher 1990), supported by Thule Air Base (now Pituffik) in Avanersuaq, north-west Greenland, constructed in 1951–2 (Vaughan 1991: 132–50).

The war of the weather stations inevitably extended to Russia's Northern Sea Route. The western terminus of this seaway, Murmansk, was fiercely attacked and bombarded by the Germans. In the pocket of a dead German soldier's uniform was found a ticket for a celebration banquet in the *Arktika* restaurant once the city had surrendered (Metel'skiy 1978: 19). It never did surrender. The route's numerous Polar stations were supplied by I.D. Papanin, now Glavsevmorput's chief, with extra provisions and machine guns and grenades, and a special detachment of the Soviet Northern Fleet was formed to escort convoys along the route. But there was no stopping a trickle of U-boats penetrating north of Novaya Zemlya into the Kara Sea to lay mines, prey on whatever shipping they could find, and come to the surface to shell the Polar stations. Fortunately for the Russians the season when this was possible was short, but in each of the three late summers of 1942–4 German U-boats scored some successes. In July–August 1942 they attacked the Polar stations at Malyye Karmakuly in south-west Novaya Zemlya (Map 24), mys Zhelaniya, at the northern tip of Novaya Zemlya, and on ostrov Uyedineniya (Lonely Island) (Map 26). In 1942 and 1943, in spite of some losses, the Russians claimed that ninety-two ships got through the western section of the Northern Sea Route unscathed. In 1944 one of the half-dozen U-boats active in the Kara Sea torpedoed the transport ship *Marina Raskova* with 354 men, women and children on board, of whom 256 were saved by search planes, but 61 other ships, carrying 251,000 tons of freight, were said to have got through safely.

While German U-boats tried and failed to interrupt the flow of traffic on the Northern Sea Route, her surface ships had even less success. In summer 1942 the heavy cruiser *Admiral Scheer* passed the northern tip of Novaya Zemlya and steamed slowly east across the northern Kara Sea in intermittent fog toward Vil'kitskiy Strait. On 23 August her reconnaissance plane spotted a convoy of twenty-one merchant ships escorted by the icebreakers *Lenin* and *Krasin* anchored near the western approaches to the strait, awaiting suitable ice conditions to pass eastwards through it. The *Scheer* raced toward them but was hampered by fog and ice and even more by the loss of her plane, which deprived her of knowledge of ice conditions, making her situation extremely dangerous. On 25 August she sighted a Russian ship which she might hope to intercept in order to obtain ice intelligence. It was the *Aleksandr Sibiryakov*, which had made the historic west to east transit through the Northern Sea Route in 1932 and was now bound for Severnaya Zemlya with supplies and personnel for the Polar stations on ostrov Domashniy and at Arctic Cape (mys Arkticheskiy; Map 25). On ostrov Domashniy, veteran polyarnik Boris Aliksandrovich Kremer and two colleagues were waiting to be relieved after a year at the station. Ordered by the *Scheer* to switch off her wireless, the *Sibiryakov*'s radio operator instead tried to warn the Polar station on Dikson Island of the presence of an enemy warship. Ordered to stop his ship, First Lieutenant Anatoliy Alekseyevich Karachava's reply was to open fire on the *Scheer*, which hopelessly outgunned the *Sibiryakov*. Although Russian accounts refer to Fascist pirates destroying peaceful ships, in fact the Russian icebreakers in Arctic seas had been formed into a special squadron of the White Sea Fleet, their officers automatically becoming naval officers. One salvo from the *Scheer* was enough to engulf the *Sibiryakov* in flames. The crew hastily destroyed ice charts and other secret documents and scuttled the ship. Most of the hundred or so people on board perished. Eighteen were taken prisoner. One managed to reach an uninhabited islet on a piece of wreckage and survived there for thirty-four days before being rescued by a Soviet pilot. On 27 August the *Scheer* made an attempt to destroy the Dikson Polar station, but was foiled. Hydrologist Mikhail Somov, who became a famous post-war polyarnik, and a colleague had withdrawn to the tundra carrying the station's secret codes and documents in sacks; the shipping in the port of Dikson had taken refuge in the shallows of the Yenisey; and the guns of the shore batteries and of two icebreakers opened fire on the *Scheer* so effectively that she withdrew behind a smokescreen. There were no more attacks by surface ships on the Northern Sea Route (Armstrong 1958: 98–101, Barr 1975b, Kanevskiy 1976: 46–79, Gordiyenko 1980; and see references in Horensma 1991: 168).

RESEARCH

The era of geographical exploration in the Arctic, mostly by individuals, has been succeeded in the twentieth century by the era of scientific research, mostly by teams. Signs of this development were apparent in the nineteenth century on Spitsbergen, which was the scene of a series of Swedish scientific expeditions (Thorén 1978), and in the Barents Sea, where the Dutch expedition ship *Willem Barents* made scientific cruises in and after 1878 (Mörzer Bruyns 1985, 1986). But the Danes were the pioneers who persisted. Before they had even completed the exploration of Greenland's coast, they founded the Commission for Geographical and Geological Research in Greenland, later the Commission for Scientific Research in Greenland, which began its work in 1878. The first Arctic scientific periodical, the prestigious *Meddelelser om Grønland*, began publication in 1876. These institutions survive to this day after more than a century of excellent work. In 1906–7 an Arctic station for the study of Greenland's flora and fauna was established at Godhavn (now Qeqertarsuaq). In the 1930s, expeditions to the Arctic, like those of the University of Oxford to Spitsbergen (Binney 1925) and the University of Michigan to west Greenland (Hobbs 1930, Carlson 1942) were much more involved in scientific research than exploration. The Second International Polar Year of 1932–3, which concentrated on geophysics and meteorology, encouraged this tendency. Research, which at first was promoted by universities, was soon being furthered by Polar institutes which were either linked to universities, like the Scott Polar Research Institute in Cambridge (1920) and the Arctic Institute of North America at Montreal, then Calgary, Alberta, Canada (1945), or established by governments as independent institutes, like St Petersburg's Arctic and Antarctic Research Institute and the Polar institutes in Oslo, Copenhagen, Rome, Paris and elsewhere.

Not all research in the Arctic is as spectacular as the Russian drifting ice stations in the Arctic Ocean, or the recovery by the international Greenland Ice Core Project of the last two hundred thousand years of the climatic and environmental history of the Earth from ice cores drilled out of the Inland Ice of Greenland. The latter culminated in July 1992, when solid rock was struck 3,029 m (9,938 ft) below the surface (Olsen 1993, Nielsen 1993). A glance at journals like *Polar Record* and *Arctic*, published respectively by the Scott Polar Research Institute and the Arctic Institute of North America, and at the annual reports of these and other institutes, reveals a very wide range of current Arctic research projects. At Cambridge, these include studies of glaciers and sea ice, of shamanism and reindeer herders in the Siberian north, and of the Northern Sea Route. At Calgary in 1992, the Arctic Institute of North America was supporting archaeological research on Ellesmere Island, while at its Devon Island research station long-term studies of the changes in the flora and fauna in the twelve thousand years since the land there became ice-free were in progress. In 1992 the newsletter of the newly established (1990) Danish Polar Centre reported on research in progress in Greenland. It mentions studies of Arctic insects as indicators of climatic change, excavation of a Saqqaq culture site near Sisimiut (Map 18), research on the feeding biologies of the wolf and the musk ox in Greenland and on the distribution of lichens, investigation of the relationship between the Greenland Inland Ice and changes in the sea level, of regional variations in Greenlandic fur boots, and of the effect of the introduction of cash into the east Greenlandic susbsistence economy. Direct government support for Arctic research occurred on a large scale after the Second World War when the United States Office of Naval Research organized an elaborate programme of research in the Arctic, both at drifting ice stations in the Arctic Ocean (Rodahl 1955, Sater 1968, Johnson 1983) and at the Naval Arctic Research Laboratory at Point Barrow, Alaska (Reed and Ronhovde 1971), not without military considerations in mind. Parallel Russian programmes were discussed in Chapter 9.

PROTECTING THE ENVIRONMENT

Increasingly, in the last decade especially, scientific research in the Arctic has been concerned with conservation. Nature reserves and national parks have been established and their ecosystems studied, and conservation programmes have brought the two largest Arctic animals, the Polar bear (Amstrupp and Wiig 1991) and the musk ox (Klein *et al.* 1984) back from the verge of extinction by European hunters. In 1974–5 the musk ox was successfully reintroduced into the Taymyr Peninsula (*Soviet Weekly*, 9.1.1982) when thirty animals were taken there from Canada and Alaska. Much research has gone into assessing the threats posed to the environment by atmospheric and marine pollution, oil and gas exploration, and the like. Atmospheric pollution in the Arctic (Sturges 1991) is most apparent in the smog or so-called Arctic Haze which occurs during the late winter and early spring. The pollutants that form it include sulphur dioxide and chlorinated hydrocarbons from industrial complexes far to the south. Barrow, Alaska, has been found to have springtime aerosol concentrations as high as those in many cities in the rest of the United States. Marine pollution was evidenced by a 1988 study that found that the level of toxic chemicals (PCBs) was much higher in the milk of women from the Canadian eastern Arctic than in that of women living farther south, no doubt because of the sea mammals in the Inuit diet (Riewe 1992). Fears have been expressed about nuclear pollution in the Barents Sea from the dumping of nuclear waste and of nuclear reactors from ships during the Soviet period, if not subsequently (*New Scientist*, 2 and 30 January, 13 February and 4 September 1993). Oil and gas exploitation has already devastated tundra at Prudhoe Bay in Alaska, and much larger areas in Yamal and elsewhere in Russia.

Problems associated with global warming are also receiving increasing attention, including its effects on the permafrost, known to be shrinking in Siberia, and on the sea ice of the Arctic Ocean. Measures have been taken by all Arctic countries to protect the environment against tourists, at whose behest aircraft and motorized sledges are said to zoom about, frightening wildlife (Hall 1987: 219). Norway, for example, has published a booklet of environmental regulations for the Spitsbergen Archipelago and Jan Mayen which prohibit the removal of artefacts from ancient campsites or burials, insist on the removal of garbage, prohibit the use of poison, leg-hold traps and snares, prohibit the firing of shots and the sounding of ships' sirens within 1 km (½ mile) of seabird breeding colonies, and impose severe restrictions on the use of vehicles. Special rules apply to the outlying districts and islands of the archipelago, all of which have been designated nature reserves or national parks (Vaughan 1992: 349–53).

CITIES

The city, which the Russians introduced into the Arctic in the twentieth century, is by definition detrimental to the environment. Compared to Murmansk and Noril'sk, Thule Air Base with its 10,000 inhabitants in the 1950s, and Fairbanks, with 23,000 inhabitants in the early 1980s, seem like villages. Fairbanks is actually south of the Arctic Circle. Even Tromsø in Norway, for long the largest town within the Arctic Circle, which had fifty thousand inhabitants in 1980, cannot compare with the Russian giants. Murmansk, with 419,000 inhabitants in 1985, was only founded in 1916. Noril'sk is even younger, dating from 1935, but had 180,000 inhabitants fifty years later (Prokhorov 1988: *s.v.*). Murmansk is primarily a port and naval base. Noril'sk is a mining centre and industrial complex. Winter temperatures there drop to -50°C (-58°F) and blizzards are frequent. Noril'sk's street lamps are four times brighter than those in more southerly Russian cities. Its streets are kept clear of snow by an army of earth movers and dump trucks. The houses, built on stilts because of the permafrost, have triple-glazed windows and are heated for some 288 days in the year by means of local natural gas. Double salaries are the rule and fur clothing in winter is essential (*Soviet Weekly*, 7 February 1987).

SPORT

Sport in the Arctic usually takes the form of a test of endurance and is essentially a twentieth-century phenomenon, though the heyday of Arctic big-game hunting was the late nineteenth century. Although the walrus and narwhal were among favoured prey, the Polar bear was the supreme prize. The accolade for the most dedicated and successful Polar bear hunter should perhaps be accorded to the Englishman Frederick G. Jackson, whose three successive overwinterings in Franz Josef Land between 1894 and 1897 were funded by newspaper magnate Alfred Harmsworth, later Lord Northcliffe, founder of Britain's first mass circulation newspapers, the *Daily Mail* and *Daily Mirror*. While exploring the archipelago's coast, Jackson and his friends shot no fewer than seventy-three

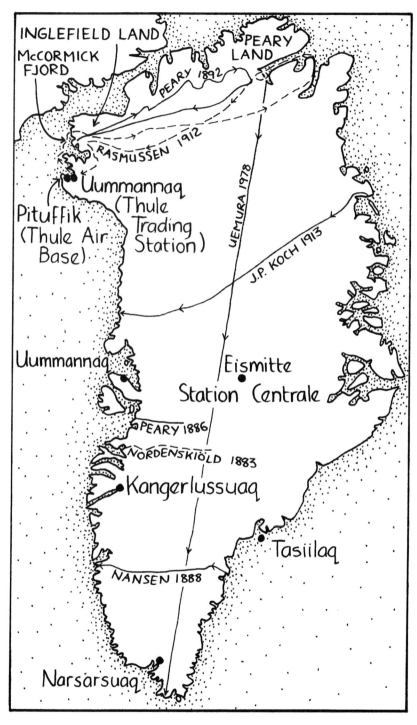

INGLEFIELD LAND

PEARY LAND

McCORMICK FJORD

PEARY 1892

RASMUSSEN 1912

Uummannaq (Thule Trading Station)

Pituffik (Thule Air Base)

UEMURA 1978

J.P. KOCH 1913

Uummannaq

Eismitte
Station Centrale

PEARY 1886

NORDENSKIÖLD 1883

Kangerlussuaq

Tasiilaq

NANSEN 1888

Narsarsuaq

Map 30. Greenland.

bears; he even offered a reward of two shillings and sixpence to any member of his party reporting a bear seen which he was able to shoot (Jackson 1899: 84, 328–62). Dog-sledge racing is another popular Arctic sport, but the most famous race, the Iditarod Trail, in Alaska, dates only from 1925. The route, rather over 1,500 km (1,000 miles) in length, varies from year to year but always starts at Anchorage and ends at Nome (Map 31). The generous prize money is distributed between the first twenty finishers. For four successive years, 1985–8, the race was won by a woman, and in 1986–8 the winner was the same woman, Susan Butcher (Alaska Almanac 1989: 88–9). Cycling has not yet become popular in the Arctic, though in autumn 1929 Gleb Leont'yevich Travin cycled the length of Russia's Arctic Ocean shore from Kola to Uelen (Metel'skiy 1978: 91). The history of jogging has not yet been put together, but, for the record, the Soviet Union's most northerly jogging club in the 1980s, at Murmansk, was called the 'Polar Bears' (*Soviet Weekly*, 7 May 1983). Mountain climbing has long been popular in the Arctic; in 1962 a group of Swiss enthusiasts climbed nearly fifty peaks in north-west Spitsbergen (Nünlist 1966).

Although they can now sometimes be achieved on tourist trips (in 1991 the Russian icebreaker *Sovetskiy Soyuz* took a hundred tourists to the North Pole) (Fisher 1992), reaching the North Pole, voyaging through the North-West Passage, and crossing Greenland's Inland Ice, are still challenging enough to attract sporting adventurers. In July 1992 the Danish Polar Centre newsletter listed fourteen 'Sporting Expeditions' in Greenland that year, most of which involved mountain climbing or long-distance ski-ing over the Inland Ice. In 1988 eight different expeditions traversed the Inland Ice to celebrate the hundredth anniversary of Nansen's crossing, two of which, both Norwegian, tried to be exact replicas of the original, using identical equipment, clothes and provisions. Since Nansen's crossing, which was one of the shortest, over fifty expeditions have crossed the Inland Ice, the most popular route being the shortest, namely from Ammassalik (Tasiilaq) to Søndre Strømfjord (Kangerlussuaq). The longest crossing of all was made in 1978 from the northern to the southern tip of the Inland Ice by the Japanese adventurer Naomi Uemura, alone, on skis with a dog sledge (Kjems 1981, Jensen 1988, Hagen 1990). Transits of the North-West Passage (Pullen and Swithinbank 1991) have mostly been made by Canadian government ships or icebreakers, but sporting yachtsmen have taken up the challenge. In 1977 Flemish yachtsman Willy de Roos took his 13 m (40 ft) ketch *Williwaw* through from east to west in a single navigation season (de Roos 1980). The American whaling historian and curator of ethnology at the Old Dartmouth Historical Society Whaling Museum, New Bedford, Massachusetts, John Bockstoce (1991), made the transit from west to east in his yacht *Belvedere* over several seasons between 1983 and 1988.

The Arctic's supreme sporting challenge is probably to reach the North Pole on the surface, over the sea ice, if possible without mechanical assistance of any kind, and return. In 1901 the great chemist D.I. Mendeleyev (1834–1907) described attempts to reach the North Pole as 'a noble sport' (Vodopiyanov, no date: 80). Table 6 lists some of the successful expeditions there up to the time of writing.

Date	Leader	Method of transport	Comment
21.04.1908	Frederick Cook + 2	Dog sledge	Not generally accepted
06.04.1909	Robert Peary + 5	Dog sledge	Has been disputed
19.04.1968	Ralph Plaisted + 3	Motorized sledge	Confirmed by aircraft (see Kuralt 1969: 188)
06.04.1969	Wally Herbert + 3	Dog sledge	Started from Point Barrow, and continued to the Spitsbergen Archipelago (Herbert 1969)
19.05.1971	Guido Monzino + 19	Dog sledge	Confirmed by air (Monzino 1971, 1987). Stopped at US base on ice island T3 on way back.
30.04.1978	Naomi Uemura	Dog sledge	Solo. Poor weather forced return by aircraft (Uemura 1978)
31.05.1979	Dmitriy Shparo + 6	Skis	Confirmed by aircraft. Route was via Soviet drifting station SP 24 (Snegirev 1985)
02.05.1986	Will Steger + 5	Dog sledge	Confirmed by aircraft (Steger and Schurke 1987)
11.05.1986	Jean-Louis Etienne	Skis	Solo. Confirmed by radio signals (Etienne 1986, Imbert 1986)
04.1987	Shinji Kazamas	200cc Yamaha motorcycle	Solo
04.1988	Dmitri Shparo + 12	Skis	From Novaya Zemlya to Ellesmere Island via North Pole. Confirmed by aircraft, Joint Soviet-Canadian expedition
13.05.1989	Robert Swan + 7	Skis	Members drawn from six different countries
04.05.1990	Erling Kagge + 2	Skis	Unsupported. One member withdrew, injured (Ousland 1991)

Table 6.   Some successful surface expeditions to the North Pole. From Gilberg 1989, with additions.

ELEVEN

The Search for Minerals

The exploitation of some of the Arctic's supposedly renewable resources has been discussed earlier in this book: the whale fisheries in Chapters 4 and 8; the trade in furs in Chapter 6. Non-renewable resources in the form of gold, metal and other ores, coal, oil and gas, and fossil ivory, have all been mined in significant amounts in the Arctic, and in much larger quantities in the sub-Arctic. However, the boundary between the two is not very precise, and no Arctic history could afford to omit the Klondike and Nome gold rushes, or the mining of cryolite in Greenland, even though both took place some way south of the Arctic Circle. (This chapter is based on Miles and Wright 1978.)

EARLY ORE SEEKERS

Martin Frobisher was not the only Arctic explorer to be tempted by the prospect of enhancing his own and his patron's profits by the discovery of precious metals or their ores. In 1605 and 1606, John Cunningham and James Hall, employed by King Christian IV of Denmark in the exploration of Greenland, found a vein of mica which was at first mistaken for silver ore (Gad 1970: 219–20). It was investigated again by an English expedition to Greenland led by James Hall until 22 July 1612, when he was killed by a Greenlander in revenge for kidnapping Greenlanders on earlier expeditions there with the Danes. William Baffin, the expedition's pilot, describes how on 24 July 1612 they 'found diuers places where the Danes had digged; it was a kind of shining stone, which, when our goldsmith, James Carlisle, had tried, it was found of no value' (Markham 1881: 25). Another explorer's search for precious metals which ended in tragedy was that of James Knight, governor of York Factory, who in 1719 embarked with two ships on a voyage for the Hudson's Bay Company to search for minerals, as well as to find the North-West Passage and expand trade. His two ships vanished into Hudson Bay and their fate – shipwreck and death on Marble Island – (Map 8) was only ascertained years later (Rich 1958: 445–6, Geiger and Beattie 1993).

HISTORIC GOLD RUSHES

In the second half of the nineteenth century, besides the settlers and trappers who were venturing into the northern wilderness of Alaska and north-western Canada, prospectors seeking gold made their way along the trails and were soon

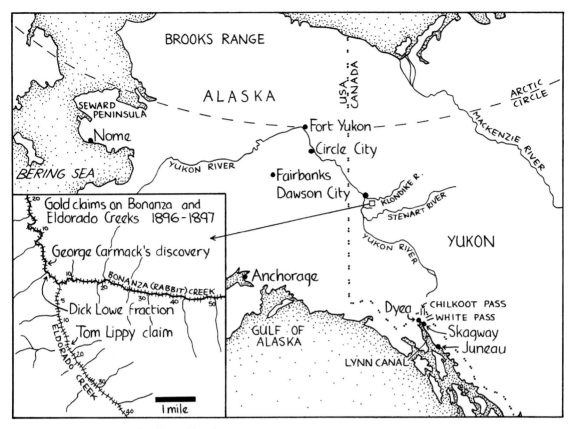

Map 31. The Klondike gold rush.

penetrating as far as the Arctic. Already in the 1860s a Hudson's Bay Company clerk at Fort Yukon, on the great bend of the Yukon River where it just touches the Arctic Circle, reported that the local missionary had seen 'so much gold' along a small river not far away 'that he could have gathered it with a spoon' (Berton 1972: 5; for what follows see Winslow 1952, Cunynghame 1953, Harris 1972, Berton 1972, Bronson 1977). The accuracy of this and other reports was soon confirmed by the prospectors themselves who, from the early 1870s, penetrated to the valley of the upper Yukon in Canada in ones and twos with shovels, pans and grubstakes of beans and bacon on their backs, either via the Mackenzie, or up the broad waterway of the Yukon all the way from its mouth, or from the south via one of the inlets along the coast of the Gulf of Alaska in Alaska's so-called Panhandle. Here, at Juneau, gold was discovered in 1880 and American prospectors were further encouraged. By 1886 dozens of them had crossed the Chilkoot and White Passes from Alaska into Canada, and many had struck lucky at the confluence of the Stewart River with the Yukon, where in a single year they were said to have panned out $100,000-worth of good quality placer gold. Ten years later, on 16 August 1896, an American, George Washington

Carmack (or one of his companions), picked up a sizeable gold nugget on the bank of a tributary of the Klondike River called Rabbit Creek. It was soon renamed Bonanza Creek, for his discovery had started the Klondike gold rush.

At first this could only be an isolated local phenomenon, for the upper Yukon Valley was cut off from the rest of the world by thousands of miles of wilderness. Within weeks, every prospector in the region converged on Bonanza Creek and neighbouring Eldorado Creek to stake his claim. Within six months almost the entire length of both creeks was staked with claims, each of which, according to the law, covered both sides of the creek up to a length of 1,000 ft (304 m) for a discovery claim, that is the first claim made in a certain area, and 500 ft each for adjoining claims. Every claim was legally registered and numbered by the local Canadian authorites, who quickly arrived on the scene, though nearly all the miners were Americans, and the township of Dawson City that now sprung up at on the confluence of the Klondike and the Yukon, less than 320 km (200 miles) south of the Arctic Circle, was virtually an American town. That autumn and winter the inhabitants of other Yukon mining settlements like Circle City migrated to it, and by April 1897 it boasted a population of 1,500. There was a shortage of everything at Dawson City that winter, except for gold. Prices soared, salt fetched its weight in gold, and gold dust was the only currency. The rest of the world only heard about the extraordinary happenings on the Klondike when the first two ships of the 1897 navigation season descended the Yukon from Dawson City and connected with two ocean-going steamers going to Seattle and San Francisco. Aboard them were over eighty prospectors who had staked their claims in Bonanza and Eldorado Creeks the previous autumn, and then spent an extremely cold and rough winter camping out and panning gold, or, when the creeks froze, excavating gravel and sand ready for panning in the spring. No one realized at the start that these two creeks contained more placer gold than any others in the world. On Eldorado, the average worth of claims One to Forty was estimated to be around $500,000. One prospector sold half of claim Two for $800, then bought it back later for $15,000. Claim sixteen had been staked and then abandoned. It was re-staked by Thomas Lippy of Seattle and brought him $1,530,000. In January 1897 a prospector called Dick Lowe was offered a tiny claim, only 80 ft (24 m) wide, by the Canadian government surveyor William Ogilvie who, when re-surveying Bonanza and Eldorado creeks, found some small parcels of land that had been staked out in excess of the permitted claims. After vainly trying to sell it for $900, Lowe decided to work it himself. The first shaft he sank yielded nothing, but the next produced $45,000 in one week, and the claim eventually earned him some $400,000. Ogilvie could have had it himself, but he was an honest civil servant doing his job and had no interest in gold.

There never was another group of successful gold-seekers to compare with the first eighty people who arrived in Seattle and San Francisco on the steamers *Portland* and *Excelsior*, bringing passengers from Dawson City, in July 1897. The ships' decks creaked with the weight of gold, carried in suitcases, grips, wooden boxes, tin cans and sewn-up blankets. Tom Lippy and his wife disembarked with a bulging suitcase, weighing over 200 lb (90 kg), full of gold. Less fortunate passengers still carried $10,000 or $15,000 worth of gold – a fortune in those days.

The arrival of these two ships triggered a world-wide stampede to the Klondike in 1897–8. 'Klondike or bust!' was on every lip 'and red-lettered lapel buttons with the phrase "Yes I'm going this spring" enjoyed a brisk sale' (Berton 1972: 108).

It seems that of the hundred thousand or so men and women who set out on the trails to the Klondike in 1897–8, less than half actually reached Dawson City, and many of these late-comers were too late even to find a claim worth staking out. They had to face indescribable difficulties. The most-used trail led over the dreaded Chilkoot Pass, and the Canadian authorites would only admit into Canada prospectors bringing with them a one-ton grubstake, sufficient to last them a year; for starvation threatened that winter in overcrowded Dawson City. The route to the Chilkoot began at the gold-rush township of Dyea, a few miles from Skagway. The pass in winter was a snow-covered icy slope with a gradient of one in three, up which the prospectors had to struggle in single file on steps cut in the ice for nearly three-quarters of a mile, with heavy packs on their backs. The ascent took several hours and few could carry more than around 35 kg (75 lb) at a time, so that each prospector had to toboggan back down the slope and struggle up it again with another load, until up to forty climbs had been made, before the entire one-ton grubstake was at the top. Soon primitive tramways and endless chains of buckets were rigged up by entrepreneurs, who probably made more money that way than they would have done panning gold. Once over the Chilkoot Pass, the prospectors had to build makeshift boats to navigate themselves across lakes and through rapids, 1,280 km (800 miles) down the Yukon to Dawson City.

Many of the original eighty gold-seekers lost their fortunes as quickly as they had gained them. Some drank themselves to death, few had problems spending their money. Dick Lowe drank too much and married a dance-hall girl who helped to ruin him. In 1905 he was selling water by the bucket in Fairbanks, Alaska. Tom Lippy sold his claim in 1903, made a trip round the world, became a respected and philanthropic citizen of Seattle, but was bankrupt when he died in 1931. For most prospectors the excitement of finding gold was more important than becoming rich. As poet Robert Service put it (quoted in Nelson 1958: 9):

> There's gold, and its haunting and haunting;
>   It's luring me on as of old;
> But it isn't the gold that I'm wanting
>   So much as just finding the gold.

The Klondike gold rush fizzled out almost as quickly as it had started. In the autumn of 1898 placer gold was found on the Snake River and its tributaries in the south of the Seward Peninsula, 240 km (150 miles) south of the Arctic Circle and 1,280 km (800 miles) west of Dawson City. By summer 1899 a new stampede for gold had begun and when, on 27 July 1899, news that gold had been found on the beach at the mouth of the Snake River reached Dawson City, two thousand men and women, representing about half the population, left within a month to help found a new shanty town called Nome on the shore of the Bering Sea. By the end of the summer of 1900 there were said to be 12,488 men and women camping out along the beach, and the population of Nome and its environs was thought to have totalled 18,000. It was said that two years of gold digging at Nome brought $8,000,000 to the United States treasury – more than the purchase price of Alaska. Thereafter, beach gold became harder to win, but prospectors wandering far and wide found gold in many other places in Alaska, and the country's gold production continued to increase.

ARCTIC GOLD PRODUCTION AND EXPLORATION

The Russians had sold all the gold in Alaska to the United States for a song, but they had plenty of their own. The infamous Kolyma fields, exploited by the forced labour of exiles from the late-nineteenth century onwards, were far south of the Arctic Circle (Conquest 1979). Since the Second World War gold has been found and exploited in Chukotka. The famous Komsomol'skiy placer, not far from Pevek, began producing gold in 1958, and from 1959 on gold was being won in the valley of the Malyy Anyuy River. In 1978 it was estimated that more than half the Soviet Union's gold came from these placers and from one at Polyarnyy. In Arctic Alaska, scattered placer mines and one lode mine along the southern foothills of the Brooks Range were expected to produce between $5,000,000 and $10,000,000 annually through the late 1980s (Miller 1984: 67–8). In east Greenland, in 1990, as part of a gold exploration programme begun in 1986, a hole bored in the Kangerlussuaq Fjord area (Map 33) found gold at a concentration of 2.6 g (0.09 oz) of gold per ton of material over a depth of 1.5 metres (4½ ft), as well as a layer giving 3.5 g (0.12 oz) per ton of platinum and 1.6 g (0.05 oz) per ton of gold. This hole was only 12 km (7½ miles) from the already discovered Skærgård gold field, which also has platinum. The estimated value of the gold and platinum found in this area has been put at $130 billion. It looks as though gold mining may start in earnest soon in east Greenland in what could become the world's richest gold mine (Sinding and Poole 1991).

COAL-MINING ON SPITSBERGEN

Jonas Poole, sent to Spitsbergen by the Muscovy Company in 1610 to look for whales and walruses, reported 'Sea-coales which burnt very well' in King's Bay (Kongsfjorden). Later, Spitsbergen coal was well known to the Dutch whalers, who would lay in a stock for the voyage home (Scoresby 1820a: 149). Nineteenth-century Swedish expeditions made detailed investigations of seams in various places; the Scottish yachtsman James Lamont (1876: 275–83, 292–3) coaled his ship in Advent Bay (Adventfjorden) and King's Bay in 1859; and in 1898 Scottish explorer W.S. Bruce took samples of Spitsbergen coal back to Scotland. In spite of the difficulties of coal mining in the Arctic, which include the need for an overwintering work force, the very short, or, in bad ice-years, non-existent navigation season, the permafrost, and the freezing of stock piles, two Norwegian companies began operations in Spitsbergen in 1899–1900, encouraged by the absence of coal mines in Norway. In the summer of 1899 Søren Zakariassen sailed his sloop out of Tromsø (Map 29) to Advent Bay in Ice Fjord (Isfjorden), loaded it with coal, sold the coal that autumn in Tromsø, and founded the Ice Fjord Coal Company in Oslo that winter. But when he returned to Advent Bay in the summer of 1900 to stake a claim he found that the Trondheim-Spitsbergen Coal Company had fenced in a large area and erected placards proclaiming its private ownership.

In the summer of 1901 an American visitor arrived in Spitsbergen, namely Michigan industrialist John M. Longyear, who disembarked from a tourist steamer in Bell Sound (Bellsund) with his wife and five children and, fascinated by the place, exclaimed 'It looks to me like a gold country'. He further noted that 'Spitsbergen now belongs to no country, and if coal or gold are found here some nation will hasten to colonise it' (Dole 1922a: 192). Longyear and his associates bought up the Trondheim-Spitsbergen Coal Company's claim in Advent Bay, registered the Arctic Coal Company of Boston with $100,000 capital, and even mined some coal in the summer of 1905 to sell to visiting steamers. Competitors were brushed aside. A Bergen Coal Company briefly appeared in Advent Bay in the summer of 1904. The Sheffield-based Spitsbergen Coal and Trading Company mined 500 tons of coal on the north shore of the mouth of Advent Bay

Plate 25. Coal mine at Longyear City, now Longyearbyen, Spitsbergen (Brown 1920: 232). This photograph, showing the stock of coal mined during the winter, the wire ropeway from the mine, and a ship loading at the jetty, was probably taken by the Scottish Polar explorer W.S. Bruce (Speak 1992), when the Arctic Coal Company of Boston, USA, was still working the mine (Speak pers. comm.).

in 1906. In the winter of 1907/8 the Arctic Coal Company left a wintering party of some fifty men in the tourist hotel. This had been put up around 1886 on the south shore of the head of Advent Bay, alongside a group of wooden buildings that soon became known as Longyear City (Longyearbyen). A solitary, forty-five–year-old Norwegian woman apparently helped with housework and cooking. According to the Americans, no alcohol and no personal firearms were allowed in Longyear City and all went well there, while a serious mutiny disrupted the Spitsbergen Coal and Trading Company's mine across the bay, where around sixty Scandinavian and ten British workers were allowed to carry firearms and enjoyed a winter supply of fourteen thousand bottles of beer. This British mining operation was abandoned in 1909. The Arctic Coal Company ran into all kinds of difficulties, especially from Norwegian claim-jumpers, encouraged by the Norwegian government. Difficulties were also created by the bureaucratic delaying tactics of the Norwegian government, by the bad ice conditions which seriously interfered with shipping in 1910, by strikes, and, in 1913, by the arrival of the Russians, likewise intent on mining coal. Indeed, the Arctic Coal Company never really got under way and made no profits. Instead of the hoped-for annual production of 100,000 tons, a mere 26,000 tons were sold in 1911 and only 37,678 tons in 1913. Longyear's last visit was in 1914. The work force was evacuated soon afterwards, and in 1916 the mine and its buildings were sold to the Store Norske Spitsbergen Kulcompagni, which had increased annual production to around 450,000 tonnes by the 1970s.

It was not long before the Russians, perhaps because of their history of hunting and trapping activities on Spitsbergen, became interested in the coal. They made their first serious move toward joining the international coal rush there in 1912, by sending V.A. Rusanov in the *Herkules*, commanded by Captain A.S. Kuchin, with the future 'director of the Arctic' Rudol'f L. Samoylovich and other geologists, on a tour of inspection along the Spitsbergen coast. They staked out claims in four different places. Then, while Samoylovich returned home on a cruise ship, Rusanov set out eastwards with ten companions on a voyage along the Northern Sea Route in the *Herkules*, never to be heard of again (Barr 1984). In 1913 J.M. Longyear was surprised to find a party of twenty Russians with tents, digging out coal on the shore of Ice Fjord, some 13 km (8 miles) from Longyear City. A large building, on which was flying the Russian flag, had been erected next to an Arctic Coal Company claim post, which had been broken and mutilated. The leader of the Russian party introduced himself as Rudol'f Samoylovich of the Grumant Mining Company of St Petersburg, and admitted he had inspected the American mine the year before as a tourist. Longyear informed Samoylovich that he was trespassing, but the United States embassy in St Petersburg failed to unearth the address of the Grumant Company, which in fact had only been set up that year. The name Grumant, which the Russians gave to their mine, was the old-time Pomors' name for Spitsbergen. The first 80 tons of coal were shipped from Grumant in 1913 in the *Mariya*. By 1932, a year after the Grumant enterprise had been taken over by the Soviet state combine Arktikugol, annual production was 20,000 tons. The head office of Arktikugol was in Moscow. It also had an office in Arkhangel'sk, but its supply base was in Murmansk. It was

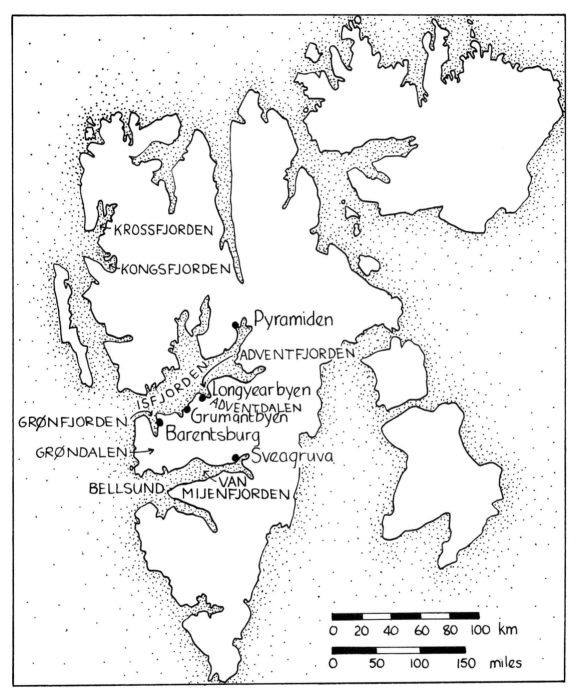

Map 32. Coal mining on Spitsbergen.

responsible for the running of the Soviet coal mines on Spitsbergen and in the Pechora region.

After the First World War, when coal prices were high, the Dutch, who had no coal of their own and whose whalers had been familiar with Spitsbergen for centuries, also turned their attention to Spitsbergen coal. A Rotterdam shipowner, Hendrik Hermann Dresselhuys, helped to set up the Nederlandsche Spitsbergen Compagnie, Nespico for short, in 1921, and himself became director. Beside the old Ice Fjord Coal Company claims, Nespico was able to buy the Green Harbour mine, on the east coast of Grønfjorden, which a Russian company was working, so that 25,000 tons of coal were shipped to the Netherlands in the summer of 1921. The mine and adjoining settlement were renamed Barentsburg after the Dutch explorer. In the winter of 1921/2, in place of the 100 or so Russians of the previous winter, Nespico staffed the mine with 230 persons – 11 officials, apparently Dutch, 147 German foremen and workers, 68 Norwegians, and one Dutch fitter. They had with them five wives and one child. In 1924–5 almost four hundred persons overwintered, including Dresselhuys and his family. But coal production stuck at 65,00 tons in 1924, capital diminished, and the mine soon ceased production. In 1927–8 three caretakers wintered: a German, a Norwegian and a Dutchman. Dresselhuys tried but failed to sell the mine to the Norwegians. Then, in 1931, engineer B.D. Alewijnse, on a tour of inspection at Barentsburg, came across a party of Russian geologists there, and offered them the lot for 3 million guilders. In the end Dresselhuys let it go to Arktikugol for 1¼ million guilders, and Alewijnse and a group of technicians helped the Russians to re-start mining in 1932–3. In 1935 Arktikugol's Spitsbergen mines, Grumant and Barentsburg, produced 400,000 tons of coal for the Soviet Union, and in 1936 the figure was over 1,000,000 tons.

Since the Second World War only Russians and Norwegians have mined coal on Spitsbergen. While Grumant has been 'temporarily' closed down since 1961, Barentsburg and another mine, Pyramid (Pyramiden), continued in operation. Pyramid, first claimed by a Swedish company in 1910, was acquired by the Grumant Company in 1927, and developed by Arktikugol from 1939. At the time of writing, the Russians have opened new mines on land leased from Norway in the Grøndal area. Longyearby was still the centre of Norwegian mining operations on Spitsbergen, but a large new mine had also been developed by the Store Norske Spitsbergen Kulkompagni at Sveagruva in Van Mijenfjord. This was originally a Swedish mine, bought by Store Norske in 1934. The small Kongsfjord coalfield was worked at Ny-Ålesund by a Norwegian company from 1917 until 1962, when a disastrous explosion caused the closure of the mine. In 1993, coal production in Spitsbergen was probably higher than it had ever been. Neither the Russians nor the Norwegians seemed likely, for political as well as economic reasons, to cease their own coal-mining operations there, or to encourage anyone else to begin (Brown 1920: 215–57, Dole 1922, Brown 1923: 258–67, Hoel 1966, 1967, Rylnikov 1983, Gnilorybov 1988).

CRYOLITE FROM GREENLAND

From time immemorial the Greenlanders were familiar with the mineral cryolite, also called ice-stone or Greenland spar, which melts in the flame of a blubber

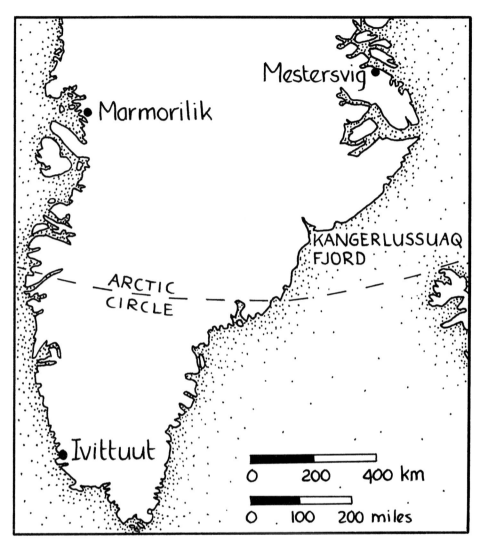

Map 33. Mining in Greenland.

lamp and was found only at Ivittuut (formerly Ivigtut) in south-east Greenland (Bøgvad 1950: 99–102). In 1794 it became known to the Danes and, from the mid-nineteenth century, the export of cryolite yielded substantial revenues, by way of a tax on production, for the Royal Greenland Trade Department. The mine soon took the form of a gigantic pit with perpendicular sides, which was eventually about 70 m (250 ft) deep. Managed at first by a group of small firms, one of which, in the first half of the twentieth century, was the Pennsylvania Salt Manufacturing Company of Philadelphia, the mine provided employment for up to three hundred persons. The cryolite was used as a source of sodium, in aluminium production, and in the glass and ceramics industries. By 1962 this unique ore body was mined out, though shipments from stockpiles to Copenhagen, where the ore was processed, continued for another twenty years. Thus the world's only important source of cryolite was exhausted in a little more than a hundred years.

MINES IN THE RUSSIAN ARCTIC

Naturally, since about two-thirds of the world's Arctic lands are within the boundaries of the Russian Federation, Arctic Russia's known mineral resources are greater than those of any other Arctic region. Only the merest sketch can be given here of some of the main centres of mineral production. The Kola Peninsula's (Kol'skiy poluostrov) metal-mining industry was developed by the Soviets before and after the Second World War, in the only part of the Russian Arctic which has a rail connection to a year-round, ice-free port, in the shape of Murmansk, as well as a rail connection with the industrialized south (Doiban *et al.* 1992). Mining cities with over ten thousand inhabitants have grown up in the Kola Peninsula near the most important mines. Olenegorsk has huge reserves of iron ore which have been exploited since 1955. At Monchegorsk, where local nickel and copper ores have been worked out, ore from Nikel', Zapolyarnyy and elsewhere is processed. Apatity and Kirovsk produce apatite and nepheline for Russian's phosphate and aluminium industries, and for export. However, in 1989 it was made known that these industrial activities had caused environmental damage on an unprecedented scale. Salt and heavy metal run-off has polluted lakes and rivers, acidification has damaged forests, and in some areas all vegetation has been destroyed.

At and around Vorkuta, in the Pechora basin, coal was first mined in 1934, and production was increased five-fold by the opening of new mines after the Second World War. By 1975 this huge coal field on the Arctic Circle was producing 242 million tons per annum. In that year a new mine operating at Vorga-Shor, near Vorkuta, was claimed to be Europe's largest coalmine. Here there is a rail connection with Moscow, but no ice-free port. The important mining centre of Noril'sk, on the southern fringe of Taymyr, has a rail link with Dudinka on the Yenisey River. Noril'sk and neighbouring Talnakh are now Siberia's most important producers of copper and nickel. As early as 1919 Lenin encouraged the Siberian Geological Committee to organize a Yenisey expedition. It was led in 1920 by Nikolay Nikolayevich Urvantsev, the later explorer of Severnaya Zemlya. Its tools were miners' picks, crowbars and shovels. It had ten pairs of boots for its fifteen men and no proper warm clothing. Rations were unadorned: each person was allowed, for a month, 12 kg (26 lb) of rye flour, 1.5 kg (3 lb) of groats, 200 g (7 oz) of butter and sugar, 400 g (14 oz) of tobacco and soap, and two boxes of matches. Besides this the fifteen men shared a pood (16.38 kg or about 36 lb) of rye rusks daily. Nevertheless, the ore the expedition sent back to Leningrad showed a high content of copper, nickel and platinum, and, within a few years, mines were opened. In the early 1930s, using forced labour, work began on the construction of Noril'sk. Production and communications improved quickly enough for the Noril'sk mines to play an important role in the Great Patriotic

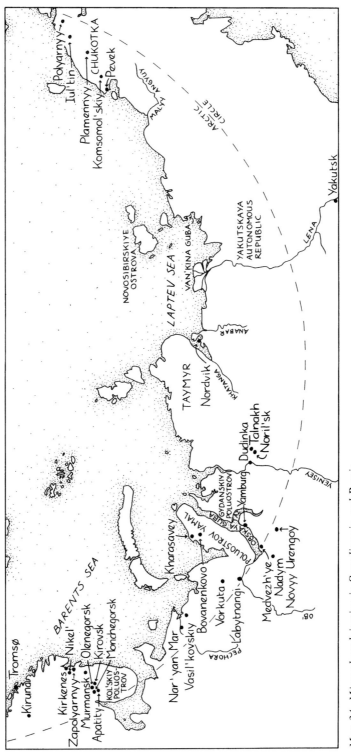

Map 34. Mineral exploitation in Scandinavia and Russia.

War; on 29 April 1942 a plane took off from Dudinka airfield with 1,110 kg (2,442 lb) of nickel for the Soviet Union's tank factories (Urvantsev 1969, Kutsev 1989: 20–1).

The potentially enormous mineral resources of the Russian Arctic Far East have so far scarcely been exploited, but some of the most valuable minerals are being worked here and there. Since 1975 tin concentrate has been recovered from the bottom of the Laptev Sea in Van'kina guba, on the north coast of Yakutia. Tin is also mined at Iul'tin and Pevek in northern Chukotka, while Iul'tin produces tungsten as well, and Plamennyy mercury.

METAL ORES IN SCANDINAVIA, GREENLAND AND CANADA

Outside the Russian Federation there are important Arctic iron-ore mines in Sweden at Kiruna and in Norway at Kirkenes (Map 34). In Greenland two lead-zinc mines have opened and closed after the exhaustion of their ore. At Mestersvig, in the east, the Blyklippen deposit was completely exhausted between 1956 and 1963 (Gilberg 1992). At Marmorilik, in the west, some mining took place from the 1860s, but it was not until 1973 that a modern mine went into production. This was the so-called Black Angel Mine, which ceased to operate in July 1990 (Sinding 1992). In the Canadian Arctic, besides a great deal of exploration and many discoveries, three important mining operations have been undertaken in the twentieth century. Between 1933 and 1940, and 1942 and 1960, the Eldorado Mine at Port Radium, near the Great Bear Lake just south of the Arctic Circle, was Canada's most northerly mine in production (Map 36). Besides silver, cobalt, copper and radium, it provided after 1942 pitch-blende for the Manhattan Project, the name given to the construction of the two atom bombs dropped on Hiroshima and Nagasaki on 6 and 9 August 1945. The Eldorado mine produced silver again between 1976 and 1981, and silver and copper were mined elsewhere in the region east of the Great Bear Lake in the 1960s and 1970s. The other two mining operations are in the Canadian Arctic Archipelago. In north-west Baffin Island, the Nanisivik lead-zinc-silver mine was opened in 1976. The Polaris lead-zinc mine on Little Cornwallis Island went into production in 1982. Its output of ore is shipped to smelters in Europe during the brief navigation season, which lasts from August to October (Nassichuk 1987).

OIL FROM ALASKA AND CANADA

Large deposits of onshore and offshore oil and gas have been discovered throughout the Arctic, and if society continues to be as dependent on oil and gas as it is now, these reserves are bound to be exploited sooner or later; sooner, if world prices rise, later if, as is the situation in the mid 1990s, oil and gas from outside the Arctic are available at a reasonable price. The first significant Arctic oilfields to be exploited extend along the coastal plain of Alaska's North Slope. Oil-seeps along the coast east of Barrow had been known since the nineteenth century, and in 1923 President Warren G. Harding designated some 95,830 sq km (37,000 square miles) of the North Slope as Naval Petroleum Reserve No. 4,

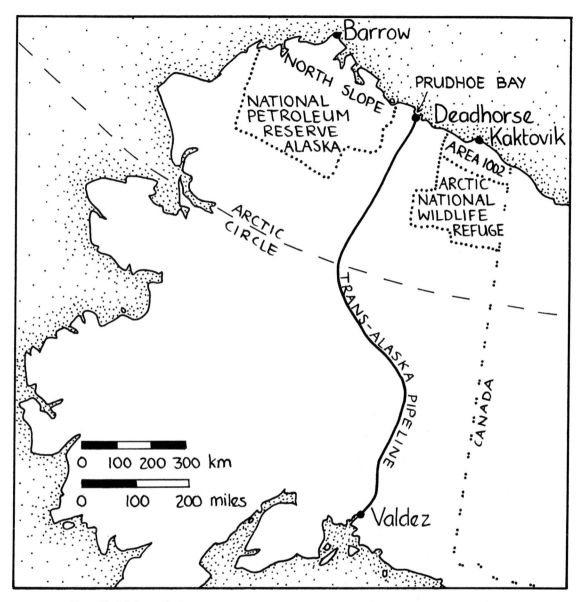

Map 35. Oil from Alaska.

closed to private exploitation. It was explored between 1944 and 1953 by the United States Navy and Geological Survey, which concluded that 'a major petroleum province existed'. Gas from this field was in use in government agency buildings in Barrow from 1949, but the local Eskimos had to wait until 1963 before it was supplied to their homes. The reserve was transferred from the Navy Department to the Department of the Interior in 1977 and renamed the United States National Petroleum Reserve Alaska. It has yet to be exploited (Alaska

Almanac 1989: 130. For what follows, see Coates 1991 and material published by the Alyeska Pipeline Service Coy.). Meanwhile, in 1968 oil had been discovered in significant quantity at Prudhoe Bay, but the planned Trans-Alaska Pipeline, to take it from the North Slope to Valdez on the south coast of Alaska, was held up by the state of Alaska's demands for taxes, by the objections of natives, whose land claims were affected, and by environmentalists. It took the world oil crisis of 1973, when Arab oil-producing countries withheld or reduced oil supplies to the West, quadrupling the price and demonstrating the vulnerability of the United States, to launch the construction of the pipeline. The workforce peaked in 1975 at 21,000 men and women, and the first oil flowed through the 1,300 km (800 miles) of 1.2 m (48 in) pipeline on 20 June 1977. Because the oil emerges at a temperature of 80° C (176° F) the pipeline has to run above ground over the tundra permafrost. Besides the pipeline, an access road had to be constructed along it and, on the shore of Prudhoe Bay, what amounted to a massive industrial complex on piles or gravel pads rose out of the flat marshy tundra, alongside dozens of oil wells and the oil town of Deadhorse. From 1977 onwards, over a million and a half barrels of crude oil passed every day through the pipeline and into tankers at Valdez. In March 1989 some two hundred thousand barrels were spilled into Prince William Sound from the tanker *Exxon Valdez*, after it struck a reef. About half the Prudhoe Bay oil was shipped to west-coast refineries and half to the east coast of the United States via the 121 km (76 mile) Trans-Isthmus Pipeline, specially built for the purpose. Prudhoe Bay became the largest single source of crude oil produced in the United States, but this immense field is now depleted, the yield is decreasing, and, by the year 2000, 90 per cent of its oil will have been used. The huge reserves of natural gas still there remain to be exploited in the future, if at all; they would probably have to be transported by pipeline via Canada (Dugger 1984, Garrett 1984).

Meanwhile, the coastal tundra around the tiny Inupiat settlement of Kaktovik looks like becoming a new Prudhoe Bay, even though it is within the Arctic National Wildlife Refuge. The problem is that, when the United States Congress passed the Alaska National Interests Land Conservation Act in 1980, which doubled the size of the refuge and designated most of it wilderness, it excluded from this designation, with an eye to future oil exploration, a 160 km (100 mile) long, 26 to 54 km (16 to 34 mile) wide stretch of coastal plain, including Kaktovik, called 'Area 1,002' after the number of the clause in the act mentioning it. In 1986 a United States Fish and Wildlife Service report to the Secretary of the Interior after five years' research in the refuge acknowledged that it formed a vital ecosystem for wildlife and a wilderness of international significance. But it recommended that 'Congress should authorize the Secretary to lease the entire 1,002 area for oil and gas exploration and development'. So far, this has not been done and disputes continue between oilmen and conservation interests, involving both state and federal governments and the native Inupiat Eskimos, organized into the Arctic Slope Regional Corporation and the Kaktovik Village Native Corporation. Meanwhile, in 1991, President George Bush's plan to start drilling in Area 1,002 was rejected by the United States Senate (*Guardian*, 8 November 1991), and in 1992–3 President Bill

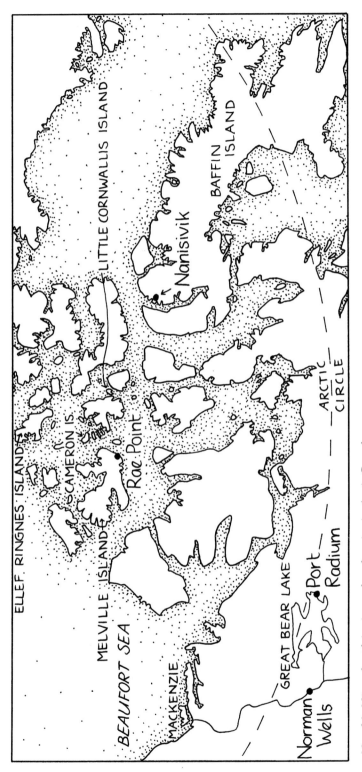

Map 36. Mineral exploitation and exploration in Arctic Canada.

ELLEF. RINGNES. ISLAND

LITTLE CORNWALLIS ISLAND

MELVILLE ISLAND

CAMERON IS.

Rae Point

Nanisivik

BAFFIN ISLAND

BEAUFORT SEA

ARCTIC CIRCLE

MACKENZIE

GREAT BEAR LAKE

Port Radium

Norman Wells

Clinton repeatedly spoke in favour of a 'development-free Arctic Refuge' (Baker 1993).

In the Canadian Arctic two important oil and gas fields have been discovered and explored, but exploited only in part: one in the Mackenzie Delta and the Beaufort Sea adjoining the delta, and the other in the Arctic Archipelago, between Melville and Ellef Ringnes Islands. In the Mackenzie Delta area, huge amounts of gas and oil had been revealed by the two hundred or so wells drilled up to 1986, when the first tanker-load of Beaufort Sea oil was delivered to Japan. Some seventy wells were drilled offshore from artificial islands, drill ships, or floating platforms, in and around the delta. In the 1970s two projects for transporting gas from the Arctic islands were cancelled, one the Arctic Pilot Project, in the form of liquified natural gas in icebreakers, the other the Polar Gas Pipeline Project, in a large-diameter overland pipeline. During the twenty-five years 1961–86, 126 wells were drilled on or among the Arctic islands between the north coast of Melville Island and the south coast of Ellef Ringnes Island, and two small shipments of oil from the Bent Horn Field on Cameron Island were shipped to Montreal. But all activity ceased in 1986, in reaction to falling world petroleum prices, and Panarctic Oils Ltd, the main company concerned, closed down its Rea Point field headquarters on Melville Island (Pimlott *et al.* 1976, Stirling and Calvert 1983, McLaren 1984, Nassichuk 1987).

GAS FROM SIBERIA

In the Russian Arctic this side of the Urals oil was already flowing by the mid-1970s from the wells at Vasil'kovskiy in the Bol'shezemel'skaya tundra, and being taken by pipeline to the port of Nar'yan-Mar on the Pechora River. During the 1980s at least four oil-drilling ships or platforms were built at Vyborg, near Leningrad, to prospect for oil and gas in the southern Barents Sea – for example in the shallow waters round Kolguyev Island. By 1990 three oil/gas fields had been found (Clarke 1991). But it is beyond the Urals, in north-western Siberia, that massive exploitation of natural gas, and major discoveries of oil reserves, have taken place. In the 1970s and 1980s the gas towns of Medvezh'ye, Nadym, and Novyy Urengoy were built on, or just south of, the Arctic Circle. This huge Urengoy gas field, probably the world's largest, became the centre, from 1978 on, of an extensive pipeline system which carried gas to many parts of the then Soviet Union (Map 34 above). One of the six pipelines radiating out from Novyy Urengoy, the East-West Pipeline from Urengoy to Paris, was constructed with Western European help in the face of rather half-hearted opposition by the Reagan administration of the United States. Work stated in 1981 and France began receiving gas through the pipeline at the beginning of 1984. No sooner was this pipeline completed than the Progress Pipeline was started, to take gas from the new town of Yamburg (1981) on a northerly extension of the Urengoy field, to the then Socialist countries of Eastern Europe. This very rapid expansion of west Siberian gas extraction, doubtless to be followed by oil, looks like moving further north in the Yamal and Gyda peninsulas, as well as in the Gulf of the River Ob', which they straddle. Already the Bovanenkovo gas field in Yamal is in the course of development, but, in the last few years, opposition from environmentalists and native peoples, as in Alaska, has begun to slow down economic development. By the 1980s ecologists were complaining that the River Ob' was emptying over 100,000 tons of spilled hydrocarbon waste into the Arctic Ocean every year, from leaky pipelines, oil droplets from flares burning off gas, and from drainage water from processing plants which carries away a huge collection of organic and inorganic chemicals: fenols, methanol, heavy metals, sulphides, chlorides. They also complained that ten years before, Yamal had been lavishly provided with sturgeon, sterlet, white salmon and other freshwater fish, but that this thriving fishery had been destroyed by pollution. Moreover, 1.3 million hectares (3.2 million acres) of good quality reindeer pasture in the Yamal area had been destroyed by the unregulated driving of tracked vehicles. Since reindeer pasture did not count as agricultural land, culprits only suffered a nominal fine of ten roubles per hectare, and it was easier for the gas/oil undertakings to pay this fine than to try to control traffic (Kutsev 1989: 175–7). In 1989, the Soviet authorities, after protests from the Nentsy and other reindeer herders in the area and from ecologists, as well as because of a shortage of capital, postponed a major pipeline project in Yamal for five to seven years. This consisted of the construction of up to ten parallel 1.5 m (5 ft) wide pipelines and a railway, to link Labytnangi on the Arctic Circle with the gasfields at Kharasavey and Bovanenkovo in the Yamal Peninsula (Map 34 above; Vitebsky 1990).

Although the search for oil and gas is continuing through much of Arctic eastern Siberia, little has been extracted so far. What may prove to be an important field, relatively easily exploited, is the so-called Yenisey-Khatanga trough which extends from the Gulf of the River Taz (Tazovskaya guba) in the west to the mouth of the Khatanga in the east; that is, right across southern Taymyr, forming a continuation eastwards of the Yamburg field on the eastern shore of the Gulf of the Taz. Gas is already being piped to Noril'sk from at least five wells between the Gulf of the Taz and the Yenisey, and research is under way on the possibility of extracting gas hydrate, that is frozen gas, in this region 250 km (150 miles) north of the Arctic Circle. At the other end of the trough, exploration has been undertaken in the Nordvik area and in the Anabar River Valley (Wilson 1989).

FOSSIL IVORY

Ivory known to have been dug out of the ground was widely distributed in the ancient world, both in China and in the Mediterranean area. Mammoth ivory reached the London market in 1611, and the eighteenth-century ivory-trading activities of Ivan Lyakhov, discoverer of the New Siberian Islands (Novosibirskiye ostrova; Map 15) were mentioned in Chapter 5. These activities, and those of subsequent dealers, can have made little impression on the huge quantity of fossil ivory still lying on, or embedded in, the ground. During three summer expeditions to the New Siberian Islands in 1882–4, Russian zoologist-explorer Aleksandr Aleksandrovich Bunge and his companions collected nearly 2,500 good quality mammoth tusks. By the end of the nineteenth century, mammoth ivory had become a cheap substitute for elephant ivory in Europe, and Hamburg was the main market. In 1908, the Yakutsk dealer Ya. F. Sannikov put the average annual output of mammoth ivory from north-east Siberia at 71,000 lb (32,000 kg) or about 450–500 tusks (Pfizenmayer 1939: 184–5). Mammoth ivory had from time immemorial been an object of barter among the native peoples of Siberia, and it was widely employed for domestic utensils and for carving. The Chukchi used it for making coats of mail (Plate 27) and the Yakuts made fine fretwork combs and caskets, knife handles and all kinds of ornamental carving with it. The New Siberian Islands (Map 15) have always been a main source of supply of mammoth ivory, and British mammoth-hunter Bassett Digby (1926: 153) describes how the tusks were found there in the early twentieth century:

> Most of the ivory hunters go up to the New Siberians in early spring, crossing the frozen sea with dog-sleds running light. The best of the harvest is in the week when the last of the snow melts, generally about the middle or end of May. Then, with the thaw, every little hillside brook is a foaming torrent, and, right and left, banks are being worn down or caving in. There are landslips, too, along the cliffs, to be searched for and examined. A gale at the time of the break-up of the ice is a godsend on certain parts of the coasts, for, driven by the wind, the massive floes, many feet thick, ride in on the top of the tide and thud like titanic battering-rams against the cliffs, bringing down fall after fall of frozen soil in which tusks are embedded.
>
> In the mudbanks west of Bolshoi Lyakhov, and on the sands of the low ground between Kotelnoi and Fadievskoi, tusks are to be found at low tide, sometimes quite a little grove of them sticking up in the sand, their drooping curve making them look, as the Yakuts graphically put it, like great candles that have been placed too near the fire.

In 1982 the Soviet government announced plans for the annual export of about ten tons of mammoth ivory, worth up to two million dollars (*Nieuwsblad van het Noorden*, 26 July 1982).

TWELVE

Who Owns the Arctic?

Most of this book so far has been devoted to the Arctic ventures and adventures of people of European extraction. Little or no mention has been made of the indigenous inhabitants of the Arctic described in Chapter 1, over whom explorers, traders and others have ridden roughshod. The rightful owners of the Arctic were allowed no rights. Their hunting territories were annexed by national states wholly alien to them, whose subjects they were forced to become. Their cultures were destroyed, their populations decimated or deported, the animals they depended on for subsistence slaughtered, even their health undermined. Their history has been a history of tragedies and disasters brought about by white people. As long ago as 1893 Fridtjof Nansen, in his book *Eskimo Life*, had foreseen the extinction of the Greenlanders: 'a declining race, which is perhaps beyond all help, since it is already stung with the venom of our civilization' (Nansen 1893b: viii). Recognizing that the impact on the Greenlanders of 'European activity in Greenland has been degeneration and decadence in every respect' (p. 338), he pleaded for the immediate withdrawal of all Danes from the country, or else 'there would be no natives left behind to inhabit the land' (pp. 338, 350). Fortunately, Nansen has been proved wrong. Not only are the Greenlanders still there after a hundred years, as well as the Danes, but so are the other Arctic peoples, and the future is brighter now for many of them than it ever has been during the last hundred years. This chapter may start with a funeral dirge, but it closes with a hint of optimism.

PAWNS OF INTERNATIONAL POLITICS

Naturally, the Arctic, just like Africa, was carved up among the powers without any reference whatever to its inhabitants. By 1900, it was generally agreed among the nations that a state could annexe any area it wished after discovering it, occupying it, and notifying other countries. In early times an explorer claimed the lands he discovered for his king or country by leaving an announcement of the claim in a cairn or on a noticeboard. In 1614 Robert Fotherby claimed Spitsbergen for King James I by setting up crosses in two places with the royal coat of arms displayed on a sixpenny piece nailed to them. He also took a piece of turf 'as a signe of lawful possession of this country'. When the Dutch arrived at one of these places they pulled down the cross, removed the sixpence, and fixed the coat of arms of their stadholder Prince Maurice of Orange-Nassau on a post

(Markham 1881: 85–6, 92, 98). In 1576 Martin Frobisher had ordered crew members who got ashore on Baffin Island to bring him something 'in token of Christian possession' on behalf of Queen Elizabeth. Flowers, grass and rocks were collected. He himself enticed an Eskimo kayaker near the ship with a hand bell but dropped the bell at the last moment, grabbed the man, and 'plucked him with main force, boate and al' out of the sea and on board. In the end three Eskimos were kidnapped and taken back to England as tokens of possession of the newly discovered land, but died shortly afterwards (Stefansson 1938a: 50–1). They were not the first Eskimos to be kidnapped by Europeans, for a woman and child had been taken in 1566, probably in west Greenland, though nothing is known of the circumstances. They were figured in a German woodcut of 1567 made in Augsburg after a lost Dutch original (Gulløv 1988: 129–46). Frobisher's acts of violence set the tone for future relations between Europeans and Eskimos, and by 1660 some thirty had been kidnapped (Gad 1970: 238). In 1605 a Danish expedition commanded by the Scot, John Cunningham, a captain in the Danish Royal Navy, was sent to west Greenland. On landing there, he knelt and thanked God for his safe arrival, then took possession on behalf of King Christian IV of Denmark 'takeinge with him both earth and stones' (Gosch 1897a: 10) as proof of the same. On both this and the 1606 expedition Greenlanders were seized by force and taken back to Denmark. One of the six captured in 1605 was shot on board ship while trying to escape; one of the five captured in 1606 jumped overboard (Gosch 1897a, Bertelsen 1945: 9–17, Gad 1970: 219–20, Møller 1985). None survived more than a few years, nor did the man and three women abducted in 1654, who were made famous by having their portraits painted in Bergen, Norway, while on their way to their doom in Denmark (Bertelsen 1945: 18–22).

West Greenland became and remained a Danish colony. In 1776 its Greenlandic inhabitants became subject to a Danish royal monopoly, in the shape of the Royal Greenland Trading Company, of all trading and navigation, as well as to a Danish royal prohibition of access to them of all unauthorized persons. East Greenland became a Danish colony in 1894, and the state monopoly was extended to include it. However, many Norwegians insisted that west Greenland was Norwegian, not Danish. It had been colonized first by Eirik the Red and other Norwegian Vikings at a time when no Eskimos were living there, and then, in 1721, by the Norwegian missionary Hans Egede when it was occupied by Eskimos. At that time Norway was united to the Danish crown. When Norway was parted from Denmark and transferred to Sweden in 1814 by the victorious allies, as a reward for Sweden's help against Napoleon (Denmark having supported the French), Greenland remained Danish. The Norwegians protested, but had to accept *de facto* Danish possession of west Greenland. However, in the second decade of the twentieth century their hunters and trappers became active along the otherwise uninhabited coast of east Greenland north of Tasiilaq (Ammassalik) (see Chapter 6 above). The Danish authorities responded by encouraging Danish activities in the disputed area and their efforts to bolster their sovereignty there led in 1924–5 to the deportation or relocation of eighty-seven Greenlandic 'volunteers' from Tasiilaq, with some west Greenlanders, to a new Danish colony in Scoresby Sound 'which would be a strong and permanent bulwark against the Norwegian annexational activities further northwards in east Greenland' (Mikkelsen 1934: 133; see also Skeie 1931, Berlin 1932, Stefansson 1943: 198–9). At The Hague, in 1933, the Greenland dispute was settled in Denmark's favour, not without a 'Greenlandic' voice, welcoming Danish sovereignty of Greenland, being heard at the International Court of Justice there. It was orchestrated by Knud Rasmussen, whose grandmother was Greenlandic (Bistrup 1936: 41–55; for this paragraph, see Smedal 1931, Preuss 1932, Ingstad 1937). Avanersuaq, or north-west Greenland (Map 4), which had been privately administered since 1910 by Knud Rasmussen, was formally annexed by Denmark in 1937 without any consultation with the local Inuhuit Eskimos. They were the last tiny group of all the world's Arctic peoples to be subjected to a national state. Their independence was further compromised when in 1950 they were instructed to send representatives to the new Provincial Council of Greenland in Nuuk (Vaughan 1991: 154). In 1953 Greenland, and the Greenlanders with it, became an integral part of the kingdom of Denmark.

The transference in 1924 of a group of east Greenlandic Eskimos from Tasiilaq to form the new settlement of Ittoqqortoormiit in Scoresby Sound, in order to bolster Danish sovereignty in east Greenland, was not by any means the first such move. Exactly the same thing had been done by the Russians, for similar reasons, in the 1870s. Then it had been the Nentsy who were the victims of power politics, and Novaya Zemlya the land in dispute. These two large Arctic islands had long

Plate 26. The Nenets Aleksandr Vylka and his family at Krestovaya guba, Novaya Zemlya in about 1920. This colony was founded in 1910, when a dwelling house, chapel, storehouse and bath-house were built (Greely 1929: 137 and illustration facing p. 138).

been regarded as within the Russian sphere of interest, but were increasingly visited by Norwegians. In 1871 it was claimed that eighty or ninety Norwegians were going to Novaya Zemlya to hunt walruses and other game, compared to only four Russians. These Norwegians were accused of decimating sea mammal populations, ruining the nests of eider ducks by taking the down, and destroying the huts and crosses erected by Russian hunters. In 1867 the Nenets Foma Vylka, with his wife Arina, their children and some companions, were selected by the tsarist government to found a colony on the south island of Novaya Zemlya. Other Nentsy were moved there in 1872 and 1878, and the settlement was thereafter effectively maintained by the Russian authorities (Armstrong 1965: 120, Pasetskiy 1980: 128–33, Barr 1985: 113, Horensma 1991: 11). In 1926, to protect its sovereignty over uninhabited Wrangel Island (ostrov Vrangelya), the Soviet government transferred some Eskimo families there from Chukotka. Apparently they got used to it but, ten years later, they recorded in a letter to *Pravda* that 'we were all sorry to leave the land of our fathers for an unknown island' (Vodopyanov, no date: 312–13).

In 1952–3 the Canadian government was responsible for what looked to some Inuit and others like a similar abuse of Arctic people in the interest of national sovereignty. Eleven Inuit families were moved from Inukjuak (Port Harrison) on the eastern shore of Hudson Bay to establish two quite new Inuit settlements – the furthest north in Canada – at the Canadian government stations of Grise Fjord on Ellesmere Island, and Resolute on Cornwallis Island. According to one version of the story these people were given the impression that they were being taken to an area of abundant game, that they would be settled together and not divided into different groups, and that they would be returned to Inukjuak within two years, if they so wished. In the event, there was so little game of the right kind that the deportees were forced to scavenge for food in the rubbish tips at the police posts. The promise of returning them to Inukjuak was not kept, in spite of their request to be returned, nor were visits to their former home made possible. And instead of being kept together, the eleven families were split into two separate groups which could not communicate with each other. Some of the people involved have insisted that they never volunteered to go but 'did not have the freedom to refuse being sent away' because they dared not, or could not, resist the all-powerful authority of the police (Nungak 1990: 37). The government's officially stated reason for this relocation or deportation was to improve the social and economic situation of the Inuit. So far it has not explained why eighty-year-old grandmother Nellie Amagoalik, disabled Anna Aqiatusuk, and some of the best Inukjuak soapstone carvers, were included among the deportees: there were no medical facilities, and there was no soapstone, at either Grise Fjord or Resolute. In the 1950s Canada was deeply concerned about her sovereignty in the Arctic, which had been formally declared by Captain J.E. Bernier during two cruises of the Dominion government steamer *Arctic* between 1906 and 1909 (Bernier 1910), and was trying to assert effective occupation there. A government official was quoted as saying in 1953 that Canada 'is anxious to have Canadians occupying as much of the north as possible and it appeared that in many cases the Eskimo were the only people capable of doing this' (Marcus 1991: 293). The

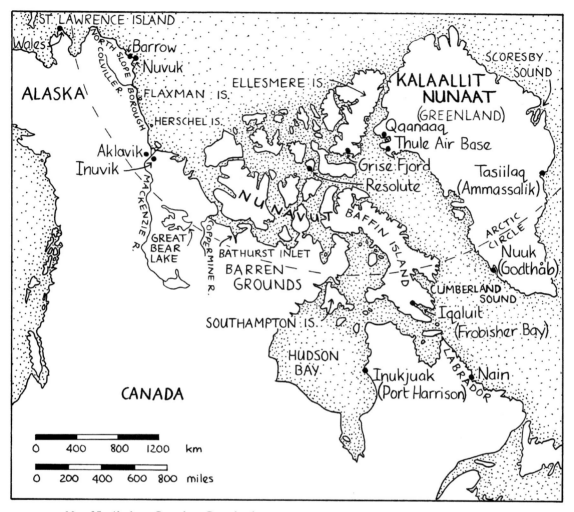

Map 37. Alaska – Canada – Greenland.

Canadian parliamentary committee on aboriginal affairs recommended in June 1990 that those relocated should receive monetary compensation for wrongs suffered, and that the government should formally acknowledge their role in the maintenance of Canadian sovereignty in the High Arctic. It remains to be seen what the end of this sorry affair will be (Nungak 1990, Grant 1991, Marcus 1991).

The sale of Alaska by Russia to the United States of America in 1867 entailed the transference of native Arctic peoples from the jurisdiction of one great power to another. Although in 1786 Empress Catherine II had claimed sovereignty over the entire north-western section of the American continent, the Russians never had penetrated, still less administered, the northern, Arctic, part of the country, inhabited by Inupiat Eskimos. These were neither consulted about, nor immediately affected by, the change of ownership. They were not conquered, nor did they sign any kind of treaty. They had no idea of what was going on. Their rights, if they had any, were ignored. In 1924 they were made citizens of the United States, whether they wished it or not (Ray 1975: 185–8, Arnold 1976: 24–6, 61–92).

TRIBUTE IN THE EURASIAN ARCTIC

For centuries, the subjection of the native Arctic peoples of Eurasia to Norwegians, Swedes and Russians was characterized by the levying of tributes in furs and other northern products. The first people on record to fall victim to this form of exploitation were the Sami. In about AD 890 , a Norwegian seafarer and landowner called Ottar, visiting King Alfred in England, gave the king detailed geographical information about Scandinavia which Alfred valued highly enough to take down and include in the preface to Orosius's world history, which he was translating into English at the time. Ottar, who 'lived furthest north of all Norwegians', reported that he owned a herd of six hundred domesticated reindeer and six decoy reindeer, which the Sami used to catch wild reindeer. Thus the Sami were acting as his reindeer herders. Their subjection to him, and no doubt to other Norwegians, is confirmed by his further report that the main source of Norwegians' income was tribute in pelts, down, walrus ivory and walrus-hide ships' cables, paid them by the Sami. 'Each one pays according to his rank; the chiefs have to pay 15 marten's skins, five reindeer skins, one bear's skin, 40 bushels of feathers, a bearskin or otterskin coat and two ship's cables each 60 ells long, one made of walrus hide the other of seal's' (Ross 1940, Jones 1984: 158–62; also Nansen 1911a: 168–80, Whitaker 1981). In Siberia the fur tribute or *yasak* was taken over by the Russians from their predecessors, the Tatars and Mongols, and it soon became an important source of wealth for the government of the tsars. It was extended throughout Siberia by means of the systematic and forcible taking of hostages from native groups not yet paying yasak. Semen or Semeyko Dezhnev, the Cossack explorer in the tsar's service, describes in a petition of 1622 addressed to his sovereign how this was done (Fisher 1981: 106):

> I, your slave, was left with twenty-four men from all these companions of mine, and twelve of these companions [following] a winter route on snowshoes and sleds failed to reach the Anandyr' because of frost, hunger, and want. Twelve men disappeared without a trace on the road. With twelve men altogether I, your slave, dragged myself to the Anandyr' River, and not wishing to die of starvation, went with these companions on an expedition to the non-tribute paying Kanauls and Khodyntsy. By God's mercy and your tsarist good fortune we took as hostages two men from the Anaul tribe, Kolupayko and Negovo; and from the Khodynskiy tribe Chokchoy; and two Chuvankiye men, Leonta and Podonets. While capturing Podonets he cut me, your slave Semeyko, on the chest with a knife. With these hostages in hand we collected your sovereign's tribute of 30 sables from their brothers and kinsmen.

The yasak remained a fur tribute until the second half of the eighteenth century, when it began to be commuted for cash and its character changed to a tax

(Armstrong 1965, Safronov 1980). Along with the tribute went trade, for any pelts surplus to the yasak were used to trade. Tribute collectors and traders went hand in hand, one person often performing both functions. These furs were, however, mainly from the sub-Arctic taiga rather than from the tundras of the true Arctic.

THE CHUKCHI RESIST

It was for the most part silently and surreptitiously that the Arctic peoples of Eurasia were persuaded to pay tribute and annexed with the land they occupied to Russia or Norway or Sweden. The Chukchi alone opposed this imperialism by force of arms. They were successful because they were more remote from Russian centres of power, and more numerous, than most other Siberian peoples. In 1701, after substantial losses, they repelled a force of twenty-four Russians with 110 Yukagir allies sent along the Chukotka coast eastwards from the Russian fort at Anadyr' to demand tribute in furs. On this occasion Chukchi men killed each other rather than be taken prisoner. From 1731 onwards, a major in the Siberian dragoon regiment stationed at Tobol'sk, Dmitriy Pavlutskiy, led a series of hard-fought campaigns against the Chukchi from his base at Anadyr', but without succeeding in levying tribute. In 1742 the imperial government ordered the total extirpation of the Chukchi and the Koryaks. The men were to be killed, the women and children shared among their Cossack conquerors. After Pavlutskiy was killed in battle in 1747 the Chukchi were said to have kept his head for a long time as a trophy. Russian sources claim that the Chukchi were warlike and aggressive. We have no written record of Chukchi attitudes to the Russians, but they are easily imagined. The Russians soon abandoned attempts to levy a tribute in furs by means of military conquest and turned instead to a more peaceful and subtle method of subjecting the Chukchi. In 1770 they dismantled their fort at Anadyr': between 1710 and 1764 it was reckoned to have cost them 1,381,000 roubles to maintain, while a mere 29,000 roubles worth of tribute had been collected by it. In 1788 the Russian authorities at Yakutsk took the first steps to organize trade with the Chukchi by holding a fair or market at the confluence of the Bol'shoy Anyuy River and the Angarka River. Later, this was transferred to Ostrovnoye on the Malyy Anyuy River, a right-bank tributary of the Kolyma, and became annual (Map 38). No objection was raised when the Chukchi had Russian citizenship imposed on them in 1789; perhaps they were not told about this (Nordenskiöld 1881b: 73–9; Antropova and Kuznetsova 1964: 803, Vdovin 1965: 102–52, Dikov 1974b: 90-1, 101–3; Müller 1986: 75–8, Forsyth 1992: 143–51).

TRADERS AMONG THE NENTSY

The disruption caused by tribute payment to the way of life of the Old World Arctic peoples was nothing compared to the devastating effect of trade, which in many cases led to the complete transformation, or even destruction, of their cultures and identities. The originally egalitarian social system of the Nentsy, based on groups or clans of reindeer-herding households, developed from the

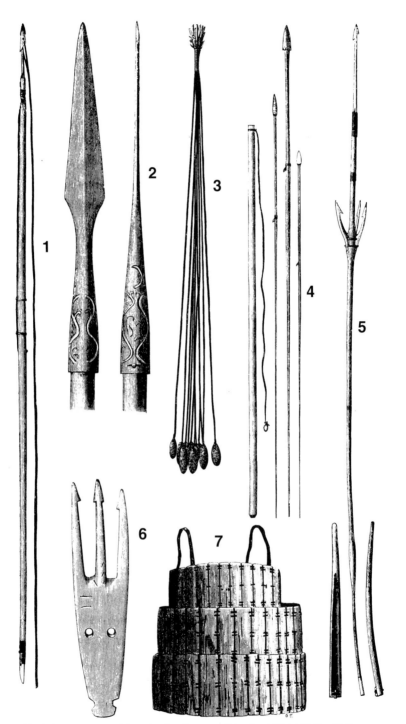

Plate 27. Chukchi weapons and hunting implements (Nordenskiöld 1881b: 105).
1. Harpoon (one-fifteenth natural size). 2. Spear found at a grave (one quarter natural size).
3. Bolas used for killing birds in flight (one-eighth). 4. Throwing spear with detachable
shaft(one-seventh). 5. Bird spear with throwing stick (one-twelfth). 6. Bone head of fish spear
or leister (one quarter). 7. Body armour consisting of coat of mail made from pieces of fossil
mammoth ivory lashed together with leather thongs (one-ninth).

eighteenth century onwards, under the impact of Russian traders backed by administrators, into a hierarchical society of rich and poor. In the second half of the nineteenth century commercial exploitation was stepped up by Russian fur-trading and fishing companies based in neighbouring cities like Arkhangel'sk and Tobol'sk, which enriched the wealthier Nentsy still further, and further exploited the poorer ones. Reindeer passed in large numbers to the wealthy few, while formerly communal pastures were privatized. Fishing waters, originally owned by a clan, then inherited by individual families, were now rented to Russian traders by heads of households. 'The catch was made by the Nentsy, who obtained all the necessary equipment and food, including bread, from the Russian trader. In return for this advance, the trader received half the catch and bought the other half at a reduced price' (Prokof'yeva 1965: 563). Inevitably, while some Nentsy households grew wealthy, many were impoverished.

FREE ENTERPRISE IN ALASKA

Among native peoples most exposed to the commercial activities of white people were the Inupiat of the northern Alaskan coast from Wales to Barrow (Map 37; Faynberg 1971: 36–68, Bockstoce 1986). Twenty years before the coastal hunting grounds of these Eskimos were formally purchased by America from Russia, American whalers had arrived there in force. In 1849 some six thousand American seamen were in offshore waters; in 1852 there were probably ten thousand and thereafter for the rest of the nineteenth century the figure rarely fell below a thousand in any one year. Between 1890 and 1905 around twenty whaleships, containing eight or nine hundred men, spent each winter somewhere along the ice-bound coast between Point Barrow (Nuvuk) and the Mackenzie Delta. These people naturally traded with the local Eskimos, as did the trading ships that accompanied them. Needing Eskimo labour to assist with whaling operations, the whalers paid for this in kind, with rifles, ammunition, flour, molasses, tobacco and rum, brandy or other liquor. Some Eskimos abandoned subsistence hunting for wage labour of this sort. In return for such products, other Eskimos used the rifles to kill large numbers of caribou to supply the whalemen with fresh meat. Thus the Eskimos helped the Americans to reduce the populations of the animals they mainly depended on for food: the bowhead, walrus and caribou, while their economy became locked in a wage-labour boom which saturated them with manufactured articles and American foodstuffs, and turned out to be short-lived. As whaling historian John Bockstoce has shown (1986: 346–7), by the mid-1870s American whalers had accounted for some 13,500 bowheads and over 100,000 walruses, and by about 1900 stocks were so depleted that the industry was on its last legs. The Inupiat way of life had been turned upside down. The introduction of reindeer herding among the Eskimos by the United States government from the 1890s onwards only served to underline this, but did help to stave off starvation (Andrews 1939, Jenness 1962, Faynberg 1971: 72–80). The inland or Nunamiut Eskimos, caught up in the same wage-labour and trading nexus, suffered similarly from the depletion of the stocks of their principal game animal, the caribou. Reduced in number, and forced to leave their hunting grounds inland and abandon their time-honoured collective caribou hunt, the Nunamiut drifted to Barrow and other coastal settlements, or were taken to Herschel Island and the Mackenzie Delta to work for a wage (Gubser 1965).

One article of trade that was especially damaging was alcohol (Ray 1975: 188–94, Hamer and Steinbring 1980). The United States authorities had prohibited the provision of liquor to Alaskan natives in 1873, but whalers and traders continued to supply it in quantity at least until about 1900. In the 1880s the whalers taught the Eskimos at Point Hope how to distil alcohol from a mixture of water, flour and molasses, and soon there were do-it-yourself 'whisky' distilleries in all the coastal villages (Jarvis 1899: 20–1). The annual cruises of United States revenue cutters from 1879 on helped to reduce the supply and home manufacture of alcohol, but Captain Healy of the *Corwin* was being over-optimistic when he reported in 1884 that 'the whisky traffic in northern Alaska has almost entirely ceased' (Healy 1889: 17). In the same report he describes finding in the bark *Northern Light* 'fifteen gallons of a vile spirituous compound' and ten gallons of American whisky, all of which the captain claimed was for his and his crew's use and not for trade (p. 11). Captain Healy also mentions that two or three 'whaling captains openly boasted of having thrown overboard one or two hundred' gallons of 'a vile compound called Honolulu rum' (p. 18) when they got wind of the *Corwin*'s presence. This alcohol did not merely make the Eskimos drunk and undermine their health, it impaired their subsistence hunt and caused many a bloody affray between them and the whalers and traders. A notorious example occurred in 1877 on the trading brig *William H. Allen*, captained by George Gilley, when some fifteen or twenty inebriated Eskimos from Wales who came on board were clubbed to death, shot, or thrown overboard to drown. At Herschel Island, on 30 November 1895, a drunken Eskimo called Pysha beat his wife and killed his baby daughter by beating her head against the wall of his house. Seized by a crowd of whalers, he was handcuffed to a post and was apparently going to be shot when the missionary, Archdeacon C.E. Whittaker, intervened. Instead, Pysha was given a hundred strokes with a dog whip, the archdeacon laying on the first dozen lashes. Deranged by this punishment, Pysha murdered eight Eskimos at Flaxman Island before being executed by the Eskimos at Barrow (Bockstoce 1986: 279; see also Finnie 1944: 40n).

While alcohol was wreaking havoc among the Eskimos, they also contracted diseases. Their population was decimated by influenza, measles and other epidemics brought by both whalers and traders. On St Lawrence Island (Map 1) in 1878–81, 1000 out of a population of 1500 Eskimos were thought to have died from starvation and smallpox. Alcohol was probably in part to blame (Hughes 1960: 12–13). On the Alaskan coast, villages were abandoned and areas depleted of inhabitants. The population of Point Barrow or Nuvuk was reckoned at 1000 in 1828, 309 in 1863, and a mere 100 in 1890 (Jenness 1962: 7).

What was left of Eskimo society in northern Alaska by the early 1900s had lost much of its egalitarian character. The formation of hierarchies of rich and poor accompanied the disintegration of subsistence hunting communities. The trapping for pelts that tended to take the place of sea mammal hunting after 1900 dispersed the Eskimos along winter trap lines and upset their traditional winter social life. They became even more dependent on 'shop' food. No wonder the Soviet scholar and anthropologist F.A. Faynberg (1971: 44–87) saw in all this nothing else but the ruin of native cultures at the hands of colonial exploitation, promoted by American capitalism. The Canadian anthropologist Diamond Jenness (1962) agreed with him, but most people at the time took it for granted that the Eskimos were being propelled from primeval ignorance, idleness and squalor towards industry, cleanliness and even civilization by the dynamic forces of the market economy.

THE RUINATION OF CANADIAN INUIT CULTURES

After their first encounters with white men, often in the shape of the British Royal Navy, in the mid-nineteenth century, the Inuit hunters of much of Arctic Canada were left very much to their own devices for a hundred years. Only in the Mackenzie Delta, and in Hudson Bay and Cumberland Sound, did the activities of whalers impinge on the Inuit in this period. In these areas the whalers' presence caused the transmission of venereal disease, tuberculosis, and acute infectious diseases to the Inuit populations and adversely affected their diet, resulting in dramatic population reductions, especially in the MacKenzie Delta (Keenleyside 1990). This whaling activity was absolutely devastating for the unfortunate inhabitants of Southampton Island (Shugliak). There, in the summer of 1902, the members of a small and distinctive Inuit group, the Sallirmiut, numbering fifty-eight persons, contracted 'a virulent gastric or enteric infection' which originated on board the Dundee whaler *Active*. It virtually wiped them out. Only one woman and four children survived. The woman was dead by 1907, and the children were adopted by a neighbouring Inuit group (Ross 1975: 114–17). The Sallirmiut disappeared from history before they had even been visited by an anthropologist.

During most of the first half of the twentieth century the principal impact of the Canadian government on many Inuit communities was the replacement of their customary law, which permitted blood feuds and the killing of insane, aggressive or otherwise unsociable people, by the white man's law, which regarded this as murder. At first, culprits were treated leniently. The Copper Eskimos who killed an American, H.V. Radford and his Canadian companion, George Street, near Bathurst Inlet in 1912 had perhaps acted under provocation, and were let off with a warning. A year later two French missionaries, Jean-Baptiste Rouvière and Guillaume Le Roux, were killed near the mouth of the Coppermine River after Le Roux, inexperienced in the Arctic and impatient with their slow progress, had apparently threatened and then assaulted their Inuit guides (Buliard 1953: 12–18 gives a very different story, but without supporting evidence or references). Acquitted of murder at a first trial in Edmonton, the two Inuit, who admitted the killing, and even disclosed that they had eaten the missionaries' livers afterwards, to make sure they were not troubled by their spirits, were tried again at Calgary and convicted of murdering Le Roux. The sentence was life imprisonment, but they were freed after a few years. More serious was the case of the two Copper

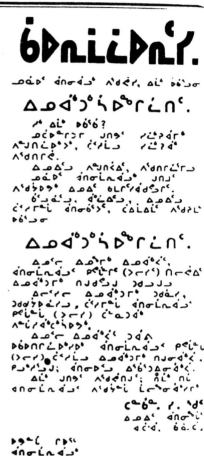

KNOW YE

The King of the Land commands you, saying:

'THOU SHALT DO NO MURDER"

Why does he speak thus?

Long ago our God made the world, and He owns the world.

The people also He made, and He owns them.

The King of the land is commanded by God to protect the people well.

The white people and Indians and Eskimos have him for their ruler. He is their ruler, therefore he commands, saying:

"THOU SHALT DO NO MURDER"

But if a man kills a man, the King sends his servants, the police, to take and kill the murderer.

But ye do not kill the murderer, nor cause him to be killed. This only the King's servants, the police, ought to do

But when a man commits murder, at once tell the King's servants, the police, and they will take and bind the murderer and the ruler will judge him.

Thus our God commands us so that you are to follow the King's command

DUNCAN C. SCOTT,
In Charge of Eskimo Affairs. Ottawa, Canada

GEORGE, R.I

Plate 28. A bilingual Canadian government poster of the 1920s (Fleming 1929: Plate 23). The Eskimo text is written in the syllabic characters invented in about 1840 by James Evans, a Methodist missionary, to enable Cree Indians to read the Bible. An Anglican missionary, Edmund J. Peck, adapted this alphabet for Inuit-Inupiaq (Inuktitut) in 1878. In 1960 the Canadian government hired a linguist, Raymond Gagné, to create a new orthography. He recommended dropping the syllabic system, and devised a new system using the Roman alphabet. But many Inuit wished to retain the syllabic alphabet and the Inuit Language Commission, appointed in 1974, worked out a dual system which remains in use to this day (Lewis 1905: 80–6, Finnie 1944: 46, Creery 1983: 11).

Eskimos tried for murder at Herschel Island in 1923, for they had between them killed four Inuit in a dispute over women, as well as a corporal of the Royal Canadian Mounted Police and an employee of the Hudson's Bay Company. It was argued that the lenient treatment so far meted out to Inuit murderers was ineffectual, and the two were hanged at Herschel Island in February 1924 (Godsell 1951: 225–95, Morrison 1986).

Such murder trials, symbols of Canadian sovereignty, were pin-pricks compared to the tragic developments that overwhelmed the Canadian Inuit in the second half of the twentieth century; some due to government action, others to government inaction; still others to the operation of market forces far away from the world of the Inuit. In the 1950s especially, the Canadian Inuit were compelled to abandon their nomadic camps and concentrate in settlements. Unlike the Alaskan Eskimos and the Greenlanders, the Canadian Inuit had no experience at all of living in villages. The government's plan was supervised by the Royal Canadian Mounted Police, who commented in 1951 on the 'destitution, filth and squalor' of the new settlements (Duffy 1988: 24). At Frobisher Bay, now Iqaluit, in the 1950s, a shanty town was built by Inuit immigrants using packing cases and discarded corrugated iron. The traditional snow house was exchanged for such structures, or for wood-frame houses covered with canvas. This concentration of the population was partly due to declining caribou numbers, which made the Inuit more dependent on imported food and clothing, only available from a shop, and partly to the collapse of the fur market, which made relief in the form of social benefits more and more essential (Duffy 1988). In the early 1950s Mackenzie Eskimo trappers could earn up to $1,000 per annum; but in the winter of 1960/1 only two of the twenty-nine trappers at Aklavik earned more than $400 (Faynberg 1971: 121). Naturally 'shop' food and social assistance could only be available in settlements. Hardest hit by declining caribou numbers were the inland Caribou Eskimo. Their subsistence depended on hunting migrating caribou in the Barren Grounds, remote from settlements, between the Great Bear Lake and Hudson Bay (Mowat 1951, Csonka 1991). The Barren Ground Inuit caribou kill is thought to have declined from a hundred thousand animals in 1948 to a mere fifteen thousand in 1957–8 (Faynberg 1971: 122). One near starving group of Caribou Eskimos was relocated in 1950 and again in 1957, and eventually had to be moved to the Hudson Bay coast (Mowat 1960). By the 1960s the Caribou Eskimo, resettled in white-dominated villages along the coast, were dependent on welfare and 'shop' food, lived in pre-fabricated government houses, had ceased to wear fur clothing, were no longer hunters and trappers, and had begun to drink. Their dogs dwindled in number, then disappeared, to be replaced by motorized sledges. Even their language was on the way out, because their children were being educated in white schools and taught English (Arima 1984: 460).

Inuit society, formerly a network of dispersed, ever-moving hunting groups, smaller, family-sized in summer, larger for collective caribou or seal hunting in autumn or winter, had been held together by kinship. It was self-supporting, sharing, and egalitarian. By 1960 this whole way of life was being undermined. The Inuit increasingly settled around Hudson's Bay Company or police posts, and depended for a living on welfare payments, handicrafts such as carving, or wage labour of some kind. In the Arctic towns they were segregated from whites and discriminated against, forming a lower stratum of society, in which they were joined by Indians and *métis*, or people of mixed race. Thus at Inuvik on the Mackenzie River in 1966–7, 600 Inuit, 200 Indians and 300 métis lived in the West End of town in dwellings lacking central heating, flush toilets and running water, while the 1,500 or so whites lived in the East End in houses with modern conveniences (Faynberg 1971: 127). No wonder Inuit health was at a low ebb in the 1950s and 1960s. In 1956 about 10 per cent of Canadian Inuit were suffering from tuberculosis, and when this was on the way to eradication in the 1960s, pneumonia took its place (Duffy 1988: 51–94). In 1958 the life expectancy of an Inuk (singular of Inuit) was said to be little more than twenty-four years and the infant mortality rate was placed at 260 deaths per 1,000 births. Chronic malnutrition was said to affect three-quarters of the population, the precise size of which was not even known to the Canadian authorities (Mowat 1960: 112–13).

GREENLAND: LA CIVILIZATION OBLIGATOIRE

Ammassalik, ou la Civilization Obligatoire was the title of French anthropologist Robert Gessain's book on the East Greenlanders of Ammassalik or, as it is now, Tasiilaq, published in 1969. Obligatory or compulsory civilization, is what he saw happening among this isolated Inuit group, ruled since 1894 by Denmark, between his first stay among them in 1934 and the second in 1965. Here, just as in Alaska and Canada, native society was being destroyed and then recreated in the image of the sovereign power, in this case Denmark. This was not so much done purposefully; it was a by-product of the American or European presence. Willy-nilly the Arctic peoples had to become civilized.

History, explains Gessain, had given the Danes the responsibility for introducing the few hundred Eskimos of Tasiilaq to the modern world. Avoiding the sudden introduction of European products, the Danes introduced the usual articles of trade step by step – rifles, clothes and cloth, foodstuffs, but no coffee, no alcohol. In 1894 a trading station was set up and wooden houses for this, a church and a handful of functionaries soon followed. Over the years the Eskimos were baptized, and the Danish presence led to an increasing proportion of métis among them. From 1957 alcohol was sold, with disastrous results. In the time-honoured way of commerce, needs were created among the Greenlanders and the means of satisfying these needs were then sold to them. Pre-fabricated wooden houses were supplied, like everything else, by the Royal Greenland Trade Department. A cash economy soon developed, with inevitable consequences. In the new system, the products of the subsistence hunt acquired a market value, and the East Greenlanders were persuaded to sell their necessities. Thus more and more seals were placed on the market. Tents were made of canvas, not sealskin, rubber replaced sealskin boots, the sealskin-covered women's boat, the umiak, almost disappeared, European clothing replaced sealskin, and seal-blubber was no longer used for heating and lighting. The killed seal was once shared out in an elaborate but precise way among kin in a society that was essentially cooperative and egalitarian. The fore parts of the carcase were shared with the hunter's father, brothers, and cousins, and the rear parts with the hunter's wife's family. By 1969, at Tasiilaq, Gessain saw only too clearly a typical European-type society developing: a hierarchy of wealth, with an 'élite' of Danish officials and well-off West Greenlanders at the top, and impoverished wage-labourers at the bottom of the scale (Gessain 1969, Faynberg 1971: 226–54).

The Greenlanders of the west coast and the Inuhuit of Avanersuaq or north-west Greenland likewise had to accept civilization from the Danes. Although Danish policy toward Greenlanders has often been held up as a model of how aboriginal peoples ought to be treated, the Greenlanders' way of life was affected and transformed in the years after the Second World War in the same way as that of the Canadian Inuit. In west Greenland in the years after 1948, the Danish government invested large sums in a modern fishing industry based on towns. To develop this, many small settlements were compulsorily evacuated, and pressure was put on Greenlanders living in small subsistence-hunting groups to move into the towns by closing schools and shops in outlying districts, and by suspending house-building there. Loans were only available for fishermen living in towns. Between 1950 and 1970 the proportion of the population living in towns increased from a half to nearly three-quarters. At the same time Greenlandic society was proletarianized, because formerly independent hunters now became lower-paid wage labourers in towns where higher-paid Danes dominated the labour market and held all the positions of responsibility. This amounted to the economic, social and political oppression of the majority of West Greenlanders, and it fostered the rise of a Danish-speaking west Greenlandic élite (Dahl 1986: 316–18). In Avanersuaq there was no fishing industry, but the tendency to concentrate in towns was greatly stimulated in 1953 when 116 Inuhuit were compulsorily moved to the settlement at Qaanaaq to make way for Thule Air Base (Map 37). In the new town of Qaanaaq, largely paid for by the United States authorities, discrimination against the Inuhuit was only too apparent. Lower down, and to the west, were Inuhuit houses, lacking sanitary arrangements and running water, and heated by coal-burning stoves. Higher up, and to the east, larger houses were built for the Danes and West Greenlanders with hot and cold running water and electricity (Vaughan 1991: 164; see also Malaurie 1991). Such contrasts in housing were soon to be found throughout the Arctic, exactly imitating on a small scale the discrimination in housing between rich and poor found in almost all the towns and cities in the rest of the world.

THE WAR ON SUPERSTITION

Not one of the states which vied with one another in annexing Arctic territory troubled at first to govern these territories themselves. Administration was either delegated to trading companies, as in Canada, Greenland and Russian Alaska, or left to missionaries. Since the Christian faith was seen as an adjunct of civil government, missionaries were often encouraged by the state. Greenland's first and most famous missionary, the Norwegian priest Hans Egede, dedicating his *Description of Greenland* to King Frederick IV of Denmark and Norway, thought that:

This little work cannot fail of a gracious Reception from Your Royal Highness, as it aims only at, and is calculated for, the Honour of God, and Your Royal Family's Exaltation. The last of which wholly depends on, and necessarily follows the first; for when the poor Greenlanders shall have learned to know and worship God, as their Creator and Redeemer, then they shall likewise learn to acknowledge and honour a Christian Sovereign as their King and Ruler. . . .

The same sort of attitude was apparent in Labrador in the 1760s, where British governor Hugh Palliser greeted Jens Haven's plans for a mission with enthusiasm, evidently because Haven had emphasised to him that the mission would 'unite this folk with the English nation' as well as converting it to Christianity (Kleivan 1966: 24–5). The American missionary-teacher Sheldon Jackson, who virtually ruled Alaska between 1884 and 1909 on behalf of the United States Bureau of Education, thought along identical lines. The native children had to be taught English to fit them 'for the social and industrial life of the white population of the United States and promote their not-too-distant assimilation', and congress supported him (Jenness 1962: 18). But Eskimos could not be civilized in this way, nor could their souls be saved, until they had been freed from the shackles of superstition. To the missionaries and the missionary societies which sent them, the richly imaginative spirit world of the Arctic peoples, the closeness and reality of the supernatural, the uplifting and other beneficial activities of the shaman, were incomprehensible. The wearing of amulets or charms was condemned as superstitious and magical. The missionary's aim was the outright destruction of the Arctic peoples' most essential spiritual convictions: the shaman, the taboo, and the belief in spirits. To him Torngak 'the spirit of evil' was an 'evil influence in the heart and life of the poor haunted Eskimo' that had to be extirpated (Davey 1905). It was partly these 'many gross Superstitions' as Egede described them (1745: 180) that led him and other missionaries to use epithets like 'unhappy', 'despicable', 'wretched' and 'miserable' in describing the Eskimos. Almost equally important was the extirpation of a whole series of social practices which were condemned as un-Christian, though they were often more or less essential to the Arctic peoples' way of life: wife-exchange, infanticide, polygamy, hunting on Sunday, and taking clothes off when indoors, to name but a few.

The long-term success of the missionaries in destroying the spirit world of the Arctic peoples and in eliminating their un-Christian customs was by no means achieved simply through spiritual propaganda. The missionaries had the good sense to work hard in the spheres of health and education. Their efforts were greatly facilitated by the commercial penetration of aboriginal societies. Conversion and trade went together: the profits from trade paid for the mission. When in 1903 the Inuhuit of Avanersuaq accepted the proposal for a permanent trading-post in their north-west Greenland hunting territories, they were easily persuaded at the same time that they should be taught the white man's customs and beliefs by a mission post (Vaughan 1991: 72–3). Hans Egede himself was not just a missionary; he was also the principal investor in a trading enterprise called the Bergen Greenland Company, which placed him in charge of on-shore buildings, trade and fishing in Greenland. He was both churchman and businessman, and most of the material needs of his mission were supplied by his company (Sollied and Solberg 1932, Bobé 1952, Gad 1973: 23–50).

Even with the help of trade, the missionaries faced serious difficulties. In trying to abolish the shaman, they sometimes inadvertently replaced him with their own persons; Egede was not entirely averse to being thought of as a shaman by the Greenlanders (Fenger 1879: 66). Some Alaskan Eskimos known to the explorer Vilhjalmur Stefansson thought that the missionary spoke the word of God in the same way as the shaman in a trance was the mouthpiece of his spirits. When a zealous missionary preached that no work should be done on Sunday, he was praised by one of the Eskimos for his wisdom: their wise men had taboos on food and drink, on clothing and methods of travel, but none of them had considered the grandiose possibility of a taboo on a *day*. A Mackenzie Eskimo that Stefansson spoke to assured him that he had no difficulty at all in believing that Christ raised people from the dead. Their own shamans could do it. Only a few years before, the great shaman Alualuk had gone to the house where Taiakpanna had died that morning, summoned his familiar spirits, performed the appropriate ceremonies, and woken Taiakpanna from the dead. Problems were caused, too, by the failure of the Alaskan missionaries to agree among themselves. For instance, Dr H.T. Marsh, the broad-minded medical missionary at Barrow, Alaska, was dismissed from his post in 1912 by the Presbyterian Board of Home Missions in New York, after years of excellent medical work. The Eskimos themselves had laid a formal complaint against him on three counts. Firstly they said, he encouraged Sabbath-breaking by telling the Eskimos that it was foolish and unnecessary to interrupt their annual whale hunt on Sundays. Then, when the Eskimos suggested that he ask God to keep the whales away on Sundays, so they did not lose an opportunity to catch one, he declared that such a prayer was inappropriate and would be unavailing. To the Eskimos, this looked as though he was teaching them that prayers were of no avail. No wonder some of these Eskimos complained that Dr Marsh was an inefficient shaman. Eskimos from other areas had told them that *their* missionaries had taught that whatever they asked of God would be granted. Thirdly, he was accused of encouraging immodesty by taking off his coat in Eskimo houses, other missionaries having taught the Eskimos that this was immodest and inadmissible (Stefansson 1919: 89–94, 407–35).

REPERCUSSIONS OF MISSIONARY ENTHUSIASM

Already in the nineteenth century astute observers like Henrik Rink and Fridtjof Nansen (1893b) had noted the harm done by missionaries in their efforts to give the Eskimos what they thought was a better spiritual and material life (Rink 1877: 136–46). Rink pointed out that the subversion of the authority of the shaman 'was the same as abolishing the only institution that could be considered to represent appointed magistrates or lawgivers'. And by removing the shamans, the missionaries removed from their natural position of influence in Greenlandic society 'the most eminent persons, both as regards intellectual abilities, personal courage, and dexterity in pursuing the national trade', namely hunting (p. 142). As for the prohibition of all kinds of public meetings and festivals, these were, in fact, the equivalent of courts of justice in which the rights, obligations and rules of Greenlandic society were laid down. Thus, Rink argued, the missionaries entirely undermined Eskimo society. In the twentieth century the Norwegian anthropologist Helge Kleivan has shown how the missionary posts of the Moravian brothers in north-east Labrador impinged negatively on Inuit society, in spite of their proclaimed and laudable aims of maintaining the Eskimos' subsistence hunt and preserving their language. This mission was established at Nain in 1769 with extensive powers: it was granted 40,469 hectares (100,000 acres) of land and exclusive trading and judicial rights over the Eskimos. A system of credits in the mission shop placed the Eskimos in debt to the mission, thus increasing their dependence on it and encouraging them to switch to a diet of 'shop' food. The missionaries brought their own boat-building equipment and showed the Eskimos how to build their own wooden boats, so that the umiak went out of use. The Eskimos were encouraged to move into wooden houses which had to be heated with a wood-burning stove in place of a blubber lamp. This caused depletion of the local timber, and time and energy had to be devoted to longer and longer journeys to collect firewood, to the detriment of the subsistence hunt. The population was concentrated in a few settlements and the Christian Eskimos were kept strictly separate from their still heathen brethen, thus undermining the essential solidarity of Eskimo society. Lastly, the notion of communal hunting territories, foreign to the missionaries, came to be replaced by the concept of private hunting lands, which became hereditary (Kleivan 1966 and Faynberg 1971: 136, 142–6).

VENIAMIN AMONG THE NENTSY

Western missionaries, with the best intentions, did lamentable harm to aboriginal societies. Eastern missions were more benign and tolerant in intention, and less far-reaching in effect. The holy fathers of the Russian Orthodox Church at Arkhangel'sk had been much disturbed at the beginning of the nineteenth century by reports from Nes' in the Kanin Peninsula (poluostrov Kanin). In most of this area there were no priests, no churches, and many heathen Nentsy. There were even cases of apostasy. A certain Vasiliy Nemtinov, who had not been to confession for fourteen years, was persuading Christian Nentsy to revert to shamanism and idolatry. On 29 January 1825 a five-man mission headed by the archimandrite Veniamin set out from Arkhangel'sk. At Mezen, on their way to Kanin to convert the heathen, they recruited a sixth man, Apitsyn Stepan, a newly converted Nenets who could read and write Russian, as interpreter. Penetrating into the foothills of the mountains of northern Kanin, the archimandrite found the head man of all the Kanin tundra, the sixty-year-old Khokholya Barakulev. In spite of the archimandrite's inducements – fine cloth, a horse brass, some beads, an axe and vodka – Khokholya resisted conversion on the grounds that he was too old to change his beliefs. Instead, he delved in a corner of the *chum*, or nomad tent, where heathen masks were kept, and read out loud from a parchment document so fast that neither the archimandrite, who had been learning Samoyed for six months, nor the interpreter, could understand a word. It was a grant of Tsar Ivan the Terrible dating from 1545, prohibiting anyone from interfering with the hunting and fishing of the Nentsy in Kanin. Now, complained Khokholya, some Mezen people had been interfering in spite of the tsar's grant, and he persuaded Veniamin to report this to the governor of Arkhangel'sk before finally permitting himself to be baptized. That summer, 420 Kanin Nentsy followed his example. The mission continued for five years, during which time Veniamin built three churches, baptized three thousand Nentsy, wrote a Samoyed grammar and dictionary, and translated the New Testament into Samoyed; but not without difficulties. Nasty stories about the mission were put about. Many Nentsy disappeared with their reindeer into the distant tundra when they heard about the mission; some even fled beyond the Urals. The persevering archimandrite planned to travel to Vaygach Island (ostrov Vaygach) to destroy the Nentsy's idols there (Plate 1) but could not find any Nentsy to accompany him, until three arrived from the northern Urals. These three, afterwards found to be escaped convicts, readily accepted baptism and took the archimandrite to Vaygach after he had plied them with vodka. Once there, they demanded more vodka, got drunk and danced around the idols. While this impious orgy was in progress, Veniamin set fire to the idols and burned them and everything with them. A cross which he then set up on the spot was found desecrated the next day. It was smeared with grease and blood, and a piece of red cloth had been attached to it. Afterwards the archimandrite was tempted to think that his mission had been a failure: he may well have been right. At any rate – fortunately no doubt for the Nentsy – his specially invented Samoyed alphabet, which combined elements of the Greek and Russian alphabets, was later dropped. Apparently the baptism of the Nentsy had absolutely no effect on their religious beliefs. The only impact of Christianity on them was that the popular patron saint of Russians in the north, St Nicholas, joined the company of ancient Nentsy deities under the name Nikola. Sacrifices of reindeer were made to him and icons with his picture on them were rubbed with reindeer fat and blood (Prokof'yeva 1964: 550, 566, 570; Vasil'yev and Geydenreykh 1977: 69–76).

SOCIALISM AMONG ARCTIC PEOPLES

Archimandrite Veniamin had missionized with the gentlest possible touch. He destroyed idols, he baptized the heathen, and he tried to introduce literacy to them. But he left their spirit world, their shamans and their material culture and social organization intact. Infinitely more far-reaching and radical than Russian orthodox Christianity was the ideology of communism or socialism, whichever one chooses to call it, which inspired the Russians to a new form of imperialism in the twentieth century in the name of their new empire, the Soviet Union. Instead of the haphazard way in which the Arctic peoples of the western hemisphere were incorporated into the white man's market systems, Christian churches and national states, those of the eastern hemisphere were overwhelmed by a well-orchestrated, all-pervading ideology backed by an elaborate bureaucracy. The entire apparatus of a giant state was determined to rid them of everything seen as their backwardness. They were to be introduced to a bright new world, a new life.

Capitalist exploitation, illiteracy, poverty, the subjection of women, and the authoritarian rule of officials would be swept away, together with shamanism, taboos, and nomadism. Within a fortnight of the October Revolution of 1917, the Declaration of Rights of the Peoples of Russia, signed by Vladimir Il'ich Lenin and Iosif Stalin, proudly proclaimed the principles of equality among the peoples of Russia, of the 'Free development of national minorities and national groups', and the 'Right of the peoples of Russia to free self-determination, up to the point of secession and the formation of an independent state' (Armstrong 1965: 192–3; on what follows see Taracouzio 1938, Armstrong 1958, Sergeyev 1965, Armstrong 1966, Gurvich 1980, Kuoljok 1985, Forsyth 1992: 283–320, and especially Vakhtin 1992).

Soviet policy toward northern peoples, the nationalities policy, was laid down in principle first and then resolutely, if not ruthlessly, applied. Already in 1922 the Soviet government had authorized an investigation of these peoples 'with a view to determining the best way of introducing them to socialism' (Armstrong 1966: 67). As soon as the last resistance to the Soviets had been crushed in 1924 a special organ to undertake the socialist reconstruction of the North was set up: the Committee for the Assistance of the Peoples of the North, or Committee of the North (*Komitet severa*) for short, which soon had sub-committees in various centres. In 1925 northern peoples were exempted from all taxes. Later, the sale of spirituous liquor to them was prohibited, but the committee's first real task was to discover exactly who the northern peoples really were. The first Soviet decree to mention them included such vague designations as the 'hordes of the tundra communities' and little-known names like the Samagirs, Manegrians, Olyutors and Kereks, which referred to local sub-groups only. As a result of some expeditions to the Soviet North in 1925, the committee was able to draw up a list of twenty-seven nationalities or ethnic groups which were formally designated 'small peoples of the north'. Among the twenty-six Siberian peoples were the Khanty, Mansi, Nentsy, Entsy, Nganasans, Dolgans, Evens, Chukchi, Koryaks and Eskimos. The only purely European people were the Sami. Omitted from this list because they were large rather than small peoples, being the most numerous, were the Komi and the Yakuts. Naturally, present-day anthropologists find it hard to accept this naive classification of northern native peoples.

The northern peoples were not brought into the administrative structure of the Soviet Union in the 1920s and 1930s without difficulties. Only after some experimentation with clan and nomadic soviets was the local soviet, an elected council, the lowest unit of self-government based on a village and surrounding area, widely established. The local soviets thus set up, which were often dominated by Russians and seldom if ever by natives, were linked together within regions of varying size, each region having its own elected self-government. Some regions were named after nationalities. It might be thought that by making the area occupied by the Nentsy into a Nentsy or Nenets Autonomous Region or Okrug in 1930, at the Nentsy's request, the authorities were implementing the principles contained in the Declaration of Rights. But, in fact, even when their own 'national' okrug was established in 1930, the Nentsy themselves made up only 44 per cent of its population. By 1959 the figure had dropped to a mere 11

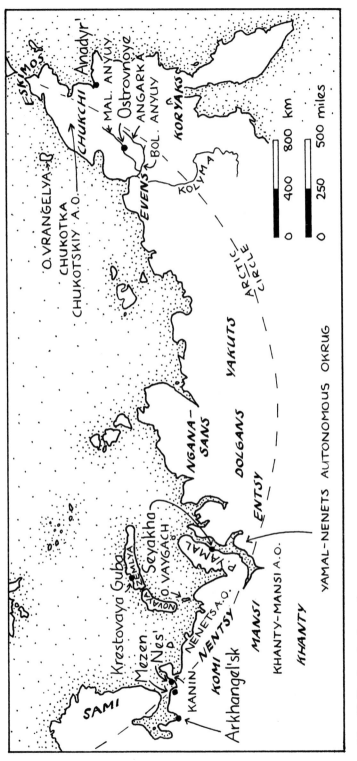

Map 38. Russian Arctic peoples.

per cent (Kuoljok 1985: 80), while in the Chukchi Autonomous Okrug in 1979 only 9.5 per cent of the population were Chukchi (Gurvich 1980: 11). Thus these apparent territorial self-governments of the northern peoples set up in 1929–30 only existed on the map or in theory, because the huge influx of Russian and other immigrants into them soon reduced the aboriginal people to small minorities. In any case, all important affairs in the Soviet Union after the 1930s were run by the highly centralized Communist Party from Moscow. Once the political and administrative framework had been laid down, this powerful organization moved in to proseletyze the northern peoples, making use from 1933 onwards of mobile units called Red Chums and Red Yarangas. These were moved around on sledges drawn by dogs or reindeer, or carried by boats (Red Boats), stopping at settlements. Besides spreading the gospel of communism, they also cared for children, provided some medical and technical help, and, among other things, campaigned against illiteracy and witchcraft: new-style missionaries. Their work went slowly: in 1938 there was said to be only one communist among the Nganasans.

Along with political restructuring went economic reorganization. From 1930, marketing was collectivized by the setting up of cooperative shops, and production by the formation of collective farms, or *kolkhozes*, and state farms, or *sovkhozes*. Even reindeer breeding was collectivized. In the Kanin Peninsula the original four kolkhozes were merged in 1960 to form a single one, called the North Pole. This comprised several herds of reindeer totalling seventeen or eighteen thousand head, each cared for by a brigade or detachment of thirty to forty Nentsy who lived in chums. The territory of the North Pole collective included nearly two million hectares of reindeer ground, rivers, lakes and marshes, 200,000 hectares of forest, and the inshore waters of the Kanin coast. From these last, the North Pole collective supplied the fish cooperative (*rybkoop*) in the settlement of Nes' with fish (Vasil'yev and Geydenreykh 1977: 12, 17, 26, 33–4). Another Arctic collective was the Yamalsky kolkhoz or Yamal collective at Seyakha on the shore of the Yamal Peninsula at 70° north. Here, excellent modern housing, a school and a power station reflected the profits made by the Nentsy reindeer herders of the collective from the sale of reindeer meat (up to a thousand tons a year) and white fox skins (almost nine thousand in 1974 alone). The collective also produced up to a thousand farmed blue fox pelts per annum. It used air transport for bringing in supplies, sending out its products, and for collecting pelts from outlying settlements (Vasil'yev and Geydenreykh 1977: 185–9). At best, the Nentsy reindeer herders in these collectives were semi-nomads, not full nomads, because they worked from a fixed base.

In the southern tip of the Chukchi Peninsula, the small, Asiatic Eskimo subsistence-hunting settlements originally scattered along the coast were evacuated or abandoned one after another between 1922 and 1960 in favour of a few larger settlements at the heads of inlets (Krupnik 1989: 36–8). Thus Chaplino was moved in 1959 to Novoye Chaplino (New Chaplino), where family subsistence hunting was replaced by collective Arctic fox-fur farming, the necessary meat for the foxes being obtained by six-man sea mammal hunting brigades (Callaway and Pilyasov 1993). Lest art be forgotten, in the 1930s and later, seasonal brigades of ivory carvers, each numbering about fifteen persons, were formed in the settlements of Chaplino, Sireniki, Naukan, Dezhnev and Uelen (Map 1; Mitlyanskaya 1976: 46).

In the Soviet Union, then, the aboriginal peoples of the north were overwhelmed by a far-reaching assimilation into the rest of Soviet society, by the replacement of their religions and beliefs with communism, and by the re-shaping of social structures through the introduction of the kolkhoz. Originally, nearly all the region's Arctic peoples were nomads, but by the time the Soviet Union was dismantled in 1991 true nomadism had all but disappeared. Lastly, the large-scale industrial opening up of the Soviet north mainly after 1960 further affected the native peoples. Huge complexes for the extraction of minerals, oil and gas based in north-west Siberia and elsewhere were developed, using Russian, Ukranian and even Bulgarian workers, while the hunting territories, fisheries and reindeer pastures of the northern peoples in areas like Yamal were overrun and destroyed. Pollution reared its ugly head on the tundra; the waters of the Gulf of the Ob' (Obskaya guba) were polluted. Everywhere populations of native peoples, dispersed and disintegrating, were drifting into the rapidly expanding towns (Kutsev 1989).

A FINAL BLOW?

In 1971 the Congress of the United States dealt what might easily have been the death blow to the native peoples of Alaska: it passed the Alaska Native Claims Settlement Act, with the intention of leaving the way clear for large-scale oil exploitation (Jorgensen 1990) and of bringing the Indians, Eskimos and Aleuts of Alaska 'into the mainstream of American life' (Berger 1985: 20) by making them 'go into business' like other good Americans. Their way of life was to be transformed from a subsistence to a cash and investment economy (Alaska Almanac 1989: 135). Needless to say, these peoples were not systematically asked for their views on this act: several native organizations supported it, but the Arctic Slope Native Association of Inupiat Eskimos opposed it. The act extinguished any aboriginal title Alaskan natives might claim to the land and any aboriginal hunting and fishing rights they might have. In return for surrendering this potential claim and these rights, which covered the entire territory of Alaska, the native peoples were granted title to 44 million acres of land, about 10 per cent of that territory. In compensation for surrendering the other 90 per cent of the territory of Alaska, the native peoples were to be paid $962.5 million, 'about three dollars an acre' (Berger 1985: 24). The land and the nearly one billion dollars made over to natives were not, however, simply given to them, either as tribal groups or individuals. The natives 'were obliged to set up corporations to serve as the vehicles for the ownership and management of this land and the money, which became corporate assets' (p. 20). Moreover, native control of the twelve regional and two hundred village corporations established by the act was only assured for twenty years: after 1991 non-natives could become voting shareholders and many of the 44 million acres 'granted' to the natives by the act could be, and almost certainly would be, sold to private individuals, including many whites. The act also laid it down that natives born on or after 18 December 1971 would receive neither cash nor shares; it only applied to natives alive when it was passed. In 1983 the Canadian judge Thomas Berger was selected by the Inuit Circumpolar Conference to head the Alaska Native Review Commission. This body was to assess the working of the Alaska Native Claims Settlement Act of 1971. Among Berger's recommendations was that tribal or local native governments should be set up to replace the village corporations and that the native land should be transferred to these new tribal governments. In the event, in 1988, substantial changes were made by congress to the 1971 act with the aim of protecting native interests (Jorgensen 1990: 291–3). However, the native peoples who once roamed undisturbed over the whole of Alaska were now virtually excluded from 90 per cent of that huge area (Arnold 1976, Berger 1985, Stenbaek 1986).

REBIRTH

The lowest point in the fortunes of Arctic peoples may have been reached in the 1960s and 1970s. Since about 1980 signs of recovery and reconstruction, especially in the political field, have been increasingly apparent. Everywhere – in Greenland, Canada, Alaska and Russia – Arctic peoples seem to be reclaiming their own (Osherenko and Young 1989: 72–109; special 1992 issue of *Études/Inuit/Studies*, vol. 16 (2), entitled 'Collective Rights and Powers'). The true, original owners of the Arctic are about to repossess it. This remarkable recovery appears to have been brought about by at least three developments. Firstly, a demographic upsurge among Arctic peoples has followed drastic nineteenth-century declines in population. Admittedly, this upsurge has been accompanied by an increase in the proportion of persons of mixed race among Arctic peoples, but these have usually been assimilated. At Tasiilaq in east Greenland the few hundred East Greenlanders of the 1880s were represented, on 1 January 1991, by 2,684 descendants. In the whole of Greenland there were 11,621 Greenlanders in 1901 and 46,691 on 1 January 1991 (Grønland 1990 Statistisk Årbog 1991: 343, 335). But the proportion of Danes in the popluation of Greenland increased from less than 5 per cent in 1950 to over 20 per cent in 1978 (Rouland 1991: 136). The population of Netsilik Eskimos in Canada jumped from about 550 in 1954 to 720 in 1967, largely under the influence of improved medical and welfare services (Balikci 1984: 429). The population of Kotzebue Sound Eskimo, inhabiting some 93,240 sq km (36,000 square miles) round the shores of Kotzebue Sound in north-west Alaska (Map 1), decreased from over 3,000 to a little over 1,000 in 1880–1900, and then increased during the twentieth century, to reach a total of 5,215 in 1980 (Burch 1984: 316). In the Russian far north, significant population increases have been made by the Nentsy, from 16,375 in 1926 to 34,700 in 1979, and the Chukchi, from 12,364 in 1926 to 15,200 in 1989, and by most other Arctic peoples, but the Russian Sami have only increased their numbers from 1,738 in 1897 to around 1,900 in 1989 (Armstrong 1965: 184, Armstrong 1990, Knapp 1992). On the other hand the Sami as a whole, living in Norway, Sweden, Finland and Russia, were thought to have increased from about 35,000 in 1960 to 42,000 in 1984 (Manker 1963, Zorgdrager 1984).

A second important cause of the new political awareness of Arctic peoples has been the cultivation of their own languages, the development of scripts or alphabets for them (Plate 28), and the fostering of literatures in those languages. In Greenland the monthly journal *Atuagagdliutit* or 'something for reading, accounts of all sorts of entertaining subjects', has been published at Nuuk since 1 January 1861 in Greenlandic. It was started by Henrik Rink (Rink 1877: 214, Banks 1975: 112, Gad 1984: 227). After earlier false starts in north America, the Inuit there are now being educated in their own language. In the early years of the Soviet Union, the cultural and educational development of the northern peoples was given high priority. From 1930 on the Institute of the Peoples of the North (*Institut Narodov Severa*) in Leningrad (now St Petersburg) developed a training programme for teachers and experts from the different nationalities and became involved in a project for the study of northern languages and the development of writing systems for them (Armstrong 1958: 119, Armstrong 1966: 57–88). After a 1932 Committee for the Study of a New Alphabet for the Peoples of the North had considered the problem, the Roman alphabet was abandoned and in 1937 a new Cyrillic-based alphabet was introduced for thirteen nationalities (Taracouzio 1938: 295–314). But a ruthless policy of 'Russification' in the 1950s and 1960s led to the widespread suppression and even, in some areas, obliteration of native languages. Only in the 1980s, when fewer than half northern children were being taught in their own language (Dahl 1990: 37), was this policy reversed. From 1989 onwards minority languages have again been officially encouraged.

Sustained by rising populations and the development of written languages, the recovery of the northern peoples has in the third place been promoted by the creation among them of educated élites. In part these have been due to miscegenation; in part they are the result of the educational and cultural programmes mentioned above. The creation of a Danish-speaking Greenlandic élite, trained in college or university in Copenhagen, was paralleled in the Soviet Union and elsewhere. The motive in each case was the same: to promote the assimilation of the native peoples into the white man's world, be it capitalist or communist. But the result has been otherwise. Chukchi writers like Tikhon Semushkin (1947) and Yuriy Rytkheu (1981) exemplify this process. Rytkheu describes how he began life in a nomad tent or *yaranga* in 1930 and graduated from Leningrad University. He became a well-known Soviet writer but remained a Chukchi at heart. 'And wherever these representatives of the northern peoples might work . . . they always remain loyal to the place from which they sprang, for in this point of the globe is concentrated their concept of the Motherland, the sense of one's native land' (Rytkheu 1981: 23). Such intellectuals among the northern peoples have become their politicians, and are spearheading their thrust towards political reconstruction and independence.

The reconstruction which all the Arctic peoples are now demanding is based on ideas which Europeans and Americans have instilled into them. The idea that land can be bought and sold, and privately or publicly owned, once entirely foreign to them, has led them to claim lands as their own. The idea of government in the shape of elected authorities, once likewise foreign to them, has led them to demand self-government. And the notion of the national state, Yuriy Rytkheu's 'Motherland', is likely to inspire them sooner or later to demand independence. So far, progress along these lines has been slow. The Greenlanders obtained a substantial measure of self-government, called Home Rule (*hjemmestyre*), from the Danes in 1979. The forty-seven thousand Greenlanders of 1991 shared this with an élite of nine thousand Danes, but the Danish élite appears to be crumbling, while the Greenlandic government in Nuuk is steadily transforming Kalaallit Nunaat into a centralized modern nation-state (Dahl 1986, Lauritzen 1983, Jull 1985, Stenbaek 1986) complete with national flag, national day, anthem and coat-of-arms (Kleivan 1991). This is at the expense both of the East Greenlanders and the Inuhuit of Avanersuaq in the north-west, who have become victims of West Greenlandic imperialism, and may relish being ruled from Nuuk no more than some Scots appreciate being ruled from Westminster. Their own distinctive dialects have been entirely overwhelmed by West Greenlandic. The Home Rule government of the social-democratic party Siumut has not yet aspired to complete independence from Denmark, though it did preside over Greenland's secession in 1985 from the European Economic Community. Nor has Siumut so far pursued its 1975 demand that Denmark recognize the aboriginal right of Greenlanders to the land they occupy. On the other hand, in Canada land claims have been linked with demands for self-government. Current negotiations for Nunavut, meaning 'our land' in Inuit-Inupiaq, seem likely to culminate in 1999 with the creation of a new Canadian province of that name, carved out of the North-West Territories, over 80 per cent of the twenty-two thousand-strong population of which will be Inuit. Linked to Nunavut is a land claim partly inspired by the Alaska Native Claims Settlement Act: the Canadian Inuit currently look like surrendering their aboriginal title to all land in Canada, in return for 18 per cent of the land in Nunavut, to be held in outright ownership, and a cash payment of $1.15 billion (Creery 1983, Anon. 1992, Bell 1992, Dickerson 1992, Pelly 1993, Dickerson and McCullough 1993).

The first native self-government set up by an Arctic people seems to have been the North Slope Borough, based on Barrow in Alaska. It was established on the initiative of the Inupiat Arctic Slope Native Association in 1972, and its 227,920 sq km (88,000 square miles) – 15 per cent of the land area of Alaska – include eight villages. About 70 per cent of its population are Inupiat Eskimos, but that proportion is declining, and some believe the borough will eventually pass out of Inupiat control. In 1970 the population of Barrow was 91 per cent Inupiat; in 1985 it was only 61 per cent Inupiat and, in the thirty-to-fifty age group, non-natives outnumbered natives. By levying taxes on the oil companies operating at Prudhoe Bay, the borough government has been able to lavish money on buildings and public services and subsidize programmes for supporting and developing the Inupiat language, various cultural activities, and the Inupiat subsistence economy. Inupiat culture has been revitalized and political awareness stimulated. The North Slope Borough has so far been an unmitigated success, but it has yet to create a self-supporting economic base before North Slope oil reserves are depleted (Morehouse and Leask 1980, Chance 1990: 173–86, Knapp and Morehouse 1991).

Not so fortunate as the Inupiat of northern Alaska are the indigenous inhabitants of the Yamal-Nenets and Khanty-Mansi autonomous regions of northern Russia, which are world suppliers of oil and gas. They have received absolutely nothing from the proceeds (Prokhorov 1989). In 1989 they founded an association called Spaseniye Yugry (Save Yugra; see Map 6) to protect their interests against the oil and gas companies (*Survival International Newsletter* 30, 1990). Soon afterwards, representatives of the peoples of the entire Russian north, taking a leaf out of the notebook of the Eskimos, who established the Inuit Circumpolar Conference in 1977 (*Polar Record* 20: 373–7, Lauritzen 1983, Jull 1989), founded the Association of Small Peoples of the Soviet North in March 1990 (Dahl 1990). They followed this up in the summer of 1991, on the eve of the collapse of the Soviet Union, by joining with others to found the Assembly of Deputies of Northern, Siberian and Far Eastern Peoples (*Severnye Prostory*, July 1991, p. 3). The programme of the Association of Small Peoples of the North noted that 'the outrages of the past decades' had led to social and economic backwardness and the 'forgetting of the cultural and spiritual values of these peoples'. It called for 'real autonomy' for the northern peoples so that they could 'plan their own present and future'. This was to be achieved in particular by the replacement of kolkhozes and sovkhozes by small family groups, and by the formation of self-governing administrative areas within the Russian Federation containing compact populations of northerners (Dahl 1990: 53–6). In October 1990 a group of Chukchi leaders announced plans for a breakaway Chukchi Autonomous Republic, to replace part of the existing Chukchi Autonomous Okrug. The new republic would no longer be part of the province or *oblast* of Magadan (Bernton 1991), and would form a separate Chukchi-dominated 'national' territory. In all parts of the Arctic then, the 1990s will surely see the aboriginal peoples rising, phoenix-like, from the ashes of the past to claim what is rightfully their own. They will use European ideas of land ownership, self-government, natural rights and, ultimately, the national state, to prevent their further assimilation into alien societies, and to remove definitively the threat of their extinction.

References

Aasgaard, G. 1946. *Svalbard under og etter Verdenskrigen*. Oslo: Norges Svalbard- og Ishavs-undersøkelser, 65. Offprinted from *Norsk Geografisk Tidsskrift* 11: 49–62.

Adams-Ray, E. (trans.) 1931. *The Andrée Diaries, being the Diaries and Records of S.A. Andrée, Nils Strindberg and Knut Fraenkel*. London: John Lane the Bodley Head. Translated from *Med Ornen mot Polen*, Stockholm 1930.

Ahlbäck, T. and J. Bergman (eds) 1991. *The Saami shaman drum: based on papers read at the Symposium on the Saami Shaman Drum . . . Åbo, Finland*. Åbo: Donner Institute for Research in Religious and Cultural History.

Akkuratov, V. 1981. 'K Polyusu otnositel'noy nedostupnosti' ['To the Pole of Relative Inaccessibility']. *Vokrug Sveta [Around the World]* 1981 (4): 30–5.

Alaska Almanac 1989. *Facts about Alaska*. Anchorage: Alaska Northwest Books.

Albrethsen, S.E. and C. Keller. 1986. 'The use of the saeter in medieval Norse farming in Greenland'. *Arctic Anthropology* 23: 91–107.

Alekseev, A.I. 1990. *The Destiny of Russian America 1741–1867*. Kingston, Ontario and Fairbanks, Alaska: Limestone Press. Translated from the Russian.

Alekseyev, A.I. 1982. *Osvoyeniye russkimi lyud'mi dal'nego vostoka i russkoy Ameriki do kontsa XIX veka [The development of the Far East and Russian America by Russian people until the end of the nineteenth century]*. Moscow: Nauka.

Alt, B.T., R.M. Koerner, D.A. Fisher and J.C. Bourgeois. 1985. *Arctic climate during the Franklin Era, as deduced from ice cores*. In: Sutherland 1985: 69–92.

Amstrupp, S.C. and O. Wiig (eds) 1991. *Polar bears. Proceedings of the Tenth Working Meeting of the IUCN/SSC Polar Bear Specialist Group*. Gland, Switzerland: International Union for the Conservation of Nature and Natural Resources.

Amundsen, R. 1908a and b. *The North West Passage: being the record of a voyage of exploration of the ship Gjøa, 1903–1907*. 2 vols. London: A. Constable. Translated from: *Nordvest-Passagen. Beretning om Gjøa-Ekspeditionen. 1903–1907*, Kristiania 1907.

Amundsen, R. 1921. *Nordostpassagen*. Kristiania: Gyldendal.

Amundsen, R. [1925]. *My Polar Flight*. London: Hutchinson.

Amundsen, R. 1927. *My Life as an Explorer*. London: William Heinemann.

Amundsen, R. and L. Ellsworth. 1925. *Our Polar Flight*. New York: Dodd, Mead & Co.

Amundsen, R. and L. Ellsworth. [1926]. *The First Flight Across the Polar Sea*. London: Hutchinson.

Ancker, P.E. 1993. 'Narsarsuaq Air Base (B.W. –1)'. *Grønland* 41: 125–252.

Anderson, D.D. 1984. *Prehistory of North Alaska*. In Damas (ed.) 1984: 80–93.

Anderson, J. 1756. *Beschryving van Ysland, Groenland en de Straat Davis*. Amsterdam: Jan van Dalen. Translated from *Nachrichten von Island, Grünland und der Strasse Davis*, Hamburg 1746.

Anderson, J. 1940–1. 'Chief factor James Anderson's Back River journal of 1855'. *Canadian Field Naturalist* 54: 63–7, 84–9, 107–9, 125–6, 134–6; 55: 9–11, 21–6, 38–44.

Anderson, J.W. 1961. *Fur Trader's Story.* Toronto: Ryerson Press.

Andrews, C.L. 1939. *The Eskimo and his Reindeer in Alaska.* Caldwell, Idaho: Caxton Printers.

Anon. 1876. *The Arctic World. Its Plants, Animals and Natural Phenomena. With a Historical Sketch of Arctic Discovery.* London: T. Nelson & Sons.

Anon. 1979. 'Notes. Archaeological find on Baffin Island'. *Polar Record* 19: 385–6.

Anon. 1992. *Summary of the agreement between the Inuit of the Nunavut Settlement Area and Her Majesty in right of Canada.* Yellowknife: Inuit Ratification Committee.

Antropova, V.V. and V.G. Kuznetsova. 1964. *The Chukchi.* In: Levin and Potopov 1964: 799–835.

Arikaynen, A.I. 1984. *Transportnaya arteriya Sovetskoy Arktiki [The Transport Artery of the Soviet Arctic].* Moscow: Nauka.

Arima, E.Y. 1984. *Caribou Eskimo.* In: Damas (ed.) 1984: 447–62.

Arlov, T.B. 1986. *Svalbard 1596–1650 i historiografisk lys.* Trondheim: University of Trondheim.

Arlov, T.B. 1987. *The historical writing about Smeerenburg.* Smeerenburg Seminar. Rapportserie no. 38, pp. 7–18. Oslo: Norsk Polarinstitutt.

Armstrong, A. 1857. *A Personal Narrative of the Discovery of the North-West Passage.* London: Hurst & Blackett.

Armstrong, T.E. 1952. *The Northern Sea Route. Soviet Exploitation of the North-east Passage.* Scott Polar Research Institute Special Publication, 1. Cambridge: Cambridge University Press.

Armstrong, T. 1958. *The Russians in the Arctic. Aspects of Soviet Exploration and Exploitation of the Far North, 1937–1957.* London: Methuen. Reprinted 1972.

Armstrong, T.E. 1965. *Russian Settlement in the North.* Cambridge: Cambridge University Press.

Armstrong, T.E. 1966. *The administration of the northern peoples: the USSR.* In: Macdonald 1966: 57–88.

Armstrong, T.E. 1980. 'The north-east passage as a commercial waterway, 1879–1979'. *Ymer* 1980: 86–130.

Armstrong, T.E. 1983. *Bering's expeditions.* In: Bater, J.H. and R.A. French (eds), *Studies in Russian Historical Geography,* pp. 175–195. London: Academic Press.

Armstrong, T.E. 1990. 'Northern peoples of the USSR, 1989'. *Polar Record* 26: 316.

Armstrong, T. 1992a. *Siberian and Arctic exploration.* In: Frost 1992: 117–26.

Armstrong T. 1992b. 'A history of the Northern Sea Route'. *International Challenges* 12 (1): 34–42.

Armstrong T. (ed.) 1975. *Yermak's Campaign in Siberia.* London: Hakluyt Society.

Armstrong T. and L.W. Brigham. 1993. 'The Northern Sea Route Project'. *Polar Record* 29: 60.

Arneborg, J. 1989. 'Nordboarkæologiens historie – og fremtid'. *Grønland* 37: 121–37.

Arnesen, O. 1929. *Roald Amundsen som han var.* Oslo: Gyldendal, Norsk Forlag.

Arnold, R. (ed.) 1976. *Alaska Native Land Claims.* Anchorage: Alaska Native Foundation.

Arutyunov, S.A., I.I. Krupnik and M.A. Chlenov. 1982. *'Kitovaya alleya'. Drevnosti ostrovov proliva Senyavina [Whale Alley. Antiquities of the islands in Senyavina Strait].* Moscow: Nauka.

Asher, G.M. (ed.) 1860. *Henry Hudson the Navigator*. London: Haklyut Society.

Astrup, E. 1898. *With Peary near the Pole*. London: Pearson. Translated from *Blandt Nordpolens naboer*, Kristiania 1895.

Back, G. 1836. *Narrative of the Arctic land expedition to the mouth of the Great Fish River and along the shores of the Arctic Ocean in the years 1833, 1834 and 1835*. Philadelphia: E.L. Carey and A. Hart.

Back, G. 1838. *Narrative of an Expedition in HMS* Terror *Undertaken with a View to Geographical Discovery on the Arctic Shores*. London: John Murray.

Baidukov, G. 1938. *Over the North Pole. The narrative of the Russian non-stop flight from Moscow to the U.S.A.* London: George G. Harrap.

Baker, F.W.G. 1982. 'The First International Polar Year, 1882–1883'. *Polar Record* 21: 275–85.

Baker, J. 1993 'Protecting an Arctic refuge. A summer of decision for the Arctic National Wildlife Refuge'. *Arctic Circle*, summer 1993.

Balchen, B., C. Ford and O. La Forge. 1945. *War below Zero. The Battle for Greenland*. London: George Allen & Unwin.

Balikci, A. 1970. *The Netsilik Eskimo*. New York: Natural History Press.

Balikci, A. 1984. *Netsilik*. In: Damas (ed.) 1984: 415–30.

Ballantyne R.M. 1857. *Hudson's Bay or Everyday Life in the Wilds of North America*. London: T. Nelson & Sons. First published 1848.

Bandi, H-G. 1969. *Eskimo Prehistory*. London: Methuen. Translated from *Urgeschichte der Eskimo*, Stuttgart 1964.

Bang, O. 1981. *Tre år i drivisen. Fridtjof Nansens polarfærd med træskibet* Fram *1893–1896*. Copenhagen: Rhodos.

Banks, M. 1975. *Greenland*. Newton Abbot: David & Charles.

Bardarson, I. 1930. *Det gamle Grønlands beskrivelse*. Ed. F. Jonsson. Copenhagen: Levin & Munksgaard.

Barr, W. 1975a. 'A tsarist attempt at opening the Northern Sea Route: the Arctic Ocean Hydrographic Expedition, 1910–1915'. *Polarforschung* 45: 51–64.

Barr, W. 1975b. 'Operation 'Wunderland'. *Admiral Scheer* in the Kara Sea, August 1942'. *Polar Record* 17: 461–72.

Barr, W. 1978. 'The voyage of the Sibiryakov, 1932'. *Polar Record* 19: 253–66.

Barr, W. 1981. 'Baron Eduard von Toll's last expedition: the Russian Polar Expedition, 1900–1903'. *Arctic* 34: 201–24.

Barr, W. 1984. 'The fate of Rusanov's *Gerkules* expedition in the Kara Sea, 1913'. *Polar Record* 22: 287–304.

Barr, W. 1985. *The expeditions of the First International Polar Year, 1882–1883*. Calgary: Arctic Institute of North America.

Barr, W. 1986. 'Wettertrupp Haudegen. The last German Arctic weather station of World War 2'. *Polar Record* 23: 143–57, 323–33.

Barr, W. 1991a. 'An introduction to Aleksandr Fedorovich Middendorf [Alexander Theodor von Middendorff] and his expedition to Taymyr 1843'. *Polar Geography and Geology* 15: 3–6.

Barr, W. 1991b. 'Background to Otto Sverdrup's voyage in the Kara Sea on board *Eclipse* in 1914–1915'. *Polar Geography and Geology* 15: 167–71

Barr, W. 1991c. *The Arctic Ocean in Russian history to 1945*. In: Brigham (ed.) 1991: 11–32.

Barr, W. 1992. 'Franklin in Siberia? Lieutenant Bedford Pim's proposal to search the Arctic coast of Siberia, 1851–1852'. *Arctic* 45: 36–46.

Barrington, D. 1818. *The Possibility of Approaching the North Pole Asserted by the Hon. D. Barrington*. New York: James Eastburn.

Barrow, J. 1818. *A Chronological history of Voyages into the Arctic regions*. London: John Murray. Reprinted Newton Abbot 1971.

Barrow, J. 1846. *Voyages of Discovery and Research within the Arctic Regions from the Year 1818 to the Present Time*. New York: Harper & Brothers.

Barry, P.S. 1992. 'The Canol Project, 1942–1945'. *Arctic* 45: 401–3.

Barthelmess, K. 1987. 'Walfangtechnik vor 375 Jahren. Die Zeichnungen in Robert Fotherby's *Journal* von 1613'. *Deutsches Schiffahrtsarchiv* 10: 289–324.

Bartlett, R.A. 1928. *The Log of Bob Bartlett*. New York and London: G.P. Putnam's Sons.

Beaglehole, J.C. (ed.) 1967a and b. *The voyage of the* Resolution *and* Discovery. *1776–1780*. 2 vols. Cambridge: Hakluyt Society.

Beattie, O. and J. Geiger. 1989. *Frozen in Time. The Fate of the Franklin Expedition*. London: Grafton Books.

Beaujeu-Garnier, J. 1990. *La Société de Géographie de Paris et l'exploration arctique. Gustave Lambert, pionnier de la conquête du Pôle*. In: Devers 1990: 129–37.

Beazley, C.R. 1897, 1901, 1906. *The Dawn of Modern Geography*. 3 vols. London: John Murray.

Beechey, F.W. 1831a and b. *Narrative of a Voyage to the Pacific and Beering's Strait, to Co-operate with the Polar Expeditions, Performed in HMS* Blossom . . . *in the Years 1825–26–27–28*. 2 vols. London: Henry Colburn and Richard Bentley.

Beechey, F.W. 1843. *A Voyage of Discovery Towards the North Pole, Performed in HM Ships* Dorothea *and* Trent, *1818*. London: Richard Bentley

Beke, C.T. (ed. and trans.) 1853. *A true description of three voyages by the North-east towards Cathay and China, undertaken by the Dutch in the years 1594, 1595, and 1596. By Gerrit de Veer*. London: Hakluyt Society. New edition: *The three voyages of William Barents to the Arctic regions*, London 1876.

Belcher, E. 1855a and b. *The Last of the Arctic Voyages; Being a Narrative of the Expedition in HMS* Assistance *during the Years 1852-53-54*. 2 vols. London: Lovell Reeve.

Bell, J. 1992. 'Nunavut: the quiet revolution'. *Arctic Circle* 2 (4): 12–21.

Bellot, J.R. 1854. *Journal d'un voyage aux mers polaires executés à la recherche de Sir John Franklin en 1851 et 1852*. Paris: Perrotin. English translation, 2 vols, London 1855.

Belov, M.I. 1956. *Istoriya otkrytiya i osvoyeniya Severnogo morskogo puti, 1. Arkticheskoye moreplavaniye s drevneyshikh vremen do serediny XIX veka* [*History of the discovery and development of the Northern Sea Route, 1. Arctic seafaring from ancient times to the mid-nineteenth century*]. Moscow: Morskoy Transport.

Belov, M.I. 1959. *Istoriya otkrytiya i osvoyeniya Severnogo morskogo puti, 3. Sovetskoye arkticheskoye moreplavaniye 1917–1932* [*History of the discovery and development of the Northern Sea Route, 3. Soviet Arctic seafaring*]. Leningrad: Morskoy Transport.

Belov, M.I. 1969. *Istoriya otkrytiya i osvoyeniya Severnogo morskogo puti, 4. Nauchnoye i khozyaystvennoye osvoyeniye Sovetskogo Severa 1933–1945* [*History of the discovery and development of the Northern Sea Route, 4. Scientific and economic exploitation of the Soviet North*]. Leningrad: Gidrometeorologicheskoye Izdatel'stvo.

Belov, M.I. 1977. *Po sledam polyarnykh ekspeditsiy* [*On the track of Polar expeditions*]. Leningrad: Gidrometeoizdat.

Belov, M.I., O.V. Ovsyannikov and V.F. Starkov. 1980. *Mangazeya*. 2 vols. Leningrad: Gidrometeoizdat.

Berger, T.R. 1985. *Village journey. The report of the Alaska Native Review Commission*. New York: Hill and Wang.

Berglund, J. 1986. 'The decline of the Norse settlements in Greenland'. *Arctic Anthropolgy* 23: 109–35.

Berlin, K. 1932. *Danmarks ret til Grønland*. Copenhagen: Nyt Nordisk Forlag and Arnold Busck.

Bernier, J.E. 1910. *Report on the Dominion of Canada Government Expedition to the Arctic Islands and Hudson Strait on Board the D.G.S.* Arctic. Ottawa: Government Printing Bureau.

Bernton, H. 1991. 'Melting the Ice Curtain, 2'. *Alaska* 57 (8): 39–43.

Bertelsen, A. 1945. 'Grønlænderne i Danmark'. *Meddelelser om Grønland* 145 (2). 211pp.

Berton, P. 1972. *Klondike. The Last Great Gold Rush.* 1896–1899. Toronto: McClelland and Stewart. Originally published 1958.

Berton, P. 1988. *The Arctic Grail. The Quest for the North West Passage and the North Pole, 1818–1909.* New York: Viking Penguin.

Bessels, E. 1875. 'L'expédition polaire Américaine sous les ordres du Capitaine Hall'. *Bulletin de la Société de Géographie* 9: 291–9.

Bessels, E. 1879. *Die amerikanische Nordpol-Expedition.* Leipzig: Wilhelm Engelmann.

Bessels, E. 1884. 'The northernmost inhabitants of the Earth. An ethnographic sketch'. *American Naturalist* 18: 861–82.

Beynen, L.R.K. 1876. *De reis der* Pandora *naar de Nordpoolgewesten in de zomer van 1875.* Amsterdam: C.F. Stemler.

Binney, G. 1925. *With Seaplane and Sledge in the Arctic.* London: Hutchinson.

Birket-Smith, K. 1929. *Jens Munk's rejse og andre danske ishavsfarter under Christian IV.* Copenhagen: C.A. Reitzel.

Birket-Smith, K. 1936. *The Eskimos.* London: Methuen.

Birket-Smith, K. (ed.) 1950a and b. *Grønlandsbogen.* 2 vols. Copenhagen: J.H. Schultz.

Bistrup, H.A.Ø. 1936. *Knud Rasmussen og Grønlandsmonopolet.* Copenhagen: Levin and Munksgaard.

Bjerre, J. [1980] *Sirius. Danmarks slædepatrulje i Nordøstgrønland.* Copenhagen: Lademann.

Blake, E.V. (ed.) 1874. *Arctic Experiences: Containing Capt. George Tyson's Wonderful Drift on the Ice-floe, a History of the* Polaris *Expedition, the Cruise of the* Tigress, *and Rescue of the* Polaris *Survivors.* New York: Harper & Brothers.

Blom, G.A. 1984. 'The participation of the kings in the early Norwegian sailing to Bjarmeland'. *Arctic* 37: 385–8.

Blond, G. 1965. *Ordeal below zero.* London: Mayflower Books. Originally published 1956.

Blyth, J.D.M. 1951. 'German meteorological activities in the Arctic, 1940–1945'. *Polar Record* 6: 185–226.

Bobé, L. 1915. 'Hollænderne paa Grønland'. *Atlanten* 4: 257–84.

Bobé, L. 1929. *History of the trade and colonization until 1870.* In: Vahl *et al.* 1929: 77–163.

Bobé, L. 1952. *Hans Egede, colonizer and missionary of Greenland.* Copenhagen: Rosenkilde and Bagger.

Bockstoce, J. 1977. *Steam whaling in the western Arctic.* New Bedford, Mass.: Old Dartmouth Historical Society.

Bockstoce, J.R. 1986. *Whales, Ice and Men. The History of Whaling in the Western Arctic.* Seattle: University of Washington Press and New Bedford Whaling Museum.

Bockstoce, J. (ed.) 1988a and b. *The journal of Rochfort Maguire. 1852–1854.* 2 vols. London: Hakluyt Society.

Bockstoce, J. 1991. *Arctic Passages. A Unique Small-boat Journey Through the Great Northern Waterway.* New York: Hearst Marine Books.

Bogoras, W. 1904. *The Jesup North Pacific Expedition, 7. The Chukchee.* New York: American Museum of Natural History. Translated into Russian, Leningrad 1934.

Bøgvad, R. 1950. *Grønland som mineralproducerende land.* In: Birket-Smith 1950b: 95–120.

Bolkhovitinov, N.N. 1990. *Russko-amerikanskiye otnosheniya i prodazha Alyaski, 1834–1867* [*Russian-American relations and the sale of Alaska, 1834–1867*]. Moscow: Nauka.

Bolotnikov. N.Ya. 1980. 'Kayur Sergey Zhuravlev' ['The dog driver S. Zhuravlev']. *Polyarnyy Krug* [*Polar Circle*]: 47–55.

Bonga, A.C. 1992. 'Robert E. Peary: a medical assessment'. *Polar Record* 28: 71–2.

Borup, G. 1911. *A tenderfoot with Peary*. New York: Frederick A. Stokes.

Bouché, M. 1952. *Groenland. Station Centrale*. Paris: Bernard Grasset.

Braat, J., J.P.F. Kok, J.H.H. de Graaff and P. Poldervaart. 1980. 'Restauratie, conservatie en onderzoek van de op Nova Zembla gevonden zestiende-eeuwse prenten'. *Bulletin van het Rijksmuseum* 1980 (2): 43–79.

Brainard, D.L. 1929. *The Outpost of the Lost. An Arctic Adventure*. Indianopolis: Bobbs-Merrill.

Brander, J. 1955. *Jan Mayen in verleden en heden*. Middelburg: J.W.den Boer.

Bray, E.F. de. 1992. *A Frenchman in Search of Franklin: de Bray's Arctic Journal, 1852–1854*. Trans. and ed. W. Barr. Toronto: University of Toronto Press.

Brebner, J.B. 1933. *The Explorers of North America. 1492–1806*. London: A. & C. Black.

Bree, P.J. van, and L. Hacquebord. 1988. *Hebben de Nederlanders de Groenlandse walvis in de Noordatlantische wateren uitgeroeid?* In: Hacquebord and Vroom 1988: 146–51.

Brigham, L.W. 1991. *Technical developments and the future of Soviet Arctic marine transportation*. In: Brigham (ed.) 1991: 125–39.

Brigham, L.W. (ed.) 1991. *The Soviet Maritime Arctic*. London: Belhaven Press and Cambridge Scott Polar Research Institute.

Brigham, L.W. 1993. 'Opening the Northern Sea Route'. *Polar Record* 29: 60–1.

Brinner, L. 1913. *Die deutsche Grönlandfahrt. Abhandlungen zur Verkehrs- und Seegeschichte im Auftrag des Hansischen Geschichtsvereins*, 7. Berlin: Karl Curtius.

Brody, H. (ed.) 1973. *Peoples of the Earth, 16. The Arctic*. Danbury Press.

Bronson, W. 1977. *The Last Grand Adventure*. New York: McGraw-Hill.

Brontman, L. 1938. *On the Top of the World. The Soviet Expedition to the North Pole, 1937*. London: Victor Gollancz.

Brosse, J. 1983. *Great Voyages of Discovery. Circumnavigators and Scientists, 1764–1843*. New York and Oxford: Facts on File Publications.

Broude, B.G. 1992. *Umberto Nobile. 1885–1978*. St Petersburg: Nauka.

Brower, C.D. 1950. *Fifty Years Below Zero. A Lifetime of Adventure in the Far North*. London: Travel Book Club. First published New York 1942.

Brown, A. (trans.) 1935. *The Voyage of the* Chelyuskin. *By Members of the Expedition*. London and New York: MacMillan. Translated from *Pokhod* 'Chelyuskina', ed. O.Yu. Shmidt *et al.*, 2 vols, Moscow 1934.

Brown, J. 1858. *The North-West Passage, and the Plans for the Search for Sir John Franklin. A Review*. London: E. Stanford.

Brown, R.N.R. 1920. *Spitsbergen. An Account of Exploration, Hunting, the Mineral Riches and Future Potentialities of an Arctic Archipelago*. Philadelphia: J.B. Lippincott.

Brown, R.N.R. 1923. *A Naturalist at the Poles*. London: Seeley, Service & Co.

Bruijn, J.R. 1981. *From minor to major concern: entrepreneurs in seventeenth-century Dutch whaling*. In: van Holk 1981: 43–53.

Brusewitz, G. 1991. A.E. 'Nordenskiöld och Nordisk Polarforskning'. *Nordenskiöld-Samfundets Tidskrift* 50: 8–17.

Bruun, D. 1902. *Kampen om Nordpolen*. Copenhagen: Det Nordiske Forlag.

Bryce, G. 1910. *The Siege and Conquest of the North Pole*. London: Gibbings & Co.

Buliard, R.P. 1953. *Inuk*. London: MacMillan.

Burch, E.S. jnr. 1984. *Kotzebue Sound Eskimo*. In: Damas (ed.) 1984: 303–19.

Burch, E.S. 1988. *The Eskimos*. London: Macdonald.

Busch, B.C. 1985. *The War Against the Seals. A History of the North American Seal Fishery*. Kingston and Montreal: McGill-Queen's University Press and Gloucester: Alan Sutton.

Bush, R.J. 1892. *Reindeer, Dogs and Snowshoes*. London: Sampson Low, Son, and Marston. Reprinted New York 1970.

Callaway, D.G. and A. Pilyasov. 1993. 'A comparative analysis of the settlements of Novoye Chaplino and Gambell'. *Polar Record* 29: 25–36.

Calvert, J. 1963. *Surface at the Pole. The Story of the USS* Skate. London: Adventurers Club. First published 1960.

Cameron, I. 1980. *The History of the Royal Geographical Society 1830–1980. To the Farthest Ends of the earth*. London: Macdonald.

Campbell, M.W. 1957. *The North West Company*. Toronto: MacMillan Company of Canada.

Cantwell, J.C. 1889. *A narrative account of the exploration of the Kowak [Kobuk] River, Alaska*. In: Healey 1889: 47–74.

Carlson, W.S. 1942. *Greenland Lies North*. New York: MacMillan.

Carlson, W.S. 1962. *Lifelines through the Arctic*. New York: Duell, Sloan and Pearce.

Carpenter, K.J. 1986. *The History of Scurvy and Vitamin C*. Cambridge: Cambridge University Press.

Caswell, J.E. 1956. *Arctic Frontiers. United States Explorations in the Far North*. Norman: University of Oklahoma Press.

Chalmers, J.W. 1960. *Fur Trade Governor. George Simpson. 1820–1860*. Edmonton: Institute of Applied Art.

Chance, N.A. 1990. *The Inupiat of Arctic Alaska: an Ethnography of Development*. Fort Worth, Texas: Holt, Reinhart and Winston.

Chard, C.S. 1963. 'The Nganasan: Wild Reindeer Hunters of the Taimyr Peninsula'. *Arctic Anthropology* 1 (2): 105–21.

Christiansen, H.C. *et al.* 1973. *Spotlights on Greenland*. Copenhagen: Royal Greenland Trade Department.

Christy, M. (ed.) 1894 a and b. *The Voyages of Captain Luke Foxe of Hull and Captain Thomas James of Bristol, in Search of a North-West Passage in 1631–1632*. 2 vols. London: Hakluyt Society.

Chubakov, K.N. 1979. *Severnyy morskoy put'* [*The Northern Sea Route*]. Moscow: Znaniye.

Chubakov, K., A. Arikaynen and M. Shevelev. 1982. 'Severnyy morskoy put' [The Northern Sea Route]'. *Morskoy Flot* [*The Fleet*] 1982 (12): 22–9.

Ciriquiain-Gaiztarro, M. 1961. *Los Vascos en la pesca de la balena*. San Sebastian: Biblioteca Vascongada de los Amigos del Pais.

Clark, G.V. 1986. *The Last of the Whaling Captains*. Glasgow: Brown, Son & Ferguson.

Clarke, B. 1964. *Polar Flight*. London: Ian Allan.

Clarke, J.W. 1991. *Oil and gas resources in the offshore Soviet Arctic*. In: Brigham (ed.) 1991: 108–22.

Claustre, D. (ed.) 1982. '"The north-West Passage, or voyage finished": a Polar play and musical entertainment'. *Polar Record* 21: 95–115.

Clavering, D.C. 1830. 'Journal of a voyage to Spitsbergen and the east coast of Greenland in HMS *Griper*'. *Edinburgh New Philosophical Journal* (new series) 9: 1–30.

Coates, P.A. 1991. *The Trans-Alaska Pipeline Controversy: Technology, Conservation and the Frontier*. London and Toronto: Associated University Presses.

Collinson, R. 1889. *Journal of HMS* Enterprise *on the Expedition in Search of Sir John Franklin's Ships by Behring Strait, 1850–55*. London: Sampson, Low, Marston, Searle & Rivington.

Conquest, R. 1979. *Kolyma. The Arctic Death Camps*. Oxford: Oxford University Press.

Conway, W.M. (ed.) 1904. *Early Dutch and English Voyages to Spitsbergen in the Seventeenth Century*. London: Hakluyt Society.

Conway, W.M. 1906. *No Man's Land. A History of Spitsbergen from its Discovery in 1596 to the Beginning of the Scientific Exploration of the Country*. Cambridge: Cambridge University Press.

Cook, F.A. 1911. *My Attainment of the Pole. Being a Record of the Expedition Which First Reached the Boreal Center, 1907–1909*. New York: Polar Publishing.

Cook, F.A. 1953. *Return From the Pole*. London: Burke.

Cook, J.A. 1926. *Pursuing the Whale. A Quarter-Century of Whaling in the Arctic*. London: John Murray.

Cooke, A. 1981. *A gift outright: the exploration of the Canadian Arctic islands after 1880*. In: Zaslow (ed.) 1981: 51–60.

Cooke, A. and C. Holland. 1978. *The Exploration of Northern Canada, 500–1920. A Chronology*. Toronto: Arctic History Press.

Corner, G.W. 1972. *Doctor Kane of the Arctic Seas*. Philadelphia: Temple University Press.

Crantz, D. 1767a and b. *The History of Greenland*. 2 vols. London: The Brethren's Society

Credland, A.G. [1979] *The* Diana *of Hull*. Hull: Kingston upon Hull Museums and Art Galleries.

Creery, I. 1983. *The Inuit (Eskimo) of Canada*. London: Minority Rights Group.

Cruwys, L. 1990. 'Henry Grinnell and the American Franklin Searches'. *Polar Record* 26: 211–16.

Cruwys, L. 1991. 'Profile: Henry Grinnell'. *Polar Record* 27: 115–19.

Cruwys, L. 1992. 'Edwin Jesse De Haven: the first US Arctic Explorer'. *Polar Record* 28: 205–12.

Csonka, Y. 1991. 'Les Ahiarmiut (1920–1950) dans la perspective de l'histoire des Inuit Caribous'. *Boreales* 46–49: 169–70.

Cunynghame, F. 1953. *Lost Trail. The Story of the Klondike Gold and the Man Who Fought for Control*. London: Faber and Faber.

Cyriax, R.J. 1939. *Sir John Franklin's Last Arctic Expedition: a Chapter in the History of the Royal Navy*. London: Methuen.

Cyriax, R.J. 1945. *Sir John Franklin's orders considered in the light of geographical knowledge when he sailed, 1845*. In: Cyriax and Wordie 1945: 169–80.

Cyriax, R.J. and J.M.Wordie. 1945. 'Centenary of the sailing of Sir John Franklin with the *Erebus* and *Terror*'. *Geographical Journal* 106: 169–97.

Dahl, J. 1986. 'Greenland: political structure of self-government'. *Arctic Anthropology* 23: 315–24.

Dahl, J. 1990 *Indigenous peoples of the Soviet North*. International Workgroup for Indigenous Affairs. Document 67. Copenhagen.

Dahl, R. 1925. *The* Teddy *Expedition. Among the Icefloes of Greenland*. New York and London: D. Appleton.

Dalgård, S. 1962. *Dansk-Norsk hvalfangst. 1615–1660*. Copenhagen: G.E.C.Gad.

Dall, W.H. 1870. *Alaska and its Resources*. Boston: Lee and Shepard.

Damas, D. 1984. *Copper Eskimo*. In: Damas (ed.) 1984: 397–414.

Damas, D. (ed.) 1984. *Handbook of North American Indians, 5. Arctic*. Washington: Smithsonian Institution.

Daniells, R. 1969. *Alexander Mackenzie and the North West*. London: Faber and Faber.

Davey, J.W. 1905. *The Fall of Torngak or the Moravian Mission on the Coast of Labrador*. London: S.W. Partridge.

Davidson, G.C. 1918. *The North West Company*. Berkeley: University of California Press.

Davies, T.D. 1990. 'New evidence places Peary at the Pole'. *National Geographic* 177: 44–61.

Davis, C.H. (ed.) 1876. *Narrative of the North Polar Expedition. US Ship* Polaris. Washington: Government Printing Office.

Dawes, P.R. 1992. 'Tema: Lauge Koch'. *Grønland* 40: 197–240.

Day, A.E. 1986. *Search for the North-West Passage. An Annotated Bibliography*. New York: Garland Publishing Inc.

De Long, E. 1884, 1883. *The Voyage of the* Jeannette. *The Ship and Ice Journals of George W. De Long*. 2 vols. Boston: Houghton, Mifflin and Company.

Deacon M. and A. Savours. 1976. 'Sir George Strong Nares. 1831–1915'. *Polar Record* 18: 127–41.

Dekker, P. 1971. *De laatste bloeiperiode van de Nederlandse Arctische walvis– en robbevangst, 1761–1775*. Zaltbommel: Europese Bibliotheek.

Dekker, P. 1975. 'Meer dan vijftig jaren' vrije handel met de Eskimo's op Groenland'. *It Beaken. Tydskrift fan de Fryske Akademy* 37:371–85.

Dement'yev, G.P. 1951. *Sokola-krechety [The Gyrfalcon]*. Moscow: Moskovskoye Obshchestvo Ispytateley Prirody. German translation: *Der Gerfalke*, Wittenberg 1960.

Demin, L.M. 1990. *Semen Dezhnev*. Moscow: Molodaya Gvardiya.

Devers, S. (ed.) 1990. *Pour Jean Malaurie*. Paris: Plon.

Devold, H. 1940. *Polarliv*. Oslo: Gyldendal Norsk Forlag.

Dickerson, M.O. 1992. *Whose North? Political Change, Political Development and Self-Government in the Northwest Territories*. Vancouver: University of British Columbia Press and Calgary: Arctic Institute of North America.

Dickerson, M.O. and K. McCullough. 1993. 'Nunavut ('Our Land')'. *Information North* 19 (2). Calgary: Arctic Institute of North America.

Digby, B. 1926. *The Mammoth and Mammoth-Hunting in North-East Siberia*. London: Witherby.

Dikov, N.N. 1971. *Naskal'nye zagadki drevney Chukotki. Petroglify Pegtymelya [Rock Engravings of Ancient Chukotka. The Pegtymel petroglifs]*. Moscow: Nauka.

Dikov, N.N. 1974a. *Chiniyskiy mogil'nik [Chini Cemetery]*. Novosibirsk: Nauka.

Dikov, N.N. 1974b. *Ocherki istorii Chukotki s drevneyshikh vremen do nashikh dney [Outlines of the History of Chukotka from Ancient Times to the Present Day]*. Novosibirsk: Nauka.

Dikov, N.N. 1979. *Drevniye kul'tury Severo-Vostochnoy Azii [Ancient Cultures of North-East Asia]*. Moscow: Nauka.

Diubaldo, R.J. 1978. *Stefansson and the Canadian Arctic*. Montreal: McGill-Queens University Press.

Divin, V.A. 1993. *The Great Russian Navigator, A.I. Chirikov*. Trans. R.H. Fisher. Fairbanks: University of Alaska Press.

Dodge, E.S. 1973. *The Polar Rosses. John and James Clark Ross and their explorations*. London: Faber and Faber.

Doiban, V.A., M. Pretes and A.V. Sekarev. 1992. 'Economic development in the Kola Region, USSR: an overview'. *Polar Record* 28: 7–16.

Dole, N.H. 1922a and b. America and Spitsbergen: *The Romance of an Arctic Coal Mine*. 2 vols. Boston: Marshall Jones.

Dongen, S. van [1929]. *Vijf jaar in ijs en sneeuw*. Amsterdam: Scheltens & Giltay.

Donovan, G.P. (ed.) 1982. *Aboriginal/subsistence whaling (with special reference to the Alaska and Greenland fisheries)*. Cambridge: Reports of the International Whaling Commission, Special Issue.

Drastrup, E. 1932. *Blandt Danske og Norske fangstmænd i NordostGrønland*. Copenhagen: Gyldendalske Boghandel and Nordisk Forlag.

Duffy, R.Q. 1988. *The Road to Nunavut. The Progress of the Eastern Arctic Inuit Since the Second World War*. Kingston, Ontario and Montreal: McGill-Queens University Press.

Dugger, J.A. 1984. *Arctic oil and gas: policy perspectives*. In: Westermeyer and Shusterich 1984: 19–38.

Dumond, D.E. 1977. *The Eskimos and Aleuts*. London: Thames and Hudson.

Eames, H. 1973. *Winner Lose All. Dr Cook and the Theft of the North Pole*. Boston and Toronto: Little, Brown and Company.

Egede, H. 1745. *A description of Greenland*. London: C. Hitch, S. Austen, J. Jackson. Translated from *Det gamle Grønlands nye Perlustration*, Copenhagen 1741.

Elbo, J.G. 1952. 'The war in Svalbard, 1940–1945'. *Polar Record* 6: 484–95.

Elbo, J.G. 1953. 'The war in Jan Mayen'. *Polar Record* 6: 735–9.

Elder, W. 1858. *Biography of Elisha Kent Kane*. Philadelphia: Childs and Peterson and New York: Sheldon, Blakeman & Co.

Ellsworth, L. 1938. *Beyond Horizons*. New York: Book League of America.

Ellsworth, L. and F.H. Smith. 1932. 'Reports of the preliminary results of the Aeroarctic Expedition with the *Graf Zeppelin*'. *Geographical Review* 22: 61–82.

Etienne, J-L. 1986. *Le marcheur du Pôle*. Paris: Robert Laffont.

Fairley, T.C. 1959. *Sverdrup's Arctic Adventures*. London: Longmans Green.

Falk, F.J. 1983. *Grönlandfahrer der Nordseeinsel Römö*. Bredstedt: Nordfriisk Instituut.

Farrar, V.J. 1937. *The Annexation of Russian America to the United States*. Washington D.C.: W.F. Roberts. Reprinted New York 1966.

Faynberg, L.A. 1971. *Ocherki etnicheskoy istorii zarubezhnogo severa*. [*Essays on the ethnic history of the foreign north*]. Moscow: Nauka.

Faynberg, L.A. 1981. *O nekotoryikh parallelyikh v kul'ture samodiytsev i eskimosov* [*On some parallels in Samoyed and Eskimo cultures*]. In: Gurvich (ed.) 1981: 128–42.

Fenger, H.M. 1879. *Bidrag til Hans Egedes og den grønlandske Missions Historie 1721–1760*. Copenhagen: G.E.C. Gad.

Ferrante, O. 1985a and b. *Umberto Nobile*. 2 vols. Rome: Claudio Tatangelo.

Fiala, A. 1906. *Fighting the Polar Ice*. New York: Doubleday, Page & Company.

Finnie, R. [1944]. *Canada Moves North*. London: Hurst and Blackett. First published New York and Toronto 1942.

Fisher, A. 1819. *Journal of a Voyage of Discovery to the Arctic Regions Performed Between 4 April and 18 November 1818 in HMS* Alexander. London: Richard Phillips.

Fisher, A. 1821. *A Journal of a Voyage of Discovery to the Arctic Regions in HM Ships* Hecla *and* Griper *in the Years 1819 and 1820*. London: Longman, Hurst, Rees, Orme and Brown.

Fisher, D.E. 1992. *Across the Top of the World*. New York: Random House.

Fisher, R.H. 1943. *The Russian Fur Trade 1550–1700*. Berkeley and Los Angeles: University of California Press.

Fisher, R.H. 1944. 'Mangazeia: a boom town of seventeenth-century Siberia'. *Russian Review* 4: 89–99.

Fisher, R.H. 1977. *Bering's Voyages: Whither and Why*. Seattle: University of Washington Press.

Fisher, R.H. 1981. *The Voyage of Semen Dezhnev in 1648: Bering's Precursor*. London: Hakluyt Society.

Fisher, R.H. 1992. *To give Chirikov his due*. In: Frost 1992: 37–50.

Fitzhugh, W.W. 1984. *Palaeo-Eskimo cultures of Greenland*. In: Damas (ed.) 1984: 528–39.

Fitzhugh. W.W. and J.S. Olin. 1993. *Archaeology of the Frobisher Voyages*. Washington: Smithsonian Institution

Fjærli, E. 1979. *Krigens Svalbard*. Oslo: Gyldendal Norsk Forlag.

Fleming, A.L. 1929. *Dwellers in Arctic Night*. Westminster: Society for the Propagation of the Gospel in Foreign Parts.

Fletcher, R.J. 1990. 'Military radar defence lines of northern north America: an historical geography'. *Polar Record* 26: 265–76.

Ford, C. 1966. *Where the Sea Breaks its Back. The Epic Story of a Pioneer Naturalist and the Discovery of Alaska*. Boston: Little, Brown & Co.

Ford, J.A. 1959. *Eskimo Prehistory in the Vicinity of Point Barrow, Alaska*. New York: Anthropological Papers of the American Museum of Natural History.

Fordham, D. 1991. 'Lead poisoning and the Franklin expedition'. *Polar Record* 27: 371.

Forsyth, J. 1992. *A History of Siberia. Russia's North Asian Colony, 1581–1990*. Cambridge: Cambridge University Press.

Fox, L. 1635. *North-West Fox; or Fox from the North-West Passage*. London: Alsop and Fawcet. Reprinted New York 1965.

Franklin, J. 1824a and b. *Narrative of a Journey to the Shores of the Polar Sea in the Years 1819–20–21–22*. 2 vols. Second edition. London: John Murray.

Franklin, J. 1828. *Narrative of a Second Expedition to the Shores of the Polar Sea in the Years 1825, 1826 and 1827. Including an Account of the Progress of a Detachment to the Eastward by John Richardson*. London: John Murray.

Fredskild, B. 1981. *The natural environment of the Norse settlers in Greenland*. In: van Holk 1981: 27–42.

Freeman, A.A. 1961. *The Case for Doctor Cook*. New York: Coward-McCann.

Friis, H. (ed.) 1976. *The Arctic Diary of Russell Williams Porter*. Charlottesville: University Press of Virginia.

Frolov, I. 1991. *The 1987 expedition of the icebreaker* Sibir' *to the North Pole*. In: Brigham (ed.) 1991: 33–44.

Frost, O.W. (ed.) 1992. *Bering and Chirikov. The American Voyages and their Impact*. Anchorage: Alaska Historical Society.

Fyllingsnes, F. 1990. *Undergongen til dei norrøne bygdene på Grønland i seinmellomalderen. Eit forskingshistorisk oversyn*. Oslo: Middelalderforum.

Gad, F. 1970, 1973, 1982. *The History of Greenland*. 3 vols. London: C.Hurst (vols 1 and 2) and Copenhagen: Nyt Nordisk Forlag and Arnold Busck (vol. 3). Translated from *Grønlands historie*, 3 vols., Copenhagen 1967–75.

Gad, F. 1984. *Grønland*. Copenhagen: Politikens Forlag.

Galbraith, J.S. 1976. *The Little Emperor. Governor Simpson of the Hudson's Bay Company*. Toronto: MacMillan of Canada.

Garrett, J.N. 1984. *Conventional hydrocarbons in the United States Arctic: an industry appraisal*. In: Westermeyer and Shusterich 1984: 39–58.

Garting, B. 1979. *Sven Andersson's Journal förd å Ångfartyget* Vega *under expeditionen åt Norra Ishavet, åren 1878–1879*. Karlskrona: Föreningen Gamla Carlscrona.

Geiger, J. and O. Beattie. 1993. *Dead Silence: the Greatest Mystery in Arctic Discovery*. London: Bloomsbury.

Georgi, J. 1934. *Mid-Ice. The Story of the Wegener Expedition to Greenland*. London: Kegan Paul, Trench, Trubner & Co.

Gessain, R. 1969. *Ammassalik ou la civilization obligatoire*. Paris: Flammarion.

Gessain, R. 1981. *Ovibos. La grande aventure des hommes et des boeufs musqués*. Paris: Robert Laffont.

Giæver, J. 1956. *Dyretråkk og fugletrekk på 74° nord*. Oslo: Tiden Norsk Forlag. Danish translation:

Mit Grønland, Copenhagen 1958. English translation: *In the Land of the Musk-Ox: Tales of Wildlife in North-East Greenland*, London 1958.

Gibson, J.R. 1992. *Supplying the Kamchatka Expeditions, 1725–30 and 1733–42*. In: Frost 1992: 90–116.

Giddings, J.L. 1968. *Ancient Men of the Arctic*. London: Secker and Warburg. Originally published New York 1967.

Gilberg, A. 1992. 'Blyminen ved Mestersvig i Østgrønland'. *Grønland* 40: 289–311.

Gilberg, R. 1989. 'Nordpolen og dens naboer'. *Grønland* 37: 61–4.

Gilder, W.H. 1881. *Schwatka's Search. Sledging in the Arctic in Quest of the Franklin Records*. New York: Charles Scribner's Sons.

Gilder, W.H. 1883. *Ice-pack and Tundra. An Account of the Search for the* Jeannette *and a Sledge Journey through Siberia*. New York: Charles Scribner's Sons.

Gillett, E. and K.A. MacMahon. 1980. *A History of Hull*. University of Hull Publications. Oxford: Oxford University Press.

Glover, R. (ed.) 1958. *A Journey from Prince of Wales's Fort in Hudson's Bay to the Northern Ocean. 1769. 1770. 1771. 1772. By Samuel Hearne*. Toronto: MacMillan of Canada.

Glushankov, I.V. 1980. *Navstrechu neizvedannomu [Towards the Unknown]*. Leningrad: Gidrometeoizdat.

Gnilorybov, N.A. 1988. *Ugol'nye shakhty na Shpitsbergene [Coal Mines on Spitsbergen]*. Moscow: Nedra.

Godfrey, W.C. 1857. *Narrative of the Last Grinnell Arctic Exploring Expedition in Search of Sir John Franklin, 1853–4–5*. Philadelphia: J.T. Lloyd.

Godsell, P.H. 1951. *Arctic Trader. The Account of Twenty Years with the Hudson's Bay Company*. London: Robert Hale. First edition London 1935.

Golder, F.A. 1914. *Russian Expansion in the Pacific, 1641–1850*. Cleveland: Clark Co.

Golder, F.A. (ed.) 1922, 1925. *Bering's Voyages*. 2 vols. New York: American Geographical Society.

Goodsell, J.W. 1983. *On Polar Trails: the Peary Expedition to the North Pole, 1908–1909*. Austin, Texas: Eakin Press.

Gordiyenko, P.A. 1980. 'Polyarnye gidrometeorologi. Vospominaniya o Velikoy otechestvennoy voyne, 1941–1945' ['Polar Meteorologists. Recollections of the Great Patriotic War']. *Chelovek i Stikhiya [Man and the Elements]*: 113–14.

Gosch, C.C.A. (ed.) 1897a and b. *Danish Arctic Expeditions, 1605–1620*. London: Hakluyt Society.

Gough, B.M. 1986. 'British-Russian rivalry and the search for the North-West Passage in the early nineteenth century'. *Polar Record* 23: 301–17.

Gough, B.M. (ed.) 1973. *To the Pacific and Arctic with Beechey. The Journal of Lieutenant George Peard of HMS* Blossom. *1825–1828*. Hakluyt Society. Cambridge: Cambridge University Press.

Graah, W.A. 1932. *Undersøgelses-reise til østkysten af Grønland*. Ed. K. Birket-Smith. Copenhagen: Gyldendalske Boghandel-Nordisk Forlag. English translation: *Narrative of an Expedition to the East Coast of Greenland*, London 1837.

Graburn, N.H.H. and B.S. Strong. 1973. *Circumpolar Peoples: an Anthropological Perspective*. Pacific Palisades, Calif.: Goodyear.

Grant, S.D. 1991. 'A case of compounded error: the Inuit Resettlement Project, 1953, and the government response, 1990'. *Northern Perspectives* 19 (1): 3–29.

Greely, A.W. 1886a and b. *Three Years of Arctic Service. An Account of the Lady Franklin Bay Expedition of 1881–1884*. 2 vols. New York: Charles Scribner's Sons.

Greely, A.W. 1929. *The Polar regions in the Twentieth Century*. London: George G. Harrap.

Green, F. 1926. Peary. *The Man Who Refused to Fail*. New York and London: G.P. Putnam's Sons.

Greve, T. 1973. *Fridtjof Nansen. 1861–1904.* Oslo: Gyldendal, Norsk Forlag.

Greve, T. 1974. *Fridtjof Nansen. 1905–1930.* Oslo: Gyldendal, Norsk Forlag.

Grierson, J. 1964. *Challenge to the Poles. Highlights of Arctic and Antarctic Aviation.* London: G.T. Foulis.

Gromov, M. 1939. *Across the North Pole to America.* Moscow: Foreign Languages Publishing House.

Grønland 1990 Statistisk Årbog. 1991. Kalaallit Nunaat. Nuuk: Atuakkiorfik.

Grønnow, B. 1986. 'Recent archaeological investigations of West Greenland caribou hunting'. *Arctic Anthropology* 23: 57–80.

Grønnow, B. 1991. 'Vejen til Grønland'. *Grønland* 39: 100–2.

Grønnow, B. and M. Meldgaard. 1991. 'De første vestgrønlændere'. *Grønland* 39: 103–44.

Gruber, R. 1939. *I Went to the Soviet Arctic.* London: Gollancz.

Gruening, E. 1954. *The State of Alaska.* New York: Random House.

Gubser, N.J. 1965. *The Nunamiut Eskimos. Hunters of Caribou.* New Haven & London: Yale University Press.

Gulløv, H.C. 1986. 'Introduction to special issue'. *Arctic Anthropology* 23: 1–16.

Gulløv, H.C. 1987. *Dutch whaling and its influence on Eskimo culture in Greenland.* In: Hacquebord and Vaughan 1987: 75–93.

Gulløv, H.C. 1988. 'Noua terra 1566. Newfoundland, Labrador og Grønland i samtidens europæiske bevidsthed'. *Grønland* 36: 129–46.

Gurvich, I.S. 1980. 'Polveka avtonomii narodnostey severa SSSR' ['Half a century of autonomous nationalities of the north of the USSR']. *Sovetskaya Etnografiya* 1980 (6): 3–17.

Gurvich, I.S. 1981. *K voprosu o parallelyakh v traditsionnoy kul'ture aborigennykh narodov Severnoy Azii i Severnoy Ameriki* [*The question of parallels in the traditional aboriginal cultures of north Asia and North America*]. In: Gurvich (ed.) 1981: 119–28.

Gurvich, I.S. (ed.) 1981. *Traditsionnye kul'tury Severnoy Sibiri i Severnoy Ameriki* [*Traditional cultures of northern Siberia and North America*]. Moscow: Nauka.

Guttridge, L.F. 1988. *Icebound: the* Jeannette *Expedition's Quest for the North Pole.* New York: Paragon House. First published New York 1987.

Gvozdetsky, N.A. 1974. *Soviet Geographical Explorations and Discoveries.* Moscow: Progress Publishers. Translated from *Sovetskiye geografischeskiy issledovaniya i otkrytiya,* Moscow 1974.

Hacquebord, L. 1980. 'The Smeerenburg project: an investigation of seventeenth-century Dutch whaling settlements on Svalbard'. *Polar Record* 20: 284–7.

Hacquebord, L. 1981. *Smeerenburg: the rise and fall of a Dutch whaling settlement on the west coast of Spitsbergen.* In: van Holk 1981: 79–132.

Hacquebord, L. 1984. *Smeerenburg. Het verblijf van Nederlandse walvisvaarders op de westkust van Spitsbergen in de zeventiende eeuw.* Groningen: University of Groningen Arctic Centre.

Hacquebord, L. 1986. 'A survey of the early Dutch exploration and exploitation of the Atlantic Arctic'. *Circumpolar Journal* 1 (2): 10–35.

Hacquebord, L. 1989. *Drie zeventiende-eeuwse overwinteringen.* In: Hacquebord *et al.* 1989: 24–39.

Hacquebord, L. 1991. 'Five early European winterings in the Atlantic Arctic (1596–1635): a comparison'. *Arctic* 44: 146–55.

Hacquebord, L. and R. de Bok. 1981. *Spitsbergen 79° N.B. Een Nederlandse expeditie in het spoor van Willem Barentsz.* Amsterdam: Elsevier.

Hacquebord, L. and W. Vroom. 1988. *Walvisvaart in de Gouden Eeuwe. Opgravingen op Spitsbergen.* Amsterdam: De Bataafsche Leeuw.

Hacquebord, L. and R. Vaughan (eds) 1987. *Between Greenland and America. Cross-Cultural Contacts and the Environment in the Baffin Bay area.* Groningen: University of Groningen Arctic Centre.

Hacquebord, L., J.R. Leinenga and J. de Korte. 1989. *Nederlanders in the Poolwinter*. Groningen: University of Groningen Arctic Centre.

Hagen, N.U. 1990. 'Den første kryssingen av Grønland: Fridtjof Nansen 1888'. *Grønland* 38: 5–31.

Hajdu, P. 1963. *The Samoyed Peoples and Languages*. Bloomington, Illinois: Indiana University.

Hakluyt, R. (ed.) 1907a–h. *The Principal Navigations, Voyages, Traffiques and Discoveries of the English Nation*. 8 vols. London: J.M. Dent & Sons.

Halifax, J. 1980. *Shamanic Voices. A Survey of Visionary Narratives*. Harmondsworth: Penguin Books. First edition 1979.

Hall, C.F. 1865. *Arctic Researches and Life Among the Esquimaux: Being the Narrative of an Expedition in Search of Sir John Franklin in 1860, 1861 and 1862*. New York: Harper & Brothers.

Hall, S. 1987. *The Fourth World. The Heritage of the Arctic and its Destruction*. London: The Bodley Head.

Hall, T.F. 1917. *Has the North Pole Been Discovered?* Boston: Richard G. Badger.

Hamer, J. and J. Steinbring (eds.) 1980. *Alcohol and Native Peoples of the North*. Washington, D.C.: University Press of America.

Hansen, J.P.H., J. Meldgaard and J. Nordqvist. 1985. *Qilakitsoq. De grønlandske mumier fra 1400-tallet*. Nuuk: Grønlands Landsmuseum and Copenhagen: Christian Ejder's Forlag.

Hansen, J.P.H. and Gulløv, H.C. 1989. *The mummies from Qilakitsoq – Eskimos in the fifteenth century. Meddelelser om Grønland. Man and Society* 12: 1–199.

Hansen T. 1970. *North West to Hudson Bay. The Life and Times of Jens Munk*. London: Collins. Translated and abridged from *Jens Munk*, 2. vols, Copenhagen 1965.

Harris, A.C. 1972. *Alaska and the Klondike Gold Fields*. Toronto: Coles Publishing Coy. Originally published 1897.

Hartwig, G. 1874. *The Polar World*. London: Longmans, Green. Translated from *Der hohe Norden*, Wiesbaden 1858.

Hassert, K. 1956. *Die Polarforschung. Geschichte der Entdeckungsreisen zum Nord- und Südpol*. Munich: Wilhelm Goldmann.

Hattersley-Smith, G. 1976. 'The British Arctic Expedition 1875–1876'. *Polar Record* 18: 117–26.

Hatting, T. 1982. 'Nordboernes husdyr'. *Grønland* 30: 252–7.

Hayes, I.I. 1860. *An Arctic Boat Journey in the Autumn of 1854*. Boston: Brown, Taggard and Chase.

Hayes, I.I. 1867. *The Open Polar Sea: A Narrative of a Voyage of Discovery Towards the North Pole in the Schooner* United States. New York: Hurd and Houghton.

Hayes, J.G. 1929. *Robert Edwin Peary. A record of his Explorations 1886–1909*. London: Grant Richards & Humphrey Toulmin.

Hayes, J.G. 1937. *The Conquest of the North Pole. Recent Arctic Exploration*. London: Thornton Butterworth. First edition, London 1934.

Healy, M.A. 1889. *Report of the Cruise of the Revenue Marine Steamer* Corwin *in the Arctic Ocean in the Year 1884*. Washington: Government Printing Office.

Helmer, J.W. 1991. 'The Palaeo-Eskimo Prehistory of the North Devon Lowlands'. *Arctic* 44: 301–17.

Henderson, D.S. 1972. *Fishing for the Whale. A Guide-Catalogue to the Collection of Whaling Relics in Dundee Museum*. Dundee: Dundee Museum and Art Gallery.

Hennig, R. 1936, 1937, 1938, 1939. *Terrae incognitae. Eine Zusammenstellung und kritische Bewertung der wichtigsten vorkolumbischen Entdeckungsreisen an Hand der darüber vorliegenden Originalberichte*. 4 vols. Leiden: E.J. Brill.

Henriksen, V. 1988. *Mot en verdens ytterste grense: vest for storhavet – Grønland og Vinland*. [Oslo]: Aschehoug.

Henson. M. 1912. *A Negro Explorer at the North Pole*. New York: Frederick A. Stokes. New edition: *A Black Explorer at the North Pole*, Omaha 1989.

Herbert, W. 1969. *Across the Top of the World. The British Trans-Arctic Expedition*. London: Longmans.

Herbert, W. 1978. *North Pole*. London: Sackett and Marshall.

Herbert, W. 1989. *The Noose of Laurels. The Discovery of the North Pole*. London: Hodder & Stoughton.

Hobbs, W.H. 1930. *Exploring About the North Pole of the Winds*. New York: G.P. Putnam's Sons.

Hobbs, W.H. 1936. *Peary*. New York: MacMillan.

Hoel, A. 1966a and b, 1967. *Svalbard: Svalbard's historie 1596–1965*. 3 vols. Oslo: Sverre Kildahls Boktrykkeri.

Holk, A.G.F.van (ed.) 1981. *Early European Exploitation of the Northern Atlantic 800–1700*. Groningen: University of Groningen Arctic Centre.

Holland, C. and J.M. Savelle. 1987. 'My dear Beaufort: a personal letter from John Ross's Arctic expedition of 1829–33'. *Arctic* 40: 66–77.

Holm, G. and V. Garde. 1887. *Den danske Konebaads-Expedition til Grønlands Østkyst*. Copenhagen: Forlagsbureauet.

Holtved, E. 1942. *Polareskimoer*. Copenhagen: Carl Allers.

Holtved, E. 1944a and b. *Archaeological Investigations in the Thule District. Meddelelser om Grønland* 141 (1 and 2). 308 and 184 pp.

Hooper, W.H. 1853. *Ten Months Among the Tents of the Tuski*. London: John Murray.

Hoppál, M. and O. von Sadovszky (eds) 1989. *Shamanism: Past and Present*. Budapest: Ethnographic Institute, Hungarian Academy of Sciences and Los Angeles: Fullerton International Society for Trans-Oceanic Research.

Horensma, P. 1985. 'Olivier Brunel and the Dutch involvement in the discovery of the North-East Passage'. *Fram. The Journal of Polar Studies* 2: 123–8.

Horensma, P. 1991. *The Soviet Arctic*. London: Routledge.

Horn, G. 1939. *Recent Norwegian Expeditions to South-East Greenland*. Oslo: Norges Svalbard- og Ishavs-undersøkelser.

Horwood, H. 1977. *Bartlett. The Great Canadian Explorer*. New York and Toronto: Doubleday.

Hovgaard, A. 1882. *Nordenskiöld's Voyage Round Asia and Europe*. London: Sampson, Low, Marston. Translated from *Nordenskiöld's rejse omkring Asien og Europa*, Copenhagen 1881.

Hovgaard, W. 1915. *The Voyages of the Norsemen to America*. New York: American Scandinavian Foundation.

Howarth, D. 1957. *The Sledge Patrol*. London: Collins.

Hrdlička, A. 1944. *Alaska Diary 1926–1931*. Lancaster, PA: Jaques Cattell Press.

Hughes, C.C. 1960. *An Eskimo Village in the Modern World*. Ithaca, New York: Cornell University Press.

Huish, R. 1835. *The Last Voyage of Capt. Sir John Ross, Knt. RN to the Arctic Regions; for the Discovery of a North West Passage; Performed in the Years 1829–30–31–32 and 33*. London: John Saunders.

Huish, R. 1836. *A Narrative of the Voyage and Travels of Captain Beechey . . . to the Pacific and Behring's Straits; Performed in the Years 1825, 26, 27 and 28*. London: W. Wright.

Hunt, W.R. 1981. *To Stand at the Pole. The Dr Cook-Admiral Peary North Pole Controversy*. New York: Stein and Day.

Hunt, W.R. 1986. *Stef. A biography of Vilhjalmur Stefansson. Canadian Arctic Explorer*. Vancouver: University of British Columbia Press.

Hunter, A. 1983. *Northern Traders. Caribou Hair in the Stew*. Victoria, British Columbia: Sono Nis Press.

Huntingdon, H.P. 1992a. 'The Alaska Eskimo Whaling Commission and other cooperative marine mammal management organizations in northern Alaska'. *Polar Record* 28: 119–26.

Huntingdon, H.P. 1992b. *Wildlife Management and Subsistence Hunting in Alaska*. London: Belhaven Press and Cambridge: Scott Polar Research Institute.

Imbert, B.C. 1986. 'Solo man-hauling journey to the North Pole'. *Polar Record* 23: 340.

Inglefield, A. 1853. *A Summer Search for Sir John Franklin; with a Peep into the Polar Basin*. London: Thomas Harrison.

Ingstad, H. 1937. *East of the Great Glacier*. New York and London: A. Knopf. Translated from *Øst for den store bre*, Oslo 1935.

Ingstad, H. 1969. *Westward to Vinland*. London: Jonathan Cape. Translated from *Vesterveg til Vinland*, Oslo 1965.

Innis, H.A. 1956. *The Fur Trade in Canada*. Toronto: University of Toronto Press.

Isachsen, G. 1925. *Grønland og Grønlands isen*. Oslo: J.W. Cappelen.

Ivanov, V.L. 1979. *Arkhipelag dvukh morey [Archipelago of two seas]*. Moscow: Mysl'.

Jackson, F.G. 1895. *The Great Frozen Land (Bolshaia zemelskiya tundra). Narrative of a Winter Journey Across the Tundras and a Sojourn Among the Samoyads*. London: MacMillan.

Jackson, F.G. 1899. *A Thousand Days in the Arctic*. New York and London: Harper and Brothers.

Jackson, G. 1978. *The British Whaling Trade*. London: Adam & Charles Black.

Jackson, G. 1981. *The rise and fall of English whaling in the seventeenth century*. In: van Holk 1981: 55–68.

Jacob, H.K. s', K. Snoeijing and R. Vaughan (eds) 1983. *Arctic Whaling. Proceedings of the International Symposium Arctic Whaling, February 1983*. Groningen: University of Groningen Arctic Centre.

James, T. 1633. *The Strange and Dangerous Voyage of Captain Thomas James*. London: John Legatt. Reprinted Toronto 1973.

Jansen, H.M. 1972. *A critical account of the written and archaeological sources' evidence concerning the Norse settlements in Greenland. Meddelelser om Grønland* 182 (4). 158 pp.

Jarvis, D.H. *et al.* 1899. *Report of the Cruise of the US Revenue Cutter* Bear *and the Overland Expedition for the Relief of the Whalers in the Arctic Ocean*. Washington: Government Printing Office.

Jasinski, M.E. 1991. 'Russian hunters on Svalbard and the Polar winter'. *Arctic* 44: 156–62.

Jenkins, J.T. 1921. *A History of the Whale Fisheries from the Basque Fisheries of the Tenth Century to the Hunting of the Finner Whale at the Present Time*. London: Witherby.

Jenness, D. 1922. *The Life of the Copper Eskimos. Report of the Canadian Arctic Expedition 1913–1918*, 12. Ottawa: F.A. Acland.

Jenness, D. 1962. *Eskimo Administration, 1. Alaska*. Montreal: Arctic Institute of North America.

Jensen, G. 1988. 'Oversigt over 100 års krydsninger af indlandsisen'. *Grønland* 36: 289–304.

Jensen, R.J. 1975. *The Alaska Purchase and Russian-American Relations*. Seattle and London: University of Washington Press.

Johansen, H. 1898. *Selv-anden paa 86° 14'. Optegnelser fra den norske polarfærd 1893–1896*. Kristiania: H. Aschehoug.

Johnson, G.L. 1983. 'The Fram Expeditions: Arctic Ocean Studies from Floating Ice, 1979–1982'. *Polar Record* 21: 583–9.

Johnson, H. 1907. *The Life and Voyages of Captain Joseph Wiggins*. London: John Murray.

Jones, A.G.E. 1992. *Polar Portraits. Collected Papers*. Whitby: Caedmon Press.

Jones, G. 1984. *A History of the Vikings*. Oxford: Oxford University Press. First published 1968.

Jones, G. 1986. *The Norse Atlantic Saga*. Oxford: Oxford University Press. First published 1964.

Jong, C. de 1972, 1978, 1979. *Geschiedenis van de oude Nederlandse walvisvaart*. 3 vols. Pretoria: University of South Africa.

Jonge, J.K.J. de 1873. *Nova Zembla. De voorwerpen door de Nederlandse zeevaarders na hunne overwintering aldaar in 1597 achtergelaten en in 1871 door kapitein Carlsen teruggevonden, beschreven en toegelicht*. The Hague: Martinus Nijhoff.

Jonge, J.K.J. de 1877. *The Barents Relics Recovered in the Summer of 1876 by Charles L.W. Gardiner*. Translated by S.R. van Campen. London: Trübner.

Jordan, R.H. 1984. *Neo-Eskimo prehistory of Greenland*. In: Damas (ed.) 1984: 540–8.

Jorgensen, J.G. 1990. *Oil Age Eskimos*. Berkeley: University of California Press.

Jull, P. 1985. *Self-Government for Northern Peoples: Canada and the Circumpolar Story*. Yellowknife: Aboriginal Rights and Constitutional Development Secretariat.

Jull, P. 1989. 'L'internationalisme arctique et Inuit'. *Études Internationales* 20: 115–30.

Kanaki, V.G. 1974. *Lyubimaya Arktika [The Beloved Arctic]*. Leningrad: Gidrometeoizdat.

Kane, E.K. 1856a and b. *Arctic Explorations: The Second Grinnell Expedition in search of Sir John Franklin, 1853, 1854, 1855*. 2 vols. Philadelphia: Childs & Peterson.

Kane, E.K. 1856c. *The United States Grinnell Expedition in Search of Sir John Franklin*. Philadelphia: Childs & Peterson. First edition New York 1853.

Kanevskiy, Z. 1977. *Direktor Arktiki [Director of the Arctic]*. Moscow: Izdatelstvo politicheskoy.

Kanevskiy, Z. 1979. *Borot'cya i iskat' [To Struggle and to Search]*. Leningrad: Gidrometeoizdat.

Kanevskiy, Z.M. 1976. *Tsena prognoza [The Price of Weather Forecasting]*. Leningrad: Gidrometeoizdat.

Kanevskiy, Z.M. 1989. *Zachem cheloveku l'dy? [Why Men on the Ice?]*. Moscow: Izdatel'stvo politicheskoy literatury.

Keenleyside, A. 1990. 'Euro-American whaling in the Canadian Arctic: its effects on Eskimo health'. *Arctic Anthropology* 27: 1–19.

Kennan, G. 1910. *Tent Life in Siberia*. London: G.P. Putnam's Sons. Originally published London 1870.

Kennedy, W. 1853. *A Short Narrative of the Second Voyage of the* Prince Albert *in Search of Sir John Franklin*. London: W.H. Dalton.

Kenyon, W.A. 1975. *Tokens of Possession. The Northern Voyages of Martin Frobisher*. Toronto: Royal Ontario Museum.

Kenyon, W.A. (ed.) 1980. *The Journal of Jens Munk, 1619–1620*. Toronto: Royal Ontario Museum.

Khoroshkevich, A.L. 1963. *Torgovlya velikova s Novgoroda pribaltikoy i zhapadnoy Evropoy v xiv–xv vekakh [The Trade of Great Novgorod with the Baltic and West Europe]*. Moscow.

Kimble, G.H.T. 1938. *Geography in the Middle Ages*. London: Methuen.

King, H.G.R. 1989. *The Arctic*. World Bibliographical Series. Oxford: Clio Press.

King, R. 1836a and b. *Narrative of a Journey to the Shores of the Arctic Ocean, in 1833, 1834 and 1835; Under the Command of Captain Back*. 2 vols. London: Richard Bentley.

King, R. 1855. *The Franklin Expedition from First to Last*. London: John Churchill.

Kirwan, L.P. 1962. *A History of Polar Exploration*. Harmondsworth: Penguin Books. Originally published as *The White Road*, London 1959.

Kish, G. 1973. *North-East Passage. Adolf Eric Nordenskiöld, his Life and Times*. Amsterdam: Nico Israel.

Kjems, R. 1981. *Horisonter af is. Erobringen af den grønlandske inlandsis*. Copenhagen: G.E.C. Gad.

Klein, D.R., R.G. White and S. Keller. 1984. *Proceedings of the First International Muskox Symposium*. Fairbanks: Biological Papers of the University of Alaska, Special Report, 4.

Kleivan, H. 1966. *The Eskimos of North-East Labrador*. Oslo: Norsk Polarinstitutt.

Kleivan, I. 1984. *West Greenland Before 1950*. In: Damas (ed.) 1984: 595–621.

Kleivan, I. 1991. 'Greenland's national symbols'. *North Atlantic Studies* 1 (2): 4–16.

Kleivan, I. and E.S. Burch jnr. *et al.* 1988. 'The work of Knud Rasmussen'. *Études/Inuit/Studies* 12 (1–2): 1–286.

Kleivan, I. and B. Sonne. 1985. *Eskimos. Greenland and Canada. Iconography of religions 8. Arctic Peoples*. Leiden: E.J. Brill.

Klutschak, H. 1987. *Overland to Starvation Cove. With the Inuit in Search of Franklin. 1878–1880*. Toronto: University of Toronto Press. Trans. and ed. by W. Barr from: *Als Eskimo unter den Eskimos: Eine Schilderung der Erlebnisse der Schwatka'schen Franklin-Aufsuchungs-Expedition in den Jahren 1878–1880*, Vienna 1881.

Knapp, G. 1992. 'Geographic distribution of northern peoples of the USSR, 1970 and 1979'. *Polar Record* 28: 47–50.

Knapp, G. and T.A. Morehouse. 1991. 'Alaska's North Slope Borough revisited'. *Polar Record* 27: 303–12.

Knuth, E. 1967. *Archaeology of the Musk-Ox Way*. Paris: Centre d'Études Arctiques et Finno-Scandinaves.

Kochetkov, V.K. 1980. 'Vysokoshirotniy eksperimental'nyy' ['High latitude experimental . . .']. *Chelovek i Stikhiya [Man and the Elements]*: 116–18.

Kohl-Larsen, L. *De Poolvlucht van de* Graf Zeppelin *in opdracht van de vereeniging Aeroarctic*. Amsterdam: Allert de Lange. Translated into Dutch from *Die Arktisfahrt des* Graf Zeppelin, Berlin 1931.

Koldewey, K. 1874. *The German Arctic Expedition of 1869–1870 and Narrative of the Wreck of the* Hansa *in the Ice*. London: Sampson Low, Marston, Low & Searle.

Kolsrud, O. 1935. *Til Østgrønlands historie*. Norges Svalbard- og Ishavs-undersøkelser, 29. Oslo: A.W. Brøgger.

Kowal, W.A., P.M. Krahm and O.B. Beattie. 1989. 'Lead levels in human tissues from the Franklin forensic project'. *International Journal of Environmental Analytical Chemistry* 35: 119–26.

Kozlowski, J. and H-G. Bandi. 1984. 'The palaeohistory of circumpolar Arctic colonization'. *Arctic* 37: 359–72.

Krabbe, T.N. 1930. *Greenland. Its Nature, Inhabitants and History*. Copenhagen: Levin & Munksgaard.

Kramer, F.E. 1992. *'Om at idleede sig blandt saa mange Skionheder en Brud'*. *Grønland* 40: 77–97.

Krenkel, E.T. 1939. *Camping at the Pole*. Moscow: Foreign Languages Publishing House.

Krogh, K.J. 1967. *Viking Greenland*. Copenhagen: The National Museum. Translated from *Eric den Rødes Grønland*, Copenhagen 1967.

Krupnik, I.I. 1989. *Arkticheskaya etnoekologiya [Arctic Ethnoecology]*. Moscow: Nauka.

Krypton, C. 1956. *The Northern Sea Route and the Economy of the Soviet North*. London: Methuen.

Kryuchkin, V. 1981. 'Leto v ledyanoy gavani' ['A summer at Ice Haven']. *Vokrug Sveta [Around the World]* 1981 (8): 14–19.

Kryuchkin, V. 1982. 'Po sledam ekspeditsii Barentsa' ['On the track of the Barentsz Expedition']. *Polyarnyy Krug [Polar Circle]*: 238–47.

Kuoljok, K.E. 1985. *The revolution in the North. Soviet ethnography and nationality policy*. Uppsala: *Acta Universitatis Upsaliensis. Studia multiethnica Upsaliensia*. Translated from *Revolutionen i Norr. Om sovjetetnografi och minoritetspolitik*, Uppsala 1979.

Kuralt, C. 1969. *To the Top of the World. The First Plaisted Polar Expedition*. London: Hutchinson.

Kushnarev, Y.G. 1990. *Bering's Search for the Strait: the first Kamchatka Expedition, 1725–1730.* Ed. and trans. E.A.P. Crownhart-Vaughan. Oregon: Oregon Historical Society Press.

Kutsev, G.F. 1989. *Chelovek na severe* [*Man in the North*]. Moscow: Izdatel'stvo politicheskoy literatury.

La Croix, R. de 1954. *Mysteries of the North Pole.* London: Frederick Muller. Translated from *Les disparus du Pôle.*

Lachambre, H. and A. Machuron. 1898. *Andrée's Balloon Expedition in Search of the North Pole.* New York: Frederick A. Stoke & Company.

Laguna, F. de. 1977. *Voyage to Greenland. A Personal Initiation into Anthropology.* New York: W.W. Norton.

Laktionov, A.F. 1955. *Severnyy Polyus. Ocherk istorii puteshestviy k tsentry Arktiki* [*The North Pole. A History of Journeys to the Centre of the Arctic*]. Moscow: Morskoy Transport.

Lamb, W.K. (ed.) 1970. *The Journals and Letters of Sir Alexander Mackenzie.* Hakluyt Society. Cambridge: Cambridge University Press.

Lamont, J. 1876. *Yachting in the Arctic Seas or Notes on Five Voyages of Sport and Discovery in the neighbourhood of Spitsbergen and Novaya Zemlya.* London: Chatto and Windus.

Lanman, C. 1885. *Farthest North; or the Life and Explorations of Lieutenant James Booth Lockwood, of the Greely Arctic Expedition.* New York: D. Appleton.

Lantzeff, G.V. and R.A. Pierce 1973. *Eastwards to Empire: Exploration and Conquest on the Russian Open Frontier, to 1750.* Montreal: McGill-Queen's University Press.

Larsen, H.A. 1967. *The Big Ship.* Toronto and Montreal: McClelland & Stewart.

Larson, L.M. 1917. *The King's Mirror. Speculum Regale. Konungs skuggsjá. Scandinavian Monographs*, 3. New York.

Lauridsen, P. (ed.) 1883. *Jens Munks* Navigatio Septentrionalis. Copenhagen: Gyldendal.

Lauritsen, B. 1984. *Fangstmandsliv og de danske fangstkompagnier i Nordøstgrønland. 1919–1952.* Copenhagen: Komma.

Lauritzen, P. 1983. *Oil and Amulets. Inuit: a People United at the Top of the World.* Breakwater Books. Translated from *Olie og amuletter; i Knud Rasmussens slædespor,* Copenhagen 1979.

Le Goff, J. 1990. *Le merveilleux nordique médiéval.* In: Devers 1990: 21–7.

Le Roy, P.L. 1766. *Rélation des aventures arrivées à quatre matelots russes jettés par une tempête près de l'isle deserte d'Ost-Spitsbergen, sur laquelle ils ont passé six ans et trois mois.* St Petersburg.

Le Roy, P.L. 1774. *A narrative of the singular adventures of four Russian sailors, who were cast away on the desert island of East-Spitsbergen.* . . . In: J. Staehlin von Storcksburg, *An Account of the New Northern Archipelago Lately Discovered by the Russians in the Seas of Kamchatka and Anadir,* pp. 41–118. London: C. Heydinger.

Lebedev, A.A. and I.P. Mazuruk. 1991. *Nad Arktikoy i Antarktikoy* [*Above the Arctic and Antarctic*]. Moscow: Mysl'.

Leslie, A. 1879. *The Arctic Voyages of Adolf Erik Nordenskiöld. 1858–1879.* London: MacMillan.

Leslie, J., R. Jameson and H. Murray. 1835. *Narrative of Discovery and Adventure in the Polar Seas and Regions.* Edinburgh: Oliver and Boyd.

Levere, T.H. 1993. *Science and the Canadian Arctic. A Century of Exploration 1818–1918.* Cambridge: Cambridge University Press.

Levin, B. 1982. 'Otto Yul'yevich Shmidt – uchenyy-entsiklopedist' ['academic-encyclopedist']. *Nauka i Zhizn'* [*Science and Life*] 1982(3): 50–6.

Levin, M.G. and L.P. Potapov (eds) 1964. *The Peoples of Siberia.* Chicago: University of Chicago Press. Translated from *Narody Sibiri,* Moscow 1956.

Lewin, W.H. 1935. *The Great North Pole Fraud.* London: C.W. Daniel.

Lewis, A. 1905. *The Life and Work of the Rev. E.J. Peck Among the Eskimos*. London: Hodder & Stoughton.

Lidegaard, M. 1985. *Hans – en eskimo*. Copenhagen: Nyt Nordisk Forlag, Arnold Busck.

Lidegaard, M. 1991. *Grønlands historie*. Copenhagen: Nyt Nordisk Forlag, Arnold Busck.

Lied, J. 1945. *Prospector in Siberia: the Autobiography of Jonas Lied*. New York: Oxford University Press.

Liljeqvist, G.H. 1987. *The balloon flight of Salomon A. Andrée aiming at reaching the North Pole*. In: Malaurie 1987: 217–29.

Lillingston, F.G.I. 1876. *The Land of the White Bear: Being a Short Account of the* Pandora*'s Voyage During the Summer of 1875*. Portsmouth: J. Griffin and London: Simpkin, Marshall and Co.

Limcher, A.L. (ed.) 1982. 'Perv'ii skvoznoi. Iz dnevnika L.F. Limcher, vracha ekspeditsii na ledokol'nom parokhode *Aleksandr Sibiryakov*' ['The first through voyage. From the diary of L.F. Limcher, expedition doctor on the icebreaking steamer *A. Sibiryakov*']. *Polyarnyy Krug* [*Polar Circle*]: 181–92.

Lindeman, M. 1869. *Die arktische Fischerei der deutschen Seestädte. 1620–1868*. Gotha: Justus Perthes.

Lindeman, M. and O. Finsch. 1875. *Die zweite Deutsche Nordpolarfahrt in den Jahren 1869 und 1870*. Leipzig: F.A. Brockhaus.

Linklater, E. 1972. *The Voyage of the* Challenger. London: John Murray.

Liversidge, D. 1960. *The Third Front. The Strange Story of the Secret War in the Arctic*. London: Souvenir Press.

Lloyd, C. 1970. *Mr Barrow of the Admiralty. A life of Sir John Barrow, 1764–1848*. London: Collins.

Lønø, O. 1972. *Norske fangstmenns overvintringer, 1. 1795–1892*. Oslo: Norsk Polarinstitutt.

Lønø, O. 1976. *Norske fangstmenns overvintringer, 3. 1892–1905*. Oslo: Norsk Polarinstitutt.

Loomis, C.C. 1972. *Weird and Tragic Shores. The Story of Charles Francis Hall, Explorer*. London: MacMillan.

Lubbock, B. 1937. *The Arctic Whalers*. Glasgow: Brown, Son & Ferguson.

Lynnerup, N., J. Arneborg and J.P. Hart Hansen. 1991. 'Norse anthropological remains'. *Polar Record* 27: 132–3.

Lyon, G.F. 1824. *The Private Journal of Captain G.F. Lyon of HMS* Hecla *During the Recent Voyage of Discovery under Captain Parry*. London: John Murray. Reprinted 1980.

Lyon, G.F. 1825. *A Brief Narrative of an Unsuccessful Attempt to Reach Repulse Bay, Through Sir Thomas Rowe's Welcome, in HMS* Griper, *in the Year 1824*. London: John Murray.

Lyon, W.K. 1987. *Submarine exploration of the North Pole region. History, problems, positioning and piloting*. In: Malaurie 1987: 313–28.

Maat, G.J.R. 1981. *Human remains at the Dutch whaling stations on Spitsbergen*. In: van Holk 1981: 153–201.

M'Clintock, F.L. 1859. *The Voyage of the* Fox *in the Arctic Seas. A Narrative of the Discovery of the Fate of Sir John Franklin and his Companions*. London: John Murray. Revised edition London 1869.

Macdonald, R. St J. (ed.) 1966. *The Arctic Frontier*. Toronto: University of Toronto Press.

M'Dougall, G.F. 1857. *The Eventful Voyage of HM Discovery Ship* Resolute *to the Arctic Regions in Search of Sir John Franklin . . . in 1852, 1853, 1854*. London: Longman, Brown, Green, Longmans & Roberts.

MacGahan, J.A. 1876. *Under the Northern Lights*. London: Sampson Low, Marston, Searle & Rivington.

McGhee, R. 1978. *Canadian Arctic Prehistory*. Toronto: Van Nostrand Reinhold.

McGhee, R. 1984. *Thule prehistory of Canada*. In: Damas (ed.) 1984: 369–76.

McGhee, R. 1987. *The relationship between the medieval Norse and Eskimos*. In: Hacquebord and Vaughan 1987: 51–60.

McGovern, T.H. 1981. *The economics of extinction in Norse Greenland*. In: T.M.L. Wigley, M.J. Ingram, and G. Farmer (eds). *Climate and History*, Cambridge: Cambridge University Press, pp. 404–33.

McGovern, T.H. 1991. 'Climate, correlation and causation in Norse Greenland'. *Arctic Anthropology* 28: 77–100.

MacInnes, T. (ed.) 1932. *Klengenberg of the Arctic. An Autobiography*. London and Toronto: Jonathan Cape.

MacKay, D. 1937. *The Honourable Company. A History of the Hudson's Bay Company*. London: Cassell.

McLaren, A.S. 1984. 'Transporting Arctic petroleum: a role for commercial submarines'. *Polar Record* 22: 7–23.

McLaren, A. 1987. *The Arctic submarine: its evolution and scientific and commercial potential*. In: Malaurie 1987: 329–41.

MacLaren, I.S. 1993. 'Samuel Hearne and the printed word'. *Polar Record* 29: 166–7.

MacMillan, D.B. 1918. *Four Years in the White North*. New York and London: Harper & Brothers.

MacMillan, D.B. 1934. *How Peary Reached the Pole*. Boston and New York: Houghton Mifflin.

Magnus, O. 1555. *Historia de gentibus septentrionalibus*. Rome: Joannes Maria de Viottis.

Magnusson, M. and H. Pálsson (trans.) 1965. *The Vinland Sagas. The Norse Discovery of America*. Harmondsworth: Penguin.

Makeyev, V., V. Pitul'ko and A. Kasparov. 1992. 'Ostrova De-Longa: an analysis of palaeoenvironmental data'. *Polar Record* 28: 301–6.

Malaurie, J. 1956. *The Last Kings of Thule. A Year Among the Polar Eskimos of Greenland*. London: George Allen & Unwin. Translated from *Les deniers rois de Thule*, Paris 1955. New edition, New York 1982.

Malaurie, J. (ed.) 1987. *Pôle Nord 1983. Tenth Colloquy of the Centre d'Études Arctiques*. Paris: Centre National de la Recherche Scientifique.

Malaurie, J. 1990. *Ultima Thulé*. Paris: Bordas.

Malaurie, J. 1991. *Les Esquimaux Polaires, Nord-Ouest du Groenland, 1818–1989*. In: Malaurie (ed.) 1991: 47–97.

Malaurie, J. (ed.) 1991. *Arctique horizon 2000: les peuples chasseurs et éleveurs. Deuxième dialogue franco-soviétique*. Paris: Centre National de la Recherche Scientifique.

Manker, E. 1954. *Les Lapons des montagnes suédoises*. Paris: Gallimard. Translated from *De svenska fjällapparna*, Stockholm 1947.

Manker, E. 1963. *People of Eight Seasons*. Gothenburg: Tre Tryckare Cagher.

Marcus, A.R. 1991. 'Out in the cold: Canada's experimental Inuit relocation to Grise Fjord and Resolute Bay'. *Polar Record* 27: 285–96.

Marcus, G.J. 1980. *The Conquest of the North Atlantic*. Woodbridge: Boydell Press.

Markham, A.H. 1875. *A Whaling Cruise to Baffin's Bay and the Gulf of Boothia. And an Account of the Rescue of the Crew of the* Polaris. Second edition. London: Sampson Low, Marston, Low & Searle.

Markham, A.H. 1878. *The Great Frozen Sea. A Personal Narrative of the Voyage of the* Alert *during the Arctic Expedition of 1875–6*. Third edition. London: Daldy, Isbister & Co.

Markham, A.H. 1879. *Northward Ho!* London: MacMillan.

Markham, A.H. 1891 *Life of Sir John Franklin and the North-West Passage*. London: George Philip & Son.

Markham, A.H. (ed.) 1880. *The Voyages and Works of John Davis*. London: Hakluyt Society.

Markham, A.H. (ed.) 1881. *The Voyages of William Baffin, 1612–1622*. London: Hakluyt Society.

Markham, C.R. 1873. *The Threshold of the Unknown Region*. London: Sampson Low, Marston, Low & Searle.

Markham, C.R. 1877. *A Refutation of the Report of the Scurvy Committee*. Portsmouth: J. Griffin.

Markham, C.R. 1889. *A Life of John Davis the Navigator. 1550–1605*. London: George Philip.

Markham, C.R. 1921. *The Lands of Silence: a History of Arctic and Antarctic Exploration*. Cambridge: Cambridge University Press.

Marucci, G. 1980. *Les peuples de l'Arctique*. Paris: Atlas.

Meletinskiy, E.M. 1981. *Paleoaziatskiy epos o Borone i problema otnosheniy Severo-Vostochnoy Azii i Severo-Zapadnoy Ameriki v oblasti fol'klora* [*The paleoasiatic raven epos and problems of the relationship between north-east Asian and north-west American folklore*]. In: Gurvich (ed.) 1981: 182–200.

Melville, G.W. 1896. *In the Lena Delta*. Boston: Houston, Mifflin and Co. First published Boston 1885.

Meriot, C. 1984. 'The Saami peoples from the time of the voyage of Ottar to Thomas von Westen'. *Arctic* 37: 373–84.

Metel'skiy, G. 1978. *Po kromke dvukh okeanov* [*On the Edge of Two Oceans*] Moscow: Mysl'.

Miethe, A. and H. Hergesell. 1911. *Mit Zeppelin nach Spitzbergen*. Berlin: Bong & Co.

Mikkelsen, E. 1934. *De Østgrønlandske Eskimoers historie*. Copenhagen: Gyldendalske Boghandel-Nordisk Forlag.

Miles, P. and N.J.R. Wright. 1978. 'An outline of mineral extraction in the Arctic'. *Polar Record* 19: 11–38.

Miller, F.T. 1928. *Byrd's Great Adventure. One Thousand Years of Polar Exploration*. London: Stanley Paul.

Miller, T.P. 1984. *Mineral resources: Arctic Alaska*. In: Westermeyer and Shusterich 1984: 59–74.

Milton Freeman, M.R. 1976a, b, and c. *Inuit Land Use and Occupancy Project*. 3 vols. Ottawa: Ministry of Supply and Services.

Mirsky, J. 1954. *Elisha Kent Kane and the Seafaring Frontier*. Boston: Little, Brown and Co.

Mirsky, J. 1970. *To the Arctic! The Story of Northern Exploration from Earliest Times to the Present*. Chicago and London: University of Chicago Press. Originally published 1934.

Mitlyanskaya, T.B. 1976. *Khudozhniki Chukotki* [*Chukchi Artists*]. Moscow: Izobrazitel'noye iskusstvo.

Mittelholzer, W. 1925. *By Airplane towards the North Pole. An Account of an Expedition to Spitzbergen in the Summer of 1923*. London: George Allen and Unwin. Translated from *Im Flugzug dem Nordpol entgegen*, Zürich 1924.

Mochanov, Yu.A. 1977. *Drevneyshiye etapy zaseleniya chelovekom severo- vostochnoy Azii* [*Early Stages in the Colonization of North-East Asia*]. Novosibirsk: Nauka.

Møhl, J. 1982. 'Ressourceudnyttelse fra norrøne og eskimoiske affaldslag belyst gennem knoglematerialet'. *Grønland* 30: 286–95.

Molett, W.E. 1989. 'Analysis of Admiral Peary's trip to the North Pole'. *Navigation* 36: 139–46.

Møller, J.K. 1985. 'Jens Bielkes grønlandsberetning. 1605'. *Grønland* 33: 117–48.

Monberg, J. 1990. 'Nordboernes sømærker og stednavne på Grønland i middelalderen'. *Grønland* 38: 220–4.

Monzino, G. 1971. 'Cosi ho conquistato il Polo Nord'. *Tempo* 33 (29): 32–40, (30): 29–37, (31): 28–35.

Monzino, G. 1987. *The Italian Guido Monzino Expedition to the North Pole*. In: Malaurie 1987: 249–50.

Moore, S.E. 1992. 'Summer records of bowhead whales in the north-eastern Chukchi Sea'. *Arctic* 45: 398–400.

Moore, S.E. and J.T. Clarke. 1991. 'Estimates of Bowhead Whale (*Balaena mysticetus*) numbers in the Beaufort Sea during late summer'. *Arctic* 44: 43–6.

Morehouse, T.A. and L.Leask. 1980. 'Alaska's North Slope Borough: oil, money and Eskimo self-government'. *Polar Record* 20: 19–29.

Morison, S.E. 1971. *The European Discovery of America. The Northern Voyages. AD 500–1600*. New York: Oxford University Press.

Morrison, D. 1991. 'The Copper Inuit soapstone trade'. *Arctic* 44: 239–46.

Morrison, W.R. 1986. 'Canadian sovereignty and the Inuit of the central and eastern Arctic'. *Études/Inuit/Studies* 10: 245–59.

Morton, A.S. 1973. *A History of the Canadian West to 1870–71*. Second edition. Toronto: University of Toronto Press.

Mörzer Bruyns, W.F.J. (ed.) 1985a and b. *De eerste tocht van de* Willem Barents *naar de Noordelijke Ijszee, 1878*. 2 vols. Werken van de Linschoten-Vereeniging, 84, 85. Zutphen: De Walburg Pers.

Mörzer Bruyns, W.F.J. 1986. 'The Dutch in the Arctic in the late nineteenth century'. *Polar Record* 23: 15–26.

Moss, E.L. 1878. *Shores of the Polar Sea. A Narrative of the Arctic Expedition of 1875–6*. London: Marcus Ward.

Motley, J.L. 1904. *The United Netherlands. A History, 4*. London: John Murray.

Mountfield, D. 1974. *A History of the Arctic*. New York: Dial Press.

Mowat, F. 1951. *People of the Deer*. Boston: Little, Brown & Co.

Mowat, F. 1960. *The Desperate People*. London: Michael Joseph. Originally published 1959.

Müller, G.F. 1986. *Bering's Voyages: the Reports from Russia*. Ed. and trans. C. Urness. Fairbanks: University of Alaska Press.

Muller, S. 1874. *Geschiedenis der Noordsche Compagnie*. Utrecht: van der Post.

Munn, H.T. 1932. *Prairie Trails and Arctic By-Ways*. London: Hurst and Blackett.

Naber, S.P.L'H. (ed.) 1914. *Reizen van Jan Huyghen van Linschoten naar het Noorden (1594–1595)*. Werken van de Linschoten-Vereeniging, 8. The Hague: Martinus Nijhoff.

Naber, S.P.L'H. (ed.) 1917a and b. *Reizen van Willem Barents, Jacob van Heemskerck en anderen naar het Noorden, 1594–1597 . . . verhaald door Gerrit de Veer*. Werken van de Linschoten-Vereeniging, 14, 15. The Hague: Martinus Nijhoff.

Naber, S.P.L'H. (ed.) 1921. *Henry Hudson's reize onder nederlandsche vlag, 1609*. Werken van de Linschoten-Vereeniging, 19. The Hague: Martinus Nijhoff.

Naber, S.P.L'H. (ed.) 1924. *Hessel Gerritsz. Beschryvinghe van der Samoyeden landt en Histoire du pays nommé Spitsberghe*. Werken van de Linschoten-Vereeniging, 23. The Hague: Martinus Nijhoff.

Naber, S.P.L'H. (ed.) 1930. *Walvischvaarten, overwinteringen en jachtbedrijven in het Hooge Noorden. 1633–1635*. Utrecht: A. Oosthoek.

Nansen, F. 1890a and b. *The First Crossing of Greenland*. 2 vols. London: Longmans, Green. Translated from *Paa ski over Grønland*, Kristiania 1890.

Nansen, F. 1893a. 'How can the North Polar region be crossed?' *Geographical Journal* 1: 1–32.

Nansen, F. 1893b. *Eskimo Life*. London: Longmans, Green. Translated from *Eskimoliv*, Kristiania 1891.

Nansen, F. 1897a and b. *Farthest North*. 2 vols. Westminster: Archibald Constable. Translated from *Fram over Polhavet*, Kristiania 1897.

Nansen, F. 1911a and b. *In Northern Mists*. 2 vols. London: William Heinemann. Translated from *Nord i tåkeheimen*, Kristiania 1911.

Nansen, F. 1914. *Through Siberia, the Land of the Future*. London: William Heinemann.

Nansen, F. 1925. *Hunting and Adventure in the Arctic*. London: J.M. Dent. Translated from *Blant sel og bjørn*, Kristiania 1924.

Nares, G.S. 1876. *The Official Report of the Recent Arctic Expedition*. London: John Murray.

Nares, G. 1878a and b. *Narrative of a Voyage to the Polar Sea During 1875–6*. 2 vols. London: Sampson Low, Marston, Searle & Rivington.

Nassichuk, W.W. 1987. 'Forty years of northern non-renewable natural resource development'. *Arctic* 40: 274–84.

Neatby, L.H. 1966. *Conquest of the Last Frontier*. Athens, Ohio: Ohio University Press.

Neatby, L.H. 1970. *The Search for Franklin*. London: Arthur Barker.

Neatby, L.H. (ed. and trans.) 1967. *Frozen Ships. The Arctic Diary of Johann Miertsching, 1850–1854*. Toronto: MacMillan of Canada.

Neering, R. 1989. *Continental Dash. The Russian-American Telegraph*. Ganges, British Columbia: Horsdal & Schubart.

Nelson, K. 1958. *Klondy. A Daughter of the Gold Rush*. London: Robert Hale.

Newcomb, R.L. 1882. *Our Lost Explorers: the Narrative of the* Jeannette *Arctic Expedition*. Hartford, Conn.: American Publishing Co.

Newman, P.C. 1985. *Company of Adventurers, 1*. New York: Viking Penguin.

Newman, P.C. 1987. *Caesars of the Wilderness. Company of Adventurers, 2*. New York: Viking Penguin.

Newman. P.C. 1989. *Empire of the Bay: An Illustrated History of the Hudson's Bay Company*. Toronto: Madison Press.

Newman, P.C. 1991. *Merchant Princes. Company of Adventurers, 3*. Toronto: Penguin Books Canada.

Newton, A.P. 1926. *Travel and Travellers of the Middle Ages*. New York: Kegan Paul.

Niedekker, D.B. 1989. 'Benoorden Rusland om. Nederlanders op zoek naar de noord-oostpassage'. *Spiegel Historiael* 24: 253–8.

Nielsen, R.H. 1993. 'Chill warnings from Greenland'. *New Scientist*, 28 August 1993.

Nikitin, N.I. 1987. *Sibirskaya epopeya XVII veka. Nachalo osvoyeniya Sibiri russkimi lyud'mi [Siberian Epic of the Seventeenth Century. The Beginning of the Russian Opening Up of Siberia]*. Moscow: Nauka.

Nobile, U. 1928. *In volo alla conquista del segreto polare. Da Roma a Teller, Alaska, attraverso il Polo Nord*. Milan: Mondadori.

Nobile, U. 1961. *My Polar Flights. An Account of the Voyages of the Airships* Italia *and* Norge. London: Frederick Muller.

Noice, H. 1924. *With Stefansson in the Arctic*. London: George G. Harrap.

Nooter, G.W. (ed.) 1984. *Life and Survival in the Arctic*. The Hague: Government Publishing Office.

Nordal, J. and V. Kristinsson. 1975. *Iceland 874–1974*. Reykjavik: Central Bank of Iceland.

Nordenskiöld, A.E. 1881a and b. *The Voyage of the* Vega *Round Asia and Europe*. 2 vols. London: MacMillan. Translated from Vegas *färd kring Asien och Europa*, 2 vols., Stockholm 1880, 1881.

Nordenskiöld, A.E. 1885. *Den andra Dicksonska Expeditionen till Grönland*. Stockholm: F. & G. Beijers.

Nordqvist, O.A. 1983. '*Vegas*' voyage through the North-East Passage'. *Polar Geography and Geology* 7: 1–71.

Nørlund, P. 1936. *Viking Settlers in Greenland*. Cambridge: Cambridge University Press. Translated from *De gamle nordbobygder ved verdens ende*, Copenhagen 1934.

Nourse, J.E. 1884. *American Explorations in The Ice Zones*. Boston: D. Lothrop.

Nourse, J.E. (ed.) 1879. *Narrative of the Second Arctic Expedition made by Charles F. Hall*. Washington: Government Printing Office.

Nulin, G. 1982. 'Iz istorii morskogo flota. Plavaniye V.Ya. Chichagova' ['From the History of the Navy: Chichagov's Voyage']. *Morskoy Flot* [*The Fleet*] 1982 (8): 80.

Nungak, Z. 1990. 'Exiles in the High Arctic'. *Arctic Circle* 1 (2): 36–43.

Nünlist, H. 1966. *Spitsbergen. The Story of the 1962 Swiss Spitsbergen Expedition*. London: Nicholas Kaye. Translated from: *Spitzbergen*, Zurich 1963.

Nuttall, M. 1992. *Arctic Homeland. Kinship, Community and Development in Northwest Greenland*. London: Belhaven Press and Cambridge: Scott Polar Research Institute.

Odsbjerg, A. 1992. *Lauge Koch – Grønlandsforskeren*. Copenhagen: Komma & Clausen.

Oesau, W. 1937. *Schleswig-Holsteins Grönlandfahrt auf Walfischfang und Robbenschlag vom 17–19 Jahrhundert*. Glückstadt-Hamburg: J.J. Augustin.

Oesau, W. 1955. *Hamburgs Grönlandfahrt auf Walfischfang und Robbenschlag vom 17–19 Jahrhundert*. Glückstadt-Hamburg: J.J. Augustin.

Olsen, A. 1993. 'Stor succes for Paris-udstilling om iskerneboring'. *Grønland* 41: 16–17.

Olsen, K. 1965. *Et hundeliv. Oplevelser med Slædepatruljen i Nordøstgrønland under 2. Verdenskrig*. Copenhagen: Gyldendal.

Osborn, S. 1865. *Stray Leaves from an Arctic Journal or Eighteen Months in the Polar Regions in Search of Sir John Franklin's Expedition in 1850–51*. Edinburgh and London: William Blackwood and Sons. Originally published London 1852.

Osborn, S. (ed.) 1856. *The Discovery of the North-West Passage by HMS* Investigator, *Capt. R. M'Clure. 1850, 1851, 1852, 1853, 1854*. London: Longman, Brown, Green, Longmans & Roberts. Reprinted Edmonton 1969.

Osczevski, R.J. 1990. 'Frederick Cook's Polar Journey: a Reconstruction'. *Polar Record* 26: 225–32.

Osherenko, G. and O.B. Young. 1989. *The Age of the Arctic: Hot Conflicts and Cold Realities*. Cambridge: Cambridge University Press.

Ostermann, H. 1935. *De første efterretninger om Østgrønlændingerne. 1752*. Norges Svalbard- og Ishavs-undersøkelser, 29. Oslo: A.W. Brøgger.

Østreng, W. 1977. *Politics in High Latitudes. The Svalbard Archipelago*. London: C. Hurst.

Oswalt, W.H. 1979. *Eskimos and Explorers*. Novato, Calif.: Chandler & Sharp.

Ousland, B. 1991. 'The Hard Way to the North Pole'. *National Geographic Magazine* 179: 124–34.

Owen, R. 1978. *The Fate of Franklin*. London: Hutchinson.

Papanin, I.D. 1939. *Life on an Ice Floe*. New York: Julian Messner.

Parry, A. 1963. *Parry of the Arctic. The Life Story of Admiral Sir Edward Parry. 1790–1855*. London: Chatto & Windus.

Parry, E. 1858. *Memoirs of Rear-Admiral Sir W. Edward Parry*. London: Longman, Brown, Green, Longmans & Roberts.

Parry, W.E. 1821. *Journal of a Voyage for the Disovery of a North-West Passage from the Atlantic to the Pacific; Performed in the Years 1819–20 in HM Ships* Hecla and Griper *under the Orders of William Edward Parry*. Philadelphia: Abraham Small.

Parry, W.E. 1824. *Journal of a Second Voyage for the Discovery of a North-West Passage from the Atlantic to the Pacific; Performed in the Years 1821–22–23 in HM Ships* Fury and Hecla. London: John Murray.

Parry, W.E. 1826. *Journal of a Third Voyage for the Discovery of a North-West Passage from the Atlantic to the Pacific; Performed in the Years 1824–25 in HM Ships* Hecla and Fury. London: John Murray.

Parry, W.E. 1828. *Narrative of an Attempt to Reach the North Pole . . . in the Year 1827*. London: John Murray.

Pasetskiy, V.M. 1980. *Pervootkryvateli Novoy Zemli* [*The Discoverers of Novaya Zemlya*]. Moscow: Nauka.

Pasetskiy, V.M. 1982. *Vitus Bering*. Moscow: Nauka.

Pasetskiy, V.M. 1987. *Frit'of Nansen: 1861–1930*. Moscow: Nauka.

Payer, J. 1876a and b. *New Lands within the Arctic Circle. Narrative of the Discoveries of the Austrian Ship* Tegetthof *in the Years 1872–1874*. 2 vols. London: MacMillan. Translated from *Die österreichisch-ungarische Nordpol-Expedition in den Jahren 1872–1874*, Vienna 1876.

Peary, R.E. 1898a and b. *Northward over the 'Great Ice'*. 2 vols. New York: Frederick A. Stokes.

Peary, R.E. 1907. *Nearest the Pole. A narrative of the Polar Expedition of the Peary Arctic Club in the SS* Roosevelt, *1905–1906*. London: Hutchinson.

Peary, R.E. 1910. *The North Pole. Its Discovery in 1909 under the Auspices of the Peary Arctic Club*. New York: Frederick A. Stokes.

Peary, R.E. 1917. *Secrets of Polar Travel*. New York: The Century Co.

Pellham, E. 1631. *God's Power and Providence; Shewed, in the Miraculous Preservation and Deliverance of eight Englishmen, left by Mischance in Green-land, Anno 1630*. London: John Partridge. Reprinted in White 1855: 251–83.

Pelly, D.F. 1993. 'Dawn of Nunavut'. *Canadian Geographic* 113 (2): 21–9.

Petersen, H. and E. Staffeldt (eds) 1978. *Bogen om Grønland. Fortid, nutid og fremtid*. Copenhagen: Politikens Forlag.

Petersen, J.C.C. 1857. *Erindringer fra Polarlandene optegnede af Carl Petersen, tolk ved Pennys og Kanes nordexpeditioner, 1850–1855*. Copenhagen: P.G. Philipsen.

Petersen [J.C.] C. 1860. *Den sidste Franklin-Expedition med Fox, Capt. M'Clintock*. Copenhagen: Fr. Wøldikes Forlagsboghandel.

Petersen, R. 1984. *East Greenland before 1950*. In: Damas (ed.) 1984: 622–39.

Petrow, R. 1967. *Across the Top of Russia*. London: Hodder & Stoughton.

Pfizenmayer, E.W. 1939. *Siberian Man and Mammoth*. London and Glasgow: Blackie & Son. Translated from *Mammutleichen und Urwaldmenschen in Nordost-Siberien*, Leipzig 1926.

Phipps, C.J. 1774. *A Voyage Toward the North Pole Undertaken by His Majesty's Command, 1773*. London: J. Nourse. Reprinted Whitby 1978.

Pimlott, D., D. Brown and K. Sam. 1976. *Oil Under the Ice*. Ottawa: Canadian Arctic Resources Committee.

Pinkhenson, D.M. 1962. *Istoriya otkrytiya i osvoyeniya Severnogo morskogo puti, 2. Problema Severnogo morskogo puti v epokhu kapitalizma* [*History of the Discovery and Development of the Northen Sea Route in the Capitalist era*]. Leningrad: Izdatel'stvo Morskoy Transport.

Platonov, S.F. and A.N. Andreyev. 1922. *Ocherki po istorii kolonizatsii Severa* [*Studies on the History of the Colonization of the North*]. Petrograd.

Pognon. E. 1984. 'Cosmology and cartography'. *Arctic* 37: 334–40.

Popov, A.A. 1964. *The Nganasans*. In: Levin and Potapov 1964: 571–86.

Popov, S. 1982. '*Legendarnyy A. Sibiryakov*' ['The legendary *A. Sibiryakov*']. *Morskoy Flot* [*The Fleet*] 1982 (10): 22–3.

Powell, B.D. 1992. 'Lead poisoning and the Franklin Expedition'. *Polar Record* 28: 252–3.

Powell, T. 1961. *The Long Rescue*. London: W.H. Allen.

Powys, L. 1928. *Henry Hudson*. New York: Harper.

Preuss, L. 1932. 'The dispute between Denmark and Norway over the sovereignty of East Greenland'. *American Journal of International Law* 26: 469–87.

Prokhorov, A.M. 1988. *Sovetskiy entsiklopedicheskiy slovar'* [*Soviet encyclopedia*]. Moscow: Sovetskaya Entsiklopediya.

Prokhorov, B. 1989. *USSR: How to Save Yamal*. International Work Group for Indigenous Affairs. Newsletter 58: 113–28. Copenhagen.

Prokof'yeva, E.D. 1964. *The Nentsy*. In: Levin and Potapov 1964: 547–70.

Pullen, H.F. (ed.) 1979. *The Pullen Expedition in Search of Sir John Franklin: the Original Diaries, Log and Letters of Commander W.J.S. Pullen*. Toronto: Arctic History Press.

Pullen, T.C. 1981. *The development of Arctic ships*. In: Zaslow (ed.) 1981: 153–62.

Pullen, T.C. and C. Swithinbank. 1991. 'Transits of the North-West Passage, 1906–90'. *Polar Record* 27: 365–7.

Purchas, S. (ed.) 1906a and b. *Hakluytus posthumus or Purchas his Pilgrimes, 13, 14*. Glasgow: James MacLehose & Sons.

Putnam, G.P. 1930. *Andrée. The Record of a Tragic Adventure*. New York: Brewer & Warren.

Quinn, D.B. 1974. *England and the Discovery of America, 1481–1620*. London: George Allen & Unwin.

Rabo, Sh. and P. Vittenburg. 1924. *Polyarnye strany* [*The Polar regions*], *1914–1924*. Leningrad: Izdatel'skiy otdel morskogo vedomstva.

Rae, J. 1850. *Narrative of an Expedition to the Shores of the Arctic Sea, 1846–1847*. London: T. & W. Boone.

Rasky, F. 1976. *The Polar Voyagers*. Toronto: McGraw-Hill Ryerson.

Rasmussen, K. 1921. *Greenland by the Polar Sea. The Story of the Thule Expedition from Melville Bay to Cape Morris Jesup*. London: William Heinemann. Translated from *Grønland langs Polhavet*, Copenhagen 1919.

Rasmussen, K. 1933. *Across Arctic America. Narrative of the Fifth Thule Expedition*. New York and London: G.P. Putnam's Sons. Originally published 1927. Translated from *Fra Grønland til Stillehavet*, 2 vols, Copenhagen 1925, 1926.

Rawlins, D. 1973. *Peary at the North Pole. Fact or Fiction?* Washington and New York: Robert B. Luce.

Ray, D.J. 1975. *The Eskimos of Bering Strait, 1650–1898*. Seattle: University of Washington Press.

Ray, P.H. 1885. *Report of the International Polar Expedition to Point Barrow, Alaska*. US Signals Office, Arctic Publications. Washington, D.C.: Government Printing Office.

Reed, J.C. and A.G. Ronhovde. 1971. *Arctic Laboratory. A History (1947–1966) of the Naval Arctic Research Laboratory at Point Barrow, Alaska*. Washington: Arctic Institute of North America.

Reeves, R., E. Mitchell, A. Mansfield and M.McLaughlin. 1983. 'Distribution and migration of the bowhead whale', *Balaena mysticetus*, in the eastern North American Arctic'. *Arctic* 36: 5–64.

Reinke-Kunze, C. 1992. *Aufbruch in die weisse Wildnis. Die Geschichte der deutschen Polarforschung*. Hamburg: Kabel.

Remie, C. 1984. *How Ukpaktoor lost his buttock and what he got in exchange for it*. In: Nooter (ed.) 1984: 97–120.

Reynolds, E.E. 1949. *Nansen*. Harmondsworth: Penguin Books. Originally published 1932.

Rich, E.E. 1958, 1959. *The History of the Hudson's Bay Company 1670–1870*. 2 vols. London: Hudson's Bay Record Society.

Rich, E.E. 1967. *The Fur Trade and the North-West to 1857*. Toronto: McClelland & Stewart.

Rich, E.E. (ed.) 1953. *John Rae's Correspondence with the Hudson's Bay Company on Arctic Exploration 1844–1855*. London: Hudson's Bay Record Society.

Richards, R.L. 1985. *Dr John Rae*. Whitby: Caedmon Press.

Richardson, J. 1852. *Arctic Searching Expedition: a Journal of a Boat-Voyage Through Rupert's Land*

and the Arctic Sea in Search of the Discovery Ships under Command of Sir John Franklin. New York: Harper and Brothers. First edition London 1851.

Richardson, J. 1861. *The Polar Regions.* Edinburgh: Adam and Charles Black.

Richter, S. 1946. *Jan Mayen i krigsårene.* Oslo: Norges Svalbard- og Ishavs-undersøkelser, 66. Offprinted from *Norsk Geografisk Tidsskrift* 11: 63–86.

Riewe, R. 1992. 'The demise of the Great White North: environmental impacts on the circumpolar aboriginal peoples'. *Information North* 18 (4), Calgary: Arctic Institute of North America.

Riffenburgh, B. 1991. 'James Gordon Bennett, the *New York Herald* and the Arctic'. *Polar Record* 27: 9–16.

Riffenburgh, B. 1993. *The Myth of the Explorer; the Press, Sensationalism, and Geographical Discovery.* London: Belhaven Press and Cambridge: Scott Polar Research Institute.

Rink, H. 1877. *Danish Greenland, its People and Products.* London: Henry S. King.

Rink, H. (ed.) 1878. *Memoirs of Hans Hendrik the Arctic Traveller, Serving under Kane, Hayes, Hall and Nares, 1853–1876.* Translated from the Eskimo by Dr Henry Rink. London: Trübner.

Rodahl, K. 1946. *Et år under breen.* Oslo: Gyldendal Norsk Forlag.

Rodahl, K. 1949. *Vitamin sources in Arctic regions.* Skrifter 91. Oslo: Norsk Polarinstitutt.

Rodahl, K. 1955. *T-3. Beretningen om tre mænds eventyrlige ophold på en flydende is-ø ved Nordpolen.* Copenhagen: Det Danske Forlag.

Rogne, F. 1981. *Ishavsliv. Norske fangstfolk på Grønland.* Oslo: Det Norske Samlaget.

Roos, W. de 1980. *North-West Passage.* London: Hollis & Carter. Originally published in French, Paris 1979.

Ross, A.S.C. 1940. *The* Terfinnas *and* Beormas *of Ohthere.* Leeds: School of English Language. Texts and Monographs 7.

Ross, J. 1819. *A Voyage of Discovery, made under the Orders of the Admiralty, in HM Ships* Isabella *and* Alexander, *for the Purpose of Exploring Baffin's Bay, and Enquiring into the Probability of a North-West Passage.* London: John Murray.

Ross, J. 1835. *Narrative of a Second Voyage in Search of a North-West Passage and of a Residence in the Arctic Regions during the Years 1829, 1830, 1831, 1832, 1833.* London: A.W. Webster.

Ross, J. and J.M. Savelle. 1990. 'Round Lord Mayor Bay with James Clark Ross: the original diary of 1830'. *Arctic* 43: 66–79.

Ross, J. and J.M. Savelle. 1992. 'Retreat from Boothia: the original diary of James Clark Ross, May to October 1832'. *Arctic* 45: 179–94.

Ross, W.G. 1975. *Whaling and Eskimos: Hudson Bay 1860–1915.* Ottawa: National Museum of Man.

Ross, W.G. 1979. 'The annual catch of Greenland (Bowhead) whales in waters north of Canada, 1719–1915. A preliminary compilation'. *Arctic* 32: 91–121.

Ross, W.G. 1985. *Whalemen, whaleships and the search for Franklin.* In: Sutherland (ed.) 1985: 54–68.

Ross, W.G. (ed.) 1985. *Arctic Whalers. Icy Seas. Narratives of the Davis Strait Whale Fishery.* Toronto: Irwin Publishing.

Rouland, N. 1991. *L'autonomie du Groenland du droit à la réalité.* In: Malaurie 1991: 135–47.

Rowley, J.C. 1982. *The Hull Whale Fishery.* North Ferriby: Lockington.

Rumilly, R. 1980. *La compagnie du Nord-Ouest; une épopée montréalaise.* 2 vols. Montreal: Éditions Fides.

Rylnikov, A. 1983. *Spitsbergen. Archipelago of good neighbourliness.* Moscow: Novosti Press Agency.

Rytkheu, Y. 1981. *From Nomad Tent to University.* Moscow: Novosti Press Agency.

Safronov, F.G. 1980. *Russkiye promysly i torgi na severo-vostoke Azii v XVII-seredine XIXv [Russian Hunting and Trading in North-East Asia in the Seventeenth to Mid-Nineteenth Centuries].* Moscow: Nauka.

Samoylov, V.A. 1945. *Semen Dezhnev i ego vremya* [*S. Dezhnev and his Times*]. Moscow: Izdatel'stvo Glavsevmorputi.

Sater, J.E. (ed.) 1968. *Arctic Drifting Stations. A Report on Activities Supported by the Office of Naval Research*. Washington: Arctic Institute of North America.

Savel'yeva, E.A. 1983. *Olaus Magnus i ego 'Istoriya severnykh narodov'* [*O. Magnus and his 'History of Northern Peoples'*]. Leningrad: Nauka.

Savoia, L.A. di, duke of the Abruzzi. 1903a and b. *On the* Polar Star *in the Arctic Sea*. 2 vols. London: Hutchinson. Translated from *La Stella Polare nel Mare Artico, 1899–1900*, Milan 1903.

Savours, A. 1984. '"A very interesting point in geography": the 1773 Phipps Expedition towards the North Pole'. *Arctic* 37: 402–28.

Savours, A. 1987. *The British Admiralty and the Arctic*. In: Malaurie 1987: 153–78.

Savours, A. 1992. 'Lead Poisoning and the Franklin Expedition'. *Polar Record* 28: 73.

Savours, A. and M. Deacon. 1981. *Nutritional Aspects of the British Arctic (Nares) Expedition of 1875–1876 and its Predecessors*. In: Watt *et al.* 1981: 131–62.

Schilder, G. 1984. 'Development and achievements of Dutch northern and Arctic cartography in the sixteenth and seventeenth centuries'. *Arctic* 37: 493–514.

Schledermann, P. 1982. 'Nordbogenstande fra Arktisk Canada'. *Grønland* 30: 218–25.

Schledermann, P. 1990. *Crossroads to Greenland. Three Thousand Years of Prehistory in the Eastern High Arctic*. Calgary: Arctic Institute of North America.

Schley, W.S. 1887. *Report of Winfield S. Schley, Commander, US Navy, Commanding Greely Relief Expedition of 1884*. Washington: Government Printing Office.

Schley, W.S. and J.R. Soley. 1889. *The Rescue of Greely*. New York: Charles Scribner's Sons.

Schofield, B.B. 1964. *The Russian Convoys*. London: Batsford.

Schofield, E. and R.C. Nesbit. 1987. *Arctic Airmen. The RAF in Spitsbergen and North Russia in 1942*. London: William Kimber.

Schrenk, A.G. 1848, 1854. *Reise nach dem Nordosten des europäischen Russlands, durch die Tundren der Samojeden, zum Arktischen Uralgebirge*. 2 vols. Dorpat.

Schrire, C. and W.L. Steiger. 1981. 'Arctic infanticide revisited'. *Études/Inuit/Studies* 5: 111–16.

Schwerdtfeger, W. and F. Selinger. 1982. *Wetterflieger in der Arktis 1940–1944*. Stuttgart: Motorbuch Verlag.

Scoresby, W. 1815. 'On the Greenland or Polar ice'. *Memoirs of the Wernerian Society* 2: 328–36. Reprinted Whitby 1980.

Scoresby, W. 1820a and b. *An Account of the Arctic Regions*. 2 vols. Edinburgh: Archibald Constable. Reprinted New York 1969.

Scoresby, W. 1828. 'Remarks on the probability of reaching the North Pole: being an examination of the recent expedition under Captain Parry'. *Edinburgh New Philosophical Journal*, July 1828. Reprinted Whitby 1980.

Seemann, B. 1853a and b. *Narrative of the voyage of HMS* Herald *during the years 1845–51, under the command of Captain Henry Kellett*. 2 vols. London: Reeve.

Segal, L. 1939. *The Conquest of the Arctic*. London: George G. Harrap.

Seidenfaden, G. 1939. *Modern Arctic Exploration*. London: Jonathan Cape.

Selinger, F. and A. Glen. 1983. 'Arctic meteorological operations and counter-operations during World War 2'. *Polar Record* 21: 559–67.

Semushkin, T. 1947. *Children of the Soviet Arctic*. London: Travel Book Club.

Sergeyev, M.A. 1965. *The building of socialism among the peoples of northern Siberia and the Soviet Far East*. In: Levin and Potapov 1964: 487–510.

Shackleton, E. 1959. *Nansen the Explorer*. London: H.F.& G. Witherby.

Shentalinskiy, V.A. 1980. 'Konets Novoy Kolumbii' ['The End of New Columbia']. *Polyarnyy Krug* [*Polar Circle*]: 135–53.

Sherwood, M.B. 1965. *Exploration of Alaska, 1865–1900*. New Haven and London: Yale University Press. Reprinted Fairbanks 1992.

Shevelev, M.I. 1979. 'Podgotovka i osushchestvleniye pervoy vozdushnoy ekspeditsii na Severnyy Polyus' ['Preparation for and realization of the first air expedition to the North Pole']. *Letopis' Severa* [*Chronicle of the North*] 9: 38–53.

Shumilov, A. 1982. 'Zhizn' i smert' kapitan-komandora' ['The life and death of the captain-commander']. *Polyarnyy Krug* [*Polar Circle*]: 248–61.

Simmonds, P.L. 1852. *Sir John Franklin and the Arctic Regions: with Detailed Notices of the Expeditions in Search of the Missing Vessels under Sir John Franklin*. Buffalo: Geo.H. Derby.

Simmons, G. 1965. *Target: Arctic. Men in the Skies at the Top of the World*. Philadelphia: Chilton and Toronto: Ambassador Books.

Simonsen, H. (ed.) 1992. 'The Northern Sea Route'. *International Challenges* 12: 1–151.

Simpson, A. 1845. *The Life and Travels of Thomas Simpson, the Arctic Discoverer*. London: Richard Bentley. Reprinted Toronto 1963.

Simpson, T. 1843. *Narrative of the Discoveries on the North Coast of America: Effected by the Officers of the Hudson's Bay Company During the Years 1836–1839*. London: Richard Bentley.

Sinding, K. 1992. 'At the Crossroads: Mining Policy in Greenland'. *Arctic* 45: 226–32.

Sinding, K. and G. Poole. 1991. 'A multi-billion dollar gold deposit in Greenland?' *Polar Record* 27: 139–40.

Skeie, J. 1931. *Grønlandssaken*. Oslo: Olaf Norlis.

Sklokin, F. 1982. 'Poderzhi v rukakh zemnuyu os'' ['Grasping the Earth's axis']. *Polyarnyy Krug* [*Polar Circle*]: 129–39.

Skrynnikov, R.G. 1982. *Sibirskaya ekspeditsiya Yermaka* [*Yermak's Siberian expedition*]. Novosibirsk: Nauka.

Smedal, G. 1931. *Acquisition of sovereignty over Polar areas*. Skrifter 36. Oslo: Norges Svalbard- og Ishavs-undersøkelser.

Smith, C.E. 1923. *From the Deep of the Sea. Being the Diary of the Late Charles Edward Smith, Surgeon of the Whaleship* Diana *of Hull*. New York: MacMillan. First edition London 1922.

Smith, P.C. 1975. *Arctic Victory: the Story of Convoy PQ 18*. London: William Kimber.

Smolka, H.P. 1937 *Forty Thousand Against the Arctic. Russia's Polar Empire*. Revised edition. London: Hutchinson.

Snegirev, V. 1985. *On Skis to the North Pole*. New York: Sphinx Press.

Snellen, M. 1886. *De Nederlandsche Pool-Expeditie. 1882–3*. Utrecht: L.E. Bosch en Zoon.

Snow, W.P. 1851. *Voyage of the* Prince Albert *in search of Sir John Franklin*. London: Longman, Brown, Green & Longmans.

Sollied, P.R. and O. Solberg. (eds) 1932. *Bergenserne på Grønland i det 18. århundre, 1. Haabets koloni. Anlegg og beseiling. 1721–1726*. Oslo: Etnografiske Museum.

Sømod, J. 1991. 'Mønter fra Østgrønlandske handel'. *Grønland* 39: 305–8.

Sørensen, A.K. 1983. *Danmark-Grønland i det 20. århundrede – en historisk oversigt*. [Copenhagen]: Nyt Nordisk Forlag, Arnold Busck.

Speak, P. 1992. 'William Speirs Bruce: Scottish nationalist and Polar explorer'. *Polar Record* 28: 285–92.

Speck, G. 1963. *Samuel Hearne and the North-West Passage*. Caldwell, Idaho: Caxton Printers.

Spencer, A. 1978. *The Lapps*. New York: Crane, Russak.

Spencer, R.F. 1959. *The North Alaska Eskimo*. Smithsonian Institution. Bureau of American Ethnology, Bulletin 171. Washington D.C.: Government Printing Office.

Spencer, R.F. 1984. *North Alaska Coast Eskimo*. In: Damas (ed.) 1984: 320–37.

Spichkin, V.A. and V.A. Shamont'yev. 1979. *Atomokhod idet k Polyusu [Nuclear-Powered Ship Voyages to the Pole]*. Leningrad: Gidrometeoizdat.

Stackpole, E.A. (ed.) 1965. *The Long Arctic Search. The Narrative of Lieutenant Frederick Schwatka, U.S.A., 1878–1880, Seeking the Records of the Lost Franklin Expedition*. Mystic, Connecticut: Marine Historical Association.

Stamp, T. and C. Stamp. 1976. *William Scoresby. Arctic Scientist*. Whitby: Caedmon Press.

Stamp, T. and C. Stamp. 1978. *James Cook. Maritime Scientist*. Whitby: Caedmon Press.

Starokadomskiy, L.M. 1976. *Charting the Russian Northern Sea Route*. Ed. and trans. W. Barr. Montreal: Arctic Institute of North America and McGill-Queen's University Press.

Steen, E.A. 1960. *Marinens operasjoner i arktiske farvann og i Island, på Grønland, Jan Mayen og Svalbard. Norges sjøkrig 1940–5*, 7. Oslo.

Stefansson, V. 1919. *My Life with the Eskimo*. New York: MacMillan. First edition 1913.

Stefansson, V. 1922. *The Friendly Arctic. The Story of Five Years in Polar Regions*. New York: MacMillan.

Stefansson, V. 1925. *The Adventure of Wrangel Island*. New York: MacMillan.

Stefansson, V. 1935. 'Introduction to the Cheyne articles'. *Bulletin of the Geographical Society of Philadelphia* 33: 97–8.

Stefansson, V. 1939. *Unsolved Mysteries of the Arctic*. New York: MacMillan and London: George G. Harrap.

Stefansson, V. 1943. *Greenland*. London: George Harrap.

Stefansson, V. 1944. *Ultima Thule. Further Mysteries of the Arctic*. New York: MacMillan. First published 1940.

Stefansson, V. 1960. *North-West to Fortune*. London: George Allen & Unwin. First published New York 1958.

Stefansson, V. 1964. *Discovery. The Autobiography of Vilhjalmur Stefansson*. New York: McGraw-Hill.

Stefansson, V. (ed.) 1938a and b. *The Three Voyages of Martin Frobisher in Search of a Passage to Cathay and India by the North-West. AD 1576–8*. 2 vols. London: Argonaut Press.

Steger, W and P. Schurke. 1987. *North to the Pole*. New York: Ivy Books.

Steinnes, A. 1958. 'Ein nordpolsekspedisjon år 1360'. *Syn og Segn* 64: 410–19.

Stenbaek, M.A. (ed.) 1986. *Arctic Policy. Papers Presented at the Arctic Policy Conference, 19–21 September 1985*. Montreal: McGill University Centre for Northern Studies and Research.

Stewart, H. 1989. 'The Arctic Small Tool Tradition and early Canadian Arctic Palaeo-Eskimo cultures'. *Études/Inuit/Studies* 13 (2): 69–101.

Stirling, I. and W. Calvert. 1983. 'Environmental threats to marine mammals in the Canadian Arctic'. *Polar Record* 21: 433–49.

Stoklund, M. 1982. 'Nordboruner'. *Grønland* 30: 197–206.

Stolp, G.N. 1984. *Bibliografia di Umberto Nobile*. Florence: Leo S. Olschki.

Stone, I.R. 1983. 'The Crimean War in the Arctic'. *Polar Record* 21: 577–81.

Stone, I.R. 1986. 'Profile: Samuel Hearne'. *Polar Record* 23: 49–56.

Stone, I.R. 1993. 'An Episode in the Franklin search: the *Prince Albert* Expedition, 1850'. *Polar Record* 29: 127–42 and 197–208.

Storkerson, S.T. 1922. *Drifting in the Beaufort Sea*. In: Stefansson 1922: 689–703.

Stromilov, N.N. 1977. *Bpervye nad Polyusom [First at the Pole]*. Leningrad: Gidrometeoizdat.

Sturges, W.T. (ed.) 1991. *Pollution of the Arctic Atmosphere*. London and New York: Elsevier Science.

Sugden, D. 1982. *Arctic and Antarctic. A Modern Geographical Synthesis*. Oxford: Basil Blackwell.

Sutcliffe, A.J. 1985. *On the Track of Ice Age Mammals*. Cambridge, Mass.: Harvard University Press.

Sutherland, P.C. 1852a and b. *Journal of a Voyage in Baffin's Bay and Barrow Straits, in the Years 1850–1851, Performed by HM Ships* Lady Franklin *and* Sophia. 2 vols. London: Longman, Brown, Green & Longmans.

Sutherland, P.D. (ed.) 1985. *The Franklin Era in Canadian Arctic History*. Ottawa: National Museums of Canada.

Suzyumov, E.M. 1982. 'Iz istorii nauki. Vazhnyy etap. K 50-letiyu Btorogo mezhdunarodnogo polyarnogo goda' ['From the history of science. An important stage. On the occasion of the fiftieth anniversary of the Second International Polar Year']. *Chelovek i Stikiya* [*Man and the Elements*]: 136–8.

Sverdrup, H.A. 1926. *Tre aar i isen med* Maud. Oslo: Gyldendal.

Sverdrup, O. 1904a and b. New Land. *Four Years in the Arctic Regions*. 2 vols. London: Longmans, Green. Translated from *Nytland. Fire aare i arktiske egne*, Kristiania 1903.

Taracouzio, T.A. 1938. *Soviets in the Arctic*. New York: MacMillan.

Taylor, E.G.R. 1930. *Tudor Geography 1485–1583*. London: Methuen.

Tejsen, A.V.S. 1977. 'The history of the Royal Greenland Trade Department'. *Polar Record* 18: 451–75.

Thomson, G.M. 1975. *The North-West Passage*. London: Secker & Warburg.

Thorén, R. 1979. *Svenska Arktiska expeditioner under 1800-talet*. Stockholm: Marinlitteraturföreningen.

Tiander, K. 1906. *Poyezdki Skandinavov v Beloye more* [*Journeys of the Scandinavians to the White Sea*]. St Petersburg.

Tikhomirov, G.S. 1980. *K istorii ekspeditsii I.D. Papanina. Dokumental'niy ocherk* [*On the History of the Papanin Expedition. Documentary Study*]. Moscow: Mysl'.

Tillotson, J. [*c.* 1870]. *Adventures in the Ice: a Comprehensive Summary of Arctic Exploration, Discovery, and Adventure, including Experiences of Captain Penny, the Veteran Whaler*. London: John Hogg.

Toll, E. von. 1909. *Die russische Polarfahrt der* Sarja, *1900–1902*. Berlin: Georg Reimer.

Tompkins, S.R. 1945. *Alaska. Promyshlennik and sourdough*. Norman, Oklahoma: University of Oklahoma Press.

Trafton, S.J. 1989. 'Did lead poisoning contribute to deaths of Franklin Expedition members?' *Information North*, 15 (9). Calgary: Arctic Institute of North America.

Transehe, N.A. 1925. 'The Siberian Sea road. The work of the Russian Hydrographical Expedition to the Arctic, 1910–1915'. *Geographical Review* 15: 367–98.

Tranter, G.J. 1944. *Plowing the Arctic*. London: Hodder & Stoughton.

Trevor-Battye, A. 1895. *Ice-Bound on Kolguev*. Westminster: Archibald Constable.

Troup, J.A. (ed.) 1987. *The Ice-Bound Whalers*. Stromness: Orkney Press.

Tschkalow, V. 1939. *Unser Transpolarflug*. Moscow: Foreign Languages Publishing House. German translation of Chkalov, V.P., *Nash transpolyarny reys*, Moscow 1938.

Tuck, J.A. 1981. *Basque whalers in southern Labrador, Canada*. In: van Holk (ed.) 1981: 69–77.

Turley, C. 1935. *Roald Amundsen, Explorer*. London: Methuen.

Tyutenkov, A. 1979. *Arkticheskiy reys 'Sibiri'* [*The Sibir's Arctic Voyage*]. Leningrad: Lenizdat.

Uemura, N. 1978. 'Solo to the Pole'. *National Geographic Magazine* 154: 298–325.

Ulloriaq, I. 1984. 'Hvad man har hørt om de to første Nordpolsfarere'. *Grønland* 32: 61–88.

Urvantsev, N. 1933. *Severnaya Zemlya. A Short Survey of Exploration*. Leningrad: Arctic Institute.

Urvantsev, N.N. 1935. *Dva goda na Severnoy Zemle* [*Two years on Severnaya Zemlya*]. Leningrad: Izdatel'stvo Glavsevmorputi. New edition: Moscow 1969.

Urvantsev, N.N. 1969. *Noril'sk. Istoriya otkrytiya i osvoyeniya medno- nikelevykh rud sibirskogo severa* [*Noril'sk. History of the Discovery and Opening Up of the Copper-Nickel Ores of the Siberian North*]. Moscow: Nedra.

Ushakov, G.A. 1953. *Po nekhozhenoy zemle* [*On Untrodden Land*]. Moscow: Molodaya Gvardiya. New edition: Moscow 1959.

Ushakov, G.A. 1972. *Ostrov meteley* [*Island of Snow Storms*]. Leningrad: Gidrometeorologischeskoye Izdatel'stvo.

Vahl, M., G.C. Amdrup, L. Bobé, and A.S. Jensen (eds.) 1928a and b, 1929. *Greenland.* 3 vols. Copenhagen: C.A. Reitzel and London: Humphrey Milford.

Vakhtin, N. 1992. *Native Peoples of the Russian Far North.* London: Minority Rights Group.

Van der Moer, A. (ed.) 1979. *Een zestiende-eeuwse Hollander in het verre oosten en het hoge noorden. Leven, werken, reizen en avonturen van Jan Huyghen van Linschoten (1563–1611).* The Hague: Martinus Nijhoff.

Vasil'evskiy, R.S. 1987. 'The development of a maritime system of economy in the northern part of the Pacific Ocean basin'. *Études/Inuit/Studies* 11 (2): 73–90.

Vasil'yev, V.I. and L.N. Geydenreykh. 1977. *Tundra Kaninskaya* [*The Kanin Tundra*]. Moscow: Mysl'.

Vasylov, V.N. 1984. *Izbranniki dukhov* [*Chosen Ones of the Spirit*]. Moscow: Izdatel'stvo politicheskoy literatury.

Vaughan, R. 1982. 'The Arctic in the middle ages'. *Journal of Medieval History* 8: 313–42.

Vaughan, R. 1983. *Historical Survey of the European Whaling Industry.* In: s'Jacob, Snoeijing and Vaughan (eds) 1983: 121–34.

Vaughan, R. 1986. 'Bowhead whaling in Davis Strait and Baffin Bay during the eighteenth and nineteenth centuries'. *Polar Record* 23: 289–99.

Vaughan, R. 1987. *How Isolated Were the Polar Eskimos in the Nineteenth Century?* In: Hacquebord and Vaughan (eds) 1987: 95–107.

Vaughan, R. 1991. *North-West Greenland. A History.* Orono: University of Maine Press.

Vaughan, R. 1992. *In Search of Arctic Birds.* London: Poyser.

Vdovin, I.S. 1965. *Ocherki istorii i etnografii Chukchey* [*Studies in the History and Ethnogaphy of the Chukchi*]. Moscow and Leningrad: Nauka.

Venzke, J.F. 1990. 'The 1869/70 German North Polar Expedition'. *Arctic* 43: 83–5.

Vereshchagin, N.K. and Yu. Mochanov. 1972. 'Samyye severnyye v mire sledy palaeolita' ['The most northerly traces of the Palaeolithic in the world']. *Sovetskaya Arkheologiya* 1972 (3): 332–6.

Vernadskiy, V.N. 1961. *Novgorod i novgorodskaya zemlya v XV veke* [*Novgorod and the Novgorod Area in the Fifteenth Century*]. Moscow and Leningrad.

Victor, P-E. 1939. *My Eskimo Life.* New York: Simon and Schuster. Translated from *Boréal. La joie dans la nuit*, Paris 1938.

Victor, P-E. 1956. 'Winning secrets from Greenland's icecap'. *National Geographic Magazine* 1956 (1): 121–47.

Victor, P-E. 1964. *Man and the conquest of the Poles.* London: Hamish Hamilton. Translated from *L'homme à la conquête des Pôles*, Paris 1962.

Villarejo, O.M. 1965. *Dr Kane's Voyage to the Polar Lands.* Philadelphia: University of Pennsylvania Press.

Vitebsky, P. 1990. 'Gas, environmentalism and native anxieties in the Soviet Arctic: the case of Yamal peninsula'. *Polar Record* 26: 19–26.

Vize, V.Yu. 1932. *Mezhdunarodnyy polyarnyy god* [*The International Polar Year*]. Leningrad: Vsesoyuznogo Arkticheskogo Instituta.

Vize, V.Yu. (ed.) 1933. *Le Rua. Priklyucheniya chetyrekh russikh matrosov na Shpitsbergen* [*Le Roy.*

Adventures of Four Russian Sailors on Spitsbergen]. Leningrad: Izdatel'stvo Arkticheskogo Instituta. Originally published in German: *Erzählung der Begebenheiten vier russischer Matrosen, die durch einen Sturm zur Insel Ost Spitsbergen verschlagen wurden*, Riga 1760.

Vize, V.Yu. (ed.) 1936. *G. Defer [G. de Veer]. Plavaniya Barentsa [Barents's Voyage] (Diarium nauticum), 1594–1597*. Leningrad: Izdatel'stvo Glavsevmorputi.

Vodopyanov, M. *Wings over the Arctic*. Moscow: Foreign Languages Publishing House. Translated from: *Na kryl'yakh v arktiku*, Moscow 1954.

Wallace, H.N. 1980. *The Navy, the Company, and Richard King. British Exploration in the Canadian Arctic. 1829–1860*. Montreal: McGill-Queen's University Press.

Wallace, H.N. 1985. *Private Expeditions in the Search for Sir John Franklin*. In: Sutherland 1985: 42–53.

Wallis, H. *et al*. 1974. 'The strange case of the Vinland Map'. *Geographical Journal* 140: 183–214.

Watson, L. 1981. *Sea Guide to the Whales of the World*. London: Hutchinson.

Watt, J., E.J. Freeman and W.F. Bynum (eds) 1981. *Starving Sailors; the Influence of Nutrition Upon Naval and Maritime History*. London: National Maritime Museum.

Waxell, S. 1952. *The American Expedition*. London: William Hodge.

Webster, C.J. 1950. 'The economic development of the Soviet Arctic and Sub-Arctic'. *Slavonic and East European Review* 29: 177–211.

Weems, J.E. 1961. *Race for the North Pole*. London: William Heinemann.

Weems, J.E. 1967. *Peary. The Explorer and the Man*. London: Eyre & Spottiswoode.

Wegener, E. (ed.) 1939. *Greenland Journey. The Story of Wegener's German Expedition to Greenland in 1930–1931 as told by Members of the Expedition and the Leader's Diary*. London and Glasgow: Blackie and Son. Translated from *Alfred Wegeners letzte Grönlandfahrt*, Leipzig 1932.

Wellman, W. 1899. 'The Wellman Polar Expedition'. *National Geographic Magazine* 10: 481–503.

Wellman, W. 1911. *The Aerial Age*. New York: A.R. Keller.

Westermeyer, W.E. and K.M. Shusterich (eds) 1984. *United States Arctic Interests. The 1980s and 1990s*. New York and Berlin: Springer- Verlag.

Whitaker, I. 1955. *Social Relations in a Nomadic Lappish Community*. Oslo: Norsk Folkemuseum, Samiske Samlingar 2.

Whitaker, I. 1981. 'Othere's account reconsidered'. *Arctic Anthropology* 18: 1–11.

Whitaker, I. 1982. 'The problem of Pytheas' Thule'. *Classical Journal* 77: 148–64.

White, A. (ed.) 1855. *A Collection of Documents on Spitsbergen and Greenland*. London: Hakluyt Society.

Wilkes, C. 1845. *Narrative of the United States Exploring Expedition, 1838–42*. Philadelphia: Lea & Blanchard.

Wilkins, G.H. 1928. *Flying the Arctic*. New York and London: G.P. Putnam's Sons.

Willan, T.S. 1956. *The Early History of the Russia Company, 1553–1603*. Manchester: Manchester University Press.

Williams, G. 1962. *The British Search for the North-West Passage in the Eighteenth Century*. London: Longmans.

Williamson, J.A. 1962. *The Cabot Voyages and Bristol Discovery under Henry VII*. Cambridge: Hakluyt Society.

Wilson, D. 1989. *Exploration for oil and gas in eastern Siberia*. In: Wood and French 1989: 228–55.

Winslow, K. 1952. *Big Pan-Out. The Klondike Story*. London: Phoenix House.

Wood, A. and R.A. French (eds) 1989. *The Development of Siberia. People and Resources*. London: MacMillan and the School of Slavonic and East European Studies, University of London.

Woodman, D.C. 1991. *Unravelling the Franklin Mystery. Inuit Testimony*. Montreal: McGill-Queen's University Press.

Wordie, J.M. 1945. *The North-West Passage since the Last Franklin Expedition*. In: Cyriax and Wordie 1945: 180–97.

Wrangell, F. von 1844. *Narrative of an Expedition to the Polar Sea in the Years 1820, 1821, 1822 and 1823*. Ed. E. Sabine. London: James Madden.

Wright, J.K. 1925. *The Geographical Lore of the Time of the Crusades*. New York.

Wright, N. 1959. *Quest for Franklin*. London: Heinemann.

Wright, T. 1970. *The Big Nail. The Story of the Cook-Peary Feud*. New York: John Day.

Yakovlev, G.H. 1975. *Ledovye puti Arktiki* [*Ice tracks in the Arctic*]. Moscow: Mysl'.

Young, A. 1879. *The Two Voyages of the* Pandora *in 1875 and 1876*. London: Edward Stanford.

Zaslow, M. 1981. *Administering the Arctic islands 1880–1940: policemen, missionaries, fur traders*. In: Zaslow (ed.) 1981: 61–78.

Zaslow, M. (ed.) 1981. *A Century of Canada's Arctic Islands*. Ottawa: Royal Society of Canada.

Zavatti, S. 1981. *L'Italia e le regioni polari*. Ancona: Gilberto Bagaloni.

Zenzinov, V.M. and I.D. Levine. 1932. *The Road to Oblivion*. London: Jonathan Cape.

Zögner, L. 1978. 'Die kartographische Darstellung der Polargebiete bis in das 19. Jahrhundert'. *Die Erde* 109: 136–52.

Zorgdrager, C.G. 1720. *Bloeyende opkomst der aloude en hedendaagsche Groenlandsche visscherij*. The Hague: P. van Thol & R.C. Alberts.

Zorgdrager, N. 1984. *The Saami people*. In: Nooter 1984: 11–44.

Index